ALISTER E. McGRATH is professor of historical theology at Oxford University, director of the John Templeton Oxford Seminars on Science and Christianity, and principal of Wycliffe Hall, Oxford. He holds the Oxford degrees of Doctor of Divinity for his work on historical and systematic theology, and Doctor of Philosophy for his work on molecular biophysics.

A SCIENTIFIC THEOLOGY

VOLUME 2

REALITY

A SCIENTIFIC
THEOLOGY

VOLUME 2

REALITY

Alister E. McGrath

William B. Eerdmans Publishing Company
Grand Rapids, Michigan / Cambridge, U.K.

Originally published 2002 in the U.K. by
T&T Clark Ltd

A Continuum imprint

This edition published 2002 in the United States of America by
Wm. B. Eerdmans Publishing Company
255 Jefferson Ave. S.E., Grand Rapids, Michigan 49503 /
P.O. Box 163 Cambridge CB3 9PU U.K.

www.eerdmans.com

Manufactured in Great Britain

06 05 04 03 02   5 4 3 2 1

ISBN 0-8028-3926-6

FOR

JEREMY R. KNOWLES

A NATURAL PHILOSOPHER

Contents

Preface

The first volume in this trilogy exploring Christian theological method addressed the problematic question of the theological status of nature; the second now turns to consider the epistemological and ontological status of the real world, prior to exploring the question of how this may be represented theoretically in the third and final volume of the series. The three volumes of this series attempt to present an essentially linear argument from nature to theory, so that questions of how reality is represented will be dealt with virtually entirely in its final volume, even though some preliminary discussions of aspects of that topic are included in the present volume.

A scientific theology conceives the theological enterprise as a principled attempt to give an account of the reality of God, which it understands to be embedded at different levels in the world. Declining to make *a priori* prejudgements concerning what may be known of God, and the manner by which that knowledge should be established, a scientific theology approaches such questions in the light of what is actually known about God. A scientific theology thus conceives itself as an *a posteriori* discipline, responding to and offering an account of what may be known of God through revelation, taking full account of the stratified nature of that knowledge of God.

The themes of this second volume are to be set against the backdrop of radical changes in western philosophy and theology resulting from the collapse of the Enlightenment project, and the consequent fragmentation of intellectual discourse. This development has a double significance for a scientific theology, in that its formulation is rendered both more *urgent* and more *problematic*. The growing awareness of the serious flaws of both foundationalism and the cognate notion of a universal rationality has had an impact upon western thought comparable to the revolution which swept through the physical sciences through the failure of the Michelson–Morley experiment to detect the motion of the ether.[1] The collapse of the prevailing consensus demanded new ways of thinking and approaching the world, leading to the rise of both Einsteinian relativity and quantum mechanics.

A similar shift is taking place within philosophy, even though it remains unclear what its final outcome will be. The Enlightenment project has unquestionably failed; it is not obvious what will succeed it.[2] No longer can it be assumed that there is an Archimedean point of philosophical adjudication. There is little doubt that the publication of John Rawls' *Theory of Justice* (1971) marked a new interest in the Enlightenment project, particularly the advocacy of a return to a Kantian framework for moral judgements.[3] Yet Rawls' general position has been subjected to a sustained critique by Alasdair MacIntyre, who argued for a return to the Aristotelian notion of practical morality. For MacIntyre, Rawls' entire project rested on the prior assumption of the validity of the Enlightenment world-view. It was an assumption that MacIntyre believed to be fatally compromised. The solution to moral problems does not, and cannot, lie in an appeal to an allegedly universal conception of moral judgement, but in working within the tradition that supplies the framework of judgement for those posing that moral problem.[4]

One reaction to the failure of the Enlightenment project has been the systematic inversion of many of its foundational judgements. Perhaps most importantly for our purposes, the alleged 'objectivity' of knowledge has been called into question, and displaced by an increasing emphasis upon the social construction of reality. Postmodern writers have argued that our ideational worlds are free constructs of

---

[1] See A. A. Michelson and E. W. Morley, 'On the Relative Motion of the Earth and Luminiferous Ether', *American Journal of Science* 34 (1887), 333–45. For the impact of this experiment, see T. Hirosige, 'The Ether Problem, the Mechanistic World View, and the Origins of the Theory of Relativity', *Historical Studies in the Physical Sciences* 7 (1976), 3–82.

[2] For some reflections, see Gianni Vattimo, *The End of Modernity: Nihilism and Hermeneutics in Post-modern Culture.* Cambridge: Polity Press, 1991.

[3] John Rawls, *A Theory of Justice.* Cambridge, MA: Harvard University Press, 1971. For comments and assessment, see Brian Barry, *The Liberal Theory of Justice: A Critical Examination of the Principal Doctrines in A Theory of Justice by John Rawls.* Oxford: Clarendon Press, 1973; H. Gene Blocker and Elizabeth H. Smith, *John Rawls' Theory of Social Justice: An Introduction.* Athens, OH: Ohio University Press, 1980.

[4] See Roger Crisp and Michael A. Slote (eds), *Virtue Ethics.* New York: Oxford University Press, 1997.

the autonomous individual, who is unrestricted in that process of construction by external limitations or pressures.

While this particular position is open to question, to say the least, there is no doubt that the postmodern critique of the Enlightenment project has exposed some genuine weaknesses in the *grand récit* of rationality which it advocated. The Enlightenment proposed an 'objectivity' of both judgement and knowledge which overlooked the role of both history and culture in their shaping and transmission. Thus Kant's critical notion of the 'knowing subject' gives every indication of being an ideal mental construction, rather than an empirical reality, in that Kant appears to turn one of his many blind eyes to the fact that this 'knowing subject' has acquired its distinctive shape through the process of social living, shaped by a corporate tradition and socially transmitted patterns of rationality.[5]

Far from legitimating the Enlightenment's emphasis on pure 'objectivity', the natural sciences propose a spectrum of modes of interplay between 'objectivity' and 'social construction'. While physics may be taken as an instance of a natural science with a low coefficient of social construction, psychology is a clear example of such a science to make extensive use of this heuristic device. The scope of the natural sciences is such that this spectrum of possibilities is inevitable, demanding that the issue be addressed properly. Yet contrary to the postmodern trend, 'social construction' is *not* to be understood as an arbitrary determination or the pure invention of ideas on the basis of the free choice of the individual thinker or a community of discourse. The development of such constructs as 'race' or 'intelligence' represents a principled exercise in attempting to understand the world as best as possible, and to develop for this purpose whatever tools or conceptualities are best suited to the tasks of the individual natural science in question, and the level of reality it engages. Within the natural sciences, such constructs are empirically based, and represent legitimate and warranted means of gaining a tighter grasp on the reality being studied. Like hypothetical entities in theory construction, they may be held to be empirically plausible and heuristically valuable, providing their provisional status is acknowledged. This is not, it must be stressed, to prefer an instrumentalist to a realist view of the world; it is a matter of the best ordering of a realist construal of things.

[5] Heinzpeter Hempelmann, '"Keine ewigen Wahrheiten als unaufhörliche zeitliche": Hamanns Kontroverse mit Kant über Sprache und Vernunft', *Theologische Beiträge* 18 (1987), 5–33.

Three observations must be made immediately to counter possible misunderstandings at this point. As we saw earlier, 'nature' designates a wide range of entities, all of which come within the scope of the 'natural sciences'. Physics and psychology alike must be regarded as natural sciences, whose working methods and assumptions are to be critically appropriated by a scientific theology. Some sciences make greater use of social constructs than others; yet these constructs are to be understood as arising out of the experimental evidence under consideration, and are to be regarded as interpretative and predictive tools for the better understanding of the reality under investigation. They are not arbitrary, free constructions of the human imagination, but are called forth by and derive their heuristic validity from the nature of the reality under investigation. This leads to the three points we are concerned with.

1. The extent of social constructivism is dependent upon the tasks and subject-matter of the natural science in question.

2. The legitimate use of social constructions does *not* entail anti-realism, even in its weak instrumentalist version. Thus to recognize that 'intelligence' is a social construct does not mean that there is no such thing as 'intelligence'; it means that it is to be understood as a specific means of understanding a body of observational data which has a claim to reality by virtue of its explanatory and predictive fecundity, whose status is anticipated as being finally confirmed through the accumulation of additional data and inter-pretative devices.

3. Social constructs are subject to constant reappraisal and revision in the light of advancing knowledge and experimental observation.

Objectivity and social constructivism are thus not *contradictory* (as both the Enlightenment and postmodernity appear to believe, although in different ways and for different reasons). The intermingling of these notions is inevitable, given the complexity of the world which the natural sciences seek to encounter and explain.[6] Above all, a realist approach to the world is not called into question through the recognition of socially constructed aspects of the explanations offered by the natural sciences. As John Searle points out, a distinction may be made between 'brute facts' and 'social facts' – but they are still both *real*.[7] The exploration of

---

[6] The importance of the work of psychologist Jean Piaget in clarifying how young children develop the idea of 'objectivity' is of importance here: see Rachel Melkman, *The Construction of Objectivity*. Basel: Karger, 1988.

[7] John R. Searle, *The Construction of Social Reality*. New York: Free Press, 1995.

the issue of social constructs will be considered more fully in the third volume of this series; our concern here is to note that the use of such devices is consistent with – even demanded by – a realist approach to the world.

So what form of realism is most appropriate to the task of a scientific theology? One of the most distinctive features of this volume is its application of the 'critical realism' found in the writings of Roy Bhaskar to a scientific theology. Readers may be interested to know how this engagement came about. I had long been dissatisfied with certain realist accounts of pure 'objectivity' which seemed to fail to take account of either the observer's involvement in the process of knowing, or the observer's location within history, and hence at least partial conditioning by the contingencies and particularities of that location. By 1990, I had become quite clear that the Kantian tradition was seriously deficient in this respect. The increasing emphasis being placed on the role of communities and traditions seemed to me to offer at least some means of resolving this difficulty, not least through its explicit recognition of the historically situated character of reflection. The writings of Alasdair MacIntyre and others seemed to provide an important corrective to the manifest failure of the Kantian tradition to deal with this issue. However, it was not clear to me quite how this analysis could be extended to include engagement with the issues of realism in the natural sciences and theology. Indeed, some of the theological schools to embrace the idea of tradition-mediated rationality appeared to associate it, if anything, with non-realist approaches to theology, apparently believing that Locke, Hume, and Kant have rendered any form of realism philosophically indefensible.[8]

George Lindbeck's *Nature of Doctrine* illustrates the curious tendency within the Yale (or 'postliberal') school of theology to perpetuate a quite unnecessary, if not thoroughly misleading, link between a non-realist epistemology and the concept of a tradition-mediated rationality. To make this point absolutely clear: neither the failure of the Enlightenment project nor the adoption of a tradition-bound rationality implies or necessitates an anti-realism; both are perfectly consistent with a realist perspective. Yet throughout Lindbeck's discussion of cognitive approaches to Christian doctrine, there may be detected a persistent Wittgensteinian reserve concerning the external referent of doctrinal

---

[8] Janet Martin Soskice, 'Theological Realism', in W. J. Abraham and S. Holtzer (eds), *The Rationality of Religious Belief.* Oxford and New York: Clarendon Press, 1987, 105–19, especially 108–9.

statements, and a perceptible hesitation over the claims of any forms of epistemological realism.[9]

While I was able to point out some serious concerns over Lindbeck's approach in my 1990 Bampton Lectures at Oxford University, I was not at that time able to formulate a viable realist response to Lindbeck. At that stage, I simply could not see how this could be done without seriously vitiating the distinctive character of the natural sciences through a historicization of their approaches. The existing discussions of the idea of 'critical realism' within the professional science and religion community did not really seem to address the sociological point at issue, even if they were illuminating at other junctures. By about 1996, I found myself being in possession of most of the pieces I needed to create a sustainable approach to a critical realism which took account of tradition-mediated rationality – yet could not quite see how they were to be put together to yield a coherent whole.

My breakthrough came late in 1998, when I came across the third edition of Roy Bhaskar's *The Possibility of Naturalism*.[10] By the time I finished reading and annotating this work, I knew I had found a form of critical realism that took the social location of the observer seriously. The next year was taken up with a sustained engagement with Bhaskar's specific approach to critical realism, which has been developed and amplified in this work, especially its tenth chapter. It is perhaps the most significant aspect of this volume, and it is likely that my exploration of its potential for Christian theology will need to be developed further and more critically by others. I joined the 'International Association for Critical Realism' immediately, and have benefited enormously from the discussions taking place within this organization. The fact that so few theologians have interacted with this growing movement is a deeply troubling mark of the intellectual isolationism of much Christian theology, which needs to be reconsidered as a matter of some urgency.

The key to understanding how the Christian tradition relates to other traditions lies in natural theology. Although this has tended to be marginalized in recent theological discussions, the growing awareness of the critical role of traditions in mediating ideas and values promises to offer a new role to natural theology, which the present volume explores in some depth. Any given tradition is under an obligation

---

[9] George Lindbeck, *The Nature of Doctrine*. Philadelphia: Westminster, 1984, 63–7.
[10] Roy Bhaskar, *The Possibility of Naturalism: A Philosophical Critique of the Contemporary Human Sciences*. 3rd edn. London: Routledge, 1998. I encountered this work too late to include its ideas in my *Foundations of Dialogue in Science and Religion*. Oxford: Blackwell, 1999.

both to demonstrate the grounds and coherence of its own ideas and to explain those ideas which are mediated in and through other traditions. The ultimate challenge to any world-view is how it accounts for its own existence.[11] The appeal to natural theology allows the Christian tradition to offer an account of why truth, goodness and beauty are pursued in other traditions, and accounts, to a limited yet significant extent, for the specific forms that these take within those traditions.

Finally, my thanks are due to the many unseen midwives to this volume. I am grateful to the members of the Oxford Templeton Seminar in Science and Christianity over the years 1999–2001, who have provided an invaluable stimulus to my reflections on scientific theologizing. My colleagues at Oxford University have provided an outstanding intellectual environment in which to undertake research and critical theological reflection. In particular, I wish to acknowledge significant conversations with Dr Joanna McGrath, Professor Sir Roger Penrose and Professor Derick Wade, which have clarified some points of importance. Dr Darren Marks has been all that a good research assistant should be, patiently tracking down articles of relevance, and drawing my attention to others that I might have overlooked. Dr Geoffrey Green, publishing director of T&T Clark, is to be thanked for his constant encouragement. I acknowledge with gratitude a grant from the John Templeton Foundation, which made possible the research underlying this project. Without such generous support, these books could never have been written.

This work is dedicated to Professor Jeremy R. Knowles, Dean of the Faculty of Arts and Sciences at Harvard University. As my tutor in organic chemistry at Wadham College, Oxford, in the early 1970s, Knowles taught me to love the natural sciences, and to 'stoke the intellectual fires' that burned within me. I owe him more than I can ever express; this small dedication can only hint at my debt to him.

---

[11] This is one of the more troubling weaknesses of the problematic approach to naturalism found in Willem B. Drees, *Religion, Science and Naturalism*. Cambridge and New York: Cambridge University Press, 1995, 23.

PART THREE

Reality

Chapter 7

Rationality and Knowledge in Theology and the Natural Sciences

A scientific theology is concerned with knowledge of God and the world. So how is such knowledge to be acquired and confirmed? And in what ways is this knowledge modulated by the existing ideas and beliefs of the knower, and the community to which she belongs? To ask such questions is to enter into discussions which have taken place since the dawn of western civilization. The origins of a theory of knowledge can be traced back to Plato's attempt in the dialogue *Theaetetus* to distinguish 'opinion' from 'knowledge'. The intense discussion which was generated by this distinction has led to a stable consensus that knowledge may legitimately be defined as 'warranted belief'.[1] The question which naturally arises from any such definition is what form and intensity of justification is required for a belief to be regarded as 'warranted' or 'justified'.

This volume defends the view that knowledge arises through a sustained and passionate attempt to engage with a reality that is

---

[1] As Laurence Bonjour frames the issue in a major study of the nature of empirical knowledge: 'A knows that P if and only if (1) A must believe confidently that P, (2) P must be true, and (3) A's belief that P must be adequately justified.' See Laurence Bonjour, *The Structure of Empirical Knowledge*. Cambridge, MA: Harvard University Press, 1985, 9. Bonjour introduced the notion of 'epistemic responsibility' to refer to the desire to possess true beliefs, and to devise appropriate processes to lead to their establishment: Laurence Bonjour, 'Externalist Theories of Justification', *Midwest Studies in Philosophy* 5 (1980), 53–73. See further Hilary Kornblith, 'Justified Belief and Epistemically Responsible Action', *Philosophical Review* 92 (1983), 33–48. The discussion has more recently been framed in terms of 'warranted beliefs': see Alvin Plantinga, *Warrant and Proper Function*. New York: Oxford University Press, 1993; idem, *Warrant: The Current Debate*. Oxford: Oxford University Press, 1993.

encountered or made known – including the postulation of hypothetical entities or the formulation of such constructs as may appear
appropriate in rendering that reality, however provisionally. Theology,
like any responsible discipline, is accountable for its rendering of
reality, and must be called upon to reform and revise its ideas if these
can be shown to be out of line with what they purport to represent.
This presupposes and expresses a realist perspective on the world,
such as that which undergirds the successes of the natural sciences.
Theology is a principled uncovering of the spiritual structures of reality,
and a responsible attempt to represent them in a manner appropriate to their distinctive natures. Just as the natural sciences develop
a distinctive vocabulary, set of hypothetical entities and constructs to
represent the levels of reality which they encounter, so Christian
theology has evolved its own characteristic terminology, models and
conceptualities to represent the reality which is encountered and
disclosed in Jesus Christ. This is the subject of more detailed consideration in the final volume of this series, and we shall defer further
discussion of such points until then.

On such a realist view, both the natural sciences and Christian
theology regard their objects as possessing a reality and intrinsic
rationality which are to be ascertained and respected in the process of
observation and the development of theories. While the place of human
language, social location and traditions of discourse and reflection in
this process of engagement must be fully acknowledged, realism insists
that there exists an extra-linguistic reality which must be allowed to act
as the ultimate foundation and criterion of responsible human thought.
Our theories about nature are to be judged against what may be known
of nature, just as our ideas about God are to be judged against what
may be known of God.

Part of our concern in this volume is to clarify what form of realism
is to be adopted for this purpose. Given the 'variety of realisms' (Rom
Harré), which is to be preferred, and for what reasons? In due course,
we shall set out the reasons for adopting the form of 'critical realism'
developed by Roy Bhaskar and others as a means of defending realist
perspectives, while acknowledging the pervasive social location and
personal involvement of the human observer. But there is a deeper
question that must also be addressed. *Is such a realist perspective justified
in the first place?*

Many persuasive voices argue that human knowledge need not take
the form of an account of allegedly 'objective' realities outside the human
knower. Knowledge might be a human construction, representing the

historically contingent consensus that exists within a given community.[2] Theology could thus be conceived as an attempt to represent and even enhance this consensus, setting to one side as irrelevant the question of whether such ideas are extra-historical truths or objective realities.

The present chapter initiates an engagement with these questions, probing the role of tradition and communities in shaping the human response to the world. We shall consider the case for realism in more detail in chapter 9. It is, however, essential to begin our exploration of the issues of the foundations of knowledge by exploring the debate which has developed since the collapse of the Enlightenment project concerning the nature of rationality. We begin by considering Richard Rorty's case for a pragmatic approach to knowledge, based on the assertion that there is no 'objectivity' which may be grasped and represented by human philosophy. Far from being the 'mirror of nature', as the Renaissance fondly believed, Rorty holds that philosophy identifies and consolidates an existing intellectual and moral consensus within human communities.

Tradition and objectivity: the polarity of knowledge

In a paper entitled 'Solidarity or Objectivity?', Richard Rorty argues that there exist two 'principal ways in which reflective human beings try, by placing their lives in a larger context, to give sense to those lives'.[3] The first of these is the way of *solidarity*, by which people aim to give meaning to their existences by allying themselves with a community, real or imaginary, thus establishing a sense of connection and identity. Truth is about belonging and identifying – about 'what it is good for us to believe'. The second is the way of *objectivity*, which Rorty defines in terms of the quest for truth without reference to a given community. He locates the stimulus to develop this approach in the classical recognition of the diversity of communities.

> It was perhaps the growing awareness by the Greeks of the sheer diversity of human communities which stimulated the emergence of this ideal. A fear of parochialism, of being confined within the horizons of the group into which one happens to be born, a need to see it with the eyes of a stranger, helps produce the skeptical and ironic tone characteristic

---

[2] For an exploration of this idea, see Nelson Goodman, *Ways of Worldmaking*. Indianapolis, IN: Hackett Publishing Co., 1978, 138–40.
[3] Richard Rorty, *Objectivity, Relativism and Truth: Philosophical Papers*. Cambridge: Cambridge University Press, 1991, 21–34.

of Euripides and Socrates. Herodotus' willingness to take the barbarians seriously enough to describe their customs in detail may have been a necessary prelude to Plato's claim that the way to transcend skepticism is to envisage a common goal of humanity – a goal set by human nature rather than by Greek culture.

Rorty here describes a tension which can be discerned throughout human cultural history, which has resurfaced as of critical importance through the increasing emphasis being placed upon tradition-mediated rationalities following the demise of the Enlightenment project. Is true knowledge acquired through standing within a tradition, and appropriating and honouring its ideas and values? Or is it to be acquired through the pursuit of an objective realm, whose existence and nature is held to be independent of the tradition within which the searcher stands?

Rorty clearly identifies himself with those who find knowledge and values in and through solidarity. Instead of attempting to find justification for beliefs and values outside a community and its traditions, Rorty argues that we should adopt those beliefs and values which the community has found meaningful and consoling. There is no 'objective' reality outside the community, which anchors and affirms its beliefs, or which functions as a criterion by which they may be evaluated. The pragmatist 'wants solidarity to be our *only* comfort, and to be seen not to require metaphysical support'.[4]

This has major implications for a theory of knowledge, not least the decision to abjure any hope of ever grounding or justifying our beliefs. Rorty insists that we must recognize the limits placed upon us by our historical location, and thus spurn the notion that there is something extra-historical, something transcending individual traditions – an objective reality or 'thing in itself' – which constrains our thinking, such as 'the Kantian notion that there is something which is called a "structure of rationality" which the philosopher discovers and within which we have a moral duty to remain'.[5] As Rorty stresses, this means that we shall lose[6]

what Nietzsche called 'metaphysical comfort', but we may gain a renewed sense of community. Our identification with our community – our society, our political tradition, our intellectual heritage – is heightened

[4] Rorty, *Objectivity, Relativism and Truth*, 14.
[5] Richard Rorty, 'A Reply to Dreyfus and Taylor', *Review of Metaphysics* 34 (1980), 39.
[6] Richard Rorty, *Consequences of Pragmatism*. Minneapolis, MN: University of Minneapolis Press, 1982, 166.

when we see this community as ours rather than nature's, shaped rather than found, one among many which men have made. In the end, the pragmatists tell us, what matters is our loyalty to other human beings clinging together against the dark, not our hope of getting things right. [William] James, in arguing against realists and idealists that 'the trail of the human serpent is over all', was reminding us that our glory is in our participation in fallible and transitory human projects, not in our obedience to permanent nonhuman constraints.

Abandoning any sense of 'metaphysical comfort',[7] Rorty sets out the vision which has inspired western philosophy since its inception as follows:[8]

> To know is to represent accurately what is outside the mind; so to understand the possibility and nature of knowledge is to understand the way in which the mind is able to construct such representations. Philosophy's central concern is to be a general theory of representation.

Rorty has little sympathy with this position, and has spent most of his professional philosophical career attempting to demonstrate the fatuity of this outmoded epistemological enterprise. Throughout his writings, we find the same theme reiterated: classic western philosophy is fixated on issues of epistemology, which can be traced back to the Platonic obsession with universals, which underlies the absurd notion that the human mind or human language is in some way a reliable mirror of nature.

Rorty's programme is as bold as it is iconoclastic, and has attracted attention and interest primarily on account of its radical central thesis – that philosophy, as traditionally conceived, has run into the sands, and has nothing further of value to say. His radical anti-foundationalism systematically erodes any notion that our knowledge is conditioned or shaped in any way by an external reality, which may be known at least to some extent by human procedures of inquiry. Rorty clearly believes that epistemological foundationalism privileges the natural sciences, and that the rejection of any such foundationalism erodes the public credibility of any such intellectual enterprise. This sentiment resonated with the cultural mood of the 1980s, which was increasingly inclined to dispute the idea that the natural sciences were superior to other

---

[7] On this point, see Timothy Jackson, 'The Theory and Practice of Discomfort: Richard Rorty and Pragmatism', *The Thomist* 51 (1987), 270–98.

[8] Richard Rorty, *Philosophy and the Mirror of Nature*. Princeton: Princeton University Press, 1979, 3.

disciplines on account of their explanatory and predictive successes. Rorty increasingly inclined towards the view that truth was simply the 'reification of an approbative and indefinable adjective', arguing that the only proper justification for the norms of warranted assertability was the prevailing social consensus.

Humanity thus creates its own values and ideas, and is not accountable to any external objectivity for the outcome of this creative process. Rorty, here developing Michel Foucault's criticism of general ethical principles and normative standards, argues that a consequence of this communitarian or pragmatic approach to truth must be the recognition that[9]

> there is nothing deep down inside us except what we have put there ourselves, no criterion that we have not created in the course of creating a practice, no standard of rationality that is not an appeal to such a criterion, no rigorous argumentation that is not obedience to our own conventions.

Truth and morality are thus matters of social convention, created by human communities. Yet if Rorty is right, what justification could be given for opposing Nazism? Or Stalinism? Rorty finds himself unable to offer a persuasive justification for the moral or political rejection of totalitarianism, as he himself concedes. If he is right, Rorty admits, then he has to acknowledge that:

> When the secret police come, when the torturers violate the innocent, there is nothing to be said to them of the form 'There is something within you which you are betraying. Though you embody the practices of a totalitarian society, which will endure forever, there is something beyond those practices which condemns you.'

For Rorty, the truth of moral values depends simply upon their existence and acceptance within society. This view has been severely criticized as adopting an uncritical approach concerning prevailing social conventions. As Richard Bernstein points out, Rorty appears to have done little more than reify social practices, and treat these as being synonymous with 'truth':[10]

> We want to know how we are to understand 'social practices', how they are generated, sustained, and pass away. But even more important we

   [9] Richard Rorty, *Consequences of Pragmatism*, xlii.
   [10] Richard J. Bernstein, *Philosophical Profiles: Essays in a Pragmatic Mode.* Philadelphia: University of Pennsylvania Press, 1986, 53–4.

want to know how they are to be criticized. For in any historical period we are confronted not only with a tangle of social practices, but with practices that make competing demands on us. There is danger here of reifying the very idea of a social practice and failing to appreciate that our very criticisms and arguments about what is rational and irrational are constitutive of traditions and social practices.

It will be obvious that Rorty fails to take account of the insights of cultural theorists such as Antonio Gramsci on the means by which the social consensus is generated and – dare we say it? – *manipulated* by interested parties.[11] What Rorty somewhat optimistically – and surely a little naïvely? – treats as a natural consensus to be respected is regarded by Gramsci as 'hegemony' – that is, the ideological control of society through the manipulation of the ideas of a society by vested interests in such a way that they come to be regarded as natural.[12]

> Dominant groups in society, including fundamentally but not exclusively the ruling class, maintain their dominance by securing the 'spontaneous consent' of subordinate groups, including the working class, through the negotiated construction of a political and ideological consensus which incorporates both dominant and dominated groups.

Rorty thus treats a *construction* as a *given*, and falls into precisely the trap which Gramsci identifies – namely, the way in which intellectuals endorse the *status quo* without realizing it, lending it a legitimation which it ought not to possess. It is for this reason that Gramsci draws his famous distinction between the 'traditional intellectual' and the 'organic intellectual'.[13]

Rorty's views undoubtedly raise a challenge for the natural sciences. Yet the challenge raised for Rorty by those same sciences is far greater, and may be argued to constitute the reef against which his Neurathian boat finally founders. If knowledge is defined as the prevailing consensus within a community, how are we to take account of the manifest impact of scientific thinking on the thought of such a community?

---

[11] See Antonio Gramsci, *Gli intellettuali e l'organizzazione della cultura*. 6th edn. Milan: Giulio Einaudi Editore, 1955, 95–128. Note especially the significant role in creating social attitudes ascribed to journalists and the media (129–66). For comment, see David Harris, *From Class Struggle to the Politics of Pleasure: The Effects of Gramscianism on Cultural Studies*. London: Routledge, 1992.

[12] Dominic Strinati, *An Introduction to Theories of Popular Culture*. London: Routledge, 1995, 165.

[13] For the theological application of this important idea, see Alister E. McGrath, *The Future of Christianity*. Oxford: Blackwell, 2001, 146–55.

An example will highlight the issue, and indicate why Rorty's somewhat overstated case for pragmatism rests on somewhat shaky cultural foundations. Let us take the case of the impact of Darwinian thinking on western culture, particularly in the United Kingdom and the United States. The publication of Darwin's *Origin of Species* sparked off a ferocious debate within church and society, not simply over the origins of humanity, but also of its values and ideas.[14] Some of the application of Darwinian ideas may have been open to question – such as the argument that the Darwinian theme of the 'survival of the fittest' gave scientific legitimation to the capitalist model of direct economic competition,[15] or to the use of eugenics as a means of safeguarding racial identity or social competitiveness.[16] More importantly, at least for the purposes of this study, the increasing acceptance of the Darwinian account of the origins of humanity brought with it growing scepticism concerning at least some aspects of the Christian religion,[17] and an increased interest in exploring sociobiological accounts of human behaviour and ideas.[18]

It is beyond dispute that Darwinism has had a massive impact on the shaping of the ideas and values of modern western culture, and creating the consensus upon which Rorty's pragmatism ultimately rests.[19] Yet why does Darwinism have this influence? The answer is simple: *because many culturally sophisticated westerners regard it as offering a true*

[14] There is a huge literature, which merits close study. For general surveys, see Thomas F. Glick, *The Comparative Reception of Darwinism*. Austin: University of Texas Press, 1972; Richard Hofstadter, *Social Darwinism in American Thought*. Boston: Beacon, 1955; James Moore, 'Deconstructing Darwinism: The Politics of Evolution in the 1860s', *Journal of the History of Biology* 24 (1991), 353–408; Jon H. Roberts, *Darwinism and the Divine in America*. Madison: University of Wisconsin Press, 1988. Specific studies of note include: Richard Dawkins, *The Selfish Gene*. Oxford and New York: Oxford University Press, 1989; Michael Ruse, *Taking Darwin seriously: a Naturalistic Approach to Philosophy*. New York: Prometheus Books, 1998.

[15] John Laurent and John Nightingale, *Darwinism and Evolutionary Economics*. Northampton, MA: Edward Elgar, 2001.

[16] Angus McLaren, *Our Own Master Race: Eugenics in Canada 1885–1945*. Oxford: Oxford University Press, 1990.

[17] James R. Moore, *The Post-Darwinian Controversies: A Study of the Protestant Struggle to come to terms with Darwin in Great Britain and America, 1870–1900*. Cambridge: Cambridge University Press, 1979.

[18] Most notably, Edward O. Wilson, *Sociobiology: The New Synthesis*. Cambridge, MA: Harvard University Press, 1975.

[19] For the shaping of the British consensus through press coverage of the issue, see Alvar Ellegård, *Darwin and the General Reader: The Reception of Darwin's Theory of Evolution in the British Periodical Press, 1859–1872*. Chicago: University of Chicago Press, 1990. For the impact of the press on shaping social attitudes and beliefs, see Dominic Strinati, *An Introduction to Theories of Popular Culture*. London: Routledge, 1995.

account of things. Darwin's theory of evolution is widely accepted as a fact in the circles in which Rorty moves, and whose ideas he seeks to reflect as a means of enhancing social cohesion. A similar point could be made concerning the acceptance of Copernicus' heliocentrism over Ptolemy's geocentrism. Rorty's readers do not *believe* that the earth goes round the sun, or that humanity evolved: they *know* these things as facts, as the received indubitable wisdom of the age.

Rorty thus engages a consensus which is partly the response to the belief that certain scientific theories are true, and have relevance beyond the sphere of university laboratories and lecture halls. While Rorty clearly enjoys debunking the idea of philosophy as a 'mirror of nature', some such idea is subtly yet firmly embedded in the reified social consensus which he holds to be the true object of philosophy. Far from eliminating the Renaissance ideal, Rorty implicitly incorporates it into his philosophical manifesto. The social influence of the natural sciences must therefore be given due weight by philosophers who otherwise might wish to ignore or discount their theories. Yet why do such theories have such a social impact? *Because they are believed to be true*; postmodern attempts to argue that they are simply one perspective amidst countless others are not viewed as compelling. An inchoate scientific realism is implicit within the communities whose ideas Rorty values, and whose cohesion he hopes to strengthen. If truth is indeed the 'reification of an approbative and indefinable adjective', so that the only proper justification for the norms of warranted assertability was the prevailing social consensus, the social presuppositions which give rise to this consensus must be identified and be made the object of critical study. And such a study will reveal that an implicit and perhaps unacknowledged scientific realism underlies this consensus – and hence Rorty's pragmatic philosophy.

This naturally leads us on to consider the question of true knowledge according to the natural sciences.

The natural sciences and the question of knowledge

This issue of warranted knowledge is held to be of cardinal importance within the natural sciences, and the rigour with which it has been addressed is widely considered to be one of the most decisive factors contributing to their reputation for explanatory success.[20] Yet it must

---

[20] On the growth of this reputation during the Victorian period, see Richard R. Yeo, *Defining Science: William Whewell, Natural Knowledge and Public Debate in Early Victorian Britain.* Cambridge: Cambridge University Press, 1993.

be stressed that an appeal to the natural sciences in this matter is more complex and nuanced than might at first appear. It is possible to use the phrase 'natural sciences' in a loose and uncritical way, generally meaning 'the physical sciences' – that is, a mature and developed science, where the case for realism can be made with particular force.[21] Yet a scientific theology cannot rest its case solely upon the physical sciences. The challenge is to develop an account of, and identify the theological implications of, the working methods of the natural sciences as a whole, rather than privilege one specific group of those sciences as normative for the entire enterprise.

It is for this reason that the 'critical realism' developed by Roy Bhaskar is of such importance to our agenda. Bhaskar argues that each science develops methodologies appropriate to their ontologies – that is to say, that the proper working method of any given science is determined by the character of its objects of investigation, and cannot be determined *a priori* on the basis of some implicit foundationalism. Methodology is consequent upon ontology, and is hence to be determined *a posteriori*. The stratification of reality demands different working methods and assumptions across the spectrum of the sciences, despite the critical commonalities that may be identified. The stratification of the sciences is inevitably a controversial matter, but might look something like this:[22]

Psychological and Semiological Sciences
Social Sciences
Biological Sciences
Molecular Sciences

By virtue of their subject-matters, a higher degree of constructivism is implicit in psychology or the social sciences than in biology or physics. The psychologist might argue that certain psychological notions (such as emotion, intelligence and self-esteem)[23] and the social scientist that certain social categories (such as race)[24] are essentially constructed

---

[21] John Polkinghorne is an excellent example of a recent writer to press the parallels between theology and physics. For an assessment, see P. D. L. Avis, 'Apologist from the World of Science: John Polkinghorne, FRS', *Scottish Journal of Theology* 43 (1990), 485–502.

[22] Andrew Collier, *Scientific Realism and Socialist Thought*. Hemel Hempstead: Harvester Wheatsheaf, 1988, 45.

[23] For example, see J. A. Russell, 'Culture and the Categorization of Emotions', *Psychological Bulletin* 110 (1991), 426–50.

[24] Robert Young, 'The Linguistic Turn, Materialism and Race', *Alethia* 2.1 (1999), 6–11. For an attempt to argue that race is ontologically pre-given, see Linda Alcoff, 'Philosophy and Racial Identity', *Radical Philosophy* 75 (1996), 5–13. Social constructionists are surely right in arguing that notions such as 'the Negro' or 'the Female' are not inevitable

notions, whereas the physicist would argue that the electron is not. It is therefore essential to reject as simplistic from the outset the idea that *either* all scientific concepts or theories are socially constructed *or* that all such theories are the result of a direct engagement with a pre-existing reality. 'Social structures' and 'natural structures' take very different forms, with a quite distinct epistemic status.[25] Yet both are 'real' and open to analysis, if in different ways. As we have seen, it is perfectly acceptable to postulate hypothetical entities or social constructs where these are understood to be a direct result of a responsible engagement with reality, and a concern to offer the best possible account of that reality, however heuristic and provisional this may be. Yet the extent to which this takes place varies considerably from one natural science to another, with physics – surely significantly – being among the less 'constructed' such disciplines.

We shall be exploring this issue in greater detail throughout this second volume of our project. It will be obvious, however, that the question of the location of the various elements of the Christian faith on this stratified map of reality demands clarification. Barth's insistence on the distinction between 'theology' and 'religion' immediately alerts us to the fact that 'religion' designates a cultural and social phenomenon, rather than a set of ideas – more specifically, a phenomenon whose cultural characteristics are clearly shaped by social and cultural influences.[26] Christianity is embedded at a number of levels within the world – ideational, cultural and historical. The question that concerns us is how these different levels relate to one another, and how a scientific theology may claim to represent them.

Given the ontological stratification of reality, it is problematic to suggest that theology can be treated as the direct equivalent of – for example – physics in terms of its methodological and ontological

---

classifications of human beings, but are human inventions that have done more harm than good, leading to confusion rather than clarity through a process of reification. Yet to say that 'X is a social construction' does not seem to amount to more than saying that 'talking about X is not inevitable, and there are probably better ways of talking about it'.

[25] Roy Bhaskar, *The Possibility of Naturalism: A Philosophical Critique of the Contemporary Human Sciences.* 3rd edn. London: Routledge, 1998, 38.

[26] On Barth, see J. A. Veitch, 'Revelation and Religion in the Thought of Karl Barth', *Scottish Journal of Theology* 24 (1971), 1–22. For a fuller discussion of the general issue, see Daniel L. Pals, *Seven Theories of Religion.* New York: Oxford University Press, 1996; James Thrower, *Religion: The Classical Theories.* Washington, DC: Georgetown University Press, 1999; Jacques Waardenburg, *Classical Approaches to the Study of Religion: Aims, Methods and Theories of Research.* New York: De Gruyter, 1999.

assumptions. We cannot argue that because physics represents an encounter with reality which (arguably) does not make significant use of social constructed entities, the same applies to theology. The question of the location and mutual relation of theological resources within a stratified reality cannot be evaded. Yet equally, the social construction of some aspects of our interaction with reality does not negate the existence of that reality. A critical realism is sensitive to these differing strata of reality, and their implications for scientific method. It is therefore proper and necessary to engage with the natural sciences as a means of gaining at least a partial grasp of the issues underlying a realist approach to the world.

We begin our discussion of such a realist view of the world by considering the question of how knowledge of the world is gained and confirmed.

The scientific programme: corresponding coherently to reality

If there is indeed a mind-independent external world, as realists hold, the question of how we obtain and confirm knowledge of that external world becomes of central importance. The natural sciences have always insisted that the answer lies in experimentation – the observation of the natural world under monitored and controlled conditions which ensure the maximum degree of objectivity is attained.[27] As Max Planck put it: 'Experiments are the only means of knowledge at our disposal. The rest is poetry, imagination.' Even those who are supportive of a 'strong programme' in the sociology of knowledge have drawn attention to the serious misrepresentation of the scientific enterprise which it brings in its wake, apparently as its corollary – the devaluation of an engagement with nature as a means of advancing scientific knowledge.[28] One of the most serious weaknesses in the essentially sociological understanding of the development of the natural sciences advanced by Thomas Kuhn

---

[27] The subject is, of course, rather more complex than these brief statements can hope to suggest. For some of the issues, see Robert Ackermann, 'Experiment as the Motor of Scientific Progress', *Social Epistemology* 2 (1988), 327–35; Robert Ackermann, 'The New Experimentalism', *British Journal for the Philosophy of Science* 40 (1989), 185–90; J. G. Burke, *Promoting Experimental Learning: Experiment and the Royal Society 1660–1727*. Cambridge: Cambridge University Press, 1991; Allen Franklin, *The Neglect of Experiment*. Cambridge: Cambridge University Press, 1986; David Gooding, Trevor Pinch and Simon Schaffer (eds), *The Uses of Experiment: Studies in the Natural Sciences*. Cambridge: Cambridge University Press, 1989.

[28] Martin J. S. Rudwick, *The Great Devonian Controversy: The Shaping of Scientific Knowledge among Gentlemanly Specialists*. Chicago: University of Chicago Press, 1985, 450–6.

is his failure to bring out clearly just how critically important experimentation was to the emergence of new ways of thinking.

This deficiency is particularly clear in Kuhn's major study of the black-body radiation problem as it bears on the development of quantum theory,[29] which makes hardly any mention of the critical experiments which showed that there was a serious discrepancy between theoretical predictions on the basis of a classical model and the actual outcome of experimental observation. It was these discrepancies which led Planck to formulate the quantization of energy, with momentous implications for modern physical theory. Even the most elementary introduction to the development of quantum theory would treat these experimental observations as being of critical importance. Kuhn's failure to deal with this raises very serious questions concerning the credibility of the conclusions he draws from his account of this episode.[30]

Despite the enormous complexity of the relation between experiment and theory, it needs to be said that there is a widespread consensus that theory must be grounded in or consistent with experimental observations. In this sense, Planck is correct. At least in principle, theories either *account for what is already known* through experimentation or observation (sometimes referred to as 'retrodiction'), or *predict hitherto unknown results* which may be confirmed or refuted by experiments.[31] There is no doubt that the history of science provides a very large number of examples of precisely this pattern: the Compton effect provided important confirmation of the 'photon' theory of light, and resulted from an experiment designed to confirm or refute this theory. Yet other patterns can easily be discerned. For example, the advance of the perihelion of Mercury was known as a phenomenon before it was explained by Einstein's theory of relativity. Experiments can be in error, due to flaws in their design or instrumentation, thus leading to misleading conclusions.[32]

[29] Thomas Kuhn, *Black-Body Radiation and the Quantum Discontinuity*. Oxford: Clarendon Press, 1978.

[30] These experiments are discussed in the opening pages of Peter W. Atkins and R. S. Friedman, *Molecular Quantum Mechanics*. 3rd edn. Oxford: Oxford University Press, 1997, 1–2, setting the scene for the detailed theoretical analysis which follows.

[31] See the classic study of John Worrall, 'Fresnel, Poisson and the White Spot: The Role of Successful Predictions in the Acceptance of Scientific Theories', in David Gooding, Trevor Pinch and Simon Schaffre (eds), *The Uses of Experiment: Studies in the Natural Sciences*. Cambridge: Cambridge University Press, 1989, 135–57.

[32] Giora Hon, 'Is the Identification of Experimental Error contextually dependent? The Case of Kaufmann's Experiment and its Varied Reception', in Jed Z. Buchwald (ed.), *Scientific Practice: Theories and Stories of Doing Physics*. Chicago: University of Chicago Press, 1995, 170–223.

Occasionally – especially in popular accounts of the development of the sciences – actual events are made to conform to the pattern demanded by a 'theory then experiment' model. For example, the discovery of the 2.9 K background radiation by Arno Penzias and Robert Wilson in 1964 actually took place by accident, while they were working on an experimental microwave antenna at the Bell Laboratories in New Jersey. Yet at least one account of that observation interprets this as a deliberate attempt to confirm a hypothesis, thus subtly massaging the facts of history to suit the needs of a preconceived theory: 'Radio-astronomers believed that if they could aim a very sensitive receiver at a blank part of the sky that appeared to be empty, it might be possible to determine whether or not the theorists were correct.'[33] The importance of serendipity in experimental advance cannot be overlooked,[34] nor can it be misrepresented as intentionality. Yet a realistic account of scientific method is perfectly capable of explaining the accidental discovery of truth. If the real world exists independently of our recognition of its reality, it does not matter whether we discover its structures through intentional investigation or accidental encounter; the same reality is encountered.

Yet despite all the qualifications that must be entered against our broad statement that theory must be grounded in or consistent with experimental observations, the general principle holds: scientific theories must be grounded in the real world. They are accountable to the reality they purport to represent. Ontological finality thus rests with nature itself.

Yet scientific theories are not merely understood to be grounded in an external reality; the issue of internal theoretical coherence is held to be of importance. The ideas which arise from an engagement with reality should ultimately be consistent with each other. The general consensus on this matter within the natural sciences can be summarized in terms of the programme of 'corresponding coherently to reality' – which is to say, that scientific theories should be grounded in the bedrock of an engagement with the real world, and that the theories resulting from this engagement should be internally consistent. The idea of coherence can thus be articulated in terms of intra-systemic consistency, or a broader notion of coherence which takes into account a broader range of issues – as in Paul Thagard's notion of

---

[33] F. M. Branley, *The Electromagnetic Spectrum*. New York: Crowell, 1979, 100.
[34] Aharon Kantorovitch and Yuval Ne'eman, 'Serendipity as a Source of Evolutionary Progress in Science', *Studies in History and Philosophy of Science* 20 (1989), 505–30.

'explanatory coherence'.[35] Thagard offers a theory of explanatory coherence where propositions hold together because of their explanatory relations, established through the operation of principles such as symmetry, explanation, analogy, contradiction, competition and acceptability.

Alfred North Whitehead argued that metaphysical views should satisfy both *empirical* and *logical* criteria before gaining acceptance. The empirical criterion is that philosophical theses should apply adequately to experience; the logical criterion is that they should be consistent and coherent with each other. In effect, Whitehead comes close to melding correspondence and coherentist approaches to knowledge, insisting upon both intra-systemic and extra-systemic criteria in theory choice. Adequacy of scientific theories could thus be tested *formally* by a consistency analysis via mathematical proofs and *empirically* by experimental procedures. The consistency analysis presupposes a concise formalization of a theory in the language of mathematics and logic – raising the critically important issue of mathematical realism, to which we shall turn in a later chapter – but since it disregards the issue of correspondence with reality, it is only to be regarded as necessary, but not sufficient for theoretical adequacy. It is perfectly possible to postulate an internally consistent system which has no adequate grounding in reality. To be taken seriously, a theory must resonate with what may be observed, and be internally consistent.

This kind of approach finds widespread acceptance within the natural sciences, presumably because it combines an insistence upon the empirical foundations of scientific knowledge with the belief that the scientific theories developed on the basis of the analysis of experience should be internally consistent. It also finds much support among theologians. Thus Wolfhart Pannenberg's theological programme could be stated in terms of demonstrating on the one hand the internal coherence of Christian doctrines, and on the other the external coherence or consistency of those doctrines with the world of reality and other intellectual disciplines.[36] While some philosophers have insisted that we are obligated to accept either a correspondence or a coherentist approach to justified belief, there are excellent reasons for suggesting that both can be seen as intrinsic elements of a robust view of reality.

---

[35] Paul Thagard, *Conceptual Revolutions.* Princeton, NJ: Princeton University Press, 1993.
[36] Wolfhart Pannenberg, *Systematic Theology.* 3 vols. Grand Rapids, MI: Eerdmans, 1991–8, vol. 1, 21–2.

Latent within Whitehead's brief statement are two criteria, whose interplay has been the subject of considerable debate within the philosophical community. The two criteria are (1) being appropriately grounded in the real world, and (2) being possessed of an appropriate degree of internal consistency. How those criteria are to be defined, and whether they are complementary or contradictory, remains a matter of considerable debate. For example, W. F. Sellars' philosophy can be argued to be a complex meld of foundationalist and coherentist elements, based on the perception that neither is adequate on its own.

Sellars points this out in his oft-cited study 'Empiricism and the Study of Mind', in which he explores the interplay of an image of foundationalism (an elephant standing on a tortoise) and an image of coherentism (a serpent whose tail is in its mouth). The former, Sellars argues, is a mythical representation of the need for a foundation for knowledge; the elephant has to stand on *something*. The latter is to be seen as representing the unbroken circle which is characteristic of the ideas of a coherent philosophy. As Arthur Kenyon Rogers pointed out, the justification of a belief on this approach rests on its 'inclusion within a coherent system'.[37] Yet each of these approaches, Sellars insists, is deficient:[38]

> One seems forced to choose between the picture of an elephant which rests on a tortoise (what supports the tortoise?) and the picture of a great Hegelian serpent of knowledge with its tail in its mouth (where does it begin?). Neither will do.

Although Sellars is sometimes taken to be an anti-foundationalist, the situation is not quite that simple. As William Alston points out, Sellars seems to advocate a 'sort of synthesis of foundationalism and coherentism'.[39] The synthesis seems perfectly viable, not least on account of the well-known weaknesses of both accounts of justified beliefs.

Correspondence theories of truth may be broken down into three fundamental components, by which sentences of a certain type are true or false in virtue of:[40]

[37] Arthur Kenyon Rogers, *What is Truth? An Essay in the Theory of Knowledge.* New Haven, CT: Yale University Press, 1923, 12.

[38] Wilfrid Sellars, *Science, Perception and Reality.* New York: Humanities Press, 1962, 170.

[39] William P. Alston, 'What's Wrong with Immediate Knowledge?', *Synthese* 55 (1983), 73–96. See also James Cornman, 'Foundational versus Nonfoundational Theories of Empirical Justification', *American Philosophical Quarterly* 14 (1977), 287–97, who notes that Sellars can be taken as a foundationalist in certain respects.

[40] Here following Michael Devitt, *Realism and Truth.* Oxford: Blackwell, 1984.

1. their structure;

2. the referential relations between parts of the sentences and some reality; and

3. the nature of this reality.

Correspondence theories of truth would generally be affirmed to hold in respect to certain types of statements (such as those deriving from the natural sciences) while not in the case of others (particularly those which derive from ethics). The second issue noted here concerns the nature of the referential relation. Various theories have been proposed to explain this relation, including causal accounts (such as those found in the writings of F. I. Dretske, Hilary Putnam and Saul Kripke)[41] and more recently teleofunctional accounts (Ruth Millikan).[42] The third point concerns the nature of the reality to which the parts of the sentences correspond. A realist will hold that this reality is objective and mind-independent, whereas an idealist could take the view that it is objective yet not mind-independent. It is thus important to appreciate that the term 'correspondence theory' embraces quite a diverse range of options.

The defence of realism mounted throughout this work allows us to affirm that it is important that scientific theories or Christian doctrines correspond to an extra-systemic reality. The coherentist position, taken on its own, is perfectly capable of validating an internally consistent world-view which makes no significant point of contact with the real world, or which evades such contact altogether. Coherency does not guarantee truth – merely logical consistency. A belief can be consistent with all other beliefs within a system, and yet have no independent supporting evidence. A scientific theology affirms the critical importance of both extra-systemic reference and intra-systemic consistency, holding that a proper grasp of spiritual reality will ensure both.

This point is of no small importance theologically. The noted Anglican theologian Charles Gore – whose works have been shamefully neglected of late – often spoke of the 'coherence of Christian doctrine'.[43] Yet Gore never for one moment supposed that the credibility of Christian doctrine rested upon that coherence alone; its supreme

---

[41] See Saul A. Kripke, *Naming and Necessity*. Oxford: Blackwell, 1980; Hilary Putnam, *Representation and Reality*. Cambridge, MA: MIT Press, 1991.

[42] Ruth G. Millikan, *Language, Thought and other Biological Catagories: New Foundations for Realism*. Cambridge, MA: MIT Press, 1984.

[43] See especially his 1891 Bampton Lectures: Charles Gore, *The Incarnation of the Son of God*. London: John Murray, 1922.

foundation and criterion was its adequacy as an expression of the Christian understanding of the significance of Jesus Christ, as presented in Scripture and the Christian experience.[44] Christian dogma was possessed of a certain coherence precisely because it corresponded, however faintly, to the reality of the living God, incarnate in Jesus Christ. The coherence of Christian doctrine was a direct consequence of its ultimate grounding in God's self-being and self-disclosure. Gore was quite clear that human language was simply not capable of adequately reflecting the glory of God, being forced to use analogies and images to point to the greater reality which they mirror.[45]

Coherentism has its weaknesses, as we have seen. Yet in recent years, certain fundamental criticisms have been brought against the notion of knowledge being grounded in some kind of objective reality. As the criticisms directed against classical foundationalism – which seem to me to be unassailable – are often misunderstood to imply the rejection of any attempt to 'ground' knowledge in the external world, it is clearly of considerable importance to establish precisely what 'classical foundationalism' designates, and why it is now regarded as outmoded. As we shall see, this critique of foundationalism represents a serious difficulty for the Enlightenment project – but not for the notion, characteristic of the natural sciences, that knowledge may be held to be grounded in reality. To explore this matter further, we must turn our attention to the notion of the 'foundations of knowledge'.

The rise and fall of classical foundationalism

It has become a commonplace to speak of the 'foundations of knowledge' or 'the foundations of philosophy', as if this represented a self-evident truth. The rhetoric of such phrases is of no small importance. After all, if something lacks a foundation, is it not irrational, arbitrary or disreputable? To suggest that there is no such foundation immediately seems to call into question the reliability of a belief. It is hardly surprising that many have reacted with astonishment, even outrage, to the suggestion that no foundation is necessary for Christian theology.

---

[44] Charles Gore, *The Incarnation of the Son of God*, 21–6; 96–106. For similar themes in the theology of this important period in British theology, see H. P. Liddon, *The Divinity of our Lord and Saviour Jesus Christ*. London: Longmans, Green & Co., 1903; H. R. Mackintosh, *The Doctrine of the Person of Jesus Christ*. Edinburgh: T&T Clark, 1913.

[45] A point explored in more detail by his theological successors within Anglicanism: Austin Farrer, *A Rebirth of Images: The Making of St John's Apocalypse*. London: Dacre Press, 1949; Eric L. Mascall, *Existence and Analogy*. London: Darton, Longman & Todd, 1966.

This concern is entirely justified, and demonstrates the signal failure of both academic theology and philosophy to *explain* their ideas to a wider public. In view of the widespread misunderstandings which accompany the growing rejection of foundationalism, this chapter will offer far more explanatory material than is normally found in such academic discussions. It is essential to explain and justify the ideas which have led many to suggest that properly warranted beliefs do not necessarily require a foundation at all.

To begin with, we may explore the origins of the imagery of a 'foundation'. Why is our thinking about proper knowledge so heavily conditioned by the image of a building resting on a foundation? The implication of the image is clear: without a secure foundation, the building will collapse. The image has been of particular importance to Christian theology, in that a number of biblical passages use metaphors drawn from the construction of buildings to make the point that a life not secured by the living presence of God is unstable and corrigible (Luke 6:47–9; 1 Corinthians 3:12). Yet these familiar images are not intended to be used in connection with the issue of how true knowledge is to be found and acquired. The image of a building resting upon secure foundations is, however, to be found liberally scattered throughout the writings of Descartes, where it assumes an epistemically decisive function.

The classical foundationalist bases her approach to knowledge on three fundamental assumptions:

1. That there are foundational or basic beliefs which guarantee their own truth, which are accessible to any rational person, irrespective of their historical or cultural context;

2. That a series of mediate or non-basic beliefs may be derived from these immediate or basic beliefs;

3. That the connection between immediate and mediate beliefs is 'truth preserving'; in other words, that the truth of basic beliefs may be preserved in moving to non-basic beliefs.

It will be clear that further discussion is required at every point. For example, what mechanisms can ensure that the certainty of basic beliefs is transferred to non-basic beliefs? And in what category – basic or non-basic beliefs – are religious ideas, such as belief in God, to be placed? And in what ways may the truth of the premises of deduction and induction themselves be justified? This final question has been of especial importance, and requires further comment.

Perhaps the most immediately obvious available answer is that these premises are themselves justified on the basis of previous deductive or inductive arguments. Yet this initially promising line of argument leads to the possibility of an infinite regression, in which justification of the truth of these prior premises is sought, leading to a demand for justification of the premises on which these themselves rest . . . and so forth, *ad infinitum* and *ad nauseam*. Bonjour sets out the viable possibilities for dealing with this issue as follows.[46]

1. The regress might terminate with beliefs which are offered as justifying premises for earlier beliefs but for which no justification of any kind, however implicit, is available when they are challenged in turn.

2. The regress might continue indefinitely 'backwards', with ever more new empirical premise-beliefs being introduced, so that no belief is repeated in the sequence and yet no end is ever reached.

3. The regress might circle back upon itself, so that if the demand for justification is pushed far enough, beliefs which have already appeared as premises (and have themselves been provisionally justified) earlier in the sequence of justificatory arguments are again appealed to as justifying premises.

4. The regress might terminate because 'basic' empirical beliefs are reached – beliefs which have a degree of epistemic justification which is not inferentially dependent on other empirical beliefs and thus raises no further issue of empirical justification.

The essential point is that the 'basic beliefs' do not themselves require demonstration or justification; they function as axioms, self-evident truths which may be used to derive other beliefs (provided that the means used ensures that their truth is preserved in subsequent beliefs). As Bonjour argues:[47]

> The central thesis of epistemological foundationalism as understood here, is the twofold thesis: (a) that some empirical beliefs possess a measure of epistemic justification which is somehow immediate or intrinsic to them, at least in the sense of not being dependent, inferentially or otherwise, on the epistemic justification of other empirical beliefs; and (b) that it is these 'basic beliefs', as they are sometimes called, which are the ultimate source of all justification for *all* of empirical knowledge.

---

[46] Bonjour, *The Structure of Empirical Knowledge*, 22–3.
[47] Bonjour, *The Structure of Empirical Knowledge*, 17.

So what beliefs might count as foundational? Given their critical role in the construction of a philosophical or theological system, the veracity of such beliefs must be beyond doubt. The answers provided by René Descartes initially seemed to offer an unshakeable foundation for philosophical reflection.

Deduction from basic beliefs as the foundation of knowledge?

The strongly foundationalist approach of the Enlightenment can be argued to rest upon Descartes' insistence that any true 'knowledge' would be infallible, incorrigible and indubitable – that is to say, that it would be immune from error, refutation and doubt. There exists a privileged category of 'aristocratic beliefs', upon which all others are ultimately determined.[48] Where earlier philosophers tended simply to assume that there were adequate foundations for philosophical inquiry, Descartes believed it was essential to *establish* them, not least because of his growing awareness through personal travel of the cultural location and situatedness of many apparently 'universal' beliefs. So what strategies or mechanisms are appropriate to preserving the truth of premises? The two methods which secure truth and minimize error are deductive and inductive (by which I shall also understand abductive) reasoning. Deductive reasoning secures true conclusions relative to the truth of the premises, while inductive reasoning operates with the arguably less secure truth-preserving criteria of 'reasonableness', 'warrantedness' or 'probability'. Not surprisingly, deductive inference from secure epistemic foundations was regarded by Descartes as the only means by which mediate knowledge could be established while preserving the truth of its foundations. Without foundations, can knowledge be anything other than mere opinion?[49]

The rigidity of Descartes at this point has been the subject of much comment. Was not Descartes being unduly restrictive in allowing deduction as the only method to generate further justifiable beliefs? Why only deduction? Why not concede that various inductive methods could also be brought to bear upon the 'obvious' or 'self-evident', yielding further justified beliefs? The answer appears to be that Descartes was primarily concerned with what can be justified with *certainty*. Since

[48] Nicholas Rescher, *A System of Pragmatic Idealism.* Princeton, NJ: Princeton University Press, 1992, 161.
[49] For a good account of this 'Cartesian anxiety', see Richard J. Bernstein, *Beyond Objectivism and Relativism: Science, Hermeneutics, and Praxis.* Philadelphia: University of Pennsylvania Press, 1991, 8–20.

it is widely held that induction cannot yield certainties, it is not difficult to understand Descartes' decision to recognize deduction as the only valid means of connecting immediate and mediate knowledge. Most later foundationalists, however, have been prepared to allow inductive methods to generate justified beliefs, while generally agreeing with Descartes that deduction was the most reliable mechanism for preserving the truth of basic beliefs.

It will thus be clear that, although the harshness of Descartes' judgement has been widely criticized, with many critics pointing to the significant role played by inductive and probabilistic inference in human reasoning, there remains little consensus on what to put in the place of the Cartesian criteria.[50] This is not to say that there has been a shortage of suggestions. The most important attempts to defend foundationalism in recent times have made an appeal to experience as providing basic beliefs, moving away from the Cartesian view that propositions are the foundational beliefs to the quite distinct notion that subjective experiential states may be seen as constituting 'self-evident' or 'basic' beliefs. Whereas many popular accounts of foundationalism imply that 'basic' beliefs are propositional, experiential construals of foundationalism take their cue from subjective human perceptions.[51]

Experience as the foundation of knowledge?

An appeal to human experience as the foundation of knowledge is found in Paul Moser's important work *Knowledge and Evidence* (1989).[52] Moser rejects all accounts of basic beliefs that involve these beliefs being self-probable; that they depend upon an infinitely regressing chain of probable propositions for their probability; or that they are made probable by a circular chain of propositions. Rather, Moser's version of foundationalism attempts to ground justification in human experience, so that subjective experiential states are accepted as non-propositional probability-maker or truth-guarantors.

Now it must be conceded immediately that Moser's construal of foundationalism is not typical in every respect. For example, he does not require certainty at the basis of the justificatory structure, in contrast

---

[50] See F. L. Will, *Induction and Justification: An Investigation of Cartesian Procedure in the Philosophy of Knowledge*. Ithaca, NY: Cornell University Press, 1974.

[51] For some useful reflections, see Dirk-Martin Grube, 'Religious Experience after the Demise of Foundationalism', *Religious Studies* 31 (1995), 37–52.

[52] Paul K. Moser, *Knowledge and Evidence*. Cambridge: Cambridge University Press, 1989, 52–63.

to the classical foundationalism of Descartes, or the more recent construals of C. I. Lewis and Roderick Chisholm.[53] All that is required is that the proposition be a decisively better explanation than its possible competitors. Note also that nothing in Moser's system requires or makes use of self-justifying propositions.

To some, Moser's is a curious form of foundationalism, if it is a form of foundationalism at all. Yet Moser's position must be defined as 'foundationalist', in that the process of justification derives from a single starting point: all justification (at least, all *empirical* justification) is traced back to non-propositional, perceptual experience. It is important to note here that not all justification is to be understood as a matter of relations between propositions, contrary to the claims of coherence theories of justification, in that one form of justification has to do with relations between non-propositional experiential contents and propositions. Human perception can give rise to justified propositions if those propositions have strong explanatory power relative to the perceptual experiences. On the basis of such basic, justified propositions, other propositions can be justified by means of deductive and other inductive inferences. While most will be impressed by the differences between Moser and Descartes, there are still recognizable continuities between them. Above all, human experience is allowed to play a fundamental role in the process of justification.

This appeal to experience as foundational has played a major role in Christian theology since the Enlightenment. Many nineteenth-century religious writers resorted to the argument that a universal human religious experience could act as the foundation of a theological system. Thus F. D. E. Schleiermacher developed an approach to theology based on *das Gefühl*, the immediate human self-consciousness. The general human consciousness of being dependent is, according to Schleiermacher, recognized and interpreted within the context of the Christian faith as a sense of total dependence upon God. This 'feeling of absolute dependence (*das Gefühl schlechthinniger Abhängigkeit*)' constitutes the starting point for Christian theology.[54]

[53] Roderick M. Chisholm, *Theory of Knowledge*. 3rd edn. Englewood Cliffs, NJ: Prentice-Hall International, 1989. See further Ernest Sosa (ed.), *Essays on the Philosophy of Roderick M. Chisholm*. Amsterdam: Rodopi, 1979.

[54] W. Schulze, 'Schleiermachers Theorie des Gefühls und ihre religiöse Bedeutung', *Zeitschrift für Theologie und Kirche* 53 (1956), 75–103; F. W. Graf, 'Ursprüngliches Gefühl unmittelbarer Koinzidenz des Differenzen: Zur Modifikation des Religionsbegriffs in der verschiedenen Auflagen von Schleiermachers Reden über die Religion', *Zeitschrift für Theologie und Kirche* 75 (1978), 147–86.

As A. E. Biedermann later commented, Schleiermacher's theology may be regarded as the subjection of the deep inner feelings of humanity to critical inquiry.

During the heydey of the Enlightenment, the Cartesian foundationalist programme enjoyed a virtually uncritical reception. The widespread acceptance of the necessity and propriety of these 'epistemic immunities' led to a growing conviction that any knowledge worthy of the name was rather restricted in scope, and did not include many traditional forms of knowledge.[55] An excellent example of this is provided by the growing scepticism of the eighteenth century concerning the epistemic value of history. An increasing acceptance of the importance of the Cartesian 'epistemic immunities' led to the conclusion that history – here understood to include both historical figures and events – could not give access to the incorrigible kind of knowledge that was essential for a rational religious or philosophical system. How can the move from historical truth (which is essentially a collection of accidents and contingencies) to the necessary and universal truths of reason take place? Many theologians who bought into the Cartesian agenda, such as G. E. Lessing, argued that historical and rational truth were incommensurable, with the former being fallible, corrigible and dubitable.[56] It could easily be dispensed with for theological purposes.

This development had no small importance for the traditional Christian view that the history of Jesus of Nazareth, when rightly interpreted, was of fundamental importance to Christian theology. Was not Jesus of Nazareth both the foundation and criterion of any authentically Christian theology, as Martin Luther and others had argued? Lessing argued otherwise. Theology was called upon to conform to the wisdom of the age, and operate within the standards demanded of the Enlightenment community in general – namely, that its knowledge should be infallible, incorrigible and indubitable.

Since the history of Jesus of Nazareth simply did not have the epistemic status necessary to yield infallible, incorrigible and indubitable knowledge, Enlightenment writers argued that it could not be allowed to have any foundational or normative role. By its very nature, history could not act as the foundation of knowledge:[57]

---

[55] G. H. R. Parkinson, *Truth, Knowledge and Reality: Inquiries into the Foundations of Seventeenth-Century Rationalism.* Wiesbaden: Steiner Verlag, 1981.

[56] See Gordon E. Michalson, *Lessing's Ugly Ditch: A Study of Theology and History.* University Park: Pennsylvania State University Press, 1985. On Lessing in general, see Henry Allison, *Lessing and the Enlightenment.* Ann Arbor, MI: University of Michigan, 1966.

[57] G. E. Lessing, 'On the Proof of the Spirit and Power', in H. Chadwick (ed.), *Lessing's Theological Writings.* Stanford: Stanford University Press, 1956, 53–5.

If no historical truth can be demonstrated, then nothing can be demonstrated by means of historical truths. That is: accidental truths of history can never become the proof of necessary truths of reason . . . That, then, is the ugly broad ditch (*garstiger breiter Graben*) which I cannot get across, however often and however earnestly I have tried to make the leap.

Lessing's phrase 'an ugly broad ditch' between faith and history – or, more strictly, between what is to be regarded as epistemically foundational and what is not – has been seen as summing up the gulf fixed between traditional and rationalist approaches to Christian theology, and is to be seen as a landmark in modern theology. But it is a landmark that has been moved, and now discarded.

Frege: the failure of foundationalism in mathematics

One of the most significant contributing factors to this development has been the failure of foundationalism in mathematics, perhaps the area of human thought in which it should reign supreme. So what are the foundations, upon which mathematics rests securely? This question came to be of critical importance in the later nineteenth century, and was given careful attention by Gottlob Frege.[58] For Frege, arithmetic was founded in logical principles which were available to any rational being, irrespective of their historical or cultural location. The laws of logic were thus foundational, the 'laws of the laws of nature', as Frege put it. In the first volume of his *Grundgesetze der Arithmetik* (1893–4), Frege demonstrated that logic was the universal foundation of mathematics – a remarkable achievement, which seemed to mark the triumph of foundationalism as a philosophical system and of logic as the basis of human knowledge.

Except that Bertrand Russell wrote to Frege as the second volume of this massive work was going to press, pointing out an error. In his autobiography, Russell explained how, in the spring of 1901, he began to 'consider those classes which are not members of themselves, and to ask whether the class of such classes is or is not a member of itself. I found that either answer implies its contradictory. At first I supposed that I should be able to overcome the contradiction quite easily, and that probably there was some trivial error in the reasoning. Gradually, however, it became clear that this was not the case'. To understand the point at issue, let A be defined as the set of all sets that are not their

---

[58] Gideon Makin, *The Metaphysics of Meaning: Russell and Frege on Sense and Denotation.* London: Routledge, 2000, 135–78.

own elements. Assuming $A \in A$ leads to a contradiction for, by definition, A does not contain itself. However, assuming $A \notin A$ implies that A satisfies the definition and, hence, $A \in A$, which is an impossibility.[59] Or to put this more formally, that:

$$- (Ex)(y) \ (Rxy < = > - Ryy)$$

At first, Russell appears to have believed that this was simply an irritatingly trivial problem. As his research progressed, however, he began to realize its devastating implications for Frege's new philosophy of mathematics. The Paradox dealt a body-blow to Frege's system, from which it never recovered. It inspired Russell and Alfred North Whitehead to undertake a salvage operation. In their *Principia Mathematica* (1910), they argued for a different approach to logic, which avoided the problem faced by Frege. Yet the inelegance of the work convinced many that this foundationalist approach had failed. It there existed foundations for mathematics, they must lie elsewhere. Some sought this foundation in set theory; in due course, this also proved a dead end. The result was a crisis of confidence in the very idea of the 'foundations of mathematics'. As Reuben Hersh summarized the situation in two points:[60]

1. The unspoken assumption in all foundationist viewpoints is that mathematics must be a source of indubitable truth;

2. The actual experience of all schools – and the actual daily experience of mathematicians – shows that mathematical truth, like other kinds of truth, is fallible and corrigible.

Elsewhere, Hersh develops this theme in greater detail:[61]

> We are still in the aftermath of the great foundationist controversies of the early twentieth century. Formalism, intuitionism and logicism each left its trace in the form of a certain mathematical research program than ultimately made its own contribution to the corpus of mathematics itself. As *philosophical* programs, as attempts to establish a secure foundation for mathematical knowledge, all have run their course and petered out or dried up.

---

[59] For a good discussion of the background to this episode, see Ray Monk, *Bertrand Russell: The Spirit of Solitude*. London: Jonathan Cape, 1996, 142–4; 142–4. For the Paradox itself, see Reinhardt Grossmann, 'Russell's Paradox and Complex Properties', *Nous* 6 (1972), 153–64.

[60] Reuben Hersh, 'Some Proposals for Reviving the Philosophy of Mathematics', *Advances in Mathematics* 31 (1979), 31–50.

[61] Reuben Hersh, 'Introducing Imre Lakatos', *Mathematical Intelligencer* 1 (1978), 148–51.

The failure of the three great foundationalism programmes of the early twentieth century – formalism, intuitionism and logicism – have left a deep impact on the philosophy of mathematics in particular, and the general philosophical discussion of foundationalism in general. If mathematics does not have a foundation, what does? Yet, as Hilary Putnam pointed out in an important article, why should anyone think that mathematics needs a 'foundation' to work properly?[62] Answering this question emphatically in the negative, he argues that mathematics can be regarded as quasi-empirical, so that one can speak of 'mathematical realism' with as much justification as one can affirm 'scientific realism'.

While Frege's programme in mathematics remains of considerable interest and importance, the collapse of its foundationalism seems total and irredeemable. The consequences of this for a scientific theology are almost entirely positive, as will become clear from what follows.

Frege and the linguistic turn in philosophy

If Frege was right in his strongly foundationalist programme, the intellectual foundations of a dialogue in science and religion, and above all the habitability of the intellectual space we have designated 'a scientific theology', would have been fatally eroded. Wentzel van Huyssteen identifies the importance of this point as follows:[63]

Foundationalism, as the thesis that our beliefs can be warranted or justified by appealing to some item of knowledge that is self-evident or beyond doubt, certainly eliminates any possibility of discovering a meaningful epistemological link between theology and the other sciences. The claim that knowledge rests on foundations is the claim that there is a privileged class of beliefs that are intrinsically credible and that are able, therefore, to serve as ultimate terminating points for chains of justification.

Frege's mathematical philosophy is widely regarded as marking a fundamental turn in modern philosophy, in which the traditional concern for epistemology is displaced by the philosophy of language.[64] The 'linguistic turn' in philosophy, which can be argued to be initiated through Frege, marked an end to the philosophical trend which had valued and fostered an engagement between philosophy and the

---

[62] Hilary Putnam, 'Mathematics without Foundations', *Journal of Philosophy* 64 (1967), 5–22.
[63] Wentzel van Huyssteen, *Essays in Postfoundationalist Theology*. Grand Rapids, MI: Eerdmans, 1997, 226.

natural sciences. This important trend, which can be seen in many works of philosophy from the sixteenth to the nineteenth century – such as Ernst Haeckel's brilliant exploration of the epistemological and ethical implications of the natural sciences[65] – was brought to an abrupt halt through Frege's opposition to what he regarded as illegitimate intrusions on the part of biology (especially Darwinism) and psychology. Philosophy is a pure discipline, which should not be bastardized through inappropriate intimacies or matings with the natural sciences (or any other intellectual disciplines, for that matter).

It would be an overstatement to suggest that the early-twentieth-century reconfiguration of philosophy was entirely due to Frege's influence. The 'linguistic turn' in philosophy can only partly be ascribed to Frege's influence; even then, this is often indirect – for example, through the influence of his lectures upon Ludwig Wittgenstein and Rudolf Carnap. Bertrand Russell and Moritz Schlick can be argued to have derived their analytical philosophies independently of Frege. However, as Philip Kitcher has so compellingly argued, some of the cardinal theses of the emerging antinaturalism of this critical period can be seen to rest on Frege's writings.[66] There is a direct lineage from 'Frege, leading through Russell, Wittgenstein and Carnap to the professional philosophy practised in Britain, North America, Australasia and Scandinavia in the postwar years'. A new way of reading the earlier philosophical tradition developed, with Leibniz, Hume and Kant being read through Fregean-Wittgensteinian spectacles as 'analytical philosophers *manqués*'. For example, Bertrand Russell's *Philosophy of Leibniz* (1900) offers a markedly post-Fregean reading of this classic philosopher, apparently without any sense of irony or anachronism.

The outcome of this Fregean purge of the influence of the natural sciences within philosophy is best seen in Wittgenstein's *Tractatus Logico-Philosophicus*. In this landmark text, Wittgenstein systematically and deliberately insulates philosophical analysis from any contamination by these disciplines.[67]

[64] Richard Rorty, *The Linguistic Turn: Essays in Philosophical Method.* Chicago: University of Chicago Press, 1992; Amitabha Das Gupta, *The Second Linguistic Turn: Chomsky and the Philosophy of Language.* Frankfurt am Main: Peter Lang, 1996.

[65] Ernst Haeckel, *Die Welträtsel: Gemeinverständliche Studien über monistische Philosophie.* Bonn: Emil Strauss, 1899. For an excellent study of the generally positive interaction of philosophy and the natural sciences in the seventeenth century, see Maurice Mandelbaum, *Philosophy, Science and Sense-Perception: Historical and Critical Studies.* Baltimore, MD: Johns Hopkins University Press, 1964.

[66] Philip Kitcher, 'The Naturalists Return', *Philosophical Review* 101 (1992), 53–114.

[67] Ludwig Wittgenstein, *Tractatus Logico-Philosophicus.* London: Routledge & Kegan Paul, 1992, 74–6.

4.111 Philosophy is not one of the natural sciences (*Naturwissenschaften*).

4.112 The object of philosophy is the logical clarification of thoughts . . .

4.1121 Psychology is no nearer related to philosophy, than is any other natural science. The theory of knowledge (*Erkenntnistheorie*) is the philosophy of psychology . . .

4.1122 The Darwinian theory has no more to do with philosophy than has any other hypothesis of natural science.

4.113 Philosophy defines (*begrentzt*) the disputable sphere of natural science.

Wittgenstein's programme thus opens the way for two significant developments. In the first place, the natural sciences are held to have no relevance for philosophical analysis. At first sight, this seems to sit ill at ease with the obvious respect for physics which one finds in the writings of Carnap and Schlick. Nevertheless, one can argue that both these writers distance themselves from the empirical origins of physical concepts, preferring to use physics as a useful case study for demonstrating the necessity and power of logical analysis. In the second place, Wittgenstein clearly intimates that philosophy has the potential to bring clarity of thought and analysis to the hitherto rather confused approaches of the natural sciences. A good dose of *Erkenntnistheorie* is just what psychologists and biologists need to make sense of things.

Frege's apparent successful analysis of mathematical proofs thus led others to try to extend them to other fields of inquiry – perhaps most notoriously in A. J. Ayer's *Language, Truth and Logic*, which concluded, on the basis of a rather superficial survey of one or two scientific issues, that 'philosophy must develop into the logic of science'; only then could the philosopher get on with the much-needed task of 'clarifying the concepts of contemporary science'.[68] Epistemological issues were reduced to questions of logic, conceptual analysis or grammar. Whereas once the conclusions of the natural sciences were seen as significant and welcome stimuli to philosophical reflection, philosophy was now viewed as an autonomous analytical discipline which was capable of sorting out the philosophically naïve natural scientists. The new emphasis on knowledge as logical analysis was applied to the natural scientists by fundamentally anti-naturalist philosophers, resulting in a wave of publications advocating the clarification of the 'logic of

---

[68] A. J. Ayer, *Language, Truth and Logic*. London: Victor Gollancz, 1946, 201–2.

science'.[69] This 'logic' entailed that the methodological principles of the natural sciences could be reformulated to conform to Frege's preferred mathematical idiom, and were held to apply invariably across intellectual domains, irrespective of their respective subject-matters. A development within this tradition which dates from after Frege is the insistence upon the *a priori* nature of any such philosophical analysis, with the analysis of language itself being seen as fundamental importance.

The Fregean programme can be said to have dominated English-language philosophy for decades, and had a generally negative impact on any attempt to use the natural sciences as an epistemological paradigm. Logical positivism and certain other interesting dead ends in philosophy are grounded in a refusal to accept that the idea of *a priori* foundations of knowledge – as, for example, in logical analysis – is fatally compromised. Yet the demise of foundationalism has led to the widespread rejection of the linguistic turn in general, and Frege's programme in particular. The rejection of any constructive engage-ment with psychology and biology in the name of philosophical purity has generally been abandoned as quite unrealistic. As Kitcher points out:[70]

> How could our psychological and biological capacities *fail* to be relevant to the study of human knowledge? How could our scientific understand-ing of ourselves – or our reflections on the history of the sciences – support the notion that answers to skepticism and organons of methodology (or, indeed, anything very much) could be generated *a priori?*

This rejection of the approaches which lie behind the critiques of religion and religious language found in A. J. Ayer's *Language, Truth and Logic*[71] opens the way, not simply to a rediscovery of the intellectual integrity of theology, but also to the appeal to the natural sciences as *ancilla theologiae.*

Does the rejection of classic foundationalism entail relativism?

Foundationalism has been rejected by virtually every major epis-temologist and philosopher of science of the last half of the century,

---

[69] Kitcher rightly identifies the following works of the philosophy of science as reflecting this trend: Rudolf Carnap, *Logical Aspects of Probability.* Chicago: University of Chicago Press, 1950; Ernest Nagel, *The Structure of Science: Problems in the Logic of Scientific Explanation.* London: Routledge & Kegan Paul, 1979; Carl G. Hempel, *Aspects of Scientific Explanation.* New York: Free Press, 1965; Israel Scheffler, *The Anatomy of Inquiry: Philosophical Studies in the Theory of Science.* New York: Alfred A. Knopf, 1963. It is also legitimate to include K. R. Popper, *The Logic of Scientific Discovery.* New York: Science Editions, 1961, in this category.

[70] Kitcher, 'The Naturalists Return', 58.

[71] Ayer, *Language, Truth and Logic*, 151–8.

from the later Wittgenstein to Karl Popper, W. F. Sellars and W. V. O. Quine. The belief that foundationalism is philosophically indefensible is now so widely accepted that its demise is the closest thing to a philosophical consensus there has been for decades. Nicholas Wolterstorff points out that 'on all fronts, foundationalism is in bad shape. It seems to me that there is nothing to do but give it up for mortally ill and learn to live in its absence'.[72]

This might initially seem to imply an inexorable shift to some form of relativism, perhaps opening the way to more postmodern ways of thinking. This move has certainly been endorsed by some within the 'science and religion' community. Nancey Murphy has argued for the rejection of 'critical realism', holding that it remains wedded to an epistemological foundationalism.[73] In its place, she argues for a non-foundationalist epistemological holism, more sensitive to the nuances of postmodern culture. However, this seems to be a somewhat premature judgement. The rejection of classical foundationalism does not necessarily entail a rejection of realism, or give intellectual legitimation to any such slide into a freewheeling relativism.

This is clear from W. V. O. Quine's important 1981 essay 'Five Milestones of Empiricism'. In addition to undermining the claim that the abandoning of classic foundationalism leads to anti-realism and relativism, Quine's article additionally allows us to note a new reason for affirming the natural sciences as a dialogue partner for theology. Quine sets out the fundamental principles which he believes must apply to any philosophy which seeks to make sense of the world. It is essential to abandon the idea of a 'first philosophy' – that is, any attempt to insist that a philosophy precedes or governs the natural sciences. His vision of philosophy insists upon the[74]

> abandonment of the goal of a first philosophy. It sees natural science as an inquiry into reality, fallible and corrigible, but not answerable to any supra-scientific tribunal, and not in need of any justification beyond observation and the hypothetico-deductive method.

There is no need to posit some incorrigible epistemic foundation as the 'tribunal' on which the natural sciences are based, and with reference

---

[72] Nicholas Wolterstorff, *Reason within the Bounds of Religion*, Grand Rapids: Eerdmans, 1984, 52. See further the material brought together in John E. Thiel, *Nonfoundationalism*. Minneapolis, MN: Fortress Press, 1994.
[73] Nancey Murphy, 'Relating Theology and Science in a Postmodern Age', *CTNS Bulletin* 7/4 (1987), 1–10.
[74] W. V. O. Quine, 'Five Milestones of Empiricism', in W. V. O. Quine (ed.), *Theories and Things*. Cambridge, MA: Harvard University Press, 1981, 67–72.

to which they are judged. Notice how Quine moves decisively away from any assertion of 'epistemic immunities', which became such an obsession for the Enlightenment project. Our inquiries into reality may be 'fallible and corrigible', due to the complexities of the natural world, or our ability to comprehend it. Yet this does not pose any fatal difficulties to the scientific enterprise. Such a natural philosopher

> begins his reasoning within the inherent world theory as a going concern. He tentatively believes all of it, but believes also that some unidentified portions are wrong. He tries to improve, clarify and understand the system from within. He is the busy sailor adrift on Neurath's boat.

The philosopher, scientist or theologian – for Quine would see all as committed to more or less the same approach – is thus not in a position to lay down the conditions under which reality is encountered, but is obligated to engage with the world as it is presented. Both Christian theology and the natural sciences thus avoid the pitfall of foundationalism.

The natural scientist thus does not need to make (and, indeed, *cannot* make) *any* foundational assumptions about the world *a priori*. Rather, what knowledge of the world he comes to regard as reliable is based upon experimental investigation of the world, and reflection on what this investigation appears to disclose, which itself may be subject to further experimental investigation.

Quine's appeal to 'Neurath's boat' invokes the image of a boat which is already on the seas, to which repairs are being carried out. The boat is already there; it is already under way. But it needs to be adapted and modified, in the light of ongoing experimentation and reflection, as the journey proceeds. The scientific enterprise has already begun; it is, however, open to modification and adjustment in the light of experience. Here is the image in Neurath's own words:[75]

> We cannot start from a *tabula rasa* as Descartes thought we could. We have to make do with words and concepts that we find when our reflections begin. [Pierre] Duhem has shown with special emphasis that every statement about any happening is saturated with hypothesis of all sorts and that these in the end are derived from our whole worldview. We are like sailors who on the open sea must reconstruct their ship but are never able to start afresh from the bottom. Where a beam is taken away a new one must at once be put there, and for this the rest of the ship is

---

[75] Otto Neurath, *Empiricism and Sociology*. Dordrecht: Reidel, 1973, 198. This extract is taken from the 1921 writing *Anti-Spengler*. For a fuller statement of the image, see Otto Neurath, 'Protokollsätze', *Erkenntnis* 3 (1932), 204–14.

used as support. In this way, by using the old beams and drift-wood, the ship can be shaped entirely anew, but only by gradual reconstruction.

Neurath's image of the boat is of some importance to tradition-mediated programmes of inquiry. The critical point is that it is *not possible to step out of the boat.* There is no 'vantage point' from which we can view and evaluate our beliefs, except on the basis of our already existing beliefs. Traditions are like boats, in this sense. We cannot stand outside them; we can change traditions – thus jumping to a different Neurathian boat – or modify a tradition from within. But there is no tradition-independent vantage point from which to survey them. The belief system has its own distinctive foundations – which need not be shared with any other tradition – and it is on the basis of those distinctive foundations that repairs and modifications are to be made *in via.*

The implications of this for a theology based upon the Christian tradition are significant. Theology takes place within a tradition which is already in existence. The journey of faith has already been begun. The Christian tradition does not require to be *constituted,* for that has already taken place at its formative stage; it requires to be *consolidated* and *developed.* Yet we are not forced to accept the tradition precisely as it has been given to us; we are able to make 'running repairs' as we progress, in the light of our experience of the journey thus far, and the weaknesses and difficulties which this has exposed. Neurath thus uses the image of the boat to develop a philosophical equivalent to the theological notion of 'living tradition'.

Now that the Enlightenment view that there is a universal set of foundations, valid for all intellectual disciplines at all times, has been fatally eroded, there is no reason why each tradition-constituted rationality should not recognize and affirm its own distinctive founda-tions and criterions of judgement for its beliefs. The widespread recognition of a plurality of rationalities inevitably opens the way to the recognition of a concomitant plurality of foundations – a matter we shall explore further when dealing with the question of 'properly basic beliefs' within traditions (97–102).

Systemic metaphors: from foundations to webs

The metaphor of the foundation is not the only means of understand-ing how systems are created and supported. The metaphor of a web or tapestry points to a different – yet not necessarily incompatible – means of grounding and confirming beliefs. As this point is of some importance, we shall explore it further.

The web or tapestry metaphor eliminates the 'base-superstructure' distinction, and proposes in its place an interconnected network of beliefs, each of which depends upon others for its plausibility. Truth thus comes to be predicated of the system as a whole, rather than its individual elements. One might thus speak of a 'conceptual scheme' (Donald Davidson) or a 'web of belief' (W. V. O. Quine). Whereas Cartesians focused on aspects of a system, detached from the system as a whole, a non-foundationalist would deal with the interconnected beliefs taken as a whole. The issue is the truth of the system, not the truths of its individual constituents.

This point was set out clearly by Arthur Kenyon Rogers (1868–1936), in a classic discussion of the role of coherency in theory or system evaluation.[76]

> Mere logic never by any possibility can add more certainty to the conclusion than existed in the premises. Its ideal, therefore, is to carry back proof to more and more general premises, until at last its finds something in its own right on which it can rest, and from which then a derivative certainty passes to the consequences. The idea of *system*, on the contrary, implies that certainty grows continually as new facts are added.

Rogers thus argues that foundationalism is unable to make the best use of additional evidence which does not fall into the category of basic beliefs. Certainty is derived from basic, not from non-basic, premises. The flux of certainty is from the foundations upwards; there is no downwards movement. The metaphor of a system allows the evidential weight of (non-basic) facts to play a full role in establishing the truth of the whole, rather than merely its individual fragments. Certainty results from an accumulation of facts.

> The possibility of this depends, not on logical deduction from what is self-evident, but on a *coincidence* of evidence. In other words, when we see that two independent beliefs corroborate one other, the confidence we have in both is increased . . . The essence of the validation lies not in the passing on of an equal measure of certainty due to the process of inference, but to the *increase* of certainty due to the confluence of evidence.

A coherentist approach to truth thus holds that a belief is justified to the extent that it coheres with the remainder of the beliefs within the system. This is not to say that coherentism is a viable position in its own right; there is every risk that an internally consistent system could

---

[76] Arthur Kenyon Rogers, *What is Truth? An Essay in the Theory of Knowledge.* New Haven, CT: Yale University Press, 1923, 12–13.

be devised which has no connection with the real world. Yet with the demise of foundationalism, a new interest in alternative epistemic strategies had grown apace.

For there is little doubt that foundationalism – at least, in its classic forms – has died. News of this death seem to have been slow to reach certain people. There is also an interesting debate over whether this death is good news or bad news. Should the theological community rejoice or mourn? One philosopher who has no doubt about the excellence of this development is Richard Rorty, who sets out an anti-foundationalist alterative. To his critics, however, Rorty's exploration of anti-foundationalist approaches to knowledge shows how the rejection of foundationalism seems to open the door to an approach to truth which does little more than endorse prevailing social conventions and preferences (see 6–11).

Rorty's views raise important questions concerning the consequences of the rejection of foundationalism. Is there not a risk that the demise of foundationalism will open the door to a pure relativism in matters of philosophy, ethics, theology and the natural sciences? In short, does the collapse of confidence in foundationalism entail an abandonment of a realist epistemology? It is here that the natural sciences offer an important insight, which allows us to begin to see how an account of justification may be offered which combines correspondence and coherence, without being obliged to make assumptions which would be regarded as constituting an outmoded foundationalism.

It is widely accepted within the natural sciences that classic foundationalism represents a flawed account of both scientific theory and practice. *Yet to reject foundationalism is not to reject realism.* Foundationalism in the natural sciences takes the form of the prior determination of criteria of robustness and consistency, rather than a willingness to allow such criteria to be suggested or determined by the natural world itself. Attempts to lay down in advance criteria for scientific knowledge are constantly frustrated by the failure of nature to comply with such *a priori* demands. As James Cushing points out in his magisterial account of the complexities of scientific theory construction and choice:[77]

> A foundationist approach attempts to lay down certain principles that *must* be adhered to. These are based on *a priori* arguments or upon requirements necessary if one is to avoid the possibility of contradiction.

[77] James T. Cushing, *Quantum Mechanics: Historical Contingency and the Copenhagen Hegemony.* Chicago: University of Chicago Press, 1994, 4.

However, this project has not fared well when applied to actual scientific practice. In the real world that practice must often be content with a non-contradiction, arranged through a process of accommodating our initially hoped-for demands with what nature will sustain.

A priori determination of how knowledge may be acquired and verified is rendered otiose by the requirement to ascertain what the world is actually like before we can lay down how it is to be investigated, and what criteria of coherence may be applied to any ensuing knowledge. At least some preliminary understanding of what the world is like – which may be revised in the light of a continuing engagement with its structures – is essential if we are to determine what constitutes realistic and appropriate 'rules of engagement'. *These cannot be laid down in advance, in that there is no tradition-independent manner of determining what they should be.* To insist upon deploying *a priori* ideas in this way is to run the risk of imposing potentially arbitrary criteria of coherence and resilience on a world whose inner structures cry out for quite different criteria to be developed – in other words, that we use *a posteriori* criteria, which are themselves grounded in an engagement with the world. To stress this point: criteria for scientific knowledge must be grounded in what nature will permit, thus possessing an *a posteriori* rather than *a priori* character.

This observation is of critical importance in dealing with the question which arises from the growing rejection of classic foundationalism: *does the rejection of foundationalism necessarily entail the concomitant rejection of realism?* It allows a firm and emphatically negative response to this question, by making the point that correspondence with reality does not depend upon *a priori* beliefs, but upon *a posteriori* conclusions resulting from an empirical engagement with the real world. To abandon foundationalism is not to abandon a correspondence theory of truth, and thus become reliant solely upon a coherentist account of truth.

Yet some in the theological world have prematurely come to this conclusion, arguing that the failure of foundationalism entails a reliance on coherentist accounts of truth. The importance of this issue to our theme is perhaps best seen by exploring a recent approach to Christian theology developed by a group of writers associated with Yale Divinity School, which involves the rejection of experientially grounded foundationalisms in favour of a coherentist account of Christian doctrine. The result makes the theological vulnerability of coherentism abundantly clear, and reinforces the need to ensure that theological systems are grounded in an extra-systemic engagement with reality, in addition to attempting to achieve intra-systemic consistency. We shall explore this issue at length in what follows.

Postliberalism and the foundations of theology: coherent yet ungrounded?

During the 1990s, it was widely believed that one of the more promising theological developments of the decade was the new style of theology then in the process of emerging from Yale Divinity School. The movement came to be known as 'postliberalism', not least because of its emphatic assertion that the working assumptions of classic liberal Protestantism had become eroded through a series of developments. The time had come to turn away from this outmoded style of theologizing, and pursue alternative visions.

Postliberalism was initially associated with Yale Divinity School, and particularly with theologians such as Hans Frei, Paul Holmer, David Kelsey and George Lindbeck.[78] While it is not strictly correct to speak of a 'Yale school' of theology, it is fair to point our that there are sufficient 'family resemblances' between a number of the approaches to theology to emerge from Yale during the late 1970s and early 1980s to justify this way of referring to the approach, even through it has now come to be known in other terms.[79] Postliberal trends have become well established within North American and British academic theology since about 1990,[80] even though they have not been subjected to quite the critical evaluation that they merit – both in terms of its intrinsic importance as a theological methodology, and in terms of its vulnerability to certain fundamental theological criticisms.[81] Indeed, it is likely

[78] Writings which illustrate this approach include Hans Frei, *The Identity of Jesus Christ.* Philadelphia: Fortress Press, 1975; Paul Holmer, *The Grammar of Faith.* New York: Harper & Row, 1978; David Kelsey, *The Uses of Scripture in Recent Theology.* Philadelphia: Fortress Press, 1975; George Lindbeck, *The Nature of Doctrine: Religion and Theology in a Postliberal Age.* Philadelphia: Westminster Press, 1984.

[79] As pointed out by Brevard Childs, *The New Testament as Canon.* Philadelphia: Fortress Press, 1984, 541.

[80] See Charles L. Campbell, *Preaching Jesus: New Directions for Homiletics in Hans Frei's Postliberal Theology.* Grand Rapids, MI: Eerdmans, 1997; David G. Kamitsuka, *Theology and Contemporary Culture: Liberation, Postliberal and Revisionary Perspectives.* Cambridge: Cambridge University Press, 1999; Daniel Liechty, *Theology in Postliberal Perspective.* London: SCM Press, 1990.

[81] There are some useful observations in Miroslav Wolf, 'Theology, Meaning and Power: A Conversation with George Lindbeck on Theology and the Nature of Christian Difference', in T. R. Philips and D. L. Okholm (eds), *The Nature of Confession: Evangelicals and Postliberals in Conversation.* Downers Grove, IL: InterVarsity Press, 1996, 45–66.

that the judgement of history will be that postliberalism has been productive ethically – witness the massive achievement of Stanley Hauerwas[82] – but relatively sterile theologically.

It is widely agreed that the most important theological work to emerge from this school is George Lindbeck's *The Nature of Doctrine* (1984). One of the most tantalizing aspects of this work is that Lindbeck clearly intends it to be read as a *pre-theological* text, rather than an essay in systematic theology. There are thus parallels between Lindbeck's book and the *Scientific Theology* project, in that both are clearly conceived as essays in theological method, even if one is rather more extended than the other.

Lindbeck's work is to be regarded as outlining a research programme, rather than articulating its mature outcome. It may reasonably be pointed out that the work was published in 1984, allowing what most reasonable people would regard as ample time for the subsequent application of its approach. Yet Lindbeck himself has not yet produced a substantial work which indicates evidence of a transition from pre-theological enquiry to theological statement. Inevitably, this makes it difficult to judge how successful the 'Yale school' is in its theological methodology. If I might be allowed a personal reflection, I first engaged with the methodology underlying Lindebeck's *The Nature of Doctrine* in my Bampton Lectures at Oxford in 1990,[83] and have found myself constantly frustrated by the subsequent theological barrenness of the Yale school. When will it deliver what it promises?

It is my view that the Yale school will not be able to deliver any significant theological constructions, due to its failure to address the issue of the grounding of the Christian theological tradition. Lindbeck's *Nature of Doctrine* attracted considerable interest on its publication, with numerous lines of criticism being developed – each of which, if appropriated, could have led to a positive outcome through a strengthened theological programme.[84] I see no systematic attempt to

---

[82] See Stanley Hauerwas, *The Peaceable Kingdom: A Primer in Christian Ethics.* Notre Dame, IN: University of Notre Dame Press, 1984; idem, *Character and the Christian Life: A Study in Theological Ethics.* Notre Dame, IN: University of Notre Dame Press, 1994. More generally, see Arne Rasmusson, *The Church as Polis: From Political Theology to Theological Politics as exemplified by Jürgen Moltmann and Stanley Hauerwas.* Lund: Lund University Press, 1994.

[83] Alister E. McGrath, *The Genesis of Doctrine: A Study in the Foundations of Doctrinal Criticism.* Oxford: Blackwell, 1990, 14–34.

[84] The following early criticisms are of especial importance: Lee Barrett, 'Theology as Grammar: Regulative Principles of Paradigms and Practices', *Modern Theology* 4 (1988), 155–72; James J. Buckley, 'Doctrine in the Diaspora', *The Thomist* 49 (1985), 443–59. Gordon E. Michaelson, 'The Response to Lindbeck', *Modern Theology* 4 (1988), 107–20; Colman

engage these issues from within the Yale school, and judge that this movement has run into the sands – in part, because it offers an inherently unstable methodology which is ultimately pragmatist, yet clearly yearns to be realist.

Lindbeck's vision of theology as an enterprise to be undertaken within the believing tradition has much to commend it, and is not dissimilar to the methodology espoused in the *Scientific Theology* project. Yet Lindbeck runs into certain difficulties at an early stage, and never quite manages to resolve them.

1. Theology is presented in essentially pragmatic terms as the ideas which are current within the Christian community. Yet the very idea of a 'living tradition' points to the facts of doctrinal development, and theological reformation and reformulation. Lindbeck's proposal leads him into substantially the same dead end as Rorty, in that he is denied 'metaphysical comfort' precisely when his enterprise demands it.[85]

2. Lindbeck fails to articulate any means by which the Christian tradition may offer an account of the ideas and beliefs of other traditions. That is to say, he does not develop any mechanism by which Christian theology may be seen to offer a meta-traditional account of the rationalities embedded in its own and in rival traditions. There is no element of 'correlation' in Lindbeck's account of the tasks of theology.

3. Lindbeck develops a 'cultural-linguistic' approach to doctrine which he believes takes into account the insights of the social sciences, and facilitates dialogue between theology and these disciplines. But what of the *natural* sciences? Lindbeck's account of doctrine is seriously skewed through allowing some (contentious) doctrines of certain social scientists to influence him, and failing to appreciate the counterbalancing impact of the natural sciences, particularly in regard to the propriety and

O'Neill, 'The Rule Theory of Doctrine and Propositional Truth', *The Thomist* 49 (1985), 417–42; D. Z. Phillips, 'Lindbeck's Audience', *Modern Theology* 4 (1988), 133–54; William C. Placher, 'Revisionist and Postliberal Theologies and the Public Character of Theology', *The Thomist* 49 (1985), 392–416''; Geoffrey Wainwright, 'Ecumenical Dimensions of George Lindbeck's "Nature of Doctrine"', *Modern Theology* 4 (1988), 121–32.

[85] On Rorty at this point, see Jackson, 'The Theory and Practice of Discomfort: Richard Rorty and Pragmatism', Jackson offers some pertinent comments on Lindbeck.

intellectual viability of what Lindbeck styles 'cognitive-propositionalist' approaches to doctrine. (As a matter of interest, Lindbeck's manifest failure at this point is one of the factors which led me to decide to develop the project of 'a scientific theology'.)

These are important points, and will be discussed later in the present project. These criticisms are offered prior to a more detailed engagement with Lindbeck to set his theological enterprise in context, and indicate from the outset why I believe it is necessary to develop an alternative strategy to Lindbeck. The ideas which arguably underlie Lindbeck – such as Alasdair MacIntyre's emphasis on the role of tradition – can be developed more fruitfully by returning *ad fontes*, rather than engaging with them as they are encountered at second hand in Lindbeck.

With these points in mind, we may turn to a detailed engagement with Lindbeck's *The Nature of Doctrine*.

Lindbeck's rejection of foundationalism

One of the most significant arguments developed by Lindbeck is that liberal theology, through a sense of obligation to ground itself in the discourse and thought of the public arena – such as philosophical concepts or 'common human experience' – has inadvertently and improperly locked itself into an outmoded philosophical foundationalism. Lindbeck represents this liberal approach in terms of a 'commitment to the foundational enterprise of uncovering universal principles or structures', whether these turn out to be metaphysical, existential or otherwise.[86] The impulse, which is fundamentally apologetic in intent, is to find a common base for Christian theology and public discourse by a prior analysis of human knowledge, culture or experience. The merit of this critique is probably most evident in the case of Paul Tillich, whose apologetic theology is widely regarded by his critics as dictated by extra-biblical and non-Christian concerns, and inadequately grounded in the particularities of the Christian tradition.[87]

Lindbeck's proposal to extricate theology from this self-imposed quagmire rests upon a threefold characterization of approaches to Christian doctrine, two of which he regards as hopelessly outmoded,

---

[86] Lindbeck, *The Nature of Doctrine*, 129.

[87] For a positive assessment of Tillich at this point, see John P. Clayton, *The Concept of Correlation: Paul Tillich and the Possibility of a Mediating Theology*. Berlin: De Gruyter, 1980.

and the third of which he clearly considers to hold the key to future theological reflection.[88] He defines these as:

1. The *cognitive-propositionalist* model, which regards doctrines as making unwarranted cognitive truth claims, falsely asserting that doctrines make objective statements concerning reality;

2. The *experiential-expressive* model, which holds that doctrines are outward expressions of an identifiable core experience common to all Christian traditions, and possibly all world religions.

3. The *cultural-linguistic* model, which is basically a form of co-herentism. Lindbeck's dependence at this point upon a Wittgensteinian approach to language can clearly be noted, particularly his views on 'intratextuality' and the nature of truth.[89]

Lindbeck's critique of cognitive approaches to theology

We begin by exploring Lindbeck's brief and inadequate dismissal of cognitive approaches to theology. What Lindbeck terms a *cognitive-propositional* understanding of doctrine treats doctrines as 'informative propositions or truth claims about objective realities'.[90] Lindbeck argues that this approach is to be rejected as voluntarist, intellectualist and literalist, suggesting that those who are unwise enough to 'perceive or experience religion in cognitivist fashion' are those who 'combine unusual insecurity with naïveté'.[91] This somewhat hasty dismissal of a cognitive approach to doctrine seems to be based upon a highly questionable understanding of the 'cognitive-propositional' position, apparently grounded upon the belief that those inclined towards this position hold that it is possible to state the objective truth about God definitively, exhaustively and timelessly in propositional form. This cannot be considered to be an adequate representation of this position, in either its classical or post-critical forms. It fails to register the historical

---

[88] For details and analysis, see Brad J. Kellenberg, 'Unstuck from Yale: Theological Method after Lindbeck', *Scottish Journal of Theology* 50 (1997), 191–218.

[89] Lindbeck, *The Nature of Doctrine*, 63–72; 113–23. Note the clear parallels with his colleague Paul Holmer's reading of Wittgenstein at this point: Paul Holmer, 'Wittgenstein and Theology', in D. M. High (ed.), *New Essays on Religious Language*. New York: Oxford University Press, 1969, 25–35. For further reflections, see Joseph M. Incandela, 'The Appropriation of Wittgenstein's Work by Philosophers of Religion: Towards a Reevaluation and an End', *Religious Studies* 21 (1985), 457–74.

[90] Lindbeck, *The Nature of Doctrine*, 16.

[91] Lindbeck, *The Nature of Doctrine*, 21.

and linguistic sophistication of cognitive approaches to doctrine.[92] For example, Lindbeck's suggestion that the 'cognitive-propositional' approach to doctrine treats any given doctrine as 'eternally true'[93] fails to take account of the evident ability of proponents of this approach to reformulate, amplify or supplement a doctrine with changing historical circumstances.[94] Lindbeck attributes an unmerited inflexibility to cognitive approaches to doctrine through playing down the notion of 'relative adequacy' of doctrinal statements, where 'adequacy' can be assessed in terms of both the original historical context of a doctrinal formulation and whatever referent it is alleged to represent.

An episode from historical theology will help illuminate this point. Most theologians of the medieval period understood dogma as a dynamic concept, a 'perception of divine truth, tending towards this truth' (*perceptio divinae veritatis tendens in ipsam*). It is certainly true that certain medieval writings do indeed suggest that doctrine may be treated virtually as if they were Euclidean theorems: Alan of Lille's *Regulae theologiae* and Nicholas of Amien's *De arte catholicae fidei* are excellent examples of this genre dating from the twelfth century.[95] Nevertheless, a considerably more nuanced approach to the nature of theological statements is much more characteristic of Christian theology in the patristic and medieval periods.

Theology is here recognized to be concerned in the first place with the clarification of the manner in which affirmations about God are derived, and in the second place, with how they relate to analogous affirmations drawn from the more familiar world of the senses. It is an attempt to achieve conceptual clarity, to avoid confusion through subjecting statements concerning God to close scrutiny. What does the word 'God' stand for? How does the statement 'God exists', relate to the apparently analogous affirmation that 'Socrates exists'? What reasons might be adduced for suggesting that 'God is righteous'? And how does this statement relate to the apparently analogous statement 'Socrates is righteous'? [96]

[92] It might also reasonably be pointed out that it pays inadequate attention to what it means to suggest that religious claims are 'cognitive' in the first place: an excellent discussion of this point (published too late to be available to Lindbeck) may be found in James Kellenberger, *Cognitivity of Religion: Three Views*. London: Macmillan, 1985.

[93] Lindbeck, *The Nature of Doctrine*, 47. But compare the important concessions grudgingly made at 80, 105.

[94] Brian A. Gerrish, 'The Nature of Doctrine', *Journal of Religion* 68 (1988), 87–92.

[95] Gillian R. Evans, *Alan of Lille: The Frontiers of Theology in the Later Twelfth Century*. Cambridge: Cambridge University Press, 1983, 64–80.

[96] For a study of this specific issue, see Alister E. McGrath, *Iustitia Dei: A History of the Christian Doctrine of Justification*. 2nd edn. Cambridge: Cambridge University Press, 1998, 51–70.

Thus Alan of Lille (to note one of the more propositionalist of medieval theologians) is concerned with identifying the ways in which we might be misled by theological affirmations – for example, by treating them as descriptions of physical objects, or assuming that terms and conceptualities relating to God possess the same meanings as in everyday discourse.[97] Underlying such attempts to achieve clarity of concepts and modes of discourse is the recognition that doctrinal affirmations are to be recognized as perceptions, not total descriptions, pointing beyond themselves towards the greater mystery of God himself.

For such theologians, doctrines are reliable, yet incomplete, descriptions of reality. Their power lies in what they represent, rather than what they are in themselves. The point at which interrogation is appropriate concerns whether such doctrines are adequate (to the strictly limited degree that this is possible) representations of the independent reality to which they allegedly relate. Given that they cannot hope to represent it in its totality, and given the inevitable limitations attending any attempt to express in words something which ultimately lies beyond them, is the particular form of words employed the most reliable conceivable?

As many theologians have noted, the Nicene controversy is an obvious example of a struggle to articulate insights in this manner. If an experience is to be articulated in words, in order to communicate or to attempt a communal envisioning of this experience, some form of a 'cognitive-propositionalist' dimension is inevitable. Yet this is not to reduce the experience to words, but simply to attempt to convey it through words. Charles Gore made this point firmly in his 1891 Bampton Lectures at Oxford, widely regarded as a classic statement of the necessary nature and limits of the Christological dogma:[98]

> [Our dogmatic language] is as good as human language can be, but it is not adequate. Human language never can express adequately divine realities. A constant tendency to apologize for human speech, a great element of agnosticism, an awful sense of unfathomed depths beyond the little that is made known, is always present to the mind of theologians who know what they are about, in conceiving or expressing God. 'We see', says St Paul, 'in a mirror, in terms of a riddle'; 'we know in part'. 'We are compelled,' complains St Hilary, 'to attempt what is unattainable, to climb where we cannot reach, to speak what we cannot utter; instead

---

[97] See Evans, *Alan of Lille*, 33–6 for an excellent analysis.
[98] Charles Gore, *The Incarnation of the Son of God*, 105–6.

of the mere adoration of faith, we are compelled to entrust the deep
things of religion to the perils of human expression.'

The same basic principle is expressed in such diverse locations as the
apophatic elements of the Greek patristic tradition and John Henry
Newman's 'principle of reserve': doctrines cannot hope to do justice to
what they express, but they are nevertheless necessary and proper means
of preserving and communicating the mystery of faith.[99]

Lindbeck's dismissal of cognitive-propositional approaches to
doctrine is thus premature, and is not satisfactorily grounded in an engagement with the Christian tradition. Lindbeck's critique of 'cognitive'
approaches to doctrine does not do justice to the classical theological
tradition; it also rests upon a limited and somewhat puzzling choice of
dialogue partners. There is no doubt that he has listened to some *social*
scientists, such as Clifford Geertz, particularly his essay 'Religion as a
Cultural System'.[100] But what of the *natural* sciences? Lindbeck appears
to overlook the fact that the natural sciences also offer cognitive-
propositional approaches to reality in terms of theories which may be
stated in explicitly mathematical terms. It is astonishing that Lindbeck
should not have considered the implications of the cognitive dimensions
of the natural sciences at this point, when they so clearly pose a
potentially damaging – and possible fatal – challenge to his thinking.

Lindbeck's coherentist account of doctrine

So much for Lindbeck's critique of cognitive approaches to theology.
What of his own positive statements on the matter? Here we need to
consider Lindbeck's *cultural-linguistic* model of doctrine. Lindbeck
suggests, paralleling Wittgenstein, that religions may be compared to
languages, with religious doctrines functioning as grammatical rules.
Religions are cultural frameworks or mediums which engender a
vocabulary and precede inner experience.[101]

---

[99] Andrew Louth, *Discerning the Mystery: An Essay on the Nature of Theology*. Oxford:
Clarendon Press, 1983; Robin C. Selby, *The Principle of Reserve in the Writings of John Henry
Cardinal Newman*. London: Oxford University Press, 1975.
[100] Clifford Geertz, 'Religion as a Cultural System', in D. R. Cutler (ed.), *The Religious
Situation*. Boston: Beacon Press, 1968, 639–88. This is the first volume in what was intended
to be an annual report on the state of global religion. For some critical comments on his
approach, see Volker Gottowik, *Konstruktionen des Anderen: Clifford Geertz und die Krise
der ethnographischen Repräsentation*. Berlin: Reimer, 1997; Fred Inglis, *Clifford Geertz: Culture,
Custom and Ethics*. Cambridge: Polity Press, 2000.
[101] Lindbeck, *The Nature of Doctrine*, 33. The entire section (32–41) should be consulted
to ensure this extract is properly contextualized. For an exploration of the issue, see Lee C.
Barrett, 'Theology as Grammar: Regulative Principles or Paradigms and Practices', *Modern
Theology* 4 (1988), 155–72.

A religion can be viewed as a kind of cultural and/or linguistic framework or medium that shapes the entirety of life and thought ... It is not primarily an array of beliefs about the true and the good (although it may involve these), or a symbolism expressive of basic attitudes, feelings or sentiments (though these will be generated). Rather, it is similar to an idiom that makes possible the description of realities, the formulation of beliefs, and the experiencing of inner attitudes, feelings and sentiments. Like a culture or language, it is a communal phenomenon that shapes the subjectivities of individuals rather than being primarily a manifestation of those subjectivities. It comprises a vocabulary of discursive and nondiscursive symbols together with a distinctive logic or grammar in terms of which this vocabulary can be meaningfully deployed.

Just as a language is correlated with a form of life (as Wittgenstein pointed out in relation to 'language games'), so a religious tradition is correlated with the form of life it engenders and reflects.

It will be clear that the concept of *intra-systemic consistency* plays a critical role in Lindbeck's understanding of theology. Doctrines regulate religions, in much the same way that grammar regulates language, with the objective of ensuring coherence and consistency within a cultural or linguistic system. Lindbeck thus de-emphasizes the ideational content of a doctrinal statement in order to stress its formal function.[102] Lindbeck illustrates this point with reference to Shakespeare's *Hamlet*: the statement 'Denmark is the land where Hamlet lived' makes no claim to ontological truth or falsity, but is to be viewed as a statement concerning the internal ordering of the elements of Shakespeare's narrative.[103] Narrative in itself is neither fact nor fiction: it is a vehicle for either or both. Fact-like narratives are not necessarily factual.[104] Only if the narrative is taken as *history* are any claims being made concerning the ontological truth or falsity of this statement. Thus the Bible may, Lindbeck suggests, be read as a 'vast, loosely-structured non-fictional novel', the canonical narrative of which offers an identity description of God. Developing this point, Lindbeck suggests – citing the parable of the prodigal son as an example – that the 'rendering of God's character' is not necessarily dependent upon the facticity of the scriptural story.

Lindbeck insists that doctrines regulate the language of a religious community, yet seems markedly reluctant to allow that they have

---

[102] For a not totally unproblematic account of how language functions in this respect, see Earl M. Herrick, *Sociolinguistic Variation: A Formal Model.* University, AL: University of Alabama Press, 1984.

[103] Lindbeck, *The Nature of Doctrine*, 65.

[104] For Hans Frei's discussion of the relation of 'fact-likeness' to 'factuality', see Frei, *The Eclipse of Biblical Narrative*, 187.

anything to do with God, or even with reality in general. This is perhaps one of the most baffling aspects of Lindbeck's approach to doctrine, which has led many to conclude that he is anti-realist in outlook.[105] For example, consider his views on the role of Creeds:[106]

> A creed may function regulatively (doctrinally) and yet not propositionally. It seems odd to suggest that the Nicaenum in its role as a communal doctrine does not make first-order truth claims, and yet this is what I shall contend. Doctrines regulate truth claims by excluding some and permitting others, but the logic of their communally authoritative use hinders or prevents them from specifying positively what is affirmed.

This somewhat startling insight, I fear, was denied to the church fathers who formulated the Nicaenum. Lindbeck is quite right when he suggests that it 'seems odd' to suggest that doctrine merely regulates truth-claims, rather than making them in the first place. It seems odd because it is not what the Christian tradition has understood itself to be doing, despite Lindbeck's attempts to redirect it or reinterpret it on this point. Applied consistently, Lindbeck's approach renders doctrine incapable of making any cognitive, propositional or even intelligible statements about God:[107]

> Meaning is constituted by the uses of specific language rather than being distinguishable from it. Thus the proper way to determine what 'God' signifies, for example, is by examining how the word operates within a religion and thereby shapes reality and experience rather than by first establishing its propositional or experiential meaning and reinterpreting or reformulating its uses accordingly.

Doctrine is to be understood as the language of the Christian community, a self-perpetuating idiolect which, since it cannot refer to God, cannot be reformed against a knowledge of God. Lindbeck seems to suggest that conceiving theology as the grammar of the Christian language entails the abandonment of any talk about God as an independent reality and any suggestion that it is possible to make truth claims (in an ontological, rather than intra-systemic, sense) concerning

---

[105] For a counterposition, see the spirited response of Jeffrey Hensley, 'Are Postliberals Necessarily Antirealists? Reexamining the Metaphysics of Lindbeck's Postliberal Theology', in T. R. Philips and D. L. Okholm (eds), *The Nature of Confession: Evangelicals and Postliberals in Conversation*. Downers Grove, IL: InterVarsity Press, 1996, 69–80.

[106] Lindbeck, *The Nature of Doctrine*, 19.

[107] Lindbeck, *The Nature of Doctrine*, 114.

him. Lindbeck thus argues that theology is a 'second-order' activity which does not make truth claims, this function being reserved for 'first-order' assertions.[108]

> Just as grammar by itself affirms nothing either true or false regarding the world in which language is used, but only about language, so theology and doctrine, to the extent that they are second-order activities, assert nothing either true or false about God and his relation to creatures, but only speak about such assertions.

So theology is 'talk about talk about God', not 'talk about God'. One sees here immediately the classic position of a certain type of social scientist, who holds that the language and behaviour of natural scientists is open to social scientific research, whereas the 'reality' those scientists believe they are encountering and representing is meaningless or irrelevance. It is the language and conventions of the community which is interesting, not the subject it believes itself to be considering.

Lindbeck thus appears to suggest that his 'cultural-linguistic' approach to doctrine may dispense with the question of whether the Christian idiom has any external referent. This is an admirable statement of the perspective of pragmatism, coherentism or postmodernism in general, and shows that Lindbeck was thoroughly tuned in to the ideas of the 1980s. Language *functions* within a cultural and linguistic world; it does not necessarily, however, *refer* to anything. Doctrine is concerned with the internal regulation of the Christian idiom, ensuring its consistency. The question of how that idiom relates to the external world is considered to be improper. Lindbeck offers by way of illustration a comparison between an Aristotelian and non-Aristotelian grammarian. Both would be in agreement that proper sentences have certain components, such as a subject and an object. The Aristotelian would then argue that this sentence somehow 'mirrors' reality, whereas the non-Aristotelian would hold that this grammatical affirmation has no necessary ontological implications. In a similar way, Lindbeck argues, the Christian theologian may remain 'grammatically orthodox' without making any metaphysical claims, by contenting herself with following the rules, rather than accepting their ontological implications.[109]

---

[108] Lindbeck, *The Nature of Doctrine*, 65.
[109] Lindbeck, *The Nature of Doctrine*, 106.

Yet this raises important theological questions. Lindbeck appears to treat the Christian theological tradition, including its doctrines, as something which is *given*. There is no perceived need to explain how it came to be in its classic or present form, or take account of the demonstrable fact that Christian doctrines have *developed* over two thousand years.[110] Some of those developments will have to be recognized as inappropriate and inauthentic, and revised or removed in the course of ongoing theological reflection, in much the same way as the sixteenth-century Reformation aimed to purge theology of some theological beliefs and ecclesiastical practices that it regarded as inauthentic and inadequately grounded in Scripture.[111]

Lindbeck's essentially coherentist or pragmatic approach to doctrines is only viable if the 'teachings regarding beliefs and practices that are considered essential to the identity or welfare of the group' are *stable*. If his method is indeed capable of dealing with the patently obvious *development* of Christian theory and praxis – and I do not believe that it is, due to its lack of an extra-linguistic *grounding* – Lindbeck has omitted to explain how this might be the case. But how can we evaluate the Christian idiom, except by undertaking a rigorous study of what it purports to represent, interpret or convey? Intra-systemic consistency may be a necessary condition of Christian authenticity; it is most emphatically not a sufficient condition. To revert to an example used by Lindbeck, it is one thing to ensure that the term 'Denmark' is consistently employed within the context of Shakespeare's *Hamlet*. Yet this cannot excuse at least a preliminary engagement with the question of how this 'Denmark' relates to the definite and identifiable geographical and political reality, located in the world of human experience, also known as 'Denmark'. How does Shakespeare's Denmark relate to the Denmark of the real world?

This question recurs at just about every juncture of Lindbeck's analysis. Consider his statements on Christology. It is impossible to avoid the question of how the 'Jesus' of the Christian idiom relates to the historical figure of Jesus of Nazareth. Has it any identifiable connection with him? Does it refer to him, or to something else?[112] Can it

---

[110] See Pierre Rousselot, 'Petit théorie du dévelopement du dogme', *Recherches de science religieuse* 53 (1965), 355–90.

[111] Alister E. McGrath, *The Intellectual Origins of the European Reformation*. Oxford: Blackwell, 1987, 140–74.

[112] That this is a difficult as well as an important question can be seen from such studies as N. T. Wright, *Jesus and the Victory of God*. London: SPCK, 1996; Luke Timothy Johnson, *The Real Jesus: The Misguided Quest for The Historical Jesus and the Truth of the Traditional Gospels*. San Francisco: HarperSanFrancisco, 1997; Gregory W. Dawes, *The Historical Jesus*

be shown to originate from him – or is it an independent construction of the human mind? Lindbeck appears to illustrate neatly what Rowan Williams identifies as one of the most serious weaknesses of modern theology – the perennial tendency 'to be seduced by the prospect of bypassing the question of how it *learns* its own language'.[113] The possibility which Lindbeck seems unwilling and unable to consider is that the discourse which he identifies Christian doctrine as regulating may be based upon an historical misunderstanding; that it may signify nothing other than the accidental forms of historical 'givenness', giving it a socio-historical rootedness which vitiates its wider validity; that it may represent a serious misrepresentation, or even a deliberate falsification, of historical events; that it may represent a completely spurious interpretation of the significance of Jesus of Nazareth. The Christian idiom cannot simply be taken as 'given': it must be interrogated concerning its historical and theological credentials. The historically demonstrated phenomenon of the *development* of Christian doctrine and practice undermines Lindbeck's approach, by exposing that the 'givens' on which Lindbeck's system depends is corrigible.

Lindbeck's attitude to the Christian tradition appears uncomfortably similar to Bultmann's ahistorical approach to the Christian *kerygma*:[114] both are assumed just to be there, given, lying beyond challenge or justification. The interrogation to which the 'New Quest of the Historical Jesus' subjected Bultmann's kerygmatic Christology[115] must be extended to Lindbeck's understanding of the nature of doctrine. Lindbeck's doctrine, like Bultmann's *kerygma*, is not something that is just there, demanding that we take it or leave it: it is something which purports to represent adequately and accurately the significance of an historical event, and is open to challenge concerning its adequacy as an interpretation of that event. The Reformation and the Enlightenment are obvious historical instances of received doctrines being challenged concerning their historical credentials. In the end, Lindbeck's view of Christian theology is dangerously close to C. I. Lewis' famous metaphor

---

Quest: Landmarks in the Search for the Jesus of History. Louisville, KY: Westminster/John Knox Press, 2000.

[113] Rowan Williams, 'Trinity and Repetition', *Modern Theology* 2 (1986), 197–212; 197.

[114] J. M. de Jong, *Kerygma: een onderzoek naar de vooronderstellingen van de theologie van Rudolf Bultmann.* Assen: Van Gorcum, 1958.

[115] For the issues of this increasingly distant debate, see James M. Robinson, *A New Quest of the Historical Jesus.* London: SCM Press, 1959; Hans-Werner Bartsch, *Kerygma and Myth: A Theological Debate.* London: SPCK, 1962.

of the group of drunken sailors. None of them is capable of standing up on their own; but by holding on to each other, they achieve a modest degree of corporate stability denied to the individual members.

Lindbeck's cultural-linguistic approach to doctrine sets aside both epistemological realism and a correspondence theory of truth, apparently on the basis of the belief that these have been discredited by philosophical discourse. Yet this is clearly not so. It is indeed the case that what we might term 'naïve' correspondence theories of truth are treated with something approaching amusement within the professional theological community. Yet there is no shortage of philosophers prepared to defend more sophisticated correspondence theories of truth. An excellent example of this may be found in the writings of Laurence Bonjour, where we find a correspondence theory of truth is held in tandem with a coherentist theory of justification. Perhaps more worryingly, Lindbeck's tantalizingly brief references to correspondence theories of truth raise the question of whether he has confused these with the much-criticized *identity* theory of truth.[116]

Lindbeck's pragmatism or coherentism – his 'cultural-linguistic' approach could be categorized in either manner – merely raises all the objections that have been recited at length within the extended philosophical debate over the merits of correspondence and coherentist approaches to truth within the philosophical literature, without advancing that discussion in any meaningful manner.[117] Apparently unaware of the steady advances made by realist theories of knowledge in the past decades, dependent to no small extent on the explanatory successes of the natural sciences, Lindbeck appears to have drawn the quite erroneous conclusion that the belief that language, in some way and to some extent, refers to extra-systemic realities is no longer taken seriously by cultured people. Yet this rests upon a misreading of the situation, which has led Lindbeck to draw what are increasingly seen to be hasty conclusions concerning the viability of realist approaches.

Moving on from Lindbeck

So where do we go after Lindbeck? Nearly twenty years have passed since the publication of *The Nature of Doctrine*. Nothing of note has

---

[116] On which see Thomas Baldwin, 'The Identity Theory of Truth', *Mind* 100 (2001), 35–52; Julian Dodd, *An Identity Theory of Truth*. New York: St Martin's Press, 2000.

[117] See Joseph Ratner, 'The Correspondence Theory of Truth', *Journal of Philosophy* 32 (1935), 141–52; Nicholas Rescher, *The Coherence Theory of Truth*, Washington, DC: University Press of America, 1982; Bertrand Russell, 'On the Nature of Truth', *Proceedings of the Aristotelian Society* 7 (1907), 228–49; Ralph C. S. Walker, *The Coherence Theory of Truth: Realism, Anti-Realism, Idealism*. London: Routledge, 1989.

emerged from the Yale school to persuade its potential audience that some major new consolidation of an initially promising approach is due. Rather than attempt to repristinate this failed enterprise, I propose to take some of Lindbeck's building blocks, add some significant others, and pursue a different course. There are several ways out of the crisis in knowledge caused by the failure of the Enlightenment project. Lindbeck has explored one route, which is now being seen increasingly as a dead end. But there are other ways out.

In order to understand the way in which the quest for theological integrity will be pursued from this point onwards, we shall set out the problems arising from Lindbeck's approach, and indicate how we propose to meet these difficulties.

First, Lindbeck seems to lapse into a form of fideism – that is, a self-contained tradition, functioning almost as an intellectual ghetto, whose language and ideas need bear no relation whatsoever to other traditions, or to public discourse as a whole.[118] As David Tracy points out in a penetrating review, Lindbeck suffers all the weaknesses of 'Barthian confessionalism' in that theology 'has to be done purely from within the confessing community'.[119] This seems to mark a retreat from any significant cultural or intellectual engagement. This serious problem – both for Barth and for Lindbeck – can be countered by positing an approach to natural theology which recognizes and emphasizes its role as a meta-traditional device, by which the Christian tradition may engage in faithful yet productive dialogue with other traditions (72–92).

Second, Lindbeck does not offer a satisfactory account of how doctrines are grounded in any reality, apparently believing that such an idea is intellectually naïve. Without such a device, he is unable to account for doctrinal development, or respond to the need for theological reformulation and revision – such as the entire theological project of the Reformation. He is also trapped in a pragmatic cage, in that his vision of the contents of Christian theology is determined by what the community currently happens to believe, without any means of probing whether such beliefs are authentic or not. This weakness can be countered by postulating that Christian theology aims to offer a coherent

---

[118] That this need not be the case with a non-foundationalist theology can be seen from the excellent study of Ronald F. Thiemann, *Revelation and Theology: The Gospel as Narrated Promise*. Notre Dame, IN: University of Notre Dame Press, 1985, in which the manner in which Christian convictions intersect with the public arena is thoughtfully explored.

[119] David Tracy, 'Lindbeck's New Program for Theology: A Reflection', *The Thomist* 49 (1985), 460–72.

account of a reality to which it ultimately refers, and reviewing whether Lindbeck has adequately understood the 'cognitive-propositionalist' approach to doctrine, or appreciated the importance of the natural sciences in this respect.

In order to construct a more reliable account of the nature of theological knowledge, we must explore the new interest in tradition-mediated rationality which has developed since about 1970, and offer a critical account of the new possibilities which have opened up since then.

One such new possibility involves the recognition that a Christian natural theology, when properly construed, offers a trans-traditional device for the interpretation of a publicly accessible entity – namely, the natural world. Earlier (vol. 1, 300–4), we concurred with Wolfhart Pannenberg's call for a public engagement with the natural world. Yet Pannenberg's approach is vulnerable on account of its failure to explicitly acknowledge the tradition-embedded character of the intellectual frameworks through which the natural order is viewed, and on the basis of which it is interpreted. The natural world which is to be interpreted may indeed be regarded as a publicly observable entity (although to far less an extent than Pannenberg seems to appreciate); nevertheless, the process of *observation* entails '*seeing nature as God's creation*'. A publicly accessible entity is thus to be observed and interpreted on the basis of a tradition-mediated framework of rationality.

For this reason, Pannenberg's approach to natural theology must be considered to be flawed. Yet a scientific theology is able to maintain the public accessibility of the natural world, while fully recognizing the tradition-specific nature of the process of observation and interpretation. For a scientific theology, a Christian natural theology represents a tradition-mediated view of reality, which possess a created capacity to function as a trans-traditional framework of rationality. It is this critically important aspect of a scientific theology which we will explore in some detail in the following chapter.

Chapter 8

Natural Theology and the Trans-Traditional Rationality of the Christian Tradition

The project of a scientific theology is set against the broad backdrop of the collapse of the *grand récit* of the Enlightenment, which took a posited – yet never demonstrated – 'universal human reason' as the foundation and criterion of its world-view. With the advent of postmodernity, the very idea of such universal categories has come under intense scrutiny. Jean-François Lyotard and others have strongly advocated the rejection of *les grand récits*, citing their tendency to lead to intellectual and moral oppression as one of the most compelling reasons for doing so.[1] The legitimacy of this appeal may be countered in various ways, most notably by pointing out that 'oppression' assumes the status of an absolute moral notion, whereas the underlying postmodern ethos permits it a much more modest role.[2]

Yet it would be unfair to reject the postmodern critique of the Enlightenment on account of some perceived incoherences in its alternative models of rationality and morality. For an integral aspect of the postmodern critique of modernity is the incoherence of its supposedly 'universal' foundations. Postmodernity proposes an

---

[1] Jean-François Lyotard, *The Postmodern Condition: A Report on Knowledge.* Manchester: Manchester University Press, 1992.
[2] See the analysis in Ben F. Meyer, 'The Philosophical Crusher', *First Things* 12 (April 1991), 9–11. See further Bernard Bergonzi, *Exploding English: Criticism, Theory, Culture.* Oxford: Clarendon Press, 1990.

alternative to *les grand récits* – such as those of Marxism[3] – because it believes that such 'metanarratives' are unjustifiable, both in terms of their intrinsic rationality and in terms of their consequences. If the universal rationality and morality which undergirded the Enlightenment can be shown to be untenable, the only viable alternative, according to most postmodern writers, is to acknowledge the merits of *all* rationalities and moralities. To its critics, this seems like the intellectual legitimation of just about anything, and represents a lapse into uncritical affirmation of whatever views happen to be represented in society at any given time. It is a form of ideological democracy – perhaps even demagoguery – rather than a serious attempt to formulate a critical account of knowledge and truth.

Yet postmodernity is not the only response to the crisis of modernity, which has led to the collapse of classic foundationalism and those philosophies and theologies which were based upon it. It is certainly true that the demise of foundationalism, which we considered in the previous chapter, raises some very serious issues for any intellectual enterprise, theological or philosophical. If there are no universally valid and globally accepted foundations for human knowledge, how is such a knowledge to be apprehended and confirmed? What alternative is there, other than postmodernity?[4] One answer is the form of critical realism, developed by Roy Bhaskar, which seems to many to constitute the way ahead, not least through taking seriously the intellectual achievements of the natural sciences. We have already seen how the natural sciences are able to maintain a realist perspective on the world, despite the collapse of foundationalism. This strongly suggests that a scientific theology might do the same. But how? And in what way?

A scientific theology attempts to offer a view of the world, including God, which is both internally consistent and which is grounded in the structures of the real world. It aims to achieve extra-systemic correspondence with intra-systemic coherence, regarding both these criteria as of fundamental importance. The present chapter sets out the manner in which the Christian tradition is able to offer a framework for viewing and encountering the world which makes a scientific theology possible.

---

[3] For documentation, see Marc Angenot, *L'utopie collectiviste: le grand récit socialiste sous la Deuxième Internationale*. Paris: Presses Universitaires de France, 1993.

[4] See Garry Potter and José López, 'After Postmodernism: The New Millennium', in José López and Garry Potter (eds), *After Postmodernism: An Introduction to Critical Realism*. London: Athlone Press, 2001, 3–16. For a reaffirmation of some central themes of modernity against the postmodern critique, see Marjorie Peloff, *Twenty-First Century Modernism*. Oxford: Blackwell, 2001.

The urgency of developing such an approach to theology is underscored by the collapse of the Enlightenment project, to which we shall turn in a moment. Yet a scientific theology is not a *post hoc* response to this failure; rather, it represents a persistent trend throughout the great tradition of Christian theology, from Athanasius to T. F. Torrance, whose importance is highlighted by the failures of its rivals.

To explore this point, we may first turn to consider the great myth of universal reason, which undergirded the rationalism of the Enlightenment. Having ascertained why the crisis with modernity has developed and the significance of the notion of tradition-mediated rationality which has largely superseded it, we will be in a position to understand the new role that a Christian natural theology has to play in the new intellectual scenario which has developed since about 1970.

The Enlightenment: a 'view from nowhere'

The fundamental theme of classic foundationalism is that certain 'basic' beliefs undergird other beliefs, which are derived from these beliefs in such a manner that their truth is preserved and transmitted. During the period of the Enlightenment, foundationalism was placed on a more rigorous foundation through the insistence of the autonomy of human reason. Based on the assumption that there is a 'universal human reason', independent of the exigencies of space, time and culture, Enlightenment writers insisted that there was one single, universal set of criteria by which the epistemic status of all beliefs, mediate or immediate, may be judged.

It was an attractive vision, and it is a mark of precisely that attractiveness – rather than its inherent plausibility, or correspondence with the evidence – that it endured for so long. Yet the myth of a universal rationality simply could not be sustained in the light of the accumulation of counterfactual evidence and argumentation, particularly in relation to the sociology of knowledge. Whereas Kant had argued, in what now seems a somewhat optimistic manner, for transcendental criteria of judgement, valid for all minds and across all cultures and traditions at all time, the empirical study of cultural rationalities disclosed a very different pattern – namely, that people possessed and possess contested and at times incommensurable notions both of what is 'rational', 'true' and 'right', and how those qualities might be justified.[5]

[5] See Ernest Gellner, *Reason and Culture: The Historic Role of Rationality and Rationalism.* Oxford: Blackwell, 1992; Raymond Murphy, *Rationality and Nature: A Sociological Inquiry into a Changing Relationship.* Boulder, CO: Westview Press, 1994; James R. Brown, *Scientific Rationality: The Sociological Turn.* Dordrecht: Reidel, 1984.

A turning point came with the publication of Peter Winch's *The Idea of a Social Science* (1958).[6] In this work, Winch argued against the traditional tendency for western social theorists to regard themselves as neutral observers and impartial judges of other cultures. Winch took as his starting point the seemingly incontrovertible dilemma posed by the impossibility of uninterpreted data. We always see things *as* something (to use N. R. Hanson's idiom). The cultural matrix of the observer has shaped her outlook, and the manner in which she interprets her own cultural world and alternative cultural possibilities. It is thus impossible to offer a 'comparison of cultures', in that the observer inevitably judges the other culture by the standards of her own, in effect descending into a form of cultural imperialism. The only way of resolving this dilemma is to locate an external, neutral vantage point from which both cultures may be judged. But where, and how, is such a vantage point to be found?

As time progressed, the answer seemed to become increasingly clear. There is no universal truth, no absolute perspective, no privileged vantage point, through which the totality of reality may be perceived. The Enlightenment appeared to take the view that human reason elevated the intelligent and enlightened individual above the shadows and clouds of traditions, and allowed the 'big picture' to be seen with unprecedented clarity. In the light of this comprehensive overview of the totality of things, reliable judgements could be made concerning religions, traditions and other such outmoded ways of thinking and behaving. Yet the Enlightenment vision died with the recognition that the Enlightenment itself was just another human tradition, possessed of the particularity and corrigibility of the rival traditions it sought to critique and judge. Far from rising above traditions, the Enlightenment simply represented yet another tradition, distinguished perhaps by its arrogance and presumption rather than its epistemic successes. It was only a matter of time before it would be humbled and chastened.

Ethnocentrism and rationality

As we have argued, one of the most basic beliefs of the Enlightenment was the autonomy of human reason, and its universal capacity to arrive at justified beliefs. This axiom of the Enlightenment was shaken to its foundations through the growing awareness that reason was not a universal, neutral medium, shared by all humanity at all times and in

[6] For the most recent edition, see Peter Winch, *The Idea of a Social Science and Its Relation to Philosophy*. London: Routledge, 1990. For details of Winch, see Colin Lyas, *Peter Winch*. Teddington: Acumen Publishing Limited, 1999.

all places, but was situationally specific. What the Enlightenment took to be universal was actually ethnocentric – even Eurocentric[7] – reflecting the historically determined views of western culture, including its canons of rationality.[8] What was once thought to be globally valid was gradually realized to be historically situated and socially constructed. The Enlightenment assumption that there was only one 'rationality', independent of time, space and culture,[9] has given way to the recognition that there are – and always have been – many different 'rationalities'. As Stephen Toulmin points out, 'the exercise of rational judgement is itself an activity carried out in a particular context and essentially dependent on it; the arguments we encounter are set out at a given time and in a given situation, and when we come to assess them they have to be judged against this background'.[10] Philip Kitcher argues that the collapse of foundationalism inevitably raises the issue of the authorities we recognize in debate.[11]

> Our knowledge is embedded in the history of human knowledge and not detachable from it. Furthermore, our reliance on the authority of others is ineluctable. Surely, as a matter of fact, all of us do depend on authorities from childhood up, but the Cartesian hope, re-enunciated by Frege in the context of mathematics, is that we could, in principle, retreat to a stove-heated room and take our cognitive lives into our own hands. If, however, the knowledge-generating power of the processes we can undergo is dependent on the endorsements and recommendations of others, if it could be subverted by the refusal of others to accept our conclusions, then there can be no Cartesian, or even Fregean reconstruction. As Quine so frequently reminds us, we are all in Neurath's boat.

[7] Heidegger thus wrote of 'the complete Europeanization of the earth and of man': Martin Heidegger, *On the Way to Language*. New York: Harper & Row, 1971, 15–16.

[8] Gary Sauer-Thompson and Joseph Wayne Smith, *The Unreasonable Silence of the World: Universal Reason and the Wreck of the Enlightenment Project*. Aldershot: Ashgate, 1997. For the implications of the failure of any attempt to find a tradition-independent and neutral vantage point – such as that assumed by the Enlightenment – for the study and evaluation of religions, see Gavin D'Costa, 'Whose Objectivity? Which Neutrality? The Doomed Quest for a Neutral Vantage Point from which to Judge Religions', *Religious Studies* 29 (1993), 79–95. Further reflections on this theme can be found in Gavin D'Costa, 'The Impossibility of a Pluralist View of Religions', *Religious Studies* 32 (1996), 223–32. But see the points made by John Hick, 'The Possibility of a Pluralist View of Religions', *Religious Studies* 33 (1997), 161–6.

[9] On which see Frederick C. Beiser, *The Sovereignty of Reason: The Defense of Rationality in the Early English Enlightenment*. Princeton, NJ: Princeton University Press, 1996. See also some of the points made in Charles McKelvey, *Beyond Ethnocentrism: A Reconstruction of Marx's Concept of Science*. New York: Greenwood Press, 1991.

[10] Stephen Toulmin, *The Uses of Argument*. Cambridge: Cambridge University Press, 1958, 183.

[11] Philip Kitcher, 'The Naturalists Return', *Philosophical Review* 101 (1992), 72–3.

The collapse of the Enlightenment project has been greeted with scarcely concealed glee on the part of many philosophers. Thus Hans-Georg Gadamer wrote scathingly of the 'Robinson Crusoe dream of the historical Enlightenment, as artificial as Crusoe himself'.[12] Paul Feyerabend took the consequences of the collapse of belief in a single, universal rationality to its obvious conclusion in his famous (and, I think, playful) comparison between a primitive tribe and the rationalists of the Enlightenment: 'There is hardly any difference between the members of a primitive tribe who defend their laws because they are the laws of the gods . . . and a rationalist who appeals to objective standards, except that the former know what they are doing while the latter does not.'[13] Playful though some of these comments may be, the implications of the death of the myth of universal rationality has major consequences for our theme.

The implications of these developments for classic foundationalism can hardly be ignored. As Nicholas Wolterstorff points out, what was thought to be 'obvious' or 'basic' was actually 'person specific' and 'situation specific'.[14] What is judged to be 'basic' thus depends on a world-view which judges that certain beliefs are self-evidently true, and others questionable. And for the Enlightenment, religious notions – such as the existence of God – were most emphatically *not* foundational, in that they were not 'obvious' or 'self-evident'. What is properly basic depends in no small degree upon the world-view of the individual thinker, or the community to which she belongs. There exists a plurality of rationalities, as a close study of traditional Indian understandings of logic and philosophy makes perfectly clear.[15] These cannot be assimilated to their western counterparts without doing serious violence to their integrity, any more than the traditional ethnocentric religions of the region can be assimilated to Christianity.[16]

---

[12] Hans-Georg Gadamer, *Truth and Method*. London: Sheed & Ward, 1975, 271.

[13] Paul K. Feyerabend, *Science in a Free Society*. London: Verso, 1983, 82.

[14] Nicholas Wolterstorff, 'Can Belief in God Be Rational if it has no Foundations?', in Alvin Plantinga and Nicholas Wolterstorff (eds), *Faith and Rationality*. Notre Dame, IN: University of Notre Dame Press, 1983, 135–86.

[15] See Karl H. Potter, and Sibajiban Bhattacharyya, *Indian Philosophical Analysis: Nyaya-Vaisesika from Gangesa to Raghunatha Siromani*. Princeton, NJ: Princeton University Press, 1992; D. P. Chattopadhyaya, *Language, Logic and Science in India: Some Conceptual and Historical Perspectives*. New Delhi: Munshiram Manoharlal, 1995.

[16] Jitendra Nath Mohanty, *Reason and Tradition in Indian Thought: An Essay on the Nature of Indian Philosophical Thinking*. Oxford: Clarendon Press, 1992, represents a particularly interesting attempt to identify the distinctives of traditional Indian philosophies through a comparison with modern western analytical and phenomenological philosophies.

Trans-historical rationality and the history of science

This same general principle is evident from a study of the history of science. Thomas Kuhn and Larry Laudan have both explored the possibility of allowing the history of the scientific enterprise to either determine what constitutes 'scientific rationality' or provide evidence for what such a rationality might look like. The basic argument lying behind this enterprise is that a robust understanding of rationality should result in a good 'fit' with the major episodes in the history of science. Prior to the publication of Kuhn's *The Structure of Scientific Revolutions* (1962), concepts of scientific rationality were largely determined by logical considerations, ultimately stemming from the emphasis on logic found in the writings of Frege and his followers. Thus verificationism can be argued to stem from Carnap's analysis of inductive logic, and falsificationism from Popper's rejection of this scheme.

Kuhn's achievement was partly to call into question whether any trans-historical 'rationality' could be discerned within the history of science.[17] Kuhn's analysis leads some to the conclusion that there is no rational basis for theory-choice, save sociological criteria such as institutional politics or generational shifts. While not all would agree with this interpretation of Kuhn, there is widespread agreement that his analysis of the development of the sciences makes it virtually impossible to affirm that there has existed, and still exists, a concept of rationality which is independent of time and space, so that scientific progress can be considered to be purely and unproblematically cumulative.

Larry Laudan provides a much more explicit engagement with the notion of rationality. In his *Progress and its Problems*, Laudan develops the idea of rationality as constituted by the somewhat poorly defined notion of 'research traditions'.[18] We should hitch our wagons to the research tradition which solves the most problems. Whereas Imre Lakatos places an emphasis upon the novel predictions of his research programmes,[19] Laudan takes the empirical fit to the data as being of

[17] For a detailed study of Kuhn, particularly the contested notion of a 'paradigm', see Paul Hoyningen-Huene, *Reconstructing Scientific Revolutions: Thomas S. Kuhn's Philosophy of Science*. Chicago: University of Chicago Press, 1993.

[18] Larry Laudan, *Progress and its Problems: Towards a Theory of Scientific Growth*. Berkeley: University of California Press, 1977.

[19] Imre Lakatos and Elie Zahar, 'Why did Copernicus' Research Program supersede Ptolemy's?', in Robert S. Westman (ed.), *The Copernican Achievement*. London: University of California Press, 1975, 354–83. For a stimulating account of what Christian theology might learn from this, see Nancey Murphy, *Theology in the Age of Scientific Reasoning*. Ithaca, NY: Cornell University Press, 1990.

decisive importance. Inevitably, this leads to historically conditioned judgements concerning rationality. While a general criterion of rationality (which is to say, a certain effectiveness in solving problems and fitting data) might be independent of time, the specific rationality which this endorses will vary from 1500 to 1800 to 1900. One is 'rational' so long as one accepts the currently most successful research tradition, aware that the future might challenge and overthrow this verdict.

Other studies by historians of science are more critical of the role of rationality. Barry Bloor, echoing the basic ideas of the 'strong programme' in the sociology of knowledge, argues that rationality plays no explanatory role whatsoever, whether in the history of science or more generally.[20] Paul Feyerabend has mounted a vigorous critique of the notion of 'scientific rationality', partly on account of his concerns that this unduly restrictive concept limits human freedom.[21] Having rejected foundationalism, Feyerabend demonstrates a marked reluctance to limit his intellectual options by attempting to clarify what is, and what is not, 'scientific'.[22] Feyerabend develops two basic arguments against the notion of a specific scientific rationality. First, a scientific rationality cannot be demonstrated to be beneficial either to the progress of science or to the pursuit of our general epistemic goals. In what at times seem like attempts at playfulness, Feyerabend sets out to demonstrate that any epistemic goal one chooses for science, whether truth or success, will only be furthered through a loose adherence to a scientific rationality. Second, he argues that a scientific rationality both hinders our epistemic goals, and is impossible to apply consistently in practice. The result of this is what seems to his critics to be degeneration into non-scientific or anti-scientific modes of thought and discourse.[23]

The scandal of particularity and religious authority

Part of the attraction of the Enlightenment project was its proclamation of the universal accessibility of rational truth. Every person, irrespective of her social or historical location, had access to rational truth.

---

[20] For the issues, see the essays collected in Andrew Pickering, *Science as Practice and Culture*. Chicago: University of Chicago Press, 1992.

[21] Paul K. Feyerabend, *Against Method*. 3rd edn. London: Verso, 1993, 231.

[22] George Couvalis, *Feyerabend's Critique of Foundationalism*. Aldershot: Avebury, 1989.

[23] For a response, see P. K. Feyerabend, *Farewell to Reason*. London: Verso, 1987. A fuller critique of Feyerabend's irrationalism can be found in David Stove, *Scientific Irrationalism: Origins of a Postmodern Cult*. New Brunswick, NJ: Transaction Publishers, 2001. For a playful exploration and theological critique of Feyerabend's ideas, see William C. Placher, *Unapologetic Theology: A Christian Voice in a Pluralistic Conversation*. Louisville, KY: Westminster/John Knox Press, 1989, 39–54.

Revelation, in contrast, was held to be vulnerable to the 'scandal of particularity'.[24] The Enlightenment criticism of the traditional Christian notion of the revelation of God in Jesus Christ partly rested on the essntially *moral* issue of its lack of universal accessibility.[25] For H. S. Reimarus and G. E. Lessing, the idea of revelation was unacceptable in that it denied access to such 'revelation' to those whose historical location was, for example, chronologically prior to the birth of Jesus of Nazareth, or geographically distant from centres of Christian mission. The force of this objection is thus primarily moral, in that the accessibility of historical or empirical truth has no direct bearing upon its veridicality. For Lessing, this point served to highlight the moral superiority of rational religion, which was able to make an appeal to the universal truths of reason.

With the advent of the insights of the sociology of knowledge, the advantages of Lessing's position have become seriously eroded, probably to the point of rendering them specious. Patterns of rationality are now seen to be socially and historically located and conditioned. 'Reason' must be taken to refer to those frameworks of rationality and preconceived notions of self-evident truths appropriate to specific social groupings at specific moments in history, rather than some universal and perennial feature of human ratiocination. Precisely the same criticism directed by Reimarus against Christianity may now be laid against Lessing's appeal to the fictitious notion of universal reason: the social location of an individual determines the intellectual options open to him or her. 'Reason' and 'revelation' are both, it seems, subject to the limitations of historicity.

The point I wish to make through this brief engagement with the history of the natural sciences is that a plurality of rationalities is, in the first place, displayed throughout the history of science, and in the second, in the interpretation of that history by recent scholarship. Rationality is a contested notion. What is 'obvious' or 'basic' is thus

---

[24] This phrase dates from the Enlightenment, but is widely used by those wishing to disinvest Christianity of its specific beliefs and their foundations. See Robert E. Cushman, *Faith Seeking Understanding*. Durham, NC: Duke University Press, 1981, 3.

[25] For the issues, see Martin Haug, *Entwicklung und Offenbarung bei Lessing*. Gütersloh: C. Bertelsmann, 1928; Raimund Lachner, *Zwischen Rationalismus und Traditionalismus: Offenbarung und Vernunft bei Jakob Frohschammer*. Münster: Lit, 1995; Adam Siegfried, *Vernunft und Offenbarung bei dem Spätaufklärer Jakob Salat: eine historisch-systematische Untersuchung*. Innsbruck: Tyrolia, 1983; Helmut Thielicke, *Offenbarung, Vernunft und Existenz: Studien zur Religionsphilosophie Lessings*. Gütersloh: Gerd Mohn, 1959; Stephan Weyer-Menkhoff, *Aufklärung und Offenbarung: zur Systematik der Theologie Albrecht Ritschls*. Göttingen: Vandenhoeck & Ruprecht, 1988.

shaped by a tradition-based rationality. The Enlightenment had its own agenda in wishing to affirm the supreme authority of reason, not least in relation to its role in breaking with tradition and institutionalized authorities.[26]

So what alternatives exist to the discredited Enlightenment project? In recent years, particular attention has been paid to the notion of tradition as a mediator of rationality, which is especially associated with Alasdair MacIntyre. In what follows, we shall consider his approach and its merits.

Alasdair MacIntyre and the role of tradition

Alasdair MacIntyre's relentless exposure of the inconsistencies and failings of the Enlightenment project has played a significant role in the abandonment of the myth of a 'universal reason' and a rediscovery of the importance of the community and its traditions in rational discourse.[27] In exploring the history of the contested notion of 'rationality', MacIntyre points out the implications of this dispute for the entire Enlightenment project:[28]

> Both the thinkers of the Enlightenment and their successors proved unable to agree as to precisely what those principles were which would be found undeniable by all rational persons. One kind of answer was given by the authors of the *Encyclopédie*, a second by Rousseau, a third by Bentham, a fourth by Kant, a fifth by the Scottish philosophers of common sense and their French and American disciples. Nor has subsequent history diminished the extent of such disagreement. Consequently, the legacy of the Enlightenment has been the provision of an ideal of rational justification which it has proved impossible to attain.

For MacIntyre, there is no universal rationality; rather, there are competing tradition-mediated rationalities, which are in conflict, and which cannot be totally detached from the traditions which mediate them.

---

[26] See the important analysis of Jeffrey Stout, *The Flight from Authority: Religion, Morality and the Quest for Autonomy*. Notre Dame, IN: University of Notre Dame Press, 1981.

[27] On this point, see the comments of L. Gregory Jones, 'Alasdair MacIntyre on Narrative, Community and the Moral Life', *Modern Theology* 4 (1987), 53–69; P. Mark Achtemeier, 'The Truth of Tradition: Critical Realism in the Thought of Alasdair MacIntyre and T. F. Torrance', *Scottish Journal of Theology* 47 (1994), 355–74. For a more general assessment, see John Horton and Susan Mendus (eds), *After MacIntyre: Critical Perspectives on the Work of Alasdair MacIntyre*. Notre Dame, IN: University of Notre Dame Press, 1994.

[28] Alasdair MacIntyre, *Whose Justice? Which Rationality?*. London: Duckworth, 1988, 6.

MacIntyre's approach must be set against a broader backdrop, which we could loosely call the 'retrieval of communitarianism'.[29] There is a growing conviction that many of the failings of late-twentieth-century society are due to the individualist rationalist tradition of the Enlightenment. This tradition, particularly as expressed in the writings of Locke and Kant, stressed personal autonomy through the advocacy of reason, individual human rights and the universalization of reason and moral values. Even as late as 1971, these ideas continued to be advocated with uncritical force. Thus Lawrence Kohlberg argued that it was possible to identify 'universal ontogenetic trends towards the development of morality' which are grounded in 'a universal inner logical order of moral concepts'.[30]

This is no longer generally accepted. There is a growing willingness to concede that humans are social beings, whose identity and values are derived from community traditions. Charles Taylor has argued that the 'three malaises of modernity' – individualism, alienation and instrumentalism – have their roots in Enlightenment individualism, and inevitably lead to a dysfunctional relationship to the world and other human beings.[31] The Enlightenment notion of 'disengaged rationality' – perhaps best seen in the idea of impartial or disinterested knowledge – inevitably entails a decision to reject the ideas and values of the community, relying instead on those derived from the autonomous human reason.[32] As Kant put it, the essence of 'Enlightenment' (*Aufklärung*) is the[33]

> . . . emergence from self-incurred immaturity. Immaturity is the inability to use one's own understanding without the guidance of another. This immaturity is self-incurred if its cause is not lack of understanding, but lack of resolution and courage to use it without the guidance of another. The motto of Enlightenment is therefore: *Sapere aude*! Have courage to use your own understanding!'

[29] For its broad delineation, see Amitai Etzioni, *The Spirit of Community: Rights, Responsibilities and the Communitarian Agenda*. London: Fontana, 1995.

[30] Lawrence Kohlberg, 'From Is to Ought: How to Commit the Naturalistic Fallacy and get away with it in the Study of Moral Development', in T. Mischel (ed.), *Cognitive Development and Epistemology*. London: Sage, 1971, 151–231; 155; 187.

[31] Charles Taylor, *The Ethics of Authenticity*. Cambridge, MA: Harvard University Press, 1992. For the argument that this Enlightenment individualism underlies the American constitution, see H. Jefferson Powell, *The Moral Tradition of American Constitutionalism: A Theological Interpretation*. Durham, NC: Duke University Press, 1993.

[32] Daniel Bell, *Communitarianism and its Critics*. Oxford: Clarendon Press, 1993.

[33] Carl J. Friedrich, *The Philosophy of Kant: Immanuel Kant's Moral and Political Writings*. New York: The Modern Library, 1977, 145–53. For Gadamer's critique of this notion, see Hans-Georg Gadamer, *Truth and Method*, 241–5.

Kant's approach pits the moral and intellectual perceptions of the enlightened individual against the traditions of the community, apparently without noting that this individual's perceptions and thoughts have been unconsciously moulded by some community or other, whether directly or indirectly.[34] Personal identity is thus at least partly socially constructed, through interaction and shared discourse with the community and its members.[35] Communitarianism rejects a purely individualist construal of both rationality and morality, and argues for the 'need to experience our lives as bound up with the good of the communities out of which our identity has been constituted'.[36]

MacIntyre's defence of traditions as the bearers and constituters of rationality and morality has thus fallen on fertile ground. While some less critical advocates of communitarianism seem blind to the fact that it can easily degenerate into conformism and conventionalism, there is no doubt that it represents a significant retrieval of a classic approach to knowledge and morality which the Enlightenment sought first to discredit, and then to discard.

The origins of MacIntyre's programme can be located in his reflections on the moral confusion within western culture. The different visions of ethics which litter the contemporary intellectual landscape represent the ethical embodiments of certain rationalities which are mediated by traditions of inquiry. Yet there is no universal rationality, no privileged vantage point or mode of thought which allows these competing traditions to be judged. Rationality as such is an impossibility;[37] what we are confronted with are different traditions, which constitute and mediate rival visions of reason and justice.[38]

The history of attempts to construct a morality for tradition-free individuals . . . has in its outcome . . . been a history of continuously

---

[34] This is a major element of the critique of Kant mounted by Johann Georg Hamann. See Heinzpeter Hempelmann, '"Keine ewigen Wahrheiten als unaufhörliche zeitliche": Hamanns Kontroverse mit Kant über Sprache und Vernunft', *Theologische Beiträge* 18 (1987), 5–33. For further reflections on Hamann's critique of the Enlightenment, see Ulrich Gaier, 'Gegenaufklärung im Namen des Logos: Hamann und Herder', in Jochen Schmidt (ed.), *Aufklärung und Gegenaufklärung in der europäischen Literatur, Philosophie und Politik von der Antike bis zur Gegenwart.* Darmstadt: Wissenschaftliche Buchgesellschaft, 1989, 261–76.

[35] See the careful argument of John Shotter, 'Becoming Someone: Identity and Belonging', in Jon F. Nussbaum and Nikolas Coupland (eds), *Discourse and Lifespan Identity.* London: Sage Publications, 1993, 5–27.

[36] Bell, *Communitarianism and its Critics,* 184. The parallels with Rorty's pragmatic agenda (5–11) will be clear.

[37] MacIntyre, *Whose Justice? Which Rationality?,* 351.

[38] MacIntyre, *Whose Justice? Which Rationality?,* 334.

contested disputes, so that there emerges no uncontested and incontestable account of what tradition-independent morality consists in and consequently no neutral set of criteria by means of which the claims of rival and contending traditions could be adjudicated.

If there are different traditions of inquiry – as an empirical survey of the situation discloses to be and *to have been* the case – and if there exist only rationalities which are internal to these traditions, then there is no means by which one tradition may judge another, save by its own internal criteria.

At first sight, this might suggest that traditions are exempt from any criticism or judgement. Yet this is not the case. MacIntyre points to traditions developing in new directions, abandoning previous approaches in the light of the recognition of tensions and inconsistencies within the tradition. Thus a tradition might be abandoned or reconstituted 'when the discrepancy between the beliefs of an earlier stage of a tradition of enquiry are contrasted with the world of things as they have come to be understood at a later stage'.[39] A tradition of inquiry thus *changes* or *collapses* in the light of perceptions of its adequacy at either the extra-systemic or intra-systemic level. There are interesting parallels here with Thomas Kuhn's account of the development of scientific theories through 'paradigm shifts', which result from both the same external and internal pressures.

MacIntyre's development of the roles of tradition in intellectual and moral inquiry has been the subject of much interest and critical examination.[40] Within the theological community, there has been particular interest in his ideas, not least because of their clear convergence with the classical Christian notion of *traditio* as the faithful handing down of ideas and values from one generation to another, linked to the institution of the Christian *ekklesia* as MacIntyre linked Aristotle's concepts of virtue and its associated rationality with the classical Greek *polis*. The ideas developed by MacIntyre can easily be correlated with the notion of 'living tradition' as developed by writers as diverse as John Henry Newman and John Meyendorff. Christian theology and ethics can be seen as interlocked within the community. As Stanley

---

[39] MacIntyre, *Whose Justice? Which Rationality?*, 357.

[40] See Robert P. George, 'Moral Particularism, Thomism, and Traditions', *Review of Metaphysics* 42 (1989), 593–605; José Manuel Curado, 'Racionalidade e teoria da mente em Alasdair MacIntyre', *Revista Portuguesa de Filosofia* 54 (1998), 429–66; Andrew Mason, 'MacIntyre on Modernity and How It Has Marginalized the Virtues', in Roger Crisp (ed.), *How Should One Live?: Essays on the Virtues*. Oxford: Clarendon Press, 1996, 191–209.

Hauerwas points out in his study of the 'church as *polis*', we do not first recognize abstract principles of natural law and then apply them to actual societies and cultures. We learn our moral principles from living societies and their traditions, which include their practices as much and more than their doctrines.[41]

Tradition and the construction of values

The beliefs and patterns of rationality which are embedded within and communicated through traditions have a major impact on shaping attitudes and expectations towards life and the world. A tradition offers an interpretative grid, a reticulate structure which may be thrown over experience, allowing those standing within it to make sense of what they observe and experience. Observation is never 'neutral' or 'theory-free'. The recognition of the role of traditions in enabling individuals and communities to construct understandings of the world and their place within it is of considerable importance.

The important role of 'personal construct theory' in making sense of and engaging with the world was first emphasized in 1955 by George Kelly.[42] Kelly argues that each individual interpreted the world in a way that reflected their personal beliefs, which entailed viewing certain events or processes in certain specific ways.[43] Among the key elements of Kelly's personal construct theory upon a number of key ideas, we may note the following:

1. The idea of 'constructive alternativism', which asserts that we all construct our own picture of the world around us, and the manner in which we relate with the world. The central assumption lying behind constructive alternativism is that the same experience or event may be interpreted in different ways, reflecting the different personal beliefs that shape our personal construction of reality. One person, who has no religious faith, may perceive the world as random, chaotic and purposeless; another, with a strongly

---

[41] Stanley Hauerwas, *In Good Company: The Church as Polis*. Notre Dame, IN: University of Notre Dame Press, 1995. See further Arne Rasmusson, *The Church as Polis: From Political Theology to Theological Politics as exemplified by Jürgen Moltmann and Stanley Hauerwas*. Lund: Lund University Press, 1994. Hauerwas derived the title of his later book from Rasmusson's work.

[42] George A. Kelly, *The Psychology of Personal Constructs*. New York: W. W. Norton, 1955.

[43] For more recent developments, see Han Bonarius, Ray Holland and Seymour Rosenberg (eds). *Personal Construct Psychology: Recent Advances in Theory and Practice*. New York: St Martin's Press, 1981.

Christian faith, may perceive that same world – including its events – as sustained and guided by the mysteries of divine providence. This allows radically different perspectives to be developed, for example, in relation to the meaning of death, and the development of coping mechanisms when confronted with the death of close friends, or one's own terminal illness.[44]

2. Constructs are essentially *hierarchical*. Some constructs are more firmly rooted and more central to an individual's personal identity than others, so that some constructs are subordinated to others. This means that certain ways of viewing the world come to play a greater role than others. Within the Christian tradition, the idea that God has created the world plays a highly significant role, in that it shapes the contours of the Christian appreciation and interpretation of both the world around them, as well as their own place within it.

Kelly's basic approach stressed that the world is 'perceived' by a person in terms of whatever 'meaning' that the individual chooses to apply to it. The individual thus creates her own ways of seeing the world in which she lives. The world does not necessarily create them for her. For Kelly, this insight was therapeutic, in that the individual has the freedom to choose a different 'meaning' of an event or development, which they find more helpful.

Our concern here is to note the critical importance of traditions as the means by which such constructs are developed and mediated, and especially to note how the Christian tradition specifically determines *that nature is viewed as creation*. This, however, is not to say that this is a 'construction' if that is taken to imply that this is merely a 'blik', a way of looking at things which happens to suit our purposes or preferences, or which we choose arbitrarily in order to demonstrate our total intellectual autonomy. For the Christian, the decision to see nature as creation is demanded by the tradition within which she stands. It is an essential element of *being* Christian, and hence of *thinking* as a Christian.

On transcending tradition

One of the decisive turns in MacIntyre's argument for a programme of 'tradition-constituted and tradition-constitutive inquiry' is his insistence that the Enlightenment project to identify and apply a 'tradition-

---

[44] Franz R. Epting and Robert A. Neimeyer, *Personal Meanings of Death: Applications of Personal Construct Theory to Clinical Practice*. Washington, DC: Hemisphere Publishing, 1984.

transcendent rationality' was, as a matter of public record, a failure. MacIntyre is aware that his rejection of a neutral transcendent viewpoint by which traditions may be judged could lead to relativism. He believes, however, that this can be countered. Let us hear MacIntyre's statement of the problem:[45]

> The relativist challenge rests upon a denial than rational debate between and rational choice among traditions is possible; the perspectivist challenge puts in question the possibility of making truth-claims from within any one tradition. For if there is a multiplicity of rival traditions, each with its own characteristic modes of rational justification internal to it, then that very fact entails that no one tradition can offer those outside it good reasons for excluding the theses of its rivals. Yet if this is so, no one tradition is entitled to arrogate to itself an exclusive title; no one tradition can deny legitimacy to its rivals.

We should not expect to find a neutral transcendental vantage point from which tradition-mediated rationalities may be evaluated, nor should we expect to identify certain 'absolute truths' as a result of our engagement with such rationalities. Convinced of the overambition of the Enlightenment project, MacIntyre commends an epistemic modesty, which he believes to have been characteristic of pre-Enlightenment eras. Thus he observes that Thomas Aquinas managed to make a series of perfectly rational judgements concerning philosophical and theological issues on the basis of his commitment to a synthesis of Aristotelian and Augustinian elements.

Yet some have argued that MacIntyre's entire project rests on a simple yet fatal inconsistency. In order to arrive at his conclusions, it is argued, MacIntyre requires a criterion which is not internal to any specific tradition, but is common to them all. In other words, MacIntyre affirms in practice what he denies in theory – that there is a 'meta-criterion' which is not unique to any one tradition, but in effect functions as a neutral vantage point.

The objection ultimately fails, as it is clear that MacIntyre does not need to invoke the idea of a meta-criterion which originates from outside traditions. It is perfectly possible to compare one tradition with another, and conclude that one is to be preferred, *without* recourse to a third arbitrating tradition. It is therefore not true that MacIntyre's approach fails to acknowledge any accountability to standards other than those which are internal to itself.

---

[45] MacIntyre, *Whose Justice? Which Rationality?*, 352.

Nevertheless, the raising of this specific objection forces closer consideration of how any given tradition is able to account for both the existence and at least something of the character of competing traditions. In effect, we are called upon to account for the commonalities which unquestionably exist between traditions, despite their radical divergences at other points, while at the same time confronting the critical question which cannot be evaded – namely, *which tradition is to be preferred, and on what grounds?*

It is at this point that we need to return to the Christian tradition, and specifically the implications of a cluster of ideas focusing on the doctrine of creation. We have already noted the robust character of a realist approach to knowledge, which accepts and affirms the objectivity of the natural world, and the human capacity to discover its patternings and relationships. Yet it may reasonably be pointed out that most realist accounts of things feel able to affirm both the stability of the objective world and the human capacity to represent it, *without* offering an explanation of how this can be the case.

As we have argued (vol. 1, 193–240), a Christian doctrine of creation offers an explanation of the ordering and stability of the external world and the human capacity to understand and represent it. Natural theology cannot be taken as an independent ground for affirming God's existence and nature, independent of revelation, but allows a sharpened awareness of the created character of the world. The human capacity to discern that the patterning of the world is a vestige of its divine creator has been attenuated (to a contested extent) through sin, but remains a subtle, if often unacknowledged influence over human reflection. Thought insightful rather than demonstrative, natural theology has important apologetic implications.

Perhaps MacIntyre's greatest achievement, from the perspective of a scientific theology, is to rehabilitate the notion that Christianity possesses a distinct yet rational understanding of reality – a coupling which the Enlightenment regarded as illegitimate or inconsistent. To deny that there is one universal rationality is not to deny that there are local rationalities; indeed, it is the existence of a plethora of the latter which undermines the credibility of the former. Specific rationalities unquestionably exist. Among them is the Christian view that humanity and the world are created by God. As studies of Christian communities to be informed by this belief have made clear, this doctrine has a significant impact on how the world is viewed and construed. In the first volume of this work, we gave careful consideration to the role of the doctrine of creation in a Christian approach to nature.

We must now explore the implications of this tradition-mediated idea.

The role of a natural theology in transcending traditions

The Christian tradition is contained in both Scripture and the pattern of ethical and theological reflection which is grounded upon Scripture, and mediated through the Christian community. We shall explore this matter further in the final volume in this series; at this stage, however, it is important to stress the way in which the Christian tradition is constituted by the witness to Jesus Christ transmitted in Scripture. The role of this tradition in determining and transmitting the distinctive ideas and values of Christianity has been stressed in a series of works by the British New Testament scholar N. T. Wright. For Wright, *Christian* theology is to be distinguished from theology in general by its particularity; more specifically – its focus upon the Christian story:[46]

> Christian theology tells a story . . . The story is about a creator and his creation, about humans made in this creator's image and given tasks to perform, about the rebellion of humans and the dissonance of creation at every level, and particularly about the creator's acting, through Israel and climactically through Jesus, to rescue his creation from its ensuing plight.

It will be clear that this narrative approach immediately secures a connection with Scripture, and does justice to its historical and narrative character in a manner which contrasts with the occasionally rather abstract and self-referential approach offered, for example, by Karl Barth in his *Church Dogmatics*. Perhaps more importantly, Wright points to the role of the Christian tradition as the means by which the Christian story is both transmitted and interpreted.

As Wright notes, part of the particularity of the Christian story concerns the doctrine of creation. As we have stressed, the doctrine of the creation of the world and humanity by God has had a profound impact upon the Christian vision of nature, which it sees as creation. Earlier (vol. 1, 241) we offered William Alston's definition of natural theology, prior to correcting this from the perspective of the Christian tradition. Alston defined natural theology as 'the enterprise of providing

[46] N. T. Wright, *The New Testament and the People of God.* Minneapolis, MN: Fortress Press, 1992, 132.

support for religious beliefs by starting from premises that neither are nor presuppose any religious beliefs'.[47] On the basis of the analysis offered in that first volume, and reinforced in the present volume, the following definition is more appropriate: natural theology is '*the enterprise of seeing nature as creation, which both presupposes and reinforces fundamental Christian theological affirmations*'.

The patristic tradition, both eastern and western, offers us a rich understanding of how the created character of the world and humanity is to be understood. For Basil of Caesarea, the created contingent structures of the world can be thought of as a set of interconnected and dynamically interrelating qualities. For Gregory of Nyssa, we are separated from our true goal, whose memory and anticipation sustains us spiritually and challenges us intellectually throughout this mortal life. As Gregory puts this in his comments on Matthew 5:1–10:[48]

> The more that we believe that 'the Good', on account of its nature, lies far beyond the limits of our knowledge, the more we experience a sense of sorrow that we have to be separated from this 'Good', which is both great and desirable, and yet cannot be embraced fully by our minds. Yet we mortals once had a share in this 'Good' which so eludes our attempts to comprehend it. This 'Good' – which surpasses all human thought, and which we once possessed – is such that human nature also seemed to be 'good' in some related form, in that it was fashioned as the most exact likeness and in the image of its prototype. For humanity then possessed all those qualities about which we now speculate – immortality, happiness, independence and self-determination, a life without drudgery or sorrow, being caught up in divine matters, a vision of 'the Good' through an unclouded and undistracted mind. This is what the creation story hints at briefly (Genesis 1:27), when it tells us that humanity was formed in the image of God, and lived in Paradise, enjoying what grew there (and the fruit of those trees was life, knowledge, and so on). So if we once possessed those gifts, we can only grieve over our sadness when we compare our previous happiness to our present misery. What was high has been made low; what was created in the image of heaven has been reduced to earth; the one who was ordained to govern the earth has been reduced to a slave; what was created for immortality has been destroyed by death; the one who lived in the joys of Paradise has ended up in this place of drudgery and illness.

---

[47] William P. Alston, *Perceiving God: The Epistemology of Religious Experience*. Ithaca, NY: Cornell University Press, 1991, 289.
[48] Gregory of Nyssa, *Commentary on the Beatitudes*, 3.

If, as Augustine insists, the human heart and mind are indeed created to know and experience God,[49] the impact of this upon autonomous human reflection on the issues of existence cannot be overlooked. The shadow of the divine will inevitably impact any allegedly 'secular' discussions of meaning and purpose, whether its true nature is acknowledged or not.[50] Western culture not only retains significant traces of a theological lexicon to which Christians can appeal; it also has an awareness, however attenuated, of a sense of transcendence which the excesses of dogmatic rationalism was never able to eliminate. The writings of C. S. Lewis and his circle are an important witness to this point.[51] As Catherine Pickstock argues in her luminous *After Writing* (1997), there is an inevitable religious culmination to western thought, whether this is made explicit or merely allowed to remain implicit.[52]

The natural theology hinted at in these paragraphs, and outlined more fully in the first volume of this series, is not to be seen as constituting a 'proof' of God's existence or the intellectual credibility of the Christian faith. This misunderstanding of the role of natural theology mars Alvin Plantinga's otherwise excellent discussion of the basicality of belief in God within the Christian tradition (99–101). As we have stressed, natural theology gains its plausibility and derives its intellectual foundations from *within* the Christian tradition. Its roots lie *intra muros ecclesiae*, even if its relevance extends *extra muros ecclesiae*. It is not a tradition-independent or autonomous intellectual discipline, in that its legitimation rests upon a Christian doctrine of creation – including the related concepts of the contingent ordering of the created world, and the epistemic and spiritual capacities of human nature.

The relevant point here is best appreciated by considering MacIntyre's discussion of how competing traditions are to be evaluated. The notion of tradition-constituted rationality means that it is impossible for one tradition to judge another in terms that would command universal assent, in that each party to this debate 'succeeds by the standards internal to its own tradition of inquiry, but fails by the standards internal to the tradition of its opponents'. This being the

[49] Augustine, *Confessiones* I.i.i.

[50] See the explorations of this theme in Fergus Kerr, *Immortal Longings: Versions of Transcending Humanity.* London: SPCK, 1997.

[51] See Corbin Scott Carnell, *Bright Shadow of Reality: Spiritual Longing in C. S. Lewis.* Grand Rapids, MI: Eerdmans, 1999; Michael D. Aeschliman, *The Restitution of Man: C. S. Lewis and the Case against Scientism.* Grand Rapids, MI: Eerdmans, 1998.

[52] Catherine Pickstock, *After Writing: On the Liturgical Consummation of Philosophy.* Oxford: Blackwell, 1997.

case, how can competing traditions be evaluated? MacIntyre offers two answers. First, each tradition is to be analysed on its own internal terms, to establish whether it is internally coherent, and whether it is able to address the questions that the tradition itself generates. We have already noted the importance of intra-systemic coherence, and will return to this point again later.

It is MacIntyre's second criterion which is of especial interest. Can questions which cannot be answered by tradition A be answered by tradition B? In other words, can tradition A recognize that tradition B is able to answer a question that tradition A has been unable to answer satisfactorily in its own history? The Christian doctrine of creation is thus of meta-traditional significance. The scientific tradition, for example, finds itself having to presuppose the uniformity and ordering of creation; Christian theology offers an account of this. The scientific tradition recognizes that the natural world has a rationality which human rationality can discern and systematize; Christian theology, however, offers an explanation of why this is the case (see the extended discussion in vol. 1, 196–218). On both MacIntyre's criteria, the Christian tradition is able to set forth a plausible claim to represent a robust and resilient account of reality.

The important point about a natural theology is that it offers us an interpretative grid by which other traditions may be addressed on the common issues of existence, enabling the coherence and attractiveness of the Christian vision to be affirmed. The exploration of this issue in the English theology of the mid-twentieth century is of particular interest. In his carefully argued work *Finite and Infinite*, Austin Farrer stresses that the human capacity for correctly comprehending the world is directly dependent upon a willingness to recognize the world as created and sustained by an infinite and transcendent being[53] – an idea not dissimilar to that found in William Temple's *Nature, Man and God* (1934).[54] H. P. Owen insisted that the intelligibility of the world, disclosed to human inquiry, can only be adequately accounted for by postulating a doctrine of creation which gives due weight to the place of 'the Godhead's created signs', including the human mind's 'nature and operations'. As a result, Owen argues, the explicability of the world to the human mind can only be accounted for by the particularities of a Christian doctrine of creation:[55]

[53] Austin Farrer, *Finite and Infinite: A Philosophical Essay*. London: Dacre Press, 1943.
[54] William Temple, *Nature, Man and God*. London: Macmillan, 1934.
[55] H. P. Owen, *The Christian Knowledge of God*. London: Athlone Press, 1969, 87–8; 143.

It must be remembered that to say that apart from God the world is finally unintelligible is to say that *everything* is finally so. An ultimate query is placed against every fact, and every explanation of every fact. It is easy to lapse into thinking that because the cosmological question is a metaphysical one – because it comes after finite explanations have been given – it refers either to the world 'as a whole' or to the 'beginning of the world'. But it refers to everything at every moment. In itself everything at every moment is enigmatic.

The essential point to make here is the following. The Christian understanding of creation, mediated through the tradition, offers both intra-systemic and extra-systemic insights. Within the Christian tradition, the doctrine offers the possibility of a heightened awareness of the nature of the world as God's creation, and represents a critically important aspect of the economy of salvation. The doctrine of creation is thus interlinked with those of redemption and consummation, yielding a coherent understanding of the historical process, and the place of humanity within it.

Yet it is the extra-systemic aspects of the doctrine of creation that particularly concern us at this point, as these converge on a natural theology. The doctrine of creation of the world and humanity is an aspect of the Christian tradition which offers predictions or retrodictions which it believes to be valid outside that specific tradition. If God has indeed created the world, imposing ordering upon it in and through the act of creation; and if God indeed has created humanity in the *imago Dei*, then some innate knowledge of God is to be expected, however attenuated, at the levels of both subjective experience and reflection on the world. Thus Calvin argued for a natural knowledge of God at two levels: an internal experience of the presence of God, and an external awareness of the ordering of nature.

The essential point is that a Christian conception of natural theology posits that something of God may be known outside the Christian tradition. The possibility of truth is grounded, not merely in the *existence* of God, but in the existence of the *Christian* God who is held to have created the world and humanity, and has not left us 'without witness' to the divine presence and activity (Acts 14:16). The impetus to quest for God is, according to the Areopagus sermon, itself grounded in the creative action of God (Acts 17:26–7). Other traditions, without necessarily realizing that they have done so, may thus base their conceptions of rationality upon an attenuated yet real perception of the nature and character of God, based upon a predisposition of the created mind to quest for such a God, and the proclivity of nature in bearing witness to that same God, in however nuanced and indirect a fashion. The doctrine of creation is thus a tradition-mediated notion which offers a framework by which the publicly accessible natural order may be interpreted and assessed.

Three ways of conceiving the way in which the Christian tradition offers what is in effect a meta-traditional 'reading' or 'conceptualization' of nature may be considered.

1. The idea, particularly associated with theologians with an affinity with the Platonic tradition, that seeds of the divine wisdom or nature were planted within the fabric of the created order, and were capable of being discerned as such by the human mind.

2. The Thomist *analogia entis*, which holds that the created order is able to offer an accommodated or refracted vision of God, particularly through analogies which ultimately rest upon the creative action of God, coupled with the faithful discernment of this analogy on the part of the observer.

3. The Barthian *analogia fidei*, which affirms the radical dependence of the created world order upon God, so that any correspondence between creation and God is established by God in the act of revelation, not by his creatures through the act of theological reflection.

It is not my concern to judge between these approaches; rather, it is to stress the manner in which nature, when interpreted in a specifically Christian manner, is held to possess a limited revelatory capacity which human reason is able to discern. It is within the Christian tradition that these intimations, hints and partial accounts are brought to their full potential and capacity, just as it is within the Christian tradition *alone* that they are rightly interpreted in terms of the partial disclosure of a God who is known and made available through Jesus Christ.

The key point is that the Christian doctrine of creation embraces three elements:

1. A creating God, who is affirmed to be possessed of certain critical attributes or characteristics.

2. A contingent created order, whose structures and ordering is the consequence of the divine nature, rather than being determined or shaped by the characteristics of the material being ordered. The Christian doctrine of creation *ex nihilo* is of particular importance in this respect (vol. 1, 159–66; 193–6).

3. A created human rationality, shaped in the *imago Dei* (vol. 1, 197–204).

As we have already stressed, this means that there is a fundamental resonance between natural human reason and the God who created both the reflecting mind and the orders of creation upon which that created rationality reflects.

A natural theology thus allows Christian theology to *position* other disciplines and traditions, rather than be forced into positions imposed by other traditions. It is able to affirm its own *récit*, and note how this allows it to position, evaluate and critique other traditions and narratives, despite the fact that, in the first place, there is no *grand récit* which commands universal assent, and in the second, that other traditions see no compelling reason to accept the Christian *récit*.

A Christian natural theology, speaking from within the Christian tradition and from a Christian – not universal – perspective offers a specific vantage point from which the intellectual landscape may be charted and explained. Though tradition-specific, it has aspirations to universality precisely because the story which it relates offers an ultimate and coherent organizing logic which accounts for its own existence, as well as that of its rivals. In short: natural theology offers and accounts for a trans-traditional rationality, which is grounded in the particularities of the Christian tradition alone.

In what follows, we shall consider how a Christian doctrine of creation, particularly as expressed in a responsible natural theology, functions as a trans-traditional rationality, offering an account of both the rationality of the Christian tradition itself, and that of other traditions. We begin by considering the case of mathematics.

Mathematics and trans-traditional rationality

Mathematics is the closest thing to a universal human language that we shall ever see. Oxford mathematician Roger Penrose's glittering work *Shadows of the Mind*[56] is widely regarded as one of the most important exercises in the philosophy of mathematics to appear in recent years. While others had sought to emphasize the correlation between mathematics and the representation of reality, Penrose devoted particular attention to the internal structures of mathematics. After exploring the implications of such things as the Riemann mapping theorem, Penrose

---

[56] Roger Penrose, *Shadows of the Mind: A Search for the Missing Science of Consciousness.* London: Vintage, 1995. For some interesting insights on the issues, see Per Lindstrom, 'Quasi-realism in mathematics', *The Monist* 83 (2000), 122–49.

asserted that the most satisfactory explanation of the beauty and structure of mathematics was that they were somehow given by God. Mathematicians therefore do not invent equations and formulas; they discover God's antecedent creations.

Penrose had developed this approach earlier in *The Emperor's New Mind*, which includes a significant account of the implications of Mandelbrot sets.[57] Playfully inverting this, Penrose writes of the land of 'Tor'Bled-nam', a remarkable world conveyed by beautiful images now known as 'fractals'. The Mandelbrot set is defined with striking simplicity by the mapping formula[58]

$$z_{n+1} = (z_n)^2 + c$$

where c is a fixed complex number. The initial members of this set can be generated simply as follows. Take the complex number $c = 0 + 0.5i$ and the complex number $z_0 = 0$. To find the next member of this series, z_1, using the formula $z_1 = (z_0)^2 + c$, we substitute 0 for z_0 and $0.5i$ for c to yield $z_1 = 0.5i$. This allows the third member of the series, z_2, to be defined as $z_2 = (z_1)^2 + c$. This leads to $z_2 = (0.5i)^2 + 0.5i = -0.25 + 0.5i$. The fourth member, z_3, can now be calculated as $z_3 = (z_2)^2 + c$, allowing the conclusion that $z_3 = (-0.25 + 0.5i)^2 + 0.5i = -0.1875 + 0.25i$. And so forth. These iterations can be carried out by computers, and generate the fascinating patterns known as 'fractals'.[59] The shape of the resulting patterns are dependent upon the initial values of z_0 and c, and are exceptionally intricate and beautiful. These patterns, however, are already present within the mapping formula of the Mandelbrot set; it was only with the advent of high-speed computing that the remarkable patterns they generated could be visualized and appreciated. Penrose sees the Mandelbrot set as a powerful confirmation of the idea that mathematics discovers relationships that are already there: 'The Mandelbrot set is not an invention of the human mind: it was a discovery. Like Mount Everest, the Mandelbrot set is just *there*!'[60] Similarly, René Thom, the French mathematician who rose to fame in the 1970s as an originator of catastrophe theory, declared that 'mathematicians should have the courage of their most profound convictions

[57] Roger Penrose, *The Emperor's New Mind: Concerning Computers, Minds and the Laws of Physics.* London: Vintage, 1990, 98–104.

[58] Lei Tan, *The Mandelbrot Set: Theme and Variations.* Cambridge: Cambridge University Press, 2000.

[59] Details in James Gleick, *Chaos: Making a New Science.* New York: Penguin, 1987.

[60] Penrose, *The Emperor's New Mind*, 124–5.

and thus affirm that mathematical forms indeed have an existence that is independent of the mind considering them'.

On the basis of his careful analysis of the theory and practice of mathematics, Penrose concludes that three worlds exist, which must somehow be correlated in the human quest for knowledge and understanding. These are the world of 'our conscious perceptions', the physical world outside us, and the 'Platonic world of mathematical forms'.[61] This third world is populated with such entities as Maxwell's electrodynamic equations, the algebra of complex numbers, and Lagrange's theorem. So how do these worlds relate? We have already seen the remarkable correspondence between mathematics and the physical world, and could provide significant examples to develop this point further (Penrose provides an analysis of Einstein's theory of general relativity as a classic instance of this point).[62]

Penrose offers the following account of the mystery of how the three worlds – Platonic, physical and mental – coinhere and correlate.[63]

> There is the mystery of why such precise and profoundly mathematical laws play such an important role in the behaviour of the physical world. Somehow the very world of physical reality seems almost mysteriously to emerge out of the Platonic world of mathematics . . . Then there is the second mystery of how it is that perceiving beings can arise from out of the physical world. How is it that subtly organized material objects can mysteriously conjure up mental entities from out of its material substance? . . . Finally, there is the mystery of how it is that mentality is able seemingly to 'create' mathematical concepts out of some kind of mental model. These apparently vague, unreliable and often inappropriate mental tools, with which our mental world seems to come equipped, appear nevertheless mysteriously able (at least when they are at their best) to conjure up abstract mathematical forms, and thereby enable our minds to gain entry, by understanding, into the Platonic mathematical realm.

The circle is thus closed – perhaps not explained, it is true, but certainly shown to be inescapable to our thinking about the world, and the manner in which those perceptions are formalized and represented.

---

[61] Penrose, *Shadows of the Mind*, 411–20. The background to Penrose's 'three mysteries' will be found in such works as Emil Heinrich du Bois-Reymond, *Über die Grenzen des Naturerkennens: Die sieben Welträtsel – Zwei Vortrage*. Leipzig: Veit, 1907.

[62] Penrose, *Shadows of the Mind*, 415.

[63] Penrose, *Shadows of the Mind*, 413–16. See also the extended discussion in M. S. Longair and Roger Penrose, *The Large, The Small, and The Human Mind*. Cambridge: Cambridge University Press, 1999.

But *why?* Why should these three worlds be related in any way? Underlying Plato's world-view is an understated cosmogony, which presupposes an implicit continuity between the ideal world and the human mind. But what if a Christian doctrine of creation were to be superimposed upon Penrose's observations? Suppose we extricate ourselves from a Platonic tradition, and immerse ourselves in the Christian tradition which views both the world and humanity as the creations of God? This would generate the following transpositions:

Penrose	Christianity
The Platonic world	The mind of God as creator
The physical world	The world as God's creation
The mental world	Humanity as God's creation

Immediately, a continuity is established between the three worlds, whose relation for Penrose, while real, is nonetheless something of an enigma.

This framework can be discerned within the writings of T. F. Torrance, particularly at those points at which Torrance links the discernment of ordering within the world with the classic concept of 'wisdom'. In a lecture published in 1991, Torrance explored the distinction between *sapientia* and *scientia* in the thought of Augustine, noting in particular the 'transcendent' role of wisdom in grasping the ordering of the world, and pointing to its origination in God.[64] The concept of 'wisdom', as developed by Augustine, is to be understood as referring to

> the unique insight that arises when the eye of the human mind discerns an invisible transcendent realm of immutable eternal truth upon which all *scientia* of the truths of the visible corporeal realm, gained through the rational operations of the human reason, are ultimately contingent.

[64] Thomas F. Torrance, 'The Transcendental Role of Wisdom in Science', in Evandro Agazzi (ed.), *Science et sagesse: Entretiens de l'Académie Internationale de Philosophie des Sciences, 1990*. Fribourg: Universitätsverlag Freiburg Schweiz, 1991, 63–80.

What the natural sciences are forced to assume – in that it cannot be formally demonstrated without falling into some form of circularity of argument or demonstration – the Christian understanding of 'wisdom' allows to be affirmed, and correlated with the existence of a transcendent creator God, responsible both for the ordering of the world and the human ability to grasp and discern it.[65]

> [The concept of order] arises compulsorily in our minds through direct intuitive contact with the intelligible nature of reality which we acknowledge to be the ultimate judge in all questions of truth and falsity, order and disorder. That is to say, our concept of order presupposes an ultimate ground of order transcending what we can comprehend but of which we are implicitly aware in the back of our mind, and under the constraint of which we generate order in all intellectual activity. Belief in order, the conviction that, whatever may appear to the contrary in so-called random events, reality is finally and intrinsically orderly, thus constitutes an ultimate regulating factor in all rational and scientific activity.

On the basis of the doctrine of creation, there is a 'fundamental harmony between the "laws of the mind" and the "laws of nature"'. Torrance stresses that this becomes especially clear in the remarkable convergence of mathematics and physics, which is grounded in the correspondence, however nuanced and imperfect, between creation to creator. The same point applies to natural law, which rests on the Christian view that it is[66]

> governed by a transcendentalist understanding of the relation of God to the creation, who does not embody his eternal *Logos* or *Reason* or *Law* in nature as his universal law, but who through the unifying and rationalizing power of his *Logos*, conceived as the Word of God, creatively imparts to the world a pervasive rational order subordinate to himself on his transcendent level as its determinant ground. Natural law thus understood refers to the God-given patterns of the universe and has to do with the intrinsic truth or objective intelligibility or order of contingent being.

We shall return to consider the importance of natural law shortly; we now turn to explore the particular place of the doctrine of the incarnation in a Christian understanding of the existence and nature of trans-traditional rationality.

---

[65] 'The Transcendental Role of Wisdom in Science', 67.
[66] Thomas F. Torrance, *Juridical Law and Physical Law: Towards a Realist Foundation for Human Law*. Edinburgh: Scottish Academic Press, 1982, 34 n. 22.

Incarnation and trans-traditional rationality

The attempt to bridge traditions began with the conversion of the Greeks, and the realization that a bridging of horizons between an essentially Palestinian gospel and a Hellenistic culture was necessary in consequence.[67] In Greek patristic theology, this bridging of traditions is firmly linked with the concept of the λόγος through which the world was created, and which became incarnate in Christ. A firm distinction is to be drawn between a full knowledge of divine things, which is a gift of grace through the revelation of God in Christ as the λόγος incarnate, and a partial knowledge which is to be had outside the Christian tradition. Thus Justin Martyr argues that Socrates knew Christ as the λόγος incarnate 'in part' (ἀπο μέρους),[68] thus leading to the conclusion that a partial and fragmentary grasp of the Christian view of reality may be had outside the Christian revelation; a full knowledge of divine things is only to be had within the Christian tradition. As Justin puts it:[69]

> Whatever all people have said well belongs to us Christians. For we worship and love, next to God, the Logos, who comes from the unbegotten and ineffable God, since it was for our sake that he became a human being, in order that he might share in our sufferings and bring us healing. For all writers were able to see the truth darkly (ἀμυδρῶς) on account of the implanted seed of the Logos which was grafted into them. Yet it is one thing to possess a seed (σπέρμα) and a likeness in proportion to one's capacity. It is quite another to possess the reality itself.

Justin thus argues that the σπέρμα τοῦ λόγου is accessible to all humanity, irrespective of tradition, precisely because the act of creation takes chronological and ontological priority over humanity, and thus transcends human traditions – which are to be viewed as aspects of the created order. Yet this is nothing but a 'seed', a 'partial' knowledge of a greater whole – which is to be had only through Christ as the λόγος incarnate.

---

[67] For some of the issues, see Aloys Grillmeier, 'Hellenisierung-Judaisierung des Christentums als Deuteprinzipien der Geschichte des kirchlichen Dogmas', *Scholastik* 33 (1958), 321–55, 528–55.

[68] Justin Martyr, *Apologia* II.x.8. See further Everett Ferguson, *Christianity in Relation to Jews, Greeks, and Romans.* New York: Garland Publishing, 1999. On this notion in Heraclitus, see Michael Bartling, *Der Logosbegriff bei Heraklit und seine Beziehung zur Kosmologie.* Goppingen: Kummerle Verlag, 1985.

[69] Justin Martyr, *Apologia* II.xiii.4–6.

For Justin, as for the Greek patristic tradition in general, there is thus a direct and critical theological link between human rationalities (the plural is perfectly acceptable) and the full disclosure of the mind of God in Christ. Plato, the Stoics and other secular writers 'saw in part the things that derive from the divine λόγος and were sown by him'; the incarnation can thus be thought of as disclosing the full truth which the seeds could at best anticipate partially and obscurely. Yet there exists a fundamental continuity between paganism and Christianity, on account of the creative activity of God at every level, including the act of ensuring that humanity was not left 'without witness' to the divine presence and activity (Acts 14:16). The Greek tradition was quite clear that those 'seeds' could be misrepresented and misunderstood. As Clement of Alexandria argued, Epicureanism was to be regarded as the 'bastard fruit of God's plantation'.[70] Nevertheless, the continuity was there for those with the perspicuity to discern it.

Historically, much attention has been paid to the role of writers such as Justin Martyr and Clement of Alexandria in developing an attitude towards classic culture which allowed the church to critically appropriate its constituent elements. By providing a theological framework which affirmed the common foundations of truth, goodness and beauty throughout the created order, while linking a failure to perceive this with human frailty or downright dishonesty, these writers were able to argue that Christianity brought to perfection the wisdom of the ancient world. There can be no question of an uncritical acceptance or wholesale rejection of the wisdom of the pagan past; Christians are called upon to identify what is good and true, and to make it their own.[71]

Important though this historical aspect of this theological development may be, it possesses significance for the theological task of today. The affirmation that the world was created through the same divine λόγος that became incarnate in Jesus Christ offers a framework which, though specific to the Christian tradition, functions as a meta-traditional principle. Christianity is able to account for the longings, reasonings

---

[70] Clement of Alexandria, *Stromateis* VI.viii.67. See further H. B. Timothy, *The Early Christian Apologists and Greek Philosophy*. Assen: Van Gorcum, 1973; Endre von Ivànka, *Plato Christianus: Übernahme und Umgestaltung des Platonismus durch die Väter*. Einsiedeln: Johannes Verlag, 1990.

[71] See, for example, C. N. Cochrane, *Christianity and Classical Culture: A Study of Thought and Action from Augustus to Augustine*. London: Oxford University Press, 1968; Jaroslav Pelikan, *Christianity and Classical Culture: The Metamorphosis of Natural Theology in the Christian Encounter with Hellenism*. New Haven, CT: Yale University Press, 1993.

and searchings of the human heart, both individually and corporately –
and above all, across traditions.

Natural theology and the trans-traditional religious quest

The importance of this point has long been appreciated in the apologetic
task of offering a theological explanation, from a Christian perspective,
of the existence of other religions. We may consider the approach
adopted by Karl Rahner to illustrate this point. In his landmark essay
'Christianity and the Non-Christian Religions', Rahner sets out a view
of the relationship between Christianity and other religions which is
grounded in a critical distinction between the natural knowledge of
God and the specifically Christian knowledge of God.[72] On the basis of
his analysis of the nature of revelation, Rahner sets out four theses
concerning non-Christian religions:

1. Christianity is the absolute religion, founded on the unique event
   of the self-revelation of God in Christ. But those who lived before
   the revelation took place at a specific time in history, or who have
   yet to hear about the event, would thus seem to be excluded from
   salvation. This is contrary to the will of God, who wishes all people
   to be saved.

2. Non-Christian religious traditions are thus valid and capable of
   mediating the saving grace of God, until the gospel is made known
   to their members, after which they are no longer legitimate from
   the standpoint of Christian theology.

3. The faithful adherent of a non-Christian religious tradition is
   thus to be regarded as an 'anonymous Christian'.

4. Christianity will not displace other religions, so that religious
   pluralism will continue to be a feature of human existence.

It is important to note that Rahner does not consider all religions to
be equal, nor that they are simply particular instances of a common
generic encounter with God or the more vague category of 'the divine'
or 'the absolute'. Christianity has an exclusive status; the question is
therefore whether other religions allow access to the same saving grace

---

[72] Karl Rahner, 'Christianity and the Non-Christian Religions', in *Theological Investiga-
tions*. vol. 5. London: Darton, Longman & Todd, 1966, 115–34. See further Geoffrey B.
Kelly, 'Unconscious Christianity and the Anonymous Christian in the Theology of Dietrich
Bonhoeffer and Karl Rahner', *Philosophy and Theology* 9 (1995), 117–49.

as Christianity. His approach allows him to suggest that the beliefs of non-Christian religious traditions are not necessarily true in their totality (although there will be points of similarity and convergence with Christianity), while allowing that they may nevertheless mediate the grace of God by the lifestyles which they evoke or encourage.[73]

Yet the relevance of natural theology goes far beyond this issue. The critical point is this: *a Christian natural theology functions as a meta-traditional device.* We are not speaking here of the hypothetical 'tradition-transcendent rationality' so effectively critiqued by MacIntyre, but of a *tradition-specific rationality* with an explanatory power allowing it to extend its scope to other traditions so that, for the Christian community it functions as a 'tradition-transcendent rationality'. This rationality argues for the intelligibility of the universe and the intelligence of humanity as its observer and interpreter – and thus offers a *de facto* explanation of why rival traditions exist. If, as a realist epistemology insists, the ordering of the universe and the human ability to grasp something of its rationality are *independent* of an acceptance of the Christian doctrine which undergirds them, it follows that a natural knowledge of God is to be expected. Yet the Christian tradition is able to offer two advantages over its rivals:

1. By offering an explanation of the world which is internally coherent, and offers an explanation of the externally observable fact that related insights may be held, at least to some extent, outside the Christian tradition;

2. By insisting that what may be known of God through nature, although in a fragmentary and potentially inconsistent manner, may be had in full through the Christian revelation, which is *specific* to the Christian tradition. It is thus particularly interesting to note that Calvin explores the relation of a natural and revealed knowledge of God through a dialogue with Cicero, representing a comparison of two great traditions – classical pagan religion and the Christian faith.[74]

---

[73] For approaches related to Rahner's, see the important statement of Vatican II, *Nostra Aetate*, 28 October 1965; in Austin Flannery (ed.), *Vatican II: Conciliar and Postconciliar Documents.* Northport, NY: Costello Publishing Company, 1975, 738–42. For a similar approach from an evangelical perspective, see Clark H. Pinnock, *A Wideness in God's Mercy.* Grand Rapids, MI: Zondervan, 1992.

[74] This argument is set out in detail in Calvin's *Institutes* I.i–v. See further Emil Grislis, 'Calvin's Use of Cicero in the *Institutes* I:1–5: A Case Study in Theological Method', *Archiv für Reformationsgeschichte* 62 (1971), 5–37.

The apologetic implications of this are considerable. In his Leslie Stephen memorial lecture at the University of Cambridge in November 1985, Georg Steiner pointed out how a natural theology, grounded in a Christian doctrine of creation, provided the basis of a meta-traditional appeal to beauty: 'there is aesthetic creation because there is *creation*'.[75] A similar point is made by Robert Jenson in exploring the way in which Jonathan Edwards finds a close correlation, if not outright identity, between God's holiness and beauty, with highly significant implications for Edwards' encounter with (and reading of) the 'book of nature'.[76] It is one of the more significant achievements of Hans Urs von Balthasar to have demonstrated that such an approach can be extended far beyond an encounter with the purely natural world to embrace the world of human culture.[77] This approach can be taken further by considering the sense of wonder elicited at the beauty of nature.

Natural theology and the trans-traditional sense of wonder

Nature possesses an ability to take our breath away. But why? The aesthetic role of a natural theology may be conceived both in terms of creating an enhanced sense of appreciation for nature within the Christian tradition, and an explanation of the experience of wonder and delight at the experience of nature inside and outside that tradition. 'The dignity of the artist lies in his duty of keeping awake the sense of wonder in the world' (G. K. Chesterton). There can be no doubt that a sense of wonder is one of the most decisive motivations for the poet, the artist, the theologian and the natural scientist. For the great philosophers of classical Athens, it led directly to philosophy – the human response to the glories of nature, resulting both in a correct understanding of the world and a good life within its bounds. Thomas Traherne wrote of the immense poetic inspiration he derived from a deep encounter with the natural world. The sight of green trees 'transported and ravished me, their sweetness and unusual

---

[75] George Steiner, *Real Presences: Is There Anything In What We Say?*. London: Faber, 1991, 67. See also Jeremy S. Begbie, *Voicing Creation's Praise: Towards a Theology of the Arts*. Edinburgh: T&T Clark, 1991, 224–8.

[76] Robert W. Jenson, *America's Theologian: A Recommendation of Jonathan Edwards*. New York: Oxford University Press, 1988, 15–18.

[77] For an analysis, see Noel O'Donaghue, 'A Theology of Beauty', in John Riches (ed.), *The Analogy of Beauty: The Theology of Hans Urs von Balthasar*. Edinburgh: T&T Clark, 1986, 1–10.

beauty made my heart to leap and almost mad with ecstasy, they were such strange and wonderful things'.[78]

The experience of a sense of wonder at the glories of the natural world is an important point of contact between Christianity and the natural sciences in particular, and the world of human experience in general. On the basis of a Christian doctrine of creation (vol. 1, 193–240), this sense of wonder is to be directly correlated with the dual origination of both the natural world and the human imaginative faculty in the mind of God. The sense of wonder which is evoked *before* any rational reflection takes place must be seen in terms of both the natural resonance of the human imagination with the mind of God as expressed in creation, and in terms of a symbolic role as a pointer to the God who created both nature and humanity, and who will bring all things together in the final consummation. This point recurs throughout the writings of Augustine, particularly his *Confessions*; it has also passed into the reflections of Romantic poetry, to which I now turn.

'Romantic imagination was a mediation between the worldly and otherworldly whose definitive act was the simulation of transcendental release.'[79] We have already noted (vol. 1, 232) Keats' insistence on the fundamental confluence of truth and beauty, as set out in his 'Ode on a Grecian Urn' (1820):

> 'Beauty is truth, truth beauty' – that is all
> Ye know on earth, and all ye need to know.

Yet Keats also offers an account of the transcendent place of a sense of wonder at nature – whether evoked by a rainbow or the starlit sky[80] – which ultimately rests upon a Christian natural theology, detached from its context yet recognizable nonetheless. In his 1820 poem 'Lamia', Keats expressed the concern that reducing nature to scientific theories empties nature of its beauty and mystery, and reduces it to something cold and clinical. An example which he cites is the Newtonian explanation of

---

[78] Thomas Traherne, *Centuries of Meditations* Third Century, iii. On some of the themes in Traherne's poetry of relevance to our topic, see Donald R. Dickson, *From the Waters of the Abyss to the Crystal Fountain: The Typology of the Waters of Life in the Poetry of Herbert, Vaughan, and Traherne*. Columbia, MO: University of Missouri Press, 1987.

[79] Alan Liu, 'Local Transcendence: Cultural Criticism, Postmodernism, and the Romanticism of Detail', *Representations* 32 (1990), 75–113; 76.

[80] On the role of the rainbow, see Philip Fisher, *Wonder, the Rainbow, and the Aesthetics of Rare Experiences*. Cambridge, MA: Harvard University Press, 1998.

the rainbow in terms of the optical diffraction of light through rain-drops.

> Do not all charms fly
> At the mere touch of cold philosophy?
> There was an awful rainbow once in heaven:
> We know her woof, her texture; she is given
> In the dull catalogue of common things.
> Philosophy will clip an Angel's wings.

These lines have provoked caustic comments from some natural scientists, including Richard Dawkins. In his *Unweaving the Rainbow* – the title of which is derived from Keats' poem – Dawkins makes it clear that he regards this as typical anti-scientific nonsense, resting on the flimsiest of foundations. A good dose of scientific thinking would have sorted Keats out in no time.[81]

> Why, in Keats' 'Lamia', is the philosophy of rule and line 'cold', and why do all charms flee before it? What is so threatening about reason? Mysteries do not lose their poetry when solved. Quite the contrary; the solution often turns out more beautiful than the puzzle and, in any case, when you have solved one mystery you uncover others, perhaps to inspire greater poetry.

Dawkins illustrates this point by drawing attention to the consequences of Newton's analysis of the rainbow:[82]

> Newton's dissection of the rainbow into light of different wavelengths led on to Maxwell's theory of electromagnetism and thence to Einstein's theory of special relativity.

The points that Dawkins makes are important and valid. Perhaps the road from Newton to Maxwell and thence to Einstein was rather more troublesome than Dawkins' prose suggests, but the connection certainly exists. And if the unweaving of the rainbow led to the discovery of such greater mysteries (presumably perfectly capable of being expressed poetically, if poets could get their minds around the rather difficult ideas involved), then how can anybody suggest it was a foolish or improper thing to do?

We can see in Dawkins' writings an attitude towards poetry akin to that espoused by the British empiricist philosopher David Hume: 'Poets

---

[81] Richard Dawkins, *Unweaving the Rainbow: Science, Delusion and the Appetite for Wonder.* London: Penguin, 1998, 41.

[82] Dawkins, *Unweaving the Rainbow*, 42.

themselves, though liars by profession, always endeavour to give an air of truth to their fictions.' A similar attitude can be found in Peter Atkins' remarkable essay 'The Limitless Power of Science':[83]

> Although poets may aspire to understanding, their talents are more akin to entertaining self-deception. They may be able to emphasize delights in the world, but they are deluded if they and their admirers believe that their identification of the delights and their use of poignant language are enough for comprehension. Philosophers too, I am afraid, have contributed to the understanding little more than poets . . . They have not contributed much that is novel until after novelty has been discovered by scientists.

For Dawkins, things are also admirably clear. Scientists tell the truth, occasionally in less than inspiring prose; poets, on the other hand, dislike and distrust science, and generally know nothing about it. Dawkins clearly believes that Keats argues that knowing how the rainbow works will destroy its beauty and our resulting sense of wonder. It would be like telling a small child that there is no Santa Claus. Now anyone can see that the rainbow remains just as beautiful if we know how it works. In fact, we can appreciate its beauty even more than before. To be fair to Keats, he wrote these words while he was a young man. When he grew up, he might have become wiser, and learned more about the sciences along the way.

Dawkins' refutation of Keats has understandably won many plaudits from his fellow-scientists, who have welcomed his dismissal of critics who claim that science's tedious and plodding message robs nature of her beauty and inspiration. I regard Dawkins' response to Keats as being unassailable *if and only if* Keats' concern was to excoriate the scientific investigation of nature and take refuge in the safety of a premodern world. When Keats is read against the background of the Romantic movement, however, the critique he offers of certain reductionist trends within the natural sciences of his day begins to take on a quite different meaning. Far from refuting Keats, Dawkins in fact confirms precisely the fears that Keats expressed. Let me explain.

The key to Keats' concern lies in his reference to 'clipping' an angel's wings. For Keats, as for the classic tradition in general, the natural world is a gateway to the realm of the transcendent. The human reason

---

[83] Peter Atkins, 'The Limitless Power of Science', in John Cornwell (ed.), *Nature's Imagination: The Frontiers of Scientific Vision.* Oxford: Oxford University Press, 1995, 122–32. For a critique of this attitude, see Mary Midgley, *Science and Poetry.* London: Routledge, 2001.

could grasp at least something of the real world, enabling the imagination to reflect on what it signified beyond itself. Keats (and the Romantic movement at large) prized the human imagination, seeing this as a faculty which allowed insights into the transcendent and sublime. Reason, in contrast, kept humanity firmly anchored to the ground, and threatened to prevent it from discovering its deeper spiritual dimensions. Romanticism encouraged a deepened appreciation of the beauties of nature, in part through a general exaltation of emotion over reason and of the senses over intellect. 'Vision or Imagination is a Representation of what Eternally Exists, Really and Unchangeably' (William Blake).

For the Romantics, the imagination led the human mind upwards, to glimpse something of its eternal destiny. Reason, for the Romantics, barred access to this spiritual world. 'The primary imagination I hold to be the living Power and prime Agent of all human Perception, and as a repetition in the finite mind of the eternal act of creation in the infinite I AM' (Samuel Coleridge Taylor). A similar theme can be found with C. S. Lewis, who once remarked that, 'while reason is the natural organ of truth, imagination is the organ of meaning'.

For Keats, a rainbow is meant to lift the human heart and imagination upwards, intimating the existence of a world beyond the bounds of experience. For Dawkins, the rainbow remains firmly located within the world of human experience. It has no transcendent dimension. The fact that it can be explained in purely natural terms is taken to deny that it can have any significance as an indicator of transcendence. The angel that was, for Keats, meant to lift our thoughts heavenwards has had its wings clipped; it can no longer do anything save mirror the world of earthly events and principles.

Dawkins' vigorous, dismissive and highly polemic rejection of religion or any human quest for the transcendent corresponds precisely to what Keats feared. Despite Dawkins' insistence, Keats had no problems with scientific explanations of the rainbow. His criticisms were directed against those who denied that the rainbow could have any *symbolic* significance, both heightening the human yearning for a transcendent realm and hinting at means of its resolution. Keats can thus be said to have protested against a certain reading of the scientific method, rather than that method itself. Dawkins' outright and premature dismissal of any transcendent dimension to life entails a reductionist materialism which denies and eliminates any transcendent dimension to life as some kind of quackery, superstition or confidence trick (to pick up on just a few of the anti-religious overstatements which grace his writings). This, it need hardly be added, constitutes precisely the misreading of the scientific method that Keats feared, and sought to forestall.

It is a matter for profound regret that Dawkins makes no attempt to empathize with Keats – to try to understand the fear that Keats expresses and its wider resonance within western culture. Keats reacted against precisely such a materialism, which he feared would rob human life of its purpose and meaning. There seems to be a certain degree of obtuseness on Dawkins' part here – a studied refusal to take Keats' concerns seriously, dismissing him as a muddled poet who just needed to take Physics 101 to get his weird ideas sorted out.

This criticism of Dawkins' reading of Keats is intended to highlight the fact that multiple readings of nature are possible, in the light of differing presuppositions. Dawkins' reading of the natural order is determined by a strongly anti-metaphysical and anti-religious scientific positivism, which clearly still lingers in at least some sections of the community of natural scientists. Keats wishes to read nature in the light of a transcendentalist framework, clearly derived from a Christian natural theology, which sees nature as possessed of a capacity to signify a transcendent dimension of reality. An appeal to the beauty of nature is thus for Keats, as for American transcendentalist writers, an indirect acknowledgement of some grander yet veiled reason and power which lies behind it.[84]

Thus the transcendent – which we might here take as trans-traditional – appeal to beauty. We shall explore this further by considering the appeal to a further member of the Platonic triad – 'goodness' – which underlies the appeal to natural theology, both classic and contemporary.

Natural law and the trans-traditional quest for goodness

Our third line of exploration is probably the most significant aspect of trans-traditional rationality. As MacIntyre stresses, traditions do not simply mediate rationalities; at their heart lie concepts of value and virtue. Moral life is rooted in the definite practices and traditions of communities. Although such traditions are not beyond critical inquiry, there is no Archimedean moral point from which universal moral judgements may be made. As MacIntyre points out in a postscript to the second edition of *After Virtue*, the virtues must be 'integrated into the

---

[84] Paul F. Boller, *American Transcendentalism, 1830–1860: An Intellectual Inquiry*. New York: G. P. Putnam, 1974; Lawrence Buell, *Literary Transcendentalism: Style and Vision in the American Renaissance*. Ithaca, NY: Cornell University Press, 1974.

overall patterns of a tradition informed by a quest for *the* good and *the* best'.[85] Yet there is a question underlying this, which relates directly to the Christian doctrine of creation of both the natural order and humanity. Where does this quest for the 'good and the best' come from? And what guides it as it develops?

One answer traditionally given is the body of law as it actually exists. This pragmatic understanding of law was set out with some enthusiasm by Oliver Wendell Holmes in his 1897 essay 'The Path of Law'. According to Holmes, the real issue was how the courts administered law; there was nothing to be gained from philosophical or metaphysical speculation of any kind. Law could be defined rather neatly as 'the prediction of what the courts will do'. A similar view can be found in the writings of more modern pragmatist writers, such as Richard Rorty and Hilary Putnam. Laws are the creation of communities, and the important thing is to understand and apply them, thus leading to a stronger sense of communitarianism.

The rise of Nazism in Germany raised some difficult questions for this viewpoint. Legal positivism came to be seen as the unquestioning acceptance of the positive laws of a community – even when that community adopted blatantly discriminatory attitudes towards racial or social groupings.[86] The situation became more focused after the Second World War, with an increasing desire to prosecute war criminals at Nuremberg for 'crimes against humanity'. As Anthony Lisska points out, a new interest in natural law began to emerge in response to the issues raised by war crimes:[87]

> If the Nuremberg trials with their accompanying charges of 'Crimes against Humanity' were to have a theoretical foundation, then one needed a radically different account of the nature of law from that proposed by the then reigning theory, legal positivism. Legal positivism, in many ways, had not advanced beyond the catchy phrase of Justinian's code – 'What pleases the prince has the force of law.' Legal positivism did not offer theoretical grounds to warrant claims like 'Crimes against Humanity' which were needed to provide justification for the war crimes trials.

[85] Alasdair MacIntyre, *After Virtue*. 2nd edn. Notre Dame, IN: University of Notre Dame Press, 1984, 275.

[86] See the important study of Ernst Wolf, 'Zum protestantischen Rechtsdenken', in *Peregrinatio II: Studien zur reformatorischen Theologie, zum Kirchenrecht und zur Sozialethik.* Munich: Kaiser Verlag, 1965, 191–206, with its analysis of the implications of 'der Rechtswillkür des Dritten Reichs'.

[87] Anthony J. Lisska, *Aquinas's Theory of Natural Law: An Analytic Reconstruction.* Oxford: Clarendon Press, 1996, 8–9.

This is one factor underlying the resurgence of interest in natural law in the closing decades of the twentieth century. Might there be some good reason to appeal to a moral ordering, capable of being reflected in human law, which was above human convention? Might a blatantly unjust law be criticized for contravening some higher authority, to which all human laws were subject? While these questions are notoriously difficult to answer, there is no doubt that many saw them as profoundly meriting serious consideration.[88]

The notion of 'natural law' was well established in the classic period, and is found in the writings of Cicero and other leading philosophers of the period.[89] For example, Augustine interacts with the notion in his *City of God*.[90] Yet it is clear that the most important historical resource for the construction of a modern natural law is Thomas Aquinas, whose views on the subject have been the subject of considerable interest in recent years. Particular attention has been given to the argument, developed by John Finnis, that natural law theory, as originally developed by Aquinas, was misunderstood or misrepresented by later generations of moral theologians. Finnis attributed to later interpreters of Aquinas – rather than to Aquinas himself – the view that natural law is to be deduced from certain metaphysical features of the world, including an understanding of the human agent and the natural end of humanity. For Finnis, this was a false move, in that it opened Aquinas' position to the criticism directed against it by Hume – namely, that the transition from metaphysics to law entails a logical fallacy, in that it is impossible to argue from fact to value, from the descriptive to the normative. For Finnis, the first principles of natural law are not to be deduced from the natural order, in that they are self-evident, and hence do not require deduction at all.[91]

A Christian doctrine of creation can be argued to set out an understanding of the relation of God, the natural order and human nature

---

[88] See, for example, John Finnis, *Natural Law and Natural Rights*. Oxford: Clarendon Press, 1980; Jacques Maritain, *The Rights of Man and the Natural Law*. San Francisco: Ignatius Press, 1986; Yves Simon, *The Tradition of Natural Law*. New York: Fordham University Press, 1965.

[89] Hadley Arkes, 'That "Nature Herself Has Placed in Our Ears a Power of Judging": Some Reflections on the "Naturalism" of Cicero', in Robert P. George (ed.), *Natural Law Theory: Contemporary Essays*. Oxford: Clarendon Press, 1992, 245–77.

[90] For some useful reflections on such ideas in the patristic period, see Jaroslav Pelikan, *Christianity and Classical Culture: The Metamorphosis of Natural Theology in the Christian Encounter with Hellenism*. New Haven, CT: Yale University Press, 1993, 136–51.

[91] For a critical assessment of Finnis' reconstruction of Aquinas on natural law, see Lisska, *Aquinas's Theory of Natural Law*, 139–65.

which lays the foundation for some trans-traditional understanding of 'goodness' or 'justice' – whether this is understood to be intuited or inferred or from the ordering of the world.[92] We have already explored some aspects of this in our discussion of the Euthyphro dilemma (vol. I, 214–18), noting how a Christian doctrine of creation allows us to posit a congruence between human morality and the mind of God. This theme has been developed by a number of natural law advocates, who argue for an ontological basis for morality and law, grounded in the doctrine of creation.

This idea is found in a number of natural law theorists, including Henry Veatch, whose reaffirmation of natural law can be seen as an explicit critique of Cartesian foundationalism. In his *Ontology of Morals* (1973), Veatch argues that Cartesian foundationalism proves incapable of providing any objective foundation for knowledge or morality, and insists that 'goodness' and 'rightness' must be reclaimed as objective features of the world before it is meaningful to talk about 'good' or 'right'.[93] This involves a reading of Aquinas which differs somewhat from that offered by Finnis, and involves grounding an ontology of creation in God as its creator.

The importance of this point has been stressed by many writers in this tradition. Vincent Cooke has developed the familiar argument that any viable understanding of natural law rests on the critical move from 'nature' as an autonomous entity to nature *seen as* creation:[94]

> The position I am arguing for is that a metaphysics of nature is quite sufficient to provide both a *ratio essendi* and *ratio cognoscendi* of moral obligation, but that a metaphysics of nature, i.e., the position that things in general, and *a forteriori* human beings, have a *telos* or purpose other than one which they conceptually set for themselves, is thoroughly implausible unless one posits a Creator God.

The Christian tradition thus posits a 'natural' sense of morality which is grounded in the ontology of creation, and which is reflected in the

---

[92] For a theological framework which links God, humanity and nature, see the extensive discussions of T. F. Torrance on the epistemological role of the incarnation: Thomas F. Torrance, *Reality and Evangelical Theology: The Realism of Christian Revelation*. 2nd edn. Downers Grove, IL: InterVarsity Press, 1999.

[93] Henry Veatch, *For an Ontology of Morals: A Critique of Contemporary Ethical Theory*. Evanston, IL: Northwestern University Press, 1973.

[94] Vincent M. Cooke, 'Moral Obligation and Metaphysics', *Thought* 66 (1991), 65–74. For similar points, see D. J. O'Connor, *Aquinas and Natural Law*. London: Macmillan, 1967, 60; Raymond Dennehy, 'The Ontological Basis of Human Rights', *The Thomist* 42 (1978), 434–63.

moral deliberations of other traditions by virtue of human beings have been created *in imagine Dei*. The implications of such a 'tradition-mediated' notion of morality have been explored with some care by Joseph Boyle,[95] who stresses that a universal conception of natural law can be stated in a manner consistent with different linguistic and cultural traditions. 'Recognition that normative claims are based upon analyses developed from within a particular tradition of enquiry does not provide a reason for thinking that these claims are not critically vindicated.' The tradition-mediated concept of natural law provides both a context for moral reflection within the Christian tradition, and a means of accounting for the 'quest for the good and the best' within other traditions.

Boyle highlights the role of the Christian community in reflecting on how the understanding of natural law is to be developed and applied.

> The practice of natural law theorists provides a paradigm of moral inquiry that is self-consciously the development of a tradition. Contemporary natural law theorists understand themselves as elaborating and applying ideas rooted in Aquinas and developed by the later scholastics. But many of them do not understand their work as simply restating a moral system whose essential construction and application is complete. Rather, they see their work as providing application of ideas developed in the tradition to actions which the earlier tradition did not have to deal with.

While the Christian doctrine of creation, and particularly its understanding of human nature, is specific to the Christian tradition, the implications of this doctrine are such that the Christian tradition is able to explicate and predict both the existence of quests for beauty, truth and goodness in other traditions, as well as offer some hints as to the forms those might take.[96]

In this section, we have surveyed how natural theology and its cousin, natural law, both arise from a Christian doctrine of creation, and offer a means of postulating a trans-traditional rationality, whether this is recognized or not within other traditions. Thus the fundamental human conviction, shared far beyond the penumbra of the Christian tradition, that truth and goodness are things that are discovered – not invented – can best be grounded in a notion of the dual creation of the world we

---

[95] Joseph Boyle, 'Natural Law and the Ethics of Traditions', in Robert P. George (ed.), *Natural Law Theory: Contemporary Essays*. Oxford: Clarendon Press, 1992, 3–30.

[96] For the development of such ideas in the thought of C. S. Lewis, see Gilbert Meilander, *The Taste for the Other: The Social and Ethical Thought of C. S. Lewis*. Grand Rapids, MI: Eerdmans, 1998, 182–214.

explore and the minds which we deploy in this process of exploration. A natural theology thus offers an important bridge between traditions, firmly grounded in the specifics of the Christian tradition, but finding a common grace in others.[97]

The whole area of natural law needs urgent theological attention. Theologians have still not caught up with the new philosophical and legal interest in this area. One aspect of natural law which might prove especially fruitful is the exploration of the relation between natural law and atonement. Can the atoning death of Christ be formulated in terms of a restoration of the disrupted moral ordering of the universe? There are certainly historical precedents for exploring this issue, even if these have proved less than satisfactory.[98] Perhaps the time has come to reopen this discussion on the basis of a renewed vision of a natural law, seen not as an autonomous discipline but as a legitimate aspect of the Christian doctrine of creation.

Basic beliefs within tradition-constituted rationalities

The growing recognition of the role of traditions in mediating and sustaining both systems of beliefs and conceptions of rationality has led to a new interest in the question of whether traditions need share the same 'basic beliefs', or whether at least some of these may be considered to be tradition-specific. We may introduce the issue by asking whether the following statement is absolutely true:

Given a line and a point not on the line, it is possible to draw exactly one line through the given point parallel to the line.

Mathematicians will recognize this immediately as Playfair's axiom, put forward by the distinguished Edinburgh mathematician John Playfair in 1795 to resolve a difficulty encountered within Euclidean geometry.[99] To many in 1795, this axiom would have been regarded as universal, indubitable and incorrigible. Nowadays, the axiom would be held to be true *within a specific tradition* – that is, the set of assumptions which constitute the Euclidean system.

[97] For the aesthetic implications of the Reformed idea of 'common grace' see Begbie, *Voicing Creation's Praise*, 87–93, with particular reference to Abraham Kuyper and Herman Bavinck.
[98] I have in mind Henry Drummond, *Natural Law in the Spiritual World*. London: Hodder & Stoughton, 1884. For criticism, see James Denney's pamphlet *On 'Natural Law in the Spiritual World'*. Paisley: A. Gardner, 1885.
[99] John Playfair, *Elements of Geometry containing the First Six Books of Euclid*. Edinburgh: Bell & Bradfute, 1795.

In non-Euclidean geometries, Euclid's fifth postulate is replaced with a counter-postulate: through a given point which is not on a line, either there is none or more than one line parallel to the given one.[100] Carl Friedrich Gauss (1777–1855), was apparently the first to arrive at the conclusion that no contradiction may be obtained in this way, possibly as early as 1817. From a letter of 1829, it seems that Gauss was somewhat reluctant to publish his research because he suspected the mathematical community of his day would not be able to accept the challenge to Euclid's geometry which his system posed. After all, had not the great philosopher Immanuel Kant stated that Euclidean geometry is the necessary outcome of human reason? In 1840, Nikolai Ivanovich Lobachevsky (1792–1856) argued that:

> All straight lines which in a plane go out from a point can, with reference to a given straight line in the same plane, be divided into two classes – into cutting and non-cutting. The boundary lines of the one and the other class of those lines will be called parallel to the given line.

Playfair's axiom thus makes no sense within a non-Euclidean system. It is not that the axiom is incoherent; it is simply that its coherence is determined and derived from a specific system of axioms, outside of which it lacks any such coherence. It is only if a specific tradition – a specific way of conceiving geometry – is falsely construed as the *only* valid geometry that Playfair's axiom can be held to be universally true, as it once was. Immanuel Kant was unwise enough to base certain key aspects of his philosophical system on the assumed universality of the truths of Euclidean geometry, not to mention Newtonian mechanics, and postulate philosophical and moral axioms which would lead to an incorrigibly true system. But it was all a foundationalist dream. The rise of non-Euclidean geometries has demonstrated beyond doubt that Playfair's axiom is only true within the set of beliefs which, taken together, constitute Euclidean geometry. *A belief may thus be properly basic within one system, but not in another.*

We could take this question further, and ask whether the existence of God is to be regarded as a basic belief? Many writers, particularly those still hanging on to the Enlightenment world-view, would argue that the existence of God can only be deduced or inferred from other beliefs, and is not itself properly basic. Yet the collapse of the myth of a

---

[100] See Richard J. Trudeau, *The Non-Euclidean Revolution*. Boston: Birkhauser, 1986. For a seminal work in the field, see David Hilbert, *Grundlagen der Geometrie*. Leipzig: Teubner, 1899.

'universal rationality' has led to a re-examination of this question, with important consequences for a scientific theology.

Alvin Plantinga, perhaps one of the most important Christian philosophers to engage with the question of the rationality of faith after the demise of classical foundationalism, poses a fundamental question to the philosophical community at large: why should not belief in God be an 'obviously properly basic' belief – at least, for Christians?[101] Plantinga's argument hinges on the recognition that although a basic belief may not be grounded on other beliefs, the belief in question is not thereby rendered groundless. For Plantinga, there is no persuasive reason why theistic belief should not be included among a list of basic beliefs – at least, within the Christian community. In arguing that belief in God is properly basic, Plantinga aims to rebut the claim made by the evidentialist objector – that the theist who has no evidence for theism is in some way 'irrational'.

The objection to Plantinga's approach from the standpoint of classical foundationalism could be framed like this. Belief in God is not basic; it is the result of reflection on other properly basic beliefs. Plantinga argues that this position thus involves two central assumptions:

1. There are properly basic beliefs; and

2. Belief in God is not one of these properly basic beliefs.

To refute this position, Plantinga aims to erode the plausibility of the second assumption.[102] When someone sees a tree, he has every right to believe that he sees that tree despite the fact that no other propositions enter into the equation of belief. Although there are no explicitly formulated basic beliefs involved, this person has every right to believe that he sees a tree. It is not a groundless belief. Perception has a critical role to play in warranted belief.

Developing this point, Plantinga sets out to explore the 'ground of justification' of a belief. He argues that there exists a principle, such that:

In condition *C*, *S* is justified in taking *p* as basic.

To illustrate the point he has in mind, Plantinga offers the following statement for discussion:

---

[101] Alvin Plantinga, 'Reason and Belief in God', in Alvin Plantinga and Nicholas Wolterstorff (eds), *Faith and Rationality*. Notre Dame, IN: University of Notre Dame Press, 1983, 16–93.

[102] See especially Alvin Plantinga, 'Is Belief in God Properly Basic?', *Nous* 15 (1981), 41–52.

I see a rose-coloured wall in front of me.

The conditions under which I am justified in believing that 'I see a rose-coloured wall in front of me' would not include my wearing rose-tinted spectacles. Plantinga argues that the only adequate way of defining 'proper basicality', in the absence of any clearly acceptable criteria, is through a process of inductive generalization based on 'examples of beliefs and conditions such that the former are obviously proper to the latter, and examples of beliefs and conditions such that the former are obviously not proper in the latter'. Yet the examples given reflect the rationality of the tradition within which they gain their plausibility.[103]

> Criteria for proper basicality must be reached from below rather than above; they should not be presented as *ex cathedra*, but argued and tested by a relevant set of examples. But there is no reason to assume, in advance, that everyone will agree on the examples. The Christian will of course support that belief in God is entirely proper and rational. Followers of Bertrand Russell and Madelyn Murray O'Haire may disagree, but how is that relevant? Must my criteria, or those of the Christian community, conform to their examples? Surely not. The Christian community is responsible to its set of examples, not to theirs.

Plantinga's approach has generated considerable discussion.[104] For our purposes, the most significant issue is not the question of the criterion of proper basicality, but Plantinga's implicit recognition of the fact that the Christian community is possessed of a distinctive rationality in which belief in God is basic. Plantinga would add the following as examples of beliefs which would be accepted as 'enabling conditions' for the basic beliefs of the Christian community:

- God is speaking to me;
- God has created all this;
- God disapproves of what I have done;
- God forgives me;
- God is to be thanked and praised.

---

[103] Plantinga, 'Is Belief in God Properly Basic?', 50.

[104] See Hunter Brown, 'Alvin Plantinga and Natural Theology', *International Journal for Philosophy of Religion* 30 (1991), 1–19; Evan Fales, 'Plantinga's Case against Naturalistic Epistemology', *Philosophy of Science* 63 (1996), 432–51; Dewey J. Hoitenga, *Faith and Reason from Plato to Plantinga: An Introduction to Reformed Epistemology*. Albany, NY: State University of New York Press, 1991.

These ideas are simply an integral part of the air that Christians breathe, and which sustains the Christian world-view.

We can see here an approach which resonates with MacIntyre's notion of tradition-mediated rationality. There is no universal rationality which allows basic beliefs to be identified on *a priori* grounds. What is 'basic' will depend upon the socially-mediated ideas, values and practices of the community to which the individual thinker belongs. As Wesley J. Robbins points out, Plantinga's claim that beliefs are 'community-relative' – and hence not absolute – marks him off from a truly foundationalist approach to knowledge.[105] This point raises certain fundamental difficulties for the suggestion that Plantinga's approach is to be regarded as 'fideist'.[106] Bredo Johnson appears to believe that universal assent can be gained for what constitutes properly basic beliefs, and that this consensus holds across different community traditions. 'Plantinga's argument from proper basicality,' he argues, 'is a very subtle, perhaps even confused form of fideism, since it attempts to provide grounds for justifying proper basicality, without doing so clearly enough to either avoid absurdity or escape the need for epistemic agreement with communities of non-believers.'

Johnson's comments might well find acceptance within the dwindling community of Enlightenment philosophers, who continue to believe that there are certain criteria of rationality which transcend the contingencies of time, space and culture. His charge of 'fideism' would carry weight for those who believe in a universal rationality; after the death of classic foundationalism, it now seems rather hollow. 'Fideism' has become little more than a pejorative way of speaking about tradition-mediated rationality by those who hanker for the good old days of the Enlightenment. But that was then; this is now. A tradition-specific rationality which is capable of accounting for the ideas of other traditions cannot be dismissed as 'fideism', especially when there is no universal rationality or globally-valid vantage point from which to judge things. The best we can hope for after the demise of foundationalism is a tradition-specific rationality which reaches beyond that tradition in its explanatory potency.

---

[105] J. Wesley Robbins, 'Is Belief in God properly basic?', *International Journal of Philosophy of Religion* 14 (1985), 241–8. This, and other considerations, could lead to the suggestion that Plantinga is better considered as a 'coherentist' rather than 'foundationalist' thinker: John Zeis, 'A Critique of Plantinga's Theological Foundationalism', *International Journal of Philosophy of Religion* 28 (1990), 173–89.

[106] A charge made by Bredo C. Johnson, 'Basic Theistic Belief', *Canadian Journal of Philosophy* 16 (1986), 455–64.

The real question is this: given that there exists a plurality of rationalities, how may we adjudicate between them without the benefit of the Enlightenment myth of a neutral vantage point, from which all may be seen, and all may be judged? One important answer to this question has been given by John Milbank. In that we wish to move beyond this response, it is important to consider it carefully.

John Milbank and the critique of secular reason: an assessment

John Milbank's *Theology and Social Theory: Beyond Secular Reason* appeared in 1989, originally as part of a series of books entitled 'Signposts in Theology'.[107] The aim of this series appears to have been to offer an introduction to some significant issues in contemporary theology. Milbank's long, difficult yet profoundly important work established itself as a major work in its own right. On publication of the paperback edition (1993), the publishers wisely omitted mention of the series of which it was originally a part; the work had established itself on its own merits – merits which sharply distinguished it from the remainder of that series.

Milbank's project is both polemical and constructive. On the one hand, he sets out to demonstrate that secular social theory is characterized by a methodological atheism, which makes it an inappropriate dialogue partner for Christian theology (assuming, of course, that dialogue is a legitimate activity for Christian theologians; Milbank has significant reservations about this). On the other, he argues passionately that, since there is no absolute rationality which allows adjudication between these traditions, a choice between secular reason and Christianity must be made on rhetorical – rather than rational – grounds.

Milbank's rhetorical turn at this juncture is of interest, and reflects a growing interest within the scholarly community concerning the way in which we are persuaded by certain forms of speech, as much as by the argument that these convey. Recent New Testament scholarship, for example, has noted how certain quite specific rhetorical devices can be discerned within the speeches of the Acts of the Apostles.[108] Of

[107] John Milbank, *Theology and Social Theory: Beyond Secular Reason*. Oxford: Blackwell, 1993. For an introduction, see David B. Burrell, 'An Introduction to *Theology and Social Theory*', *Modern Theology* 8 (1992), 319–30.

[108] See, for example, Frederick W. Danker, 'Graeco-Roman Cultural Accommodation in the Christology of Luke–Acts', in K. H. Richards (ed.), *Society of Biblical Literature 1983 Seminar Papers*. Chico, CA: Scholars Press, 1983, 391–414; Christopher Forbes, 'Comparison, Self-Praise and Irony: Paul's Boasting and the Conventions of Hellenistic Rhetoric', *New Testament Studies* 32 (1986), 1–30; William S. Kurz, 'Hellenistic Rhetoric in the Christological

particular interest for our purposes is the increasing recognition of the role of rhetoric in the shaping of a scientific consensus.[109] Without in any way suggesting that scientific theories are purely rhetorical constructions, it is increasingly being recognized that natural scientists often use rhetorical techniques to supplement the evidential case they wish to lay before their public. Thus the seminal paper of Watson and Crick arguing for the double-helix structure of DNA can be interpreted as a rhetorical, as much as an experimental, text.[110] Charles Darwin's *Origin of Species* shows a keen awareness of how best to persuade his envisaged readership of the merits of his theory at that specific juncture in history.[111] More recently, the strongly imperialist rhetoric of E. O. Wilson's rather disappointing work *Consilience: The Unity of Knowledge* has been subjected to close scrutiny to demonstrate Wilson's commitment to a 'rhetoric of conquest'.[112]

Milbank's shift from dialectical to rhetorical modes of persuasion can be seen as marking a transition from an allegedly universal form of argumentation based on the interconnection of pure ideas to a more nuanced account of the implication of social and other culture-specific elements in the process of evaluation and reception of theories. We shall have more to say about this in the final volume of this series; our attention now turns to Milbank's criticisms of the approach adopted by Alasdair MacIntyre.

Milbank as critic of MacIntyre

That there are significant affinities and connections between Milbank and MacIntyre, not to mention a fair degree of intellectual indebtedness on the part of the former, will be obvious, most notably in the clear rejection of any idea of a tradition-independent universal rationality or transcendent category of judgement. Yet Milbank has some significant criticisms to make of MacIntyre, particularly on account of the latter's

Proof of Luke–Acts', *Catholic Biblical Quarterly* 42 (1980), 171–95; Philip E. Satterthwaite, 'Acts against the Background of Classical Rhetoric', in Bruce W. Winter and Andrew D. Clark (eds), *The Book of Acts in its First Century Setting 1: Ancient Literary Setting.* Grand Rapids, MI: Eerdmans, 1993, 337–80.

[109] For a survey of recent studies of this field, see Alan G. Gross, *The Rhetoric of Science.* Cambridge, MA: Harvard University Press, 1996, vii–xxxiii.

[110] Gross, *Rhetoric of Science*, 54–65; Lawrence J. Prelli, *A Rhetoric of Science: Inventing Scientific Discourse.* Columbia, SC: University of South Carolina Press, 1989, 236–57.

[111] John Angus Campbell, 'The Polemical Mr Darwin', *Quarterly Journal of Speech* 61 (1975), 375–90.

[112] Leah Ceccarelli, *Shaping Science with Rhetoric: The Cases of Dobzhansky, Schrödinger and Wilson.* Chicago: University of Chicago Press, 2001, 113–53.

deployment of a Socratic dialectic in arguing for the 'antique under-standing of virtue'.[113] 'Can the appeal back to Plato and Aristotle then really rescue us from liberalism and secular reason?' Milbank argues that MacIntyre's strategy is ultimately deluded, in that the exposure of the intellectual failings or contradictions of secular reason will not, in the end, overthrow it. Instead, it is necessary to offer something more compelling *aesthetically*, a more attractive rather than more 'rational' vision of the world:[114]

> I want to insist against MacIntyre that at this level of 'objective' reasoning one is only talking about the inner consistency of a discourse/practice, and that in so far as Christianity is able to render such a discourse/practice more consistent, this *in no sense* necessarily suggests a new adequacy of discourse to 'reality'. Likewise, the greater coherence in the Christian account of virtue, the city and the soul does not imply, as I think it might for MacIntyre, that simply by antiquity's own criteria it should abandon its own *mythos* and embrace Christianity ... MacIntyre, of course, wants to *argue* against this stoic-liberal-nihilist tendency, which is 'secular reason'. But my case is rather that it is only a *mythos*, and therefore cannot be refuted, but only out-narrated, if we can *persuade* people – for reasons of 'literary taste' – that Christianity offers a much better story.

Dialectics, whether Socratic or otherwise, is for Milbank a 'founda-tionalist mode of metaphysics', which must be replaced, through a 'non-dialectical adjustment', with a more plausible criterion of discerning truth and virtue.

Milbank's strong vision of Christian theology as constituted by the Christian community clearly articulates a non-foundationalist under-standing of knowledge and virtue. His disagreements with MacIntyre seem to represent a demand to purge what he discerns as continuing, yet unacknowledged, foundational elements within MacIntyre's method. Yet for Milbank, the greatest difference between himself and MacIntyre is 'the role that must be accorded to Christianity and to Christian theology'.[115] The Christian community is constituted by, and proclaims, a 'true Christian metanarrative realism', which is capable of embracing all of human life and activity. It does not need to rely on other narratives, being – at least in its own eyes – the 'grand narrative'.[116]

---

[113] Milbank, *Theology and Social Theory*, 326–32.
[114] Milbank, *Theology and Social Theory*, 330.
[115] Milbank, *Theology and Social Theory*, 327.
[116] For comment, see Gerard Loughlin, 'Christianity at the End of the Story or the Return of the Master-Narrative', *Modern Theology* 8 (1992), 365–84.

For Milbank, the Christian tradition has certain virtues which subvert the Nietzschean insistence that 'difference, non-totalization and indeterminacy of being necessarily imply arbitrariness and violence'.[117]

In that the postmodern scene is populated with many different traditions and voices, having all their own distinctive perspective, the inevitable outcome is competition for attention and allegiance. On the basis of his Nietzschean construal of history, Milbank argues that his incessant competition can easily take the form of a struggle for existence. Postmodernity is a cultural chaos, leading to violence and conflict, which can only be resolved through an ordering process, whether this ordering takes the form of dominance achieved through market forces or through political sovereignty.[118]

> 9. For nihilism, the flux is a medium of perpetual conflict, a pagan *agon* where the most powerful rhetoric will temporarily triumph, only to succumb to an apparently or effectively more powerful discourse in the future. Because there are no fixed categorial areas for different discourses/ practices, they ceaselessly overlap and contest for influence. Lyotard and others rightly do not envisage a peaceful co-existence of a plurality of discourses alongside each other, without mutual interference. The best that can be hoped for is some mitigation of the severity of conflict, a set of formal rules of engagement such as is provided for by the market or bureaucracy – forms which can survive many changes in the actual content of 'truth'.

The preoccupation with violence which distinguishes Milbank's work leads him to commend the Christian tradition on account of its capacity to tolerate difference.

In order to develop this notion of a 'harmonious difference', Milbank offers a theology of retrieval, based on his reading of Dionysius the Areopagite, Maximus the Confessor, Augustine, and Scotus Erigena. These authors did not conceive of God as the one who subsumes or compresses all things into the compactness of the divine being, understanding God as the highest entity in the pyramid of existence, with all other entities subdued to God as their monarchical capstone. Rather, Milbank argues, they conceive God as the one who calls forth difference and differential relations within the creation. Thus Maximus affirms that God makes real difference possible as the 'distinction of the

---

[117] Milbank, *Theology and Social Theory*, 5.
[118] John Milbank, '"Postmodern Critical Augustinianism": A Short *Summa* in Forty Two Responses to Unasked Questions', *Modern Theology* 7 (1991), 225–37; 227.

different', or 'the God who differentiates'. God is an 'internally creative power', which is manifested in the divine ability to call differences into existence, without feeling threatened by it.

Milbank finds this point made particularly persuasively by Dionysius, who holds that precisely because God is a 'superabundant Being', God is able to posit difference and respectfully embrace it. Milbank thus concludes that it would be wrong to hypostatize God, in that this inevitably leads to disconnecting God from difference, or to opposing God to the different. God must rather be seen as the one who takes delight in inspiring harmony between and across the differentiated entities within creation. The 'unity' of God can be understood as enabling a 'transcendental peace' among the differences.[119]

> Unity, in this Christian outlook, ceases to be anything hypostatically real in contrast to difference, and becomes instead only the 'subjective' apprehension of a harmony displayed in the order of the differences, a desire at work in their midst, although 'proceeding' beyond them (as the Holy Spirit). For Dionysius, unity has become both a dynamic happening and a complex relation. It is, in fact, a transcendental peace which 'overflows in a surplus of its peaceful fecundity' and 'preserving [all things] in their distinctiveness yet linking them together'.

Christian theology thus counters the Nietzschean nihilism of foundational violence by advancing a participatory framework, an analogical poetics, a *semiosis* of peace, a metanarrative that does not require the postulate of original violence.

Milbank's critique of secular reason

Milbank's programme is complex and contested, and rests on close readings of seminal works – secular and religious – which have shaped the western tradition of reflection and discourse. *Theology and Social Theory* offers a complex 'historicizing critique' of liberalism, sociology, Marxist dialectics and post-structuralism, aiming to show that 'every supposedly objective reasoning simply promotes its own difference, and disguises the power which is its sole support'.[120] Each represents 'a particular encoding of reality', which seeks to conceal its arbitrary claims to objectivity through rhetorical devices. Milbank sets out his 'postmodern critical Augustinianism' as follows:[121]

---

[119] Milbank, *Theology and Social Theory*, 428.
[120] Milbank, *Theology and Social Theory*, 5.
[121] Milbank, '"Postmodern Critical Augustinianism": A Short *Summa* in Forty Two Responses to Unasked Questions,' 225.

1. The end of modernity, which is not accomplished, yet continues to arrive, means the end of a single system of truth based on universal reason, which tells us what reality is like.[122]

2. With this ending, there ends also the modern predicament of theology. It has no longer to measure up to accepted secular standards of scientific truth or normative rationality . . .

3. In postmodernity there are infinitely many possible versions of truth, inseparable from particular narratives. Objects and subjects are, as they are narrated in a story. Outside a plot, which has its own unique unfounded reasons, one cannot conceive how objects and subjects would be, nor even that they would be at all.

Perhaps one of Milbank's more significant observations is that 'secular reason' is itself a theological notion, in that is rests upon certain identifiable yet contested theological assumptions, most notably a voluntarist theology coupled with a 'revived paganism' derived mainly from Machiavelli.[123] Taking his cues from Nietzche's critique of philosophy, Milbank argues that this derivative 'secular reason' has been allowed to assume an improper and quite unmerited position within theological discourse. Theology, he argues, should not allow itself to be placed from outside by philosophy and by secular thought generally. Rather, theologians should learn to get over their 'false humility' in the face of modern secular reason whose challenge 'is at an end, for it is seen that it was itself made in terms of metaphysics, and of a "religion" '.[124] So-called 'explanatory' models of sociology (such as those promoted by Talcott Parsons, Niklas Luhmann and Jürgen Habermas) are in reality no more than *narrated interpretations of reality*. Turning their own weapons against them, Milbank reduces each allegedly *wissenschaftlich* explanation of things to a conglomerate of words or linguistic signs, whose covert function is to rhetorically persuade an audience of their supposedly objective truth. Allegedly 'scientific' explanations merely offer interpreted narrative accounts of things.

Milbank argues that secular modernity has called the epistemological and ontological shots on the basis of a supposedly neutral and objective approach to understanding and acting in the world. On the basis of its

---

[122] The phrasing of this suggests that Milbank might find it interesting to engage specifically with Gianni Vattimo, *The End of Modernity: Nihilism and Hermeneutics in Postmodern Culture*. Cambridge: Polity Press, 1991, on account of Vattimo's insistence that the only solution to the crisis of modernity is a rediscovery of ontology.

[123] Milbank, *Theology and Secular Reason*, 9–26, 428.

[124] Milbank, *Theology and Social Thought*, 260.

take on reality, modernity has aimed to determine both fact and value – what is real and what unreal, what is valuable and what worthless. Postmodernism has taken this trend further through relegating everything that modernity had taken as transcendent or categorical into the relativizing flux of history, language and culture. What puzzles and irritates Milbank is that so much recent theology has followed these trends, and fallen into the abyss and void of nihilism in doing so.

Responding to these linguistic and sociological turns in theology, Milbank reaffirms the autonomy and integrity of the Augustinian tradition as a resource for making sense of and living rightly within the world. He insists that we must renounce the compromises and half-measures of modern and postmodern theology, and recover a 'post-modern critical Augustinianism' in Christian faith and practice. A universal Augustinian theological epistemology, which in turn is based on an ontology of the creation of the world *ex nihilo* through the sovereign grace of God, implies that theology, as talk about God and God's world, has the opportunity and obligation to engage with any and every aspect of contemporary society.

In an important essay on the nature of knowledge, Milbank argues that the duality between revelation and reason, nature and grace, which has become so characteristic of post-Enlightenment theology and philosophy must be regarded as a fundamental theological mistake.[125] In marked contrast, Augustine conceived of faith and reason, knowledge of God and knowledge of the world as 'included within the more generic framework of participation in the mind of God'. True rationality of any kind is by definition already illumination by the logos of God, precisely because God is both the source of being and the form of truth. While revelation is to be regarded as a higher measure of such illumination, it is not in any way discontinuous with it. The reality of God thus embraces and encompasses the being of the created order within itself. We deny the manifestation of God given in Christ if we try to be Christian without seeing and interpreting the world in Christ. And we deny the truth of the world if we try to see and interpret it independently of the revelation of God in Christ. In short, the solution to the challenge of postmodernity is not to 'reinstate reason', but to 'reckon with an immense depth behind things'. As Milbank concludes this analysis:

---

[125] John Milbank, 'Knowledge: The Theological Critique of Philosophy in Hamann and Jacobi', in John Milbank, Catherine Pickstock and Graham Ward (eds), *Radical Orthodoxy*. London: Routledge, 1999, 21–37.

There are only two attitudes to this depth: for the first, like Kant, we distinguish what is clear from what is hidden: but then the depth is an abyss, and what appears, as only apparent, will equally induce vertigo. This is why critical philosophy, the attitude of pure reason itself, is also the stance of nihilism. The twist added by postmodernism is simply that appearances themselves cannot be made clearly present, but are in ceaseless flux. The second possibility is that we trust the depth and appearance as the gift of depth, and history as the restoration of this loss of depth in Christ. By comparison with *this reason* – Christianity – we can easily see the secret identity of all impersonal religions which celebrate fate or the void with the nihilism of modernity.

This strongly pessimistic take on the outcome of the Enlightenment project is echoed by many of Milbank's colleagues within the 'Radical Orthodoxy' movement – for example, Graham Ward's *Cities of God* (2000), which aims to 'read the signs of the times through the grammar of the Christian faith'. In doing so, Ward demonstrates that the postmodern attempt to create 'a world without transcendent values' has largely imploded, failing to deliver what it promised.[126]

A critique of Milbank: three concerns

So how are we to respond to Milbank? It is likely that one of the most signal services that Milbank has rendered western academic culture is to dissuade well-meaning theologians, often with a tenuous enough grasp of the Christian tradition, from launching into the kind of superficial foray into a less than half-understood sociology or psychology which has done so much to discredit theology as an academic discipline in recent years. We have had more than enough proposals for the radical revision of a half-understood Christianity on the basis of a half-understood sociology. Rumour has it that no academic sociologist of note has not thoroughly trashed them because no academic sociologist of note could be persuaded that they were worth reading. For delivering us from such superficialisms alone we must thank Milbank.

More importantly, Milbank has offered a theological intensification of the discussion of the issues raised by MacIntyre's tradition-constituted rationality, coupled with a very important exploration of what the Christian tradition has to offer that other traditions do not. Deliberately eschewing the postmodern reluctance to commit oneself to any tradition (since all are equally arbitrary), Milbank insists that there is something distinctive about the Christian tradition that lures outsiders to convert to it, offering a third voice to compete with MacIntyre's demand for a recovery of classical virtues and nihilism's violence of despair. Perhaps Milbank is not as clear as one would like on what reasons might be offered – whether these take the form of appeals to λόγος, ἦθος or πάθος (to use the categories of persuasion espoused by classical rhetoric)[127] – for preferring the Christian tradition above its rivals in the chaos of postmodernity. Nevertheless, his appeal to rhetoric rather than dialectic opens the doors to some very interesting conversations.

In turning to criticize Milbank, I must first point out our many convergences. It is clear that the natural theology which I set out in the first volume of this work plays a role similar to that of Augustine's epistemology and ontology in the writings of John Milbank. Milbank and I both affirm that a robust doctrine of creation, which affirms an ontology of the creation of the world *ex nihilo*, offers a persuasive account of the world in terms of its *ratio* to and in God, allowing the Christian narrative to be seen as a meta-discourse which *intentionally* seeks to embrace all human life and activity. (By this, I mean that the Christian theological tradition has not perverted or misrepresented its integrity in seeking to address and inform these matters.) Milbank, it is true, focuses on issues of church, society and culture where I am primarily concerned to focus on the natural sciences. Nevertheless, the continuity is there. My emphasis on the theological retrieval of nature as creation, and the ontological foundations of the dialogue between theology and the natural sciences (vol. 1, 20–5) can be seen as a transposition of Milbank's approach, rather than as its rival.

Yet there are three fundamental and interconnected differences between us. As all three require more than a little discussion, it will be helpful to set them out in summary form, before addressing them more thoroughly.

1. I cannot see how we can evade the fact that a Christian natural theology both undergirds and encourages a critical *engagement* with other traditions (or 'discourse/practices', to use Milbank's term). Yet Milbank seems to share Karl Barth's inclination to hermeticism, which insulates Christianity from its intellectual and spiritual competitors.

2. Despite his rigorous engagement with the history of western thought, Milbank seems reluctant to address the issue of how the

ideas of Christian thinkers he wishes to reappropriate – such as Augustine – developed, and the extent to which they are shaped or conditioned by their environment. Having applied an 'historicizing critique' to the rivals of Christianity, he seems curiously unwilling to apply the same tool to specific historical embodiments of Christianity – such as Dionysius or Augustine.

3. Milbank's hostility to any form of engagement with other traditions does not seem to inhibit him from approving and appropriating such engagement through surrogates.

To turn to this first of these. Milbank vigorously refuses to engage with other traditions, precisely because they do not, and cannot, share common premises. Christian discourse and practice is apparently sealed off in a hermetic container from the remainder of human life and thought. Milbank rejects MacIntyre's preoccupation with dialectic, believing it to be foundational in character, and hence inappropriate, given that there are no 'universal structures of reason'. In its place, he posits the use of rhetoric, arguing the need for those outside the Christian tradition to be *persuaded* to accept the Christian tradition. (Given Milbank's aversion to violence, it might be proper to add that he understands 'persuasion' in intellectual, not physical, terms.) The grounds of persuasion are: negatively, that non-Christian traditions are spiritually empty and devoid of meaning and depth; and positively, that Christianity has a certain appeal to people of good taste.

Yet if the entire Platonic triad of truth, goodness and beauty are tradition-specific, how can an appeal be made to an aesthetical norm? Does not Milbank's rhetoric of persuasion ultimately depend on the assumption of shared ideas or values across traditions? Is he not obliged to posit that what I recognize as beautiful and tasteful will be appreciated as such by others, who do not share my beliefs concerning God and the creation of the world? It is not simply reason which is a false universal; goodness and beauty are subject to precisely the same difficulty. The criteria by which Milbank hopes to persuade are thus linked, however indirectly, to the tradition to which he hopes to recruit those whom he persuades. This would seem to require such people to accept the values and virtues of the Christian before they can accept Christianity itself.

Yet Augustine's analysis of beauty, which is grounded in his natural theology, allows the human perception of divine beauty, however attenuated, in advance of conversion, precisely because the human mind

has been created to respond to God.[128] Augustine thus neatly avoids the
trap into which Milbank falls. Yet I would suggest that this trap is
simply a hole that Milbank has dug for himself, as a result of his failure
to consider the meta-traditional implications of a Christian doctrine of
creation, particularly the implications of a natural theology. Milbank,
however, seems to share the exclusivism of writers such as Karl Barth
and Cornelius van Til[129] who insist that there is no common ground
between faith and unbelief. Yet the same Augustine to whom Milbank
appeals for so many aspects of his thought had rather different ideas on
this matter.[130]

> Pagan learning is not entirely made up of false teachings and superstitions.
> It contains also some excellent teachings, well suited to be used by truth,
> and excellent moral values. Indeed, some truths are even found among
> them which relate to the worship of the one God. Now these are, so to
> speak, their gold and their silver, which they did not invent themselves,
> but which they dug out of the mines of the providence of God, which
> are scattered throughout the world, yet which are improperly and un-
> lawfully prostituted to the worship of demons. The Christian, therefore,
> can separate these truths from their unfortunate associations, take
> them away, and put them to their proper use for the proclamation of the
> gospel.

On my reading of a natural theology – and, I suggest, on Augustine's
– there will be *continuities*, however weak they may be; *commonalities*,
however attenuated they may be; and *correspondences*, however oblique
they may be, between Christianity and other attempts to make sense of
the world, precisely because both that world and those who attempt to
make sense of it have been created by the same God.[131] On my reading
of Milbank, he concedes no possible point of connection between
natural wisdom and the Christian tradition.[132] Yet I see a very different
scenario envisaged in the prototypical encounter of pagan wisdom and

---

[128] For a full discussion of the intricacies of Augustine's thought at this point, see Carol
Harrison, *Beauty and Revelation in the Thought of Saint Augustine.* Oxford: Oxford University
Press, 1992.

[129] On whom see E. R. Geehan, *Jerusalem and Athens: Critical Discussions on the Theology
and Apologetics of Cornelius Van Til.* Nutley, NJ: Presbyterian and Reformed Publishing
Co., 1971.

[130] Augustine of Hippo, *de doctrina Christiana*, II.xl.60–1.

[131] The classic text in this respect is Augustine's *Confessiones.* See further Wolfgang
Wieland, *Offenbarung bei Augustinus.* Mainz: Matthias–Grünewald–Verlag, 1978.

[132] I find my concerns shared by Aidan Nichols, 'Non Tali Auxilio: John Milbank's Suasion
to Orthodoxy', *New Blackfriars* 73 (1992), 326–32.

the Christian proclamation in Athens, as we find it recorded in Acts 17. Does not Paul attempt to find common ground between the gospel and pagan culture, as a means of embedding the former in the conceptualities of the latter, eventually to transform them?[133] And is not this task continued and developed by Justin Martyr and others, who manage to offer at least a plausible account of the continuities between Christianity and other traditions, and offer an ontological grounding of these commonalities?

The Christian belief that God, in creating the world, signed it with the divine likeness and created humanity with the capacity to discern its vestiges and attenuations, clearly points to a native human ability to make some hesitant autonomous guesses as to the nature and purpose of the world, including humanity, which have the potential to resonate with the great themes of the Christian tradition. The basic idea can be seen in the concept of the λόγος προφορικός, the externalized λόγος of creation, which was developed by Theophilus and other early Christian writers both as a means of encouraging dialogue with the Platonic tradition, and also as a way of accommodating its valid insights within a Christian framework.[134]

While Justin Martyr draws upon Platonic notions, the ideas that he articulates are demonstrably Christian, grounded in both Old and New Testaments. Similar ideas – though using different conceptualities – may be found in the patristic and medieval writers who play such a significant role in Milbank's project, yet who appear to envisage a rather more intimate and productive encounter with other traditions than he allows. It is a matter of historical fact that the classic theological enterprise has rested on an engagement with other disciplines and traditions – the natural sciences included – where these are viewed as *ancillae theologiae*.

I agree fully with Milbank that a Christian ontology and epistemology, grounded in a Christian doctrine of creation – yet not

---

[133] David L. Balch, 'The Areopagus Speech: An Appeal to the Stoic Historian Posidonius against Later Stoics and the Epicureans', in D. L. Balch, E. Ferguson and W. Meeks (eds), *Greeks, Romans and Christians: Essays in Honor of Abraham J. Malherbe*. Minneapolis, MN: Fortress Press, 1990, 52–79; Hans Conzelmann, 'The Address of Paul on the Areopagus', in L. E. Keck and J. L. Martyn (eds), *Studies in Luke–Acts: Essays in Honor of Paul Schubert*. Nashville, TN: Abingdon Press, 1966, 217–30; Dean Zweck, 'The *Exordium* of the Areopagus Speech, Acts 17.22, 23', *New Testament Studies* 35 (1989), 94–103.

[134] See Wilhelm Kelber, *Die Logoslehre von Heraklit bis Origenes*. Stuttgart: Verlag Urachhaus, 1958. For useful background, see Burton L. Mack, *Logos und Sophia: Untersuchungen zur Weisheitstheologie im hellenistischen Judentum*. Göttingen: Vandenhoeck & Ruprecht, 1973.

necessarily a specifically *Augustinian* variant of this doctrine – enables the Christian tradition to make sense of the existence of other traditions, and combat their truth-claims. But it does far more than this; it lays the ground for productive conversations, in that it posits commonalities and points of access to traditions which Milbank rather prematurely judges – and, I may add, determines on grounds that are not entirely Christian – to be incommensurable with the Christian tradition.

Thus Justin Martyr can be said to have allowed the Platonic tradition – seen both *sociologically* as a community of thinkers and *intellectually* as the ideas they advanced – to yield what he clearly regarded as a strengthened Christian tradition, which was well capable of accommodating this development.[135] The present project commends engagement with the tradition of the natural sciences – again, seen as both a sociological and intellectual entity – as a means of allowing consolidation through creative innovation within a tradition which is both prepared to encourage such a development, and benefit from it. It may seem strange to speak of the natural sciences as a 'tradition'. However, the growing interest on the part of sociologists in how natural scientists work – as opposed to what they publish – has led to a growing appreciation of the social role of scientific tradition in relation to rationality and especially theory choice within the scientific communities.[136] We shall be exploring this issue further in the final volume of this work, which examines the role of a tradition-based community in relation to the genesis, development and reception of theories and doctrines.

This brings us to the second concern we have, which is of an explicitly historico-theological nature. While being immensely appreciative of the stimulus Milbank offers to the recovery of an authentic Christian view of the world, I am uneasy about his constant emphasis upon returning to the 'patristic and medieval roots' of the Christian tradition. *What about the Bible?* Throughout Milbank's work, we find a curious silence about the role Scripture has to play in the Christian theological enterprise, despite the crucial role that Scripture has so obviously played in shaping the ideas of the patristic and medieval writers who he so values. It is excellent to find a recent theologian who is prepared, not simply to read and value Augustine, but to apply him to the current theological and cultural situation. Yet the insights which Milbank so

---

[135] Milbank's account of the Christian embrace of 'difference' is helpful in exploring how this takes place.

[136] See especially P. Galison, *How Experiments End.* Chicago: University of Chicago Press, 1987.

values, particularly in relation to epistemology and ontology, may be had elsewhere within the Christian tradition, and be argued to rest in a close reading of Scripture rather than being imposed by its later interpreters.

Yet my concern is not *primarily* that Milbank marginalizes Scripture, though I do regard this as a deeply troubling aspect of his writing. It is that he evades engaging the difficult question of *how Augustine's ideas came to arise out of Scripture.* Milbank presents us with refreshing and intriguing insights from the great and good of the patristic era, and beyond, and urges us to emulate and appropriate Augustine, Dionysius and other congenial thinkers. But the ideas of these theological eminencies did not come into being, as it were, *ex nihilo.* They represent the outcome of a nuanced engagement with Scripture, a tacit indebtedness to previous thinkers, and agendas – both overt and covert – concerning what views needed to be repulsed, and what others to be affirmed.

Milbank, for all his emphasis on the importance of historicizing our ideas, seems curiously reluctant to plot the trajectory of the development of Christian thought, especially in the first two centuries. He presents what I cannot help but feel is an essentially *ahistorical* account of early (and, to a lesser extent, medieval) Christianity which seems to amount to an idealized – as opposed to historicized – account of the emergence of the Christian distinctiveness which he values so greatly. Like Lindbeck, Milbank occasionally leaves one with the misleading impression that the Christian tradition is just *there*, without being attentive to the complex story of how this complex tradition *emerged.*[137] Orthodoxy is something which was *constructed* through both theological and political conflict (perhaps even 'violence', in Milbank's terms), and the process of construction must be re-examined at all points to ensure the integrity of what has been passed down to us. And inevitably, this entails an engagement with the scriptural narrative that Nicene orthodoxy purports to embody.

Our third concern builds on this point, and again rests upon my concern over Milbank's ease in accepting historical givens, without inquiring how they came into being. Milbank objects strongly to dialogue between traditions, and the appropriation of ideas from outside the Christian tradition. I have great sympathy with Milbank's agenda

---

[137] The main issues are explored with an admirable concision in Rowan Williams, 'Does it make sense to speak of pre-Nicene orthodoxy?', in Rowan Williams (ed.), *The Making of Orthodoxy.* Cambridge: Cambridge University Press, 1989, 1–23.

here, and have myself argued against the uncritical importing of theologically normative ideas and values from outside the Christian tradition. The early Christian writer who would probably have lauded Milbank's approach the most is Tertullian, who entertained dark fears and anxieties about the wisdom of allowing Jerusalem to listen to Athens. Tertullian does not seem to be mentioned in *Theology and Social Theory*. Instead, Milbank commends writers such as Augustine as models of how theology ought to be done.

Yet was it not Augustine himself who entered into dialogue with non-Christian traditions, and commended others who had done so, not least for making the intellectual riches of these traditions available to the church? Did not Augustine actually set his face *against* the theological isolationism commended by Tertullian? Augustine clearly advocates the critical appropriation of ideas, whatever their origins, seeing this as the intellectual equivalent of claiming the treasures of the Egyptians (vol. 1, 14). Milbank thus commends engagement with other traditions *by surrogate*, in that he endorses the ideas of others who themselves commended this practice and benefited from doing so.

This issue is of critical importance in the history of the first three centuries of Christianity, when the question of the interaction of the Christian community with other intellectual or religious communities was of major significance in shaping the contours of an emerging Christian world-view. While one might want to question Adolf von Harnack's overstatements concerning the influence of a Hellenistic culture on the shaping of the Christian tradition, there is no doubt that some complex negotiations and interchanges were taking place at this time.[138] It is impossible to study the development of the Christian doctrine of God at this time without noticing the traffic of ideas between different traditions and communities.[139] With the conversion of Constantine and the recognition of Christianity as *religio licita*, new forms of interaction were possible, opening up new possibilities within the Christian tradition.

To advocate a renewed Augustinianism in theology is thus to endorse a *vicarious* engagement with non-Christian traditions and communities. It is like the person who disapproves of testing cosmetics on animals,

---

[138] E. J. Meijering, *Die Hellenisierung des Christentums im Urteil Adolf von Harnack*. Amsterdam: Kampen, 1985.

[139] See Wolfhart Pannenberg, 'The Appropriation of the Philosophical Concept of God as a Dogmatic Problem of Early Christian Theology', in *Basic Questions in Theology II*. London: SCM Press, 1971, 119–83.

but is quite happy to use a cosmetic that was tested on animals long ago, on the grounds that no suffering is caused at *present* by this practice. Why not benefit from something that happened in the past, even if we no longer approve of it?

These concerns about Milbank's approach probably reflect my sensitivities as an historical theologian, who is deeply conscious of the fact that doctrine develops, that the 'given' is at least partly 'constructed', and who has a marked aversion to idealized distortions of history. Despite these concerns, which I believe can be remedied through a more historically informed and dynamic approach to the development of the Christian tradition, Milbank has confirmed many of the theological insights developed without apparent theological intent by MacIntyre. The picture which emerges possesses a striking coherency which resonates strongly with the approach I believe to be appropriate through engaging with the natural sciences as a dialogue partner for theology.

Having criticized Milbank on a number of points, I am clearly under an obligation to respond to his concerns, not least to show how it might be possible to encounter and engage rival traditions without succumbing to their informing and determining ideologies, whether these are openly acknowledged or subtly concealed. I believe that this can be done by recognizing that:

1. As a matter of historical fact, this has already been done by many of the figures who Milbank (and I, for that matter) regard as exemplary theologians. Augustine and Aquinas have both engaged critically with the Platonic and Aristotelian traditions respectively; the latter, of course, has also engaged critically with the former.[140]

2. Most accounts of the development of Christian doctrine draw attention to the importance of pressures from outside the Christian tradition as a catalyst for doctrinal reinvigoration.[141]

3. That a responsible natural theology allows us to view the exploration of other traditions as encountering ideas whose origins lie in common grace. Not every idea in other traditions is anti-Christian and destructive of the integrity of the Christian tradition.

---

[140] Etienne Gilson, 'Pourquoi saint Thomas a critiqué saint Augustin', *Archives d'Histoire littéraire et Doctrinale du Moyen Age* 1 (1926–7), 5–127.

[141] See especially John Henry Newman, *An Essay on the Development of Christian Doctrine*. London: James Toovey, 1845. For reflections, see Aidan Nichols, *From Newman to Congar: The Idea of Doctrinal Development from the Victorians to the Second Vatican Council*. Edinburgh: T&T Clark, 1990, 17–70.

Some are neutral; others may be positive. It is essential to see this as a process of *critical appropriation*, rather than uncritical rejection or affirmation, of ideas from outside the tradition.

4. That it is possible to incorporate elements whose origins lie outside the Christian tradition in a ministerial, rather than magisterial manner.

Reaffirming the Christian tradition

Our concern in the first two chapters of this volume has been to criticize, as much as to construct. We have been primarily concerned to identify dead ends in the quest for knowledge, with a view to navigating through more promising waters. The main conclusions of this analysis have been the following:

1. Classical foundationalism represents something of a dead end, and cannot be taken to provide a secure basis for theological, philosophical or scientific reflection.

2. Against the Enlightenment, it is necessary to question the notion of 'universal absolute truth'; truth is primarily constituted in and through traditions. This entails the recognition of the severe limitations placed on dialectic as a means of persuasion, and a corresponding turn to rhetoric.

3. *A priori* notions of truth, or criteria by which truth may be established, are to be set aside as an aspect of the discredited Enlightenment project. These must be replaced with *a posteriori* ideas and criteria, which are themselves generated through a growing understanding of what the world is actually like, and hence what criteria are appropriate to its investigation.

4. What is 'appropriate' depends upon what is being investigated, and cannot be determined in advance on *a priori* grounds. Each tradition or discipline potentially demands its own criteria of engagement. Methodology is ultimately dependent upon ontology.

5. The 'linguistic turn' in philosophy has been sterile, and has simply led to a philosophical disengagement from the issues addressed by the natural sciences and Christian theology.

6. Allegedly neutral, transcendent or 'objective' disciplines – such as the social sciences – are in reality no more than *narrated*

interpretations of reality which possess no privileged status permitting them to judge or police others.

The outcome of this analysis is to raise very serious questions concerning whether Christian theology has anything *fundamental* to gain through any engagement with philosophy or sociology, if these are allowed to assume a magisterial rather than ministerial role. With John Milbank, I agree that a failure to realize the true theological nature of secular philosophies has led to theological atrophy and confusion. Against John Milbank, I insist that dialogue between Christian theology and other disciplines is legitimate and desirable, partly because any respectable Christian world-view will insist that it has something to say in response to these disciplines.

Ronald Thiemann has already explored how Christians may appeal to the specific resources of their own tradition in generating approaches which, though specific to Christianity, enable the Christian theology to interact with the public arena.[142] Against David Tracy's proposal for a 'public theology' that addresses society, academy and church on the basis of a shared understanding of rationality, Thiemann argues that the Christian tradition possesses its own distinctive rationality, on the basis of which it must learn to address and interact with the public arena.[143]

On the basis of a fully orbed Christian understanding of creation, I do not see how this intellectual responsibility can be evaded. For a tradition to *develop*, it must be *stimulated* – and part of that stimulus is interaction with other traditions. The interaction with the natural sciences is perhaps the most powerful aid to theological development that is available, and it is essential to rise to this challenge, knowing that the challenge enfolds a resource.

For tradition is not a static, but a dynamic notion. The Christian tradition is a *living* tradition, grounded in the past yet seeking to renew that heritage at every point. The dynamics of the Christian tradition are such that it is constantly seeking the critical reappropriation of its own past and appropriation of insights or approaches from outside the Christian tradition where they resonate with its core values – whether one thinks of this in terms of a common revelation transcending traditions, 'robbing the Egyptians of their riches' (Augustine), or

---

[142] Ronald F. Thiemann, *Revelation and Theology: The Gospel as Narrated Promise.* Notre Dame, IN: University of Notre Dame Press, 1985.
[143] For the further development of this idea, see Ronald F. Thiemann, *Constructing a Public Theology: The Church in a Pluralistic Culture.* Louisville, KY: John Knox Press, 1991.

accumulating intellectual driftwood to strengthen the boat while it is sailing on the high seas (Neurath).

The notion of a 'living tradition' is a general feature of human culture, not a specifically Christian matter. It involves allowing a traditional format, system or approach to stimulate novelty within those parameters, rather than woodenly repeating the past.[144] This demands an encounter and engagement with stimuli which will prompt questions such as: 'Can this be done better? Is this the only way of remaining faithful at this point? Has this been tried before?' The engagement of Christian theology with the natural sciences, especially when both are viewed as *theory* and *practice* – the actions of communities, rather than the ideas of detached individuals – offers precisely such a stimulus.

As we noted in the previous chapter, one of the most problematic aspects of George Lindbeck's 'postliberal' account of doctrine is his inability to offer viable criteria by which doctrinal developments may be assessed, or by which reform of existing doctrines may be undertaken. Attention may be paid to issues of intra-systemic consistency, to ensure that theological affirmations interconnect to their full extent. At times, Lindbeck seems to endorse a pragmatic approach to theology, simply as the doctrines currently present, as a matter of fact, within the Christian community.[145] Yet this does not really do justice to the issue of what those doctrines are meant to picture or represent, and how faithfully and successfully they achieve this goal.

Yet an integral aspect of the rationalities of both the natural sciences and a scientific theology is that the development and confirmation of ideas within their traditions is shaped and sustained by an engagement with an external reality – however much our grasp of this may be modulated by the human mind, and the context in which this is located. It will be clear that this demands that we engage in some detail with the issue of realism in science and theology, a task to which we now turn.

---

[144] Examples are easily given from fields as diverse as English horticulture to Japanese arts: see, for example, David James, *Celtic Crafts: The Living Tradition.* London: Blandford, 1997; F. Howes John, Ronald Posner and David Lindroth, *Tradition in Transition: The Modernization of Japan.* New York: Macmillan, 1975.

[145] Perhaps Lindbeck has been influenced in this matter by his Yale colleague William A. Christian, *Doctrines of Religious Communities: A Philosophical Study.* New Haven, CT: Yale University Press, 1987.

Chapter 9

The Foundations of Realism in the Natural Sciences

T he pursuit of knowledge takes many paths, some of which turn out to be dead ends, despite the hopes of previous generations that they might turn out to be the intellectual equivalent of Jean Cabot's fabled Northwest Passage from Europe to the dazzling riches of India. Among those dead ends we must number the Enlightenment belief that a *fundamentum inconcussum* for incorrigible knowledge could be devised by means of a universal, historically detached human reason, the idea that an internally consistent set of beliefs must somehow be possessed of truth, and the pragmatic idea that the best that philosophy can hope to do is to consolidate the existing ideas and values of a community. All these have their merits; yet they lead nowhere – or at least, nowhere that a critically informed person believes to be habitable.

The natural sciences, however, do not fall into any of these three categories, despite the attempts of various well-meaning assimilationists to persuade them to do so – or persuade others, often from a non-scientific background, that they have in fact done so. The basic impulse of the scientific method lies in an engagement with the real world, untroubled by prior philosophical notions of what that real world ought to look like, and what human observers ought to be able to make of it. For the natural sciences, 'ontological finality' thus rests with nature itself.[1] It is the natural world itself which determines how we should investigate it, and how we are to make sense of it. Where models or other constructs are needed to rationalize a complex empirical situation,

[1] Nicholas Rescher, *Scientific Realism: A Critical Appraisal.* Dordrecht: D. Reidel, 1987, 61.

scientists are perfectly willing to use them – provided they are regarded as provisional, heuristic devices, which may need to be modified or even discarded in the light of an increasing body of observational data, or increasingly sophisticated mathematical means of interpreting them. In the end, the final verdict lies with nature itself.

The parallels with a scientific theology will be clear. Such a theology represents a faithful and disciplined response to an encounter and engagement with reality – a world which exists independently of our longings, hopes and dreams. Yet this bald statement represents only the first move in a long and complex unfolding of possibilities, demanding clarification at every stage of that process of exploration. What 'reality' are we talking about? And how is it to be known, and ultimately expressed? What alternatives are there to the view just proposed, and what reasons may be given for rejecting them?

Yet there is also a deeper issue involved, which is often treated with less than full seriousness by those committed to any form of a realist epistemology and ontology. *How is the inescapable historicity of the theologian to be incorporated into this process of engagement?* It is fatally easy to treat the theologian as if she were historically and culturally disembodied, an ahistorical mind devoid of cultural memories and values, whose reflection takes place on a timeless plane not known to or populated by other inhabitants of the historical process.

It must be stressed that the ineluctability of the social location of the theologian does not call a realist approach to knowledge into question; it does, however, raise significant – yet *answerable* – questions concerning how an encounter with reality is expressed or depicted using the living languages of humanity. While the present chapter sets out the basic theme that scientific inquiry represents an attempt to offer a faithful response to reality, the chapter which follows sets out how a 'critical realism' allows the stratification of that reality to be reflected and incorporated within both scientific and theological reflection.

We have proposed that a scientific theology treats the working methods and assumptions of the natural sciences as an appropriate *ancilla theologiae*. A central assumption of both the natural sciences and a scientific theology is that there is indeed a 'reality' independent of the human mind, which the mind is capable of grasping, while fully conceding that:

1. Our grasp of reality is always less than total;
2. Our descriptions of reality must be held to be revisable, in the light of closer approximations to the essential properties of things;

3. Models or other constructs may be required when representing or analysing this reality, or its aspects, without in any way calling that reality into question.

This belief is not regarded as an *a priori* dogma, but as the outcome of an engagement with the world which compels the natural scientist to draw the conclusion that there exists an external world which can be grasped and represented by the inquiring human mind.

Given that the existence of a mind-independent reality is of such fundamental importance to both the natural sciences and to Christian theology, it is essential to offer both a defence and explanation of the realist thesis, before moving on to explore its theological application. The material in the present chapter deals primarily with the biological and physical sciences, and does not deal in any depth with the important issues of either the *stratification of reality* or the *involvement of the knower in knowing* and their implications for both 'critical realism' and a scientific theology. We shall return to consider this issue more fully in chapter 10, before moving on to consider its theological application in chapter 11.

Realism as the working philosophy of the physical sciences

There can be little doubt that most natural scientists espouse a range of opinions which are recognizably 'realist' in their core affirmations, reflecting a common commitment to the ontological finality of the natural order. *Realism works.* That, in two brief yet highly pertinent words, is the rather pragmatic reason why most natural scientists – especially physicists – regard themselves of realists of one sort or another. It is important to note that most natural scientists do not hold to a realist point of view on account of deep reflection on the philosophical issues involved – for example, because, having read Kant's *Critique of Pure Reason* in some detail, they find his account of the transcendental method empirically implausible. The credibility of realism arises directly from the experimental method, which discloses patterns of observational behaviour which seem to be best accounted for on the basis of a realist point of view. As Michael Redhead notes:[2]

Physicists, in their unreflective and intuitive attitude to their work, the way they talk and think among themselves, tend to be realists about the

---

[2] Michael Redhead, *From Physics to Metaphysics.* Cambridge: Cambridge University Press, 1995, 9.

entities they deal with, and while being tentative as to what they say about these entities and their exact properties and interrelations, they generally feel that what they are trying to do, and to some degree successfully, is to get a 'handle on reality'.

Scientific realism is thus, at least in part, an *empirical* thesis.[3] Its plausibility and confirmations arise from direct engagement with the real world, through repeated observation and experiment. It should not be thought of primarily as a metaphysical claim about how the world is, or ought to be; rather, it is a focused and limited claim which attempts to explain why it is that certain scientific methods have worked out so well in practice. The argument for realism based upon scientific success often takes the following form:[4]

> The successes of the natural sciences are far greater than can be accounted for by chance or miracles;
>
> The best explanation of this success is that scientific theories offer true, or approximately true, accounts of reality;
>
> Therefore we should all be scientific realists.

Realism, as Hilary Putnam and others have argued,[5] is the only explanation of scientific theories and concepts which does not 'make the success of science a miracle'. Unless the theoretical entities employed by scientific theories actually existed and the theories themselves were at least approximately true of the world at large, the evident success of science (in terms of its applications and predictions) would surely be a miracle. One anti-realist response to this is to argue that the apparent success of science is explained by the fact that scientists construct the data that confirm their own theories.[6] The data is a 'social construct' which reflects the hidden agendas of the scientists, who have a vested interest in confirming their own theories. This is simply a case of self-validation, without epistemic significance. Yet this must surely lead to the conclusion that *all* theories are equally successful, in that all are socially constructed and hence self-validating. The *particular* success of

[3] But see the critical comments of Igor Douven and Jaap van Brakel, 'Is Scientific Realism an Empirical Hypothesis?', *Dialectica* 49 (1995), 3–14.

[4] André Kukla, *Studies in Scientific Realism.* Oxford: Oxford University Press, 1998, 12.

[5] Hilary Putnam, 'Three Kinds of Scientific Realism', *The Philosophical Quarterly* 32 (1982), 195–200.

[6] Bruno Latour and Steven Woolgar, *Laboratory Life: The Social Construction of Scientific Facts.* Beverly Hills, CA: Sage, 1979.

the natural sciences – as opposed to other disciplines – then remains unexplained.

A realist foundation for scientific theories removes any obligation to posit a persistent coincidence or miracles as a means of explaining the success of science.[7]

> If the phenomenalist is correct about theoretical entities, we must believe in a *cosmic coincidence*. That is, if this is so, statements about electrons, etc., are of only instrumental value: they simply enable us to predict phenomena on the level of galvanometers and cloud chambers. They do nothing to remove the *surprising character* of these phenomena . . . On the other hand, if we interpret the theory in a realist way, then we have no need for such a cosmic coincidence: it is not surprising that galvanometers and cloud chambers behave in the way they do, for if there really are electrons, etc., this is just what we should expect. A lot of surprising facts no longer seem surprising.

There thus exist real-world entities, whose existence is independent of our theoretical constructions and mental processes, against which our ideas and theories require to be tested. While socially-constructed models may require to be developed in order to depict or render such entities capable of being visualized – note the importance of the concept of *Anschaulichkeit* for writers such as Niels Bohr and Werner Heisenberg[8] – the use of such models (which is always provisional, and open to revision in the face of advancing understanding) does not undermine the 'reality' of what they aim to represent.

As we have seen, the collapse of foundationalism has not led to any perceptible faltering in the progress of the scientific enterprise, precisely because the natural sciences do not presuppose prior philosophical foundations, nor do they depend upon the allegedly secure conclusions of philosophy in developing their ideas. Philosophical analysis brings intellectual rigour and conceptual clarity to the scientific enterprise; that enterprise, however, is not ultimately dependent on any 'first philosophy' (Quine).

Yet a cluster of issues remain unanswered by such assertions, including the question of how real entities are to be distinguished from fictional entities. What is the *criterion* of reality? Keith Campbell summarizes this point as follows:[9]

---

[7] J. J. C. Smart, *Between Science and Philosophy*. New York: Random House, 1968, 39.
[8] See Werner Heisenberg, 'Über den anschaulichen Inhalt der quantentheoretischen Kinematik und Mechanik', *Zeitschrift für Physik* 43 (1927), 172–98.
[9] K. Campbell, 'Selective Realism in the Philosophy of Physics', *The Monist* 77 (1994), 27–46; 28.

This search for a criterion for the real must be understood as a search for a criterion *for us to count something as real*; it will be a principle to apply in determining whether to accord that status, given out current state of epistemic development. There need not be, and probably cannot be, any critical mark of the real itself; the real is what is, period.

It is quite one thing to determine how we might know that something is real; we must also assume that real things exist which we do not, and possible cannot, know about. It is important to avoid the 'epistemic fallacy' (Roy Bhaskar), which confuses epistemology with ontology in affirming that only what is known can be real.

Introducing realism

The term 'realism' denotes a family of philosophical positions which take the general position that there exists a real world, external to the human mind, which the human mind can encounter, understand and represent, at least in part. There is an objective world, quite apart from the human thinker, which exists independently of our thoughts, fears, longings and musings. Nevertheless, there is considerable variation within the realist camp on precisely how 'realism' is to be defined. Three general approaches are of especial importance:[10]

1. The world is mind-independent;
2. (Only) non-mental entities exist;
3. Mental and non-mental entities exist.

Each of these statements can be seen to embody a fundamentally realist thesis, through explicitly countering Berkeley's denial of the real existence of unperceived things; the second and third, however, are to be preferred, in that they acknowledge the important distinction between 'reality' and 'mind-independence'.

It should not be the occasion for surprise that the natural sciences are widely regarded as lending active support to a generally realist epistemology. Scientific theories are thus held to relate to a reality in the world, upon which they are ultimately based and with reference to which they must ultimately be judged. As Wilfrid F. Sellars has pointed out, 'to have a good reason for holding a theory is *ipso facto* to have good reasons for holding that the entities postulated by the theory exist'.[11]

---

[10] Michael Levin, 'Realisms', *Synthese* 85 (1990), 115–38.
[11] Wilfrid Sellars, *Science, Perception and Reality*. New York: Humanities Press, 1962, 97.

A thought experiment may make this point and its implications clear. By the year 2000, there was considerable anxiety concerning the appearance of 'ozone holes' in the earth's atmosphere, threatening a significant increase in the amount of potentially harmful ultraviolet radiation reaching the surface of the planet.[12] A dramatic loss of ozone in the lower stratosphere over Antarctica was first noticed in the 1980s by a research group from the British Antarctic Survey, who were monitoring the atmosphere above Antarctica using standard instrumentation.[13] They were not, of course, observing ozone directly; they were using instruments which provided data on ozone levels through the assumption of a correlation between levels of atmospheric ozone and spectroscopic parameters. The ozone levels were too low to be accounted for by the Chapman Reactions, such as:

$$O_3 + h\nu \Rightarrow O_2 + O$$

This first reaction eliminates ozone (O_3) through ultraviolet irradiation, which converts ozone to normal oxygen molecules and oxygen radicals. These radicals can then bring about additional ozone loss through a further reaction:

$$O_3 + O \Rightarrow 2O_2$$

Yet the observed levels of ozone depletion were too great to be accounted for purely by these reactions. There had to be some additional reactions, involving additional agents. It soon became clear that the problem was due to chemicals containing chlorine, particularly CFCs (chlorofluorocarbons), compounds containing bromine, other related halogen compounds, and nitrogen oxides. CFCs are an industrial product widely employed in refrigeration systems, air conditioners, aerosols, solvents and in the production of some types of packaging. Nitrogen oxides are a by-product of combustion processes, including aircraft emissions. They are all the result of human technology, not natural processes. The atmospheric breakdown of CFCs on the surface of polar stratospheric clouds leads to the presence of hydrochloric acid (HCl) and chlorine nitrate ($ClONO_2$) in the upper atmosphere. These give rise to chlorine

[12] National Research Council Panel on Stratospheric Chemistry, *Stratospheric Ozone Depletion by Halocarbons: Chemistry and Transport.* Washington, DC: National Academy of Sciences, 1979; National Research Council Committee on Impacts of Stratospheric Change, *Protection against Depletion of Stratospheric Ozone by Chlorofluorocarbons.* Washington, DC: National Academy of Sciences, 1979.
[13] Jonathan Shanklin, *The Antarctic Ozone Hole.* Cambridge: British Antarctic Survey, 1998.

radicals through ultraviolet emission, which convert ozone to oxygen molecules, as follows:

$$Cl + O_3 \Rightarrow ClO + O_2$$

On the basis of a realist interpretation of these findings, the widespread use of CFCs leads to the loss of ozone. To prevent the further loss of ozone, the levels of atmospheric CFCs must be reduced – with important implications for the policies of nations which use these widely. Realism thus offers an account of how ozone depletion arises, and what must be done to reverse this process.[14]

A non-realist interpretation is unable to establish a firm connection between the instrumental observations and the corresponding ozone levels; between ozone depletion and CFCs; and hence to offer a solution to the reduction in the ozone levels (which might, in any case, simply be an instrumental artefact). It is only if there *really* is a loss in ozone, which *really* is caused by CFCs, that reducing the levels of CFCs is *really* going to make any difference. It will come as no surprise that the major environmental agencies and organizations adopt a realist approach to the issue. Not only does it offer an accurate diagnosis of the problem; it offers a solution, irrespective of how difficult and costly it may be to put into practice.[15]

Realism and the design of experiments

In his important study 'Methodological Realism and Scientific Rationality', Jarrett Leplin demonstrated how realistic assumptions were deeply embedded in many research programmes, the methods and outcomes of which simply cannot be comprehended without a realist perspective.[16] An excellent example is provided by Robert A. Millikan's measurement of the charge of the electron. Millikan started his work on the charge of the electron in 1906, and continued his research for seven years. His 1913 article announcing the determination of the electron's charge is widely regarded as a classic in the field. He received the Nobel Prize in 1923 for his efforts.

The 'oil drop' experiment was brilliantly designed. Millikan suspended fine drops of oil which had been electrically charged by exposure

[14] K. I. Kondrat'ev, *Atmospheric Ozone Variability: Implications for Climate Change, Human Health and Ecosystems*. London: Springer, 2000.

[15] Kevin R. Gurney and Arjun Makhijani, *Mending the Ozone Hole: Science, Technology and Policy*. Cambridge, MA: MIT Press, 1995.

[16] Jarrett Leplin, 'Methodological Realism and Scientific Rationality', *Philosophy of Science* 53 (1986), 31–51.

to X-rays in a gravitational field, and superimposed an electrical field in the opposite direction. By measuring how strong an applied electric field had to be applied in order to stop the oil drop from falling, he was able to determine the charge e as Mg/E, where M is the mass of the oil drop, g the gravitational constant, and E the strength of the electrical field required to suspend the drop. Since he was able to work out the mass of the oil drop from its rate of descent in the absence of an electrical field, he could calculate the force of gravity on one drop, and hence determine the electric charge that the drop must have. By varying the charge on different drops, he noticed that the charge was always an integral multiple of 1.6×10^{-19} coulombs. He deduced that this was the quantized charge on a single electron. The most recent determination of the charge on the electron is $1.60217733 \times 10^{-19}$ coulombs, which is within 1 per cent of the value determined by Millikan in 1913.

The point made by Leplin is that Millikan's experiment is based on the supposition that electrons exist – a hypothesis which seemed to be confirmed by the electron theory of H. A. Lorentz, the cathode ray experiments of J. J. Thompson, and the ion cloud experiments of J. S. E. Townsend and H. A. Wilson. The intentionality of Millikan's experiments was clearly grounded in his belief that electrons existed, and that their fundamental charge could be determined.

> If we describe what Millikan was doing without mentioning electrons, we seem to impute to him an unaccountable, indeed a perverse interest in the amount of electric charge which X-radiation will endow an oil droplet. What was the experiment for, if not to determine the charge of the electron?

A form of realism thus permeates the experimental methodology of the natural sciences. Their rationality is predicated on realist presuppositions. Theory is accountable to an experimentally encountered and observed reality, which functions as both the foundation and criterion of scientific knowledge. In a classic discussion of this point, Frederick L. Will points out that the linguistic turn in philosophy is intensely vulnerable to the awkward fact that language is impacted and transformed by an encounter with an increasingly understood natural world.[17]

> Whether we will it or not, our language and conceptual systems, and with them the articulation of the world achieved in them, are not ordained, once and for all, by a benevolent Creator, by genetic or other

---

[17] Frederick L. Will, *Pragmatism and Realism*. Lanham, MD: Rowman & Littlefield, 1997, 37.

biological determinants, by the inexorable march in the world of the powers of production, or by common sense. Wittgenstein's approach to language, like Lindbeck's approach to doctrine, overlooks the vexatious question of how our language and conceptualities arise, and above all, the role of the stimulus of an observed external world upon their genesis and consolidation.

It is this intentional intellectual submission to an observational and experimental encounter with reality that distinguishes the natural sciences from other more speculative disciplines, particularly those un-wise enough to consider socially determined ideas or values as *a priori*.

The nature of scientific realism

Having explored some aspects of realism, and noted how some form of realism is deeply embedded within the working assumptions of the scientific community, we now need to ask what distinguishes a 'scientific realism' from realism in general. André Kukla offers a useful taxonomy of levels of reality, which allow us to clarify the issues, as follows:[18]

1. Sense data (such as 'being appeared to greenishly').
2. Commonsense objects of perception (such as sticks and stones).
3. Unobservable entities posited by scientific theories (such as electrons).
4. Timeless abstract entities (such as numbers).

For Kukla, 'commonsense realism' affirms statement (2); 'scientific realism' affirms both statements (2) and (3).[19] The central issue, on this account of matters, thus rests on whether the theoretical (or unobservable) entities posited by reliable theories are to be regarded as 'real'.

A fuller statement of a specifically '*scientific* realism' is provided by Richard Boyd. According to Boyd, there are four central elements to a scientific realism:[20]

[18] Kukla, *Studies in Scientific Realism*, 3–4.

[19] On this scheme, 'phenomenalism' may be defined as the affirmation of statement (1), and the denial of statements (2), (3) and (4). Both 'commonsense realism' and 'scientific realism' affirm statement (1), but argue that it is inadequate as an account of reality. 'Mathematical realism' (or 'mathematical Platonism') affirms all four propositions (although it must be pointed out that Plato himself would affirm (4) and deny (1), (2) and (3)). As Kukla rightly points out, boundary disputes between these four categories are inevitable.

[20] Richard Boyd, 'The Current Status of Scientific Realism', in Jarrett Leplin (ed.), *Scientific Realism*. Berkeley: University of California Press, 1984, 41–82.

1. 'Theoretical terms' (or 'non-observational terms') in scientific theories are to be thought of as putatively referring expressions. Scientific theories should thus be interpreted 'realistically'.

2. Scientific theories, interpreted in this realistic manner, are confirmable and are in fact often confirmed as approximately true by ordinary scientific evidence interpreted in accordance with ordinary methodological norms.

3. The historical development of the mature sciences is largely a matter of successively more accurate approximations to the truth concerning both observable and unobserved phenomena. Later theories tend to build on the observational and theoretical knowledge embodied in earlier theories.

4. The reality which scientific theories describe is largely independent of thoughts or theoretical commitments.

Boyd's particular approach to scientific realism rests largely on evidential considerations, and makes a particular appeal to the explanatory successes of the sciences.

This is developed further in a reflective and informed analysis of the nature of scientific realism from the Greek philosopher of science Stathis Psillos, who argues that it incorporates three distinctive elements:[21]

1. A *metaphysical* stance: the world has a definite and mind-independent natural-kind structure. The metaphysical thesis distinguishes scientific realism from anti-realist accounts of science, whether these take the form of traditional idealist and phenomenalist views of reality, or the more modern verificationist accounts of Michael Dummett and Hilary Putnam, which effectively reduce the content of the world to whatever is legitimated by a set of epistemic practices and conditions. If the unobservable entities posited by theories exist at all, they exist independently of us humans being able to be in a position to know, verify, or recognize that they exist. Existence does not depend upon observation. Instead of projecting a structure onto the world, scientific theories, and scientific theorizing in general, discover and map out an already structured and mind-independent world.

---

[21] See Stathis Psillos, *Scientific Realism: How Science Tracks Truth*. London: Routledge, 1999, *passim*.

2. A *semantic* stance: scientific theories should be taken at face value. They are to be seen as truth-conditioned descriptions of their intended domain, whether observable or unobservable, and are hence capable of being true or false. Theoretical assertions are not reducible to claims about the behaviour of observables, nor are they merely instrumental devices for establishing connections between observables. The theoretical terms featuring in theories have putative factual reference. If scientific theories are true, the unobservable entities which they posit must also be regarded as real. Scientific realism is thus to be distinguished from eliminative instrumentalist and reductive empiricist accounts, which hold that scientific theories are syntactic-mathematical constructs which lack truth-conditions, and hence any assertoric content. On this view, there is no need to assume that there is an unobservable reality behind the phenomena, or that science aims to describe any such reality.

   Reductive empiricist accounts, on the other hand, treat theoretical discourse as being little more than disguised talk about observables and their actual (and possible) behaviour. Reductive empiricism is consistent with the claim that theoretical assertions have truth-values, but it interprets their truth-conditions *reductively* – that is to say, it argues that they are fully translatable into an observational vocabulary. Reductive empiricists are thus committed to the existence of observable entities, and in so far as a certain theoretical statement is fully translated into a statement couched solely in an observational vocabulary, they allow theoretical assertions to have truth-values without this being held to imply the real existence of unobservable entities. Scientific realism, in contrast, is an ontologically and metaphysically inflationary view.

3. An *epistemic* stance: mature and predictively successful scientific theories are well-confirmed, and are (approximately) true. There is some kind of justification for the belief that theoretical assertions are true (or approximately true), and this justification derives primarily from the ampliative-abductive methods employed by scientists which in turn presupposes that there exists an objective reality, whose structures may be exposed and analysed intentionally by the working methods and assumptions of the natural sciences.[22]

---

[22] For a more detailed discussion of the importance of this point, see John Bigelow and Robert Pargetter, *Science and Necessity*. Cambridge: Cambridge University Press, 1990.

A generally realist position unquestionably represents the working assumptions of most natural scientists – assumptions which they regard as constantly confirmed by the outcome of their engagement with the external world. Yet this hardly precludes exploring challenges to this consensus, nor an attempt to clarify precisely which of the many forms of realism available is the most suited to the task of engaging with the natural world. In view of the importance of defending realism against its many critics and identifying which form of realism is most suited to the needs of a scientific theology, we shall consider the main rivals to realism in recent discussions of the status of scientific theories.

Rivals to scientific realism

The twentieth century has witnessed extensive debate over the precise status of scientific theories, which has important implications for a scientific theology. What is the relation of theory and observation? And is it legitimate to infer the existence of unobserved entities from a careful analysis of observational data? It is fair to say that the debate has increasingly moved in favour of realist approaches in recent years, despite a vigorous rearguard action by its alternatives.[23] In what follows, we shall consider the three most significant such rivals to scientific realism, and offer an evaluation of their weaknesses. We may begin by clarifying one of the points at issue.

Any attempt to engage with the natural world, whether scientific or theological, is confronted by a series of questions concerning the nature of that world, and how it is to be known.[24] The ontological question – that is, whether a natural world exists, independent of human beings and their thoughts – is critically important, and forces us immediately

---

[23] Roger Trigg, *Reality at Risk: a Defence of Realism in Philosophy and the Sciences.* 2nd edn. London: Harvester Press, 1989.

[24] Theo A. F. Kuipers, *From Instrumentalism to Constructive Realism: On Some Relations between Confirmation, Empirical Progress, and Truth Approximation.* Dordrecht: Kluwer Academic, 2000, 3–8, sets out five critical questions, the first of which is ontological, and the remaining four of which are epistemological.

   0. Does a natural world exist, independent of human beings?
   1. Can we claim to possess true claims to knowledge of the natural world?
   2. Can we claim to possess true claims to knowledge of the natural world *beyond what is observable*?
   3. Can we claim to possess true claims to knowledge of the natural world beyond what is observable, and understand claims concerning theoretical terms to refer to real entities?
   4. Does there exist a correct or ideal conceptualization of the natural world?

to confront two very different outlooks on reality. Idealism holds that a non-conceptualized natural world cannot and does not exist apart from human beings. As Kant puts it in his *Prolegomena* (1783):[25]

> Idealism consists in the assertion that there are none but thinking beings; all other things, which we think are perceived in intuition, being nothing but representations in the thinking beings, to which no object external to them corresponds in fact. Whereas I say, that things as objects of our senses existing outside us are given, but we know nothing of what they may be in themselves, knowing only their appearances, i.e., the representations which they cause in us by affecting our senses.

The general drift of this passage can be been in the subsequent idealist consensus that while matter may or may not exist, its features as we now know them are, at least in part, the result of the operation of the human mind. The reality that we come to know is itself shaped by the operations of the mind. This is perhaps the greatest strength of idealism, in that it is difficult to conceive quite how one can encounter a reality except through the mediation of the human mind. In investigating reality, we must concede that we gain access to it, perhaps to varying extents, through models or pictures which have been devised by the mind.[26]

Yet the merits of realism cannot be overlooked at this point. The human mind certainly generates ideas – yet it generates those theories *in response to what it encounters outside itself.* For the natural scientist, the force of this point is overwhelming. The mind may indeed be able to grasp the laws which govern the motions of the planets, and offer a mathematical account of their leading features. Yet the stimulus to develop such an understanding, and the raw observational material which leads to it in the first place, has its origins outside the human mind. To put the matter very simply, scientific realists tend to see science as an activity which is best described as one of discovery and explanation: scientists discover entities and laws that were already there prior to their uncovering, and use these to explain the phenomena. Anti-realists, on the other hand, tend to see science as a process of constructing theories and concepts and applying those theories and concepts to saving the phenomena.

Kant offered a 'refutation of idealism', in which he argued that our understanding of ourselves as thinking beings presupposes material

[25] Immanuel Kant, *Prolegomena zu einer jeden künftigen Metaphysik.* 7th edn. Hamburg: Felix Meiner Verlag, 1993, 41–2.
[26] For a vigorous defence of the idealist position, see John Foster, *The Case for Idealism.* London: Routledge & Kegan Paul, 1982; T. L. S. Sprigge, *The Vindication of Absolute Idealism.* Edinburgh: Edinburgh University Press, 1983.

objects, precisely because we are obligated to think of ourselves in a temporal realm or order which presupposes the existence of periodic physical processes. In other words, the existence of planetary movements, oscillating pendula or ticking clocks is required to establish the temporal order within which our minds operate. This is open to immediate criticism: for example, it is not unreasonable to point out that Kant merely succeeds in demonstrating that the mind has to *assume* such physical processes – whether they exist *independently* of the mind is quite another question. Yet Kant's conclusion is significant: 'The existence of the thing that appears is thereby not destroyed, as in genuine idealism, but it is only shown, that we cannot possibly know it by the senses as it is in itself (*wie es an sich selbst sei*).'[27]

It is clear that Kant's view of the situation opens the way to a critical realism, in which the question of the extent to which the mind's habits of thinking and representing are conditioned by cultural and social factors may be addressed. A responsible realism cannot evade the issue of how the human mind responds to what it observes, and allow for at least some degree of constructivism in its attempts to represent what it finds. Nevertheless, it is quite improper to argue that, since the mind deploys constructs to *represent* a complex reality, that *reality itself* is the pure construction of the human mind.

Idealism

The origins of the term 'idealism' can be traced back to the writings of Christian Wolff (1679–1754), who defined idealist philosophers as 'those who acknowledge only ideal objects existing in our minds, and deny the independent reality of the world and the existence of material objects'. While this definition has been subject to some erosion as philosophical debate has proceeded, the basic theme that emerges remains as significant today as in the eighteenth century. The 'reality' that we experience or encounter is not independent of the human mind, but depends for its existence upon the organizational and correlational activity of an order-imposing human mind. This is not necessarily to suggest that the human mind creates or establishes matter (although this doctrine is unquestionably held by many within the idealist camp).[28]

[27] Kant, *Prolegomena zu einer jeden künftigen Metaphysik*, 43. For an important discussion of the application of this point, see Kirstin Zeyer, *Die methodische Philosophie Hugo Dinglers und der transzendentale Idealismus Immanuel Kants*. Hildesheim: Olms, 1999.

[28] For details, see Otto Willmann, *Geschichte des Idealismus*. 3 vols. Braunschweig: Vieweg, 1907.

Most forms of idealism share the view that there is no access to reality apart from whatever the mind provides us, often going on to add that the mind can provide and reveal to us only its own contents. It will be obvious that such a philosophy will find itself in tension with the consensus within the community of the natural sciences, where it is clear that an engagement with the structures of the real world – rather than just the ideas of the human mind – is widely assumed, on account of its evident and extensive positive resonance with the experimental evidence.

It is instructive to explore the form that this philosophy takes in the writings of the influential philosopher Immanuel Kant. Kant held that idealism must be *transcendental*, which he attempted to define in terms of appearances which are to be regarded as 'mere representations (*Vorstellungen*), not as things-in-themselves (*Dinge an sich selbst*), and that time and space are therefore only sensible forms of our intuition, not determinations given as existing by themselves, nor conditions of objects viewed as things-in themselves'.[29] Kant's idealist philosophy establishes an independent order of things apart from human reason in the *transcendent object*, which impacts our senses and provides the basic material for our ideas. Despite this concession, it is clear that Kant understands human reason, understood in terms of the individual thinking subject, to create space and time. Human reason constructs the ideas of the world, God and the Absolute. Reason applies the categories of relation to phenomena and connects them through the notion of causality. It is through the legislative power of reason that phenomena become effects and causes; they are not so in themselves, but are treated as such by reason. In the same way, human reason creates the 'laws of nature', which are to be seen purely as the sum total of sensible and inner phenomena, considered in their regular connections. They are not 'discovered' within nature, but are imposed by an order-seeking and order-imposing mind.

Yet it can hardly be overlooked that some of Kant's *a priori* assumptions actually represent *a posteriori* results derived from the natural sciences. Although this insight was denied to Kant, on account of his historical location, his transcendental philosophy is strongly historically conditioned by Newtonian mechanics and Euclidean geometry, both of which he was unwise enough to take as universal truths, rather than as provisional and local ways of thinking. In one sense, Kant's

---

[29] Immanuel Kant, *Kritik der reinen Vernunft*. Frankfurt am Main: Suhrkamp Verlag, 1968, 375.

philosophy can be thought of as an object lesson in the folly of hitching a philosophy or theology to the results of the natural sciences at any given point, rendering it vulnerable to erosion or outright rejection through the ongoing process of revision which is an integral aspect of the natural sciences. Kant seems to take the fundamental results of the natural sciences of his day as being true *a priori*, and hence unrevisable.

Perhaps the most telling criticism against Kant is set out by Roy Bhaskar. Any responsible philosophy, he argues,[30]

> . . . must avoid any commitment to the content of specific theories and recognize the conditional nature of all its results. Moreover, it must reject two propositions which were central to Kant's own philosophical project, viz. that in any inquiry of the form 'what must be the case for φ to be possible,' the conclusion, X, would be a fact about us and that φ must invariably stand for some universal operation of mind. That is to say, it must reject the idealist and individualist cast into which Kant pressed his own inquiries.

While recognizing the critical role played by reason in philosophical reflection, Bhaskar insists that it cannot be understood to operate on the basis of pure reason alone.

> For it always exercises that reason on the basis of prior conceptualizations of historical practice, of some more or less determinate social form. Thus conceived, philosophy can tell us that it is a condition of scientific activities φ and ψ that the world is stratified and differentiated, X and Y. But it cannot tell us *what* structures the world contains, or *how* they differ. There are entirely matters for substantive scientific investigation.

A related line of criticism is developed by Bhaskar's colleague Andrew Collier.[31] Collier argues that idealism, particularly in the form associated with Berkeley, is plagued by a self-referential aporia, in that it cannot evade assuming what it is inclined to deny. The central argument of idealism is that 'we can't known anything except by means of our own ideas; so we can't know anything but our own ideas'. This, Collier suggests, is implausible. 'Who would be convinced by the argument: "we can't see except by means of our eyes, so we can't see anything but our eyes"?' Whereas realism is firmly and openly committed to the 'aboutness' of ideas – that is, that ideas refer – idealism, which denies this, cannot achieve any momentum without tacitly assuming it.

---

[30]　Roy Bhaskar, *The Possibility of Naturalism: A Philosophical Critique of the Contemporary Human Sciences*. 3rd edn. London/New York: Routledge, 1998, 5.

[31]　Andrew Collier, 'About Aboutness', *Alethia* 2.1 (1999), 2–5.

A clue to the impossibility of our bring trapped inside our own ideas is the point already made, that the whole language of ideas can only get going because ideas are about things, so that by denying absoluteness, idealism deprives itself of its own medium of existence. We cannot make sense of an idea, an experience or a proposition except in terms of what it is an idea of, what is experienced, what the proposition is about. Deprived of their aboutness, these things are nothings.

Collier therefore argues that the world of ideas, far from being an autonomous world within which we live and move (and are actually trapped, in that we cannot escape from their fixities), is a response to the way the world is. The 'world that ideas are about' is prior to those ideas in three respects:

1. *Ontologically*, the world existed before we started having ideas about it;

2. *Epistemologically*, we need to know about the world before we can know about our own ideas about this world;

3. *Logically*, an idea can only be defined in terms of what it is about.

The world of ideas must therefore be seen as 'a reification of an aspect of the real world'.

The obvious weaknesses of the Kantian approach has led many to seek a reformulated idealism, which retains an emphasis upon the active role of the human mind in making sense of the world, while avoiding any implication that the natural world is 'unreal' or purely a mental construction. An excellent example of this reconstructed idealism is to be found in Nicholas Rescher's concept of 'conceptual idealism'.[32] For Rescher, any human attempt to describe the world necessarily involves the human mind. It would be absurd to suggest that we can know about a 'mind-untouched' reality, precisely because we can only obtain knowledge of the world through using our minds. 'There is no clear and sharp separation between reality and the realm of thought, because our only possible route to cognitive contact with "the real world" is through the mediation of our conceptions about it, so that, for us, "the world" is inevitably "the world as we conceive it to be".' Yet, as Roger Trigg points out, it is questionable how helpful this insight really is:[33]

---

[32] Nicholas Rescher, 'Conceptual Idealism Revisited', *Review of Metaphysics* 44 (1991), 495–523.

[33] Roger Trigg, *Rationality and Science: Can Science Explain Everything?*, Oxford: Blackwell, 1993, 128. For Trigg's defence of realism at this point, see Roger Trigg, *Reality at Risk: A Defence of Realism in Philosophy and the Sciences*. 2nd edn. London: Harvester Press, 1989.

This approach characteristically attempts to build a major philosophical theory about our relationship with the physical world out of the blindingly obvious truism that we cannot think of what we cannot think of. Put more positively, the view is that we can only think of reality in the way that we can think about it. Yet although our concepts are certainly the means through which we approach the world, we are not talking about *them* when, with their aid, we try to refer to parts of reality.

A critical realism is able to take account of the interaction of the socially-conditioning of the human mind in a way that seems to be at least as satisfactory as Rescher's. We shall return to this in due course.

Positivism

The origins of positivism lie partly in a reaction within the scientific community of the nineteenth century against a perception that the natural sciences were becoming excessively preoccupied with metaphysics, even to the point of degenerating into mysticism. Positivism is characterized by a metaphysical scepticism, grounded in an emphasis upon what is directly observable. The positivist tradition in the natural sciences thus regards scientific theories as essentially nothing more than summaries of experimental data or observations. For the Austrian physicist and philosopher Ernst Mach (1838–1916), the natural sciences concern that which is immediately given by the senses. Science concerns nothing more and other than the investigation of the 'dependence of phenomena on one another'.[34] The world consists only of our sensations; knowledge is merely a conceptual organization of the data of sensory experience or observation. This led Mach to take a strongly negative view of the atomic hypothesis, in which he argued that atoms were merely theoretical constructs which cannot be perceived.[35] On being told by his colleagues that there was excellent evidence for the atomic hypothesis, Mach responded with a demand to be *shown* one. Mach was certainly prepared to concede that 'talk about atoms' could be used; it was, he argued, a useful form of shorthand, which allowed a large number of experimental observations to be categorized.

A Kantian framework seems to lie behind Mach's statements, particularly when he argued that it is impossible to move from the world of phenomena to the world of 'things in themselves'. Nevertheless,

[34] Ernst Mach, *History and Root of the Principle of the Conservation of Energy*. Chicago: Open Court Publishing Co., 1911, 63.
[35] Erwin Hiebert, 'The Genesis of Mach's Early Views on Atomism', in R. Cohen and R. Seeger (eds), *Ernst Mach: Physicist and Philosopher*. Dordrecht: D. Reidel, 1970, 79–106.

Mach allows the use of 'auxiliary concepts' which serve as bridges linking one observation with another within the world of experience. These have no real existence, and must not be thought of as actual or existing entities. They are 'products of thought' which 'exist only in our imagination and understanding',[36] and cannot be held to transcend any knowledge which arises directly through experience. The essence of Mach's argument can be summarized in terms of two fundamental principles. The first has been called 'ontological phenomenalism'. By this is meant Mach's radical rejection of the existence of any meta-physical substance (e.g., matter, mind, the 'thing in itself') underlying experience and the correlative claim that everything that exists is sensation. As Mach put it:[37]

> It is imagined that it is possible to subtract all the parts (of a compound entity) and to have something still remaining. Thus arises the monstrous notion of a thing in itself, unknowable and different from its 'phenom-enal' existence. Thing, body, matter, are nothing apart from their complexes of colours, sounds, and so forth – nothing apart from their so-called attributes . . . the world consists only of our sensations . . . we have knowledge only of sensations, and the assumption of (underlying) nuclei . . . or of a reciprocal action between them, from which sensations proceed, turns out to be quite idle and superfluous.

A difficulty here is that Mach's approach seems to rely upon a prior acceptance of certain key themes of Kant's idealist philosophy – themes which can be argued to be historically conditioned by the scientific world-view of the eighteenth century.

We now turn to deal with an alternative approach, based on essenti-ally utilitarian considerations, which seems to bypass some of the difficulties traditionally associated with idealism.

Instrumentalism

The positivist attempt to translate all scientific concepts into a set of statements about observations runs into a series of difficulties, leading many to conclude that it must be discarded. Instrumentalism might be defined as the view that scientific theories are not true descriptions of an unobservable reality, but merely useful 'instruments' which enable us to order and anticipate the observable world. It is seen by some scholars as offering the advantages of positivism – such as the rejection

---

[36] Mach, *History and Root of the Principle of the Conservation of Energy*, 50–1.
[37] Ernst Mach, *Contributions to the Analysis of the Sensations*. Chicago: Open Court, 1897, 5–6, 10.

of the idea that theoretical terms need correspond to real entities – without its drawbacks. On this view, theories are to be seen as useful tools. A scientific theory is best understood as a rule, principle or calculating device for deriving predictions from sets of observational data. A scientific theory is an instrument or function where the input is a set of observations and the output is another set of observations – the predictions.

The distinguishing feature of instrumentalism may thus be held to be the strong distinction that is drawn between statements of an *observational* nature (which may easily be identified as 'true' or 'false') and those of a *non*-observational nature which, while taking a propositional or truth-asserting form, cannot be regarded as such in reality. The basic contours of this approach can be seen from Ernest Nagel's gloss on the kinetic model of gases, which proposes that the molecules of a gas can be thought of as analogous to inelastic spherical objects, such as billiard balls:[38]

> The theory that a gas is a system of rapidly moving molecules is not a description of anything that has been or can be observed. The theory is rather a rule which prescribes a way of symbolically representing, for certain purposes, such matters as the observable pressure and temperature of a gas; and the theory shows among things how, when certain empirical data about a gas are supplied and incorporated into that representation, we can calculate the quantity of heat required for raising the temperature of the gas by some designated number of degrees (i.e., we can calculate the specific heat of the gas).

Scientific concepts, while being clearly grounded in observations of the natural world, are thus not to be identified with, or reduced to, those observations.

Perhaps the most important defence of an instrumentalist approach to scientific theories in recent years is due to Stephen Toulmin. For Toulmin, scientific theories are invented, rather than discovered. Instead of speaking about the 'existence' or 'reality' of such entities as electrons,[39] scientists should recognize that such language is not used referentially (that is, to 'refer' to a real entity). The issue has to do with how observations are organized, with a view to stimulating further research. In one sense, instrumentalism can be seen as affirming many aspects of

---

[38] Ernest Nagel, *The Structure of Science: Problems in the Logic of Scientific Explanation*. London: Routledge & Kegan Paul, 1979, 129.

[39] Stephen Toulmin, *The Philosophy of Science: An Introduction*. London: Hutchinson, 1953, 138.

the realist position, while either denying or remaining agnostic concerning its fundamental belief that theoretical terms 'refer' to an extra-theoretical entity. Thus Arthur Fine argued that both the instrumentalist and realist 'accept the certified results of science as on a par with more homely and familiarly supported claims'; what distinguishes them, he suggests, is 'what they add onto this core position'.[40]

Yet historically, instrumentalist understandings of science have often transmuted into realist understandings with the passing of time. The Copernican (and subsequently Keplerian) theory of the solar system is a case in point.[41] Initially, many scientists and non-scientists construed the Copernican heliocentric theory instrumentally as a calculating device because there were simply too many obstacles to viewing it realistically. One thinks, for example, of Andreas Osiander's preface to Copernicus' *de revolutionibus* (1543), which suggested (perhaps rather disingenuously) that the theory to be proposed was little more than a useful hypothesis. As Osiander's preface is often alluded to, rather than cited, it may be instructive to reflect on his words, which clearly propose an instrumental interpretation of the heliocentric model of the solar system:[42]

> Since the novelty of the hypotheses of this work has already been widely reported, I have no doubt that some learned people have taken grave offence because the book declares that the earth moves, and that the sun is at rest in the centre of the universe . . . But if they are willing to examine the matter more closely, they will find that the author of this work has done nothing worthy of censure. For it is the duty of an astronomer to establish the history of the celestial movements through careful and skilful observation, and then to conceive and devise causes of these motions or hypotheses about them. Now since he cannot in any way attain to the true causes, these assumed hypotheses enable those movements to be calculated correctly from the principles of geometry, both for the future and the past. The present author has performed both these duties excellently. For these hypotheses need not be true nor even probable. It is sufficient if they only provide a calculus consistent with these observations.

[40] Arthur Fine, *The Shaky Game: Einstein, Realism and the Quantum Theory*. Chicago: University of Chicago Press, 1986, 128.

[41] Michael R. Gardner, 'Realism and Instrumentalism in Pre-Newtonian Astronomy', *Minnesota Studies in the Philosophy of Science* 10 (1983), 201–65.

[42] Nicolas Copernicus, *de revolutionibus orbium coelestium libri vi* (Nuremberg, 1543), praefatio. For Copernicus' own preface to this work, see Robert S. Westman, 'Proof, Poetics and Patronage: Copernicus' Preface to *De Revolutionibus*', in David C. Lindberg and Robert S. Westman (eds), *Reappraisals of the Scientific Revolution*. Cambridge: Cambridge University Press, 1990, 167–205.

Osiander's approach won many supporters, and may possibly correspond with unstated assumptions concerning the status of astronomical theories at the time.

Yet with growing observational evidence for the heliocentric model of the solar system, an instrumentalist approach subtly changed into its realist counterpart. The weaknesses of Copernicus' theory were soon identified; once Kepler had posited that the planets orbited the sun in ellipses, rather than circles, many of the remaining loose ends and observational anomalies began to be resolved.[43] With the development of Galilean and Newtonian physics and the new observational data that became available through the invention of the telescope, the situation changed. The heliocentric theory began to be interpreted realistically, rather than instrumentally. It was not merely a convenient way of thinking about the solar system, or a convention that enabled certain useful mathematic calculations to be performed. *This was the way things were.*

A more familiar recent example may also be noted. In 1905, Albert Einstein proposed that, under certain circumstances, a beam of monochromatic light of frequency v behaved as if it consists of 'semi-corpuscular' or particle-like objects, whose energy E was given by the relationship $E = hv$, where h is Planck's constant and v the frequency of the irradiating light.[44] The 'photoelectric effect' – namely, that electrons were emitted from a metal surface when it was exposed to ultraviolet irradiation – had been known for some time. However, the precise patterns of electron emission were puzzling. Most puzzlingly, electrons were not emitted unless the frequency of the incident light exceeded a certain threshold value, no matter how intense the applied radiation might be. The natural assumption had been that the extent of photon emission would be correlated with the intensity, not the frequency, of the incoming light.

Einstein argued that these baffling features of the photoelectric effect could be explained if the emission of electrons was to be conceived as a collision between an incoming particle-like bundle of energy and an electron close to the surface of the metal. The electron could only be ejected from the metal if the incoming particle-like bundles of energy possessed sufficient energy to eject this electron. As a result, there was a

[43] Brian S. Baigrie, 'The Justification of Kepler's Ellipse', *Studies in History and Philosophy of Science* 21 (1991), 633–64; Scott A. Kleiner, 'A New Look at Kepler and Abductive Argument', *Studies in History and Philosophy of Science* 14 (1983), 279–313.

[44] Albrecht Fölsing, *Albert Einstein: A Biography*. New York: Viking, 1997, 134–54.

cut-off point, determined by the properties of the metal in question, known as the 'work function' of the metal.[45]

Einstein's theory allowed the following aspects of the observational evidence to be explained.

1. The critical factor which determines whether an electron is ejected is not the intensity of the light, but its frequency;

2. The incoming light can be treated as if it consists of particles with a definite energy or momentum;

3. The observed features of the photoelectric effect can be accounted for by assuming that the collision between the incoming photon and the metallic electron obeys the principle of the conservation of energy, so that the kinetic energy of the emitted electron (T) can be represented as $T = h\nu - \Phi$, where Φ is the 'work function' of the metal. If $h\nu$ is less than Φ, no electrons will be emitted, no matter how intense the bombardment with photons. Above this threshold, the kinetic energy of the emitted photons can be predicted to be directly proportional to the frequency of the radiation.

Einstein's theory thus predicted that the emitted electron's energy would be governed by the relationship $T = h\nu - \Phi$. In 1916, R. A. Millikan confirmed its accuracy, while expressing his personal doubts about the particle-theory of light offered by Einstein. 'Einstein's photoelectric equation . . . appears in every case to predict exactly the observed results . . . Yet the semicorpuscular theory by which Einstein arrived at his equation seems at present wholly untenable.'[46] Yet by this stage, Einstein had moved beyond an instrumentalist approach. Even by 1909, Einstein was suggesting that 'the next phase in the development of theoretical physics will bring us a theory of light that can be interpreted as a kind of fusion of the wave and particle theory'. The transition from an instrumentalist to a realist approach to photons was well and truly under way.[47]

---

[45] The 'particle-like bundle of energy' to which we have referred was designated a 'photon' by G. N. Lewis, and this term has passed into general usage.

[46] R. A. Millikan, 'Quantenbeziehungen beim photoelektrischen Effekt', *Physikalische Zeitschrift* 17 (1916), 217–21.

[47] For the subsequent debate over Einstein's realism, see Frederico Laudisa, 'Einstein, Bell and Nonseparable Realism', *British Journal for the Philosophy of Science* 46 (1995), 309–29; L. Rosenfield, 'The Epistemological Conflict between Einstein and Bohr', *Zeitschrift für Physik* 171 (1963), 242–5.

Einstein's theoretical account of the photoelectric effect suggested that electromagnetic radiation had to be considered as behaving as particles under certain conditions. It met with intense opposition, not least because it appeared to involve the abandonment of the prevailing classical understanding of the total exclusivity of waves and particles: something could be one, or the other – but not both. Even those who subsequently verified Einstein's analysis of the photoelectric effect were intensely suspicious of his postulation of what were later known as 'photons'. Einstein himself was careful to refer to the light-quantum hypothesis as a 'heuristic point of view' – that is, as something which was helpful as a model to understanding, but without any necessary existence on its part. In other words, he adopted a strictly instrumentalist approach to the matter, regarding his postulated 'semi-corpuscular' approach to light as being a useful way of thinking about the phenomenon, which allowed certain significant calculations to be made.

The reasons for Einstein's caution will be evident: the scientific world of his day was simply not prepared for such a radical new paradigm, any more than the mid-sixteenth century was prepared for a heliocentric model of the solar system. The new theory had to be smuggled in as a mere working hypothesis or useful tool. Yet those tools can easily become an accepted view of reality, once sufficient observational evidence has accumulated. There are few today who would regard Darwin's theory of natural selection as a working tool; it is now widely seen as a view of reality.

Instrumentalism thus finds itself vulnerable to historical erosion. Today's instrumentalist approach to a theory has a disconcerting habit of becoming tomorrow's view of reality. What might initially be proposed as a heuristic approach to matters, perhaps on account of sensitivities to deeply ingrained ways of thinking or to avoid alienating the scientific establishment, can evolve into a realist understanding of the way the world is.[48]

These rivals to realism have played an important role in the philosophy of science throughout the twentieth century, and are likely to continue to feature in the discussions of the twenty-first. Yet for many, their plausibility has waned. It is almost as if the debate within the philosophy of science has become transformed into which version of realism is the most appropriate, rather than whether realism is to be preferred to its alternatives. We must therefore turn to consider why

---

[48] For some of the issues, see Michael R. Gardner, 'Realism and Instrumentalism in Nineteenth-Century Physics', *Philosophy of Science* 46 (1979), 1–34.

realism has proved so attractive a theory to natural scientists, whatever problems non-experimenting philosophers or theologians may wish to raise against it.

The case for realism: the critical issues

Within the community of experimentally-active natural scientists, there is a widespread consensus that the highly impressive explanatory and predictive successes of scientific theories is the result of their offering an essentially accurate account of what is going on at the fundamental level of reality. Scientific realism is fundamentally a thesis about the nature of science as an *activity*, which contrasts the realist understanding of science as a process of discovery and explanation with the anti-realist view of science as a process of construction of theories and concepts and of saving the phenomena by using those constructed theories and concepts. On a realist understanding, scientists may properly be said to discover entities and laws which were already in existence prior to the human realization of their existence.

The distinction between theoretical and observational claims

The Vienna Circle placed considerable emphasis upon the importance of observation as the basis for human knowledge. Vigorously rejecting the metaphysical inflationism which they regarded as so unacceptable a feature of philosophy in general, and of philosophy of science in particular, they developed a programme which held that 'observational terms' (O-terms) were to be regarded as semantically and epistemologically privileged. The truth of an O-term can be determined without recourse to any theoretical or metaphysical assumption. While this emphasis on the privileged role of O-terms is particularly associated with writers such as Rudolf Carnap, it has found continuing support in more recent years.

In a series of important studies, the Princeton philosopher Bas van Fraassen argued, partly on grounds of parsimony, that the only reasonable approach to scientific theories was to hold that they are 'empirically adequate' – that is to say, that they can offer an explanation of what is observed. 'We can have evidence for the truth of a theory only via evidential support for its empirical adequacy'.[49] Van Fraassen thus

---

[49] Bas van Fraassen, 'Empiricism in the Philosophy of Science', in P. Churchland and C. Hooker (eds), *Images of Science: Essays on Realism and Empiricism.* Chicago: University of Chicago Press, 1985, 245–308; quotation at 255.

drew a distinction between a realist, who holds that science aims to give a literally true description of what the world is like, and a 'constructive empiricist', who holds that science offers theories which are empirically adequate.[50] For the latter, acceptance of a theory does not involve commitment to the truth of that theory, but to the belief that it adequately preserves the phenomena to which it relates.[51]

> To be an empiricist is to withhold belief in anything that goes beyond the actual, observable phenomena, and to recognize no objective modality in nature. To develop an empiricist account of science is to depict it as involving a search for truth only about the empirical world, about what is actual and observable . . . it must invoke throughout a resolute rejection of the demand for an explanation of the regularities in the observable course of nature, by means of truths concerning a reality beyond what is actual and observable, as a demand which plays no role in the scientific enterprise.

This leads van Fraassen to insist that the determinative factor in theory selection will always be the notion of empirical adequacy. The theory that 'electrons exist' is capable of accounting for the observational evidence; yet this in itself is not a decisive ground for preferring it over rival theories which offer equally adequate explanations of this evidence. For example, it might be possible to propose a theory that 'while all the appearances are that electrons exist, in reality they don't exist'. We might term this the 'as if' theory. For van Fraassen, it is not possible for the natural sciences to distinguish between two such rival theories, each of which is capable of preserving the phenomena. A particularly luminous example of this situation is provided by the rival claims of the Copenhagen and Bohmian schools of quantum mechanics, each of which is empirically adequate, and cannot therefore be adjudicated on strictly scientific grounds.[52]

This does not mean that van Fraassen holds that it is impossible to make judgements between two equally empirically adequate theories – for example, between 'electrons exist' and 'it just looks as if electrons exist'. For van Fraassen, judgements may be made between these theories

[50] Christopher Norris argues cogently that van Fraassen's 'constructive empiricism' is anti-realism by another name: Christopher Norris, *Against Relativism: Philosophy of Science, Deconstruction and Critical Theory.* Oxford: Blackwell, 1997, 167–95.

[51] Bas C. van Fraassen, *The Scientific Image.* Oxford: Oxford University Press, 1980, 202–3.

[52] For an exhaustive study, see James T. Cushing, *Quantum Mechanics: Historical Contingency and the Copenhagen Hegemony.* Chicago: University of Chicago Press, 1994.

– but the criteria involved are primarily pragmatic. The theory that electrons really do exist is to be preferred to its 'as if' rival on grounds of its simplicity or natural plausibility; these considerations, however, reflect the way we like theories to be, rather than constituting grounds for believing in the *truth* of that theory.

So do electrons exist? By any criterion of observability which wins van Fraassen's somewhat quirky approval, an electron lies beyond observation. Michael Levin has argued that van Fraassen's approach reduces to saying that 'experience is as if there are electrons, but that this is the strongest statement that can be made'.[53] The electron is a posited entity with explanatory force, but no ontological status. Its existence is not *required* for theories which posit it to have explanatory success, or to possess empirical adequacy. This makes him vulnerable to the telling criticism of Nicholas Rescher, who argues that van Fraassen 'tries to do for *theoretical* entities what Bertrand Russell tried to do for *fictional* entities – to reinterpret talk that is *ostensibly* about entities in terms that bear no ontological weight'.[54]

It will be clear that the critically important distinction here concerns observation and theory. Van Fraassen insists that there is an epistemologically significant difference between those entities which can be observed by the human senses, and those which cannot. Yet the critical issue which this raises can hardly be ignored: how can the intensely problematic notion of 'observability' be defined?[55]

Rudolf Carnap argued that an *O*-term can be defined as an observable quality whose presence or absence can be ascertained by an observer in a relatively short time and with a high degree of confirmation. This is a weakly defined notion, capable of embracing a generously wide range of options, and hence precluding serious engagement with the point at issue. Carl Hempel clearly believes that he has improved upon this studied vagueness when he defines *O*-terms as terms occurring in observation statements which purport to 'describe readings of measuring instruments, changes in colour or odour accompanying a chemical reaction, verbal or other kinds of overt behaviour by a given subject under specified observable conditions'.[56] However, this is virtually devoid of value, in that it fails to engage with the question of what it is that makes a given quality 'observable'.

---

[53] Michael Levin, 'Realisms', *Synthese* 85 (1990), 115–38.
[54] Nicholas Rescher, *Scientific Realism: A Critical Appraisal*. Dordrecht: Reidel, 1987, 35.
[55] For some penetrating criticisms, see Norris, *Against Relativism*, 196–217.
[56] Carl G. Hempel, *Aspects of Scientific Explanation*. New York: Free Press, 1965, 179.

A more satisfactory, yet still intensely problematic, account is pre-sented by van Fraassen himself, who offers the following definition: 'X is observable if there are circumstances which are such that, if X is present to us under those circumstances, then we observe it.'[57] A theory can thus be said to be true if 'what the theory says *about what is observable* (by us) is true'. In other words, theories aim to describe the observable, and do not require the existence of any posited unobservable entities as a prior condition for their acceptance. 'The assertion that theory T explains fact E does not presuppose or imply that T is true.'[58]

Yet van Fraassen seems to define observation in terms of the naked eye, without the intervention of any technology. This leads him to take some puzzling assertions. The moons of the planet Jupiter are 'observ-able' (even though, under normal conditions, a telescope is required to see them from earth) because it would be possible to travel to that planet, and observe the moons directly from that vantage point. Presumably van Fraassen is arguing that we do not need technology to 'see' these moons, because we could see them for ourselves if we happened to be in the right place to do so. Yet he seems to overlook the role of technology in transporting us to precisely such a vantage point.

Having allowed that we 'see' through a telescope (in that we could observe distant entities for ourselves if our physical location were to be altered), van Fraassen goes on to argue that we do not actually 'see' through microscopes, in that the entities which are alleged to be 'observed' are not themselves visible to the naked eye. So what about spectacles, worn by a substantial proportion of the human race? Does this invalidate what they observe? Or does it mean that they do not 'observe' at all without this optical correction to their vision? Van Fraassen's distinction is widely regarded as forced, artificial and decidedly less than compelling. Rom Harré here sets out some of the objections which may immediately be raised against this approach.[59]

'Observable' means 'able to be observed by an unaided human being'. To argue that something unobservable may come to be observable (and so to speak have been the same thing all along) is to violate the rules of language. So the scientific ontology must be tied to current human capacities for observation. *Percipi est esse!* Van Fraassen generously allows physicists and other simpletons to think in terms of a spurious ontology, that is the realist interpretations of their theories, provided

[57] Van Fraassen, *The Scientific Image*, 16.
[58] Van Fraassen, *The Scientific Image*, 100.
[59] Rom Harré, *Varieties of Realism.* Oxford and New York: Blackwell, 1986, 57.

they drop it when they are called upon to say something about the furniture of the world. So the back of the moon did not exist before the Apollo fly-pasts, nor did bacteria before the invention of the microscope.

As the history of science makes very clear, a number of theoretical entities which were initially proposed largely as a matter of conjecture – such as electrons, neutrinos and other subatomic particles – subsequently came to be regarded as real entities whose existence was *discovered* through a relentless process of theoretical and empirical investigation and technological advance. The realist can therefore argue that realism, including belief in the ontology which appears to be implied by scientific theories, is to be preferred on *heuristic* grounds. Science would never have arrived at its present state of predictive and explanatory success unless its theories had not been interpreted realistically.[60]

In his important essay on the 'Epistemology of Natural Science', Wesley Salmon argues that statements concerning unobservable entities can be made without the need for a special theoretical vocabulary. Salmon noted the manner in which, in investigating the phenomenon of 'Brownian motion', Jean Perrin suspended large numbers of tiny particles of gamboge (a yellow resinous substance) in water, and observed their motion with a microscope. From their behaviour, he inferred that they were being buffeted by many smaller particles. Although these particles could not be seen, their effect could be determined, allowing the value of Avagadro's number (the number of molecules in a mole of any substance) to be determined accurately across a wide range of diverse experimental situations. As Salmon notes, 'the problem of the existence of entities not even indirectly observable was essentially settled for natural science as a result of the work of Perrin and others in roughly the first decade of the twentieth century'.[61]

Taking this point further, Grover Maxwell has argued that this distinction between observational and theoretical terms and statements must be recognized as anthropocentric and historically contingent.[62] As such, this is therefore arbitrary and cannot be regarded as epistemologically significant. Maxwell offers two arguments in support of this important assertion. In the first place, what was once deemed to be

---

[60] Jarrett Leplin, 'Methodological Realism and Scientific Rationality', *Philosophy of Science* 53 (1986), 31–51.

[61] Wesley Salmon, 'Epistemology of Natural Science', in Jonathan Dancy and Ernest Sosa (eds), *A Companion to Epistemology*. Oxford: Blackwell, 1992, 280–99.

[62] Grover Maxwell, 'The Ontological Status of Theoretical Entities', *Minnesota Studies in the Philosophy of Science* 3 (1962), 3–15.

'theoretical' can become 'observational'. Thus bacteria, once postulated as theoretical entities, became observable through the invention of the microscope. To the objection that microscopic 'observations' depend on theories of optics, and are hence not 'observations' at all, Maxwell offers a model which postulates a continuous spectrum of observability. Observations of objects through something as unproblematic as glass windows – and subsequently spectacles and binoculars – are also theory-laden, even thought we have little occasion or reason to call these theories into question.[63]

> Contemporary valency theory tells us that there is a virtually continuous transition from very small molecules (such as those of hydrogen) through 'medium-sized' ones (such as those of the fatty acids, polypeptides, proteins and viruses) to extremely large ones (such as the crystals of the salts, diamonds, and lumps of polymeric plastic). The molecules in the last-mentioned are macro, 'directly observable' physical objects, but are, nevertheless, genuine, single molecules; on the other hand, those in the first-mentioned group have the same perplexing properties as subatomic particles (de Broglie waves, Heisenberg indeterminacy, etc.) Are we to say that a large protein molecule (e.g., a virus) which can be 'seen' only with an electron microscope is a little less real or exists to somewhat less an extent than does a molecule of a polymer which can be seen with an optical microscope? And does a hydrogen molecule partake of only an infinite portion of existence or reality? Although there certainly is a continuous transition from observability to unobservability, any talk of such a continuity from full-blown existence to nonexistence is clearly nonsense.

Anticipating the anti-realist reply that such things as tables and planets are in principle observable while electrons are not, Maxwell points out that the only viable answer must be stated in theoretical terms – that is, by laying down what is intrinsically beyond observation, and what is not. 'It seems odd,' he wryly comments, 'that one who is espousing an austere empiricism which requires a sharp observational-language/theoretical-language distinction (and one in which the former language has a privileged status) should need a theory in order to tell him what is observable.'

Despite van Fraassen's attempts to absolutize a relative and contingent distinction, there is obviously a *continuum of observability*, rather than an epistemically decisive and absolute separation between 'observable' and 'theoretical' or 'unobservable'. There is thus a spectrum

---

[63] Maxwell, 'The Ontological Status of Theoretical Entities', 9.

of possibilities, in which the advance of technology necessarily implies that there is an irreversible trend towards the extension of the realm of the observable. As such, the distinction between 'observable' and 'theoretical' is not grounded on epistemic issues, but on one's historical and cultural location. It is a relative, not absolute, matter. The term 'unobservable' does not mean '*intrinsically* lying beyond human observation' but '*presently* lying beyond human observation'. While van Fraassen holds that it is improper to treat unobservables as putative observables, the history of the scientific project suggests that this is precisely what happens on a regular basis through technological advance. This is not to hold that all unobservables will alter their status in this manner. Yet it is not necessary to affirm this notion in order to refute van Fraassen; it suffices to note that some have, as a matter of fact, altered their status in this manner, and that it is to be expected that others will in the future.

A final point needs to be made. The distinction between theory and observation is of considerable importance to any account of the scientific project, and is often cited by anti-realists as supportive of their case. Thus van Fraassen's denial of a theory-neutral language can be seen as a philosophical gambit designed to blunt the force of a powerful criticism directed against anti-realism – namely, that it is ultimately incoherent. In that anti-realism is obliged to give epistemic priority to the observational components of a theory than to its non-observational claims, the observational component of the theory requires to be separated and distinguished from the remainder of the theory.[64] To put it bluntly: 'there can *be* no anti-realism – not even a problematic anti-realism – without a theory-observation distinction'.[65]

Realism responds to van Fraassen's argument, and others like it, by insisting that the distinction is ultimately incoherent. As can be seen from Maxwell's critique of the distinction, and the difficulties van Fraassen encounters in maintaining it, this is an entirely plausible strategy.[66] Yet Jerry Fodor has shown that a case can be made for arguing that the theory-observation may be positively incorporated into a *realist* epistemology, and is particularly advantageous in refuting

---

[64] Kukla, *Studies in Scientific Realism*, 129–42.

[65] Kukla, *Studies in Scientific Realism*, 111.

[66] See further Jeff Foss, 'On Accepting Van Fraassen's Image of Science', *Philosophy of Science* 51 (1984), 79–92; Richard Creath, 'Taking Theories Seriously', *Synthese* 62 (1985), 317–45; Alan Musgrave, 'Constructive Empiricism Versus Scientific Realism', *Philosophical Quarterly* 32 (1982), 262–71.

Kuhnian relativism.[67] Fodor's arguments in favour of the distinction, and his appropriation of the distinction for realist purposes, is not entirely convincing.[68] Nevertheless, Fodor's approach suggests that realism is better positioned than its rivals to deal with the observational material and the task of its interpretation.

The laws of nature

Since the uniformity of nature is an unjustified (indeed, circular) assumption within any non-theistic world-view, it could be argued that there is no firm basis upon which to engage in scientific activities, other than the belief that the regularities observed locally prove universal. Bertrand Russell summarizes the problem of assuming the uniformity of nature in his *The Problems of Philosophy*:[69]

> The problem we have to discuss is whether there is any reason for believing in what is called 'the uniformity of nature'. The belief in the uniformity of nature is the belief that everything that has happened or will happen is an instance of some general law to which there are no exceptions ... But science habitually assumes, at least as a working hypothesis, that general rules which have exceptions can be replaced by general rules which have no exceptions ... Have we any reason, assuming that they (scientific laws) have always held in the past, to suppose that they (scientific laws) will hold in the future.

The problem is that without a theological basis for the uniformity of nature in the nature and being of God, there is no reliable ideational basis for induction. Russell holds that the business of science is to find uniformities, such as the law of gravitation and the laws of motion. But how can one formulate general laws of science in a world without any basis for the uniformity of nature? Russell argues that this gives rise to a serious tension, which has not been satisfactorily resolved without the charge of circularity – that is, presupposing what is to be proved.[70]

> Experience might conceivably confirm the inductive principle as regards the cases that have been already examined; but as regards unexamined cases, it is the inductive principle alone that can justify any inference from what has been examined to what has not been examined. All arguments which, on the basis of experience, argue as to the future or

---

[67] Jerry Fodor, 'Observation Reconsidered', *Philosophy of Science* 51 (1984), 23–43.

[68] See the discussion in Kukla, *Studies in Scientific Realism*, 113–28.

[69] Bertrand Russell, *The Problems of Philosophy*. London: Oxford University Press, 1912, 63–4.

[70] Russell, *The Problems of Philosophy*, 68.

the unexperienced parts of the past or present, assume the inductive principle; hence we can never use experience to prove the inductive principle *without begging the question.* Then we must either accept the inductive principle on the ground of its intrinsic evidence, or forgo all justification of our expectation about the future.

A Christian doctrine of creation holds that the uniformity of nature (and hence the possibility of induction) are grounded in the Christian understanding of the world, which posits regularity grounded in the nature of God. In an earlier discussion (vol. 1, 225–32), we considered how the notion of the 'laws of nature' are firmly grounded in a Christian doctrine of creation. They are not to be regarded as arbitrary regulations imposed upon the world from without on an occasional basis, but as a permanent expression and embodiment *within the world* of the mind of God as creator. The idea that nature is governed by 'laws' does not appear to be a significant feature of Greek, Roman or Asian conceptions of science; it is firmly entrenched within the Judeo-Christian tradition, reflecting the specifics of a Christian doctrine of creation.[71]

The regularities of nature constitute the cornerstone of the scientific nature. The phrase 'the laws of nature' is a convenient way of encapsulating the notion of a regularity *within* nature itself, which is expressed in scientific theories concerning nature. Laws of nature are not simply convenient accounts of our observations; they express something much deeper, grounded in the nature of reality itself, which these laws attempt to express. The 'laws of nature' are not inventions or human constructions; they are potentially verifiable and veridical accounts of a reality which exists independently of the human knower.[72]

That, at least, is the view of most natural scientists. The philosophical community has seen division over how these laws of nature are to be defined, and what their implications might be. As this debate has important implications for realism in both the natural sciences and Christian theology, we may consider the issues in a little detail.

[71] A. Rupert Hall, *The Scientific Revolution, 1500–1800: The Formation of the Modern Scientific Attitude.* London: Longmans, Green & Co., 1954, 172.

[72] For the philosophical debate over this issue, see William P. Alston, 'Divine Action, Human Freedom and the Laws of Nature', in Robert John Russell, Nancey Murphy and C. J. Isham (eds), *Quantum Cosmology and the Laws of Nature: Scientific Perspectives on Divine Action.* Vatican City: Vatican Observatory, 1993, 185–207; Rom Harré, *Laws of Nature.* London: Duckworth, 1993; Mark Lange, 'Armstrong and Dretske on the Explanatory Power of Regularities', *Analysis* 52 (1992), 154–9; Margaret J. Osler, 'Eternal Truths and the Laws of Nature: The Theological Foundations of Descartes' Philosophy of Nature', *Journal of the History of Ideas* 46 (1985), 349–65; Steven Weinberg, *Dreams of a Final Theory: The Search for the Fundamental Laws of Nature.* London: Hutchinson Radius, 1993.

We may begin by considering the 'conventionalist' approach to the laws of nature, sometimes also known as an 'instrumentalist' approach. This approach became influential in the late nineteenth and early twentieth centuries, and is particularly associated with Ernst Mach and Henri Poincaré (139–40). The laws of nature are not be to considered as simply empirical generalizations, but as conventions which are adopted on account of their convenience in organizing and systematizing observational data (note the convergence with a positivist approach to scientific knowledge). They are necessary, in the sense that they are true *de dicto* – by convention or definition. They are not strictly 'experimental laws', and hence cannot be refuted experimentally. On the basis of a conventionalist approach, laws of nature are to be seen as *a posteriori* conventions adopted as the best means of rationalizing the body of experimental data currently available. While this approach has generally fallen out of favour, some recognizable variants on its themes can be found in the recent writings of Bas van Fraassen and Ronald Giere.[73]

The two main difficulties faced by conventionalism may be set out as follows.

1. Its failure to account for why some alleged 'conventions' are so successful, and others not. It is always possible to appeal to the principle of underdetermination of theory by evidence, and argue that logically distinct yet empirically equivalent theories based on different conventions are conceivable. Yet it is remarkably difficult to identify genuine examples supporting this point.[74] The reason why some 'conventions' are so successful appears to be embedded in some deep-rooted correspondence with reality.

2. If the laws of nature are simply tools that scientists use to summarize data, and are hence strictly speaking neither 'true' nor 'false', then it makes little sense to speak of these being tested, confirmed or refuted. The assertion that these conventions are true *de dicto* implies that the truth of the laws of nature is essentially linguistic, rooted in the structure of human language rather than the way the world is. This appears to locate the validity of the laws of nature in the way in which humanity talks about nature, rather

[73] Bas van Fraassen, *Laws and Symmetry*. Oxford: Clarendon Press, 1989; Ronald N. Giere, 'The Skeptical Perspective: Science without the Laws of Nature', in Freidel Weinert (ed.), *Laws of Nature: Essays on the Philosophical, Scientific and Historical Dimensions*. New York: de Gruyter, 1995, 120–38. On van Fraassen, see John W. Carroll, *Laws of Nature*. Cambridge: Cambridge University Press, 1994, 96–102.

[74] See the discussion in Brian D. Ellis, 'What Science aims to do', in P. M. Churchland and C. A. Hooker (eds), *Images of Science*. Chicago: Chicago University Press, 1985, 48–74.

than the way nature is in itself. While this approach has a certain resonance with the linguistic turn in philosophy, it suffers from precisely the weakness of the main streams of twentieth-century analytical philosophy – a failure to engage with what may lie outside the limited realm of human language.

The two main approaches to the laws of nature in contemporary philosophy of science are usually referred to as the 'regularity' and 'necessity' approaches. The *regularity* theory holds that there are indeed regularities within the natural world, which are summarized by the laws of nature. These laws, however, are nothing more than a summary or description of such regularities observed within nature.[75] The approach from *necessity* argues that the laws of nature are more than mere summaries of observed regularities; the laws of nature correspond, in some way and to some extent, to objective real features of the world which underlie the way the world is presented to human observation. It will be clear that the realist account of the natural sciences is more firmly wedded to the second of these theories. Nevertheless, it is important to appreciate that both approaches ultimately rest on the assumption that the laws of nature describe important facts about reality, whether these are understood to be contingent or necessary.[76] These are frameworks which we discern within reality, rather than impose upon it.

Steven Weinberg can be regarded as summing up a widespread consensus within the community of physicists when he argues that the 'laws of physics' are true, whether we recognize them or not – even if we may get them wrong:[77]

---

[75] In older writings, this approach is sometimes referred to as the 'Humean' approach, suggesting that it is associated with David Hume. I am unpersuaded of this, and believe this represents a misreading of Hume, which assumes that his epistemological scepticism (how may we know that something is necessary?) is carried over into his conception of the laws of nature. In fact, Hume seems to have believed that the laws of nature were, in some sense, necessary, despite the difficulties this raises. For further discussion of Hume on this point, see Tom L. Beauchamp and Alexander Rosenberg, *Hume and the Problem of Causation.* New York: Oxford University Press, 1981; John P. Wright, *The Sceptical Realism of David Hume.* Minneapolis: University of Minnesota Press, 1983. For an extended discussion of Hume and 'supervenience', see Carroll, *Laws of Nature,* 28–85.

[76] For a critique of both approaches in this respect, see Nancy Cartwright, *How the Laws of Physics Lie.* Oxford: Clarendon Press, 1983. An interesting response is to be found in Alan Chalmers, 'So the Laws of Physics Needn't Lie', *Australasian Journal of Philosophy* 71 (1993), 196–205.

[77] Steven Weinberg, 'Sokal's Hoax', *The New York Review of Books,* vol. 43, no. 13 (8 August 1996), 11–15. The 'Sokal Hoax' will be discussed later in this chapter. The reference to Stanley Fish picks up on some points made in Fish's article 'Professor Sokal's Bad Joke', *The New York Times,* 21 May 1996, 23.

When I was an undergraduate at Cornell I heard a lecture by a professor of philosophy (probably Max Black) who explained that whenever anyone asked him whether something was real, he always gave the same answer. The answer was 'Yes'. The tooth fairy is real, the laws of physics are real, the rules of baseball are real, and the rocks in the fields are real. But they are real in different ways. What I mean when I say that the laws of physics are real is that they are real in pretty much the same sense (whatever that is) as the rocks in the fields, and not in the same sense (as implied by [Stanley] Fish) as the rules of baseball – we did not create the laws of physics or the rocks in the field, and we sometimes unhappily find that we have been wrong about them, as when we stub our toe on an unnoticed rock, or when we find we have made a mistake (as most physicists have) about some physical law. But the languages in which we describe rocks or in which we state physical laws are certainly created socially, so I am making an implicit assumption (which in everyday life we all make about rocks) that our statements about the laws of physics are in a one-to-one correspondence with aspects of objective reality. To put it another way, if we ever discover intelligent creatures on some distant planet and translate their scientific works, we will find that we and they have discovered the same laws.

Weinberg here anticipates some of the themes of critical realism, to which we shall return in the next chapter. Perhaps most importantly, he draws attention to the fact that these laws are independent of the observer, and may be discovered (for – unlike the rules of baseball – they are not invented or constructed) through the rational investigation of the world.

Abduction to the best explanation

A classic problem in the philosophy of science concerns how rival explanations of the world are to be evaluated. In an influential paper, Gilbert Harman argued that inductive inference could be described as 'inference to the best explanation'.[78] This process of 'inference to the best explanation' could be described as 'accepting a hypothesis on the grounds that it provides a better explanation of the evidence than is provided by alternative hypotheses'.[79]

Although Harman's influence has led to the widespread use of the phrase 'inference to the best explanation', it must be pointed out that this phrase is confusing. One can infer that X is the best explanation;

---

[78] Gilbert Harman, 'The Inference to the Best Explanation', *Philosophical Review* 74 (1965), 88–95.

[79] Paul R. Thagard, 'The Best Explanation: Criteria for Theory Choice', *Journal of Philosophy* 75 (1976), 76–92.

one cannot infer to X as the best explanation. To use the vocabulary of Charles Peirce, one can move from evidence to hypothesis by a process of *abduction*.[80] It is therefore preferable to speak of a process of 'abduction to the best explanation'.

Perhaps the best-known scientific work to make extensive use of abduction to the best explanation is Charles Darwin's *The Origin of Species*, which sets out a substantial array of observational data which can be explained on the basis of natural selection, but which cause some difficulties for the then-prevailing theory of the special creation of individual species.[81] It may be noted here that William Whewell developed the notion of 'consilience' as a measure of the explanatory power of explanations, and that Darwin was influenced considerably by this notion in his thinking.[82]

So what is the relevance of this process to the debate over realism? The matter may be put like this. If hypothesis X offers the best explanation of a series of observations, X and its associated theoretical entities must be regarded as potentially true or real. An excellent example of this principle is provided by the growing conviction within the scientific community, from around 1900, that the credibility of the belief that matter consisted of individual atoms or molecules was strongly confirmed by the fact that many independent experimental procedures ended up providing the same value of Avagadro's constant, which is the amount of substance that contains as many objects (atoms, molecules or ions) as there are atoms in exactly 12.0 grams of Carbon-12. This number can be determined experimentally to be 6.022×10^{23}.

Five independent experimental methods lead to this same result:

1. *Langmuir-Blodgett films.* When a drop of oil is placed on water, it spreads out to cover the available surface area to the point at which it is one molecule thick. The number of molecules in a given amount of oil may therefore be determined by calculating the area covered by a given weight of oil and the molecular weight of the oil in question.[83]

---

[80] K. T. Fann, *Peirce's Theory of Abduction*. The Hague: Martinus Nijhoff, 1970. Peirce also uses the term 'retroduction' to refer to this process.

[81] Michael C. Banner, *The Justification of Science and the Rationality of Religious Belief*. Oxford and New York: Oxford University Press, 1990, 125–30.

[82] Richard R. Yeo, 'William Whewell's Philosophy of Knowledge and its Reception', in Menachem Fisch and Simon Schaffer (eds), *William Whewell: A Composite Portrait*. Oxford: Clarendon Press, 1991, 175–99.

[83] W. A. Barlow, *Langmuir-Blodgett Films*. Amsterdam: Elsevier Scientific Publishing, 1980.

2. *Brownian Motion.* Jean Perrin determined Avogadro's number in the nineteenth century by studying the vertical distribution of uniform particles of gamboge – a type of resin – in colloidal suspensions. By calculating what forces would have to be in place to account for this keeping the particles suspended, he could calculate their average kinetic energy, and hence Avogadro's number.[84]

3. *Alpha Decay.* The British physicist Lord Rutherford recognized that the alpha particles produced in radioactive decay were helium nuclei. By determining the number of helium atoms that were required to make up a certain mass of helium, Rutherford calculated Avogadro's number.

4. *X-ray diffraction.* The matrix of atoms within a crystal acts like a diffraction grating, producing a distinctive diffraction pattern which allows the spacing between atoms to be determined, and hence the number of atoms in a given weight of the substance. This allows Avogadro's constant to be determined.[85]

5. *Electrochemistry.* The electrical charge which is required to discharge a mole of metal during the process of electrolysis is known as a Faraday. This can be determined empirically. Robert Millikan's 1913 measurement of the charge on the electron allows the value of Avagadro's number to be determined using the formula $F/e = N$, where F is the value of a Faraday, e is the charge on the electron, and N is Avagadro's constant.[86]

There is no convincing explanation of these converging lines of evidence other than that atoms genuinely exist, despite the reservations that Ernst Mach expressed concerning the atomic hypothesis at the end of the nineteenth century. Although this debate was very real in the 1890s, it is today treated as obscurantist and irrelevant. The atomic hypothesis is now so well established that it is widely regarded as the best explanation of the observational evidence – and hence that atoms are 'real'. Wesley Salmon's account of Perrin's experiment and its subsequent reception allows us to summarize the force of the realist case at this point:[87]

[84] A. N. Borodin and Paavo Salminen, *Handbook of Brownian Motion: Facts and Formulae.* Basel: Birkhauser Verlag, 1996.

[85] M. F. C. Ladd and R. A. Palmer, *Structure Determination by X-ray Crystallography.* New York: Plenum Press, 1993.

[86] Samuel Glasstone, *The Electrochemistry of Solutions.* London: Methuen, 1945.

[87] Salmon, 'Epistemology of Natural Science', 292–6.

In his work on Brownian movement, Jean Perrin created large numbers of tiny spheres of gamboge (a yellow resinous substance). He suspended them in water, observed their motions with a microscope, and inferred that many smaller particles were colliding with them. Without using any non-observational terms, I have just described the essentials of an epoch-making experiment on the reality of molecules, namely the ascertainment of Avagadro's number (the number of molecules in a mole of any substance) . . . The crux of the argument is this. From a series of physical experiments that are superficially extremely diverse, it is possible to infer the value of Aavagadro's number, and the values obtained in all these types of experiment agree with one another remarkably well. If matter were not actually composed of such micro-entities as molecules, atoms, ions, electrons, etc., this agreement would be an unbelievably improbable coincidence.

The morphology of this assertion demands attention. The scientific realist claims that since the existence of molecules explains this remarkable convergence in respect to Avagadro's constant better than any other, molecules must be accepted as real. That there is a 'best' explanation is seen to rest on the assumption that there exists a reality which, once grasped, is capable of offering at least a partial explanation of a variety of experimental and observational evidence. The ability of a hypothesis to explain something better than its rivals must be seen as a mark of its truth, especially when those rivals include options such as 'treating the world *as if* it is made up of molecules, while believing that in reality it is not.' 'As if' theories possess, as we have seen, a remarkable vulnerability to historical erosion, in that instrumentalist ways of viewing things often subsequently give way to realist approaches.

Classic objections to scientific realism

It is significant that realism is regarded as the default option when dealing with the natural sciences. Critiques of realism often start from the assumption that this philosophy is so deeply entrenched within the natural sciences that its *de facto* hegemony must be challenged as a matter of principle.[88] In practice, the challenges issued generally tend to introduce modifications to scientific realism, rather than its abandonment. At the opening of the twenty-first century, it seems clear that the great debates will concern what style of scientific realism will

---

[88] See the opening comments of Nancy Cartwright, 'Do the Laws of Physics State the Facts?', *Pacific Philosophical Quarterly* 61 (1980), 75–84.

dominate the agenda, in that its non-realist rivals are increasingly regarded as problematic. It is highly significant that the anti-realist case is often made *negatively*, through a critique of realism rather than *positively*, through a defence of anti-realism, and a clarification of its implications.

Nevertheless, it is important to identify the classic objections to scientific realism, and offer a response to some of the points which they make. We begin by considering the appeal to the history of science, which has been so important an aspect of the late-twentieth-century debate over realism.

Radical theory change in the history of science

One of the most important challenges to realism concerns the shifting patterns of scientific theories in the early modern period. A theory which was widely held to be necessitated by the experimental or observational evidence in 1700 is abandoned by 1900, and replaced with a quite different theory. Is this not a clear indication that the central tenet of realism is vulnerable? That the theoretical entities which were so confidently proposed by one generation are abandoned by another?

This is certainly the view of Larry Laudan. In a feisty critique of what he terms 'convergent realism', Laudan argues that the history of science offers a 'plethora of theories which were both successful and (so far as we can judge) non-referential with respect to many of their central explanatory concepts'.[89] Laudan argues that scientific realism offers a convergent understanding of the quest for truth which simply cannot be sustained with reference to history. In other words, central theoretical concepts which were believed to be referential at the time of their acceptance are no longer viewed in this way, and are now regarded as non-referring. Examples of such theories include:

- the crystalline spheres of ancient and medieval astronomy;
- the humoral theory of medicine;
- the caloric theory of heat;
- the electromagnetic ether.

Each of these theories was once judged to be successful by the criteria of their contemporaries; they have now been abandoned. How, asks

---

[89] Larry Laudan, 'A Confutation of Convergent Realism', *Philosophy of Science* 48 (1981), 19–49. For a vigorous riposte, see Clyde L. Hardin and Alexander Rosenberg, 'In Defense of Convergent Realism', *Philosophy of Science* 49 (1982), 604–15.

Laudan, can any appeal to the 'success' of a theory be taken as evidence for realism, when that 'success' may be eroded with the passage of time? 'The fact that a theory's central terms refer does not entail that it will be successful, and a theory's success is no warrant for the claim that all or most of its central terms refer.'

Laudan's critique of realism offers an account of scientific rationality which is grounded in history. Yet the status of history in this matter must be called into question. Imre Lakatos effectively makes a historicist meta-methodology the cornerstone of his methodology of scientific research programmes. We can see here one of the major themes of Thomas Kuhn's *The Structure of Scientific Revolutions* – that the appropriate warrant for the philosophy of science, in whole or in part, is not rigorous logical or philosophical analysis of scientific theories or concepts, but the history and practice of the natural sciences.[90] This is stated clearly in the opening sentence of Kuhn's *Hauptwerk*:[91]

> History, if viewed as a repository for more than anecdote or chronology, could produce a decisive transformation in the image of science by which we are now possessed.

Kuhn's approach places an emphasis upon science as an historical phenomenon which exhibits discontinuous change, which called into question whether science could be regarded as possessing a stable foundation, or whether one could meaningfully speak of scientific 'progress'.[92] Since each paradigm shift swept away its predecessor, there is no compelling case for accepting the existence of the theoretical entities which they proposed.

This viewpoint has met with growing resistance in recent years, not least because of a growing awareness of the complexity of theory change, and a willingness to question the categories in which Kuhn delineated the somewhat chequered history of the natural sciences. The degree of continuity is far greater than is often appreciated. For example, it is fatally easy to suggest that Newtonian and quantum mechanics are totally discontinuous with one another. Yet the reality is that Newtonian mechanics can be seen as a limiting case of the more general approach set out by quantum mechanics.

[90] On which see the careful studies of Paul Hoyningen-Huene, *Reconstructing Scientific Revolutions: Thomas S. Kuhn's Philosophy of Science*. Chicago: University of Chicago Press, 1993.
[91] Thomas Kuhn, *The Structure of Scientific Revolutions*. Chicago: University of Chicago Press, 1962, 1.
[92] See Israel Scheffler, *Science and Subjectivity*. Indianapolis: Bobbs Merrill, 1967.

One of the most damaging observations made concerning Kuhn's thesis is that we can speak intelligibly and coherently concerning 'advances in our ideas concerning electrons'. This statement clearly implies that there exist such things as electrons, and that our grasp on their nature and identity has firmed up over time. Otherwise we should be driven to the conclusion – which Kuhn seemed happy to accept in the first edition of *The Structure of Scientific Revolutions*, but then retracted under criticism – that writers such as Dalton, Bohr, Dirac, Heisenberg and Schrödinger were in any sense talking about the same thing in their writings, or clarifying the nature of the same entities in their experimentation.[93]

The importance of this point will be obvious. In a carefully nuanced defence of realism, Ernan McMullin argues that the case for realism may still be maintained in the face of theory change. McMullin initially points out that 'realism had to do with the existence implications of successful theories'.[94] Yet this raises the question of theories, regarded as valid in their day, yet now considered to be discredited. For McMullin, this point may be conceded, yet must be set against the considerable body of theories which have proved resilient.

> The value of this sort of reminder, however, is that it warns the realist that the ontological claim he makes is at best tentative, for surprising reversals have happened in the history of science. But the nonreversible (a long list is easy to construct here also) still require some form of (philosophic) explanation.

The main difficulty with Kuhn's thesis, however, concerns the *appeal to history* itself as a means of critiquing realism. Kuhn's historical research employs methods not totally dissimilar to those of the natural sciences. Now if such methods and styles of reasoning in the sciences fail to allow us to reach reliable conclusions, why should we trust their outcomes in a historical context? Why is it that Kuhn appears to believe that it is legitimate to consider historical categories – such as his hopelessly muddled notion of 'paradigms' – as real entities, yet decline to accord the same status to such things as electrons, for which there is clearly better evidence, not to mention a greater degree of clarity about what is being discussed?[95] As Feyerabend comments, 'why should the

[93] Norris, *Against Relativism*, 173.

[94] Ernan McMullin, 'A Case for Scientific Realism', in Jared Leplin (ed.), *Scientific Realism*. Berkeley, CA: University of California Press, 1984, 8–40.

[95] For this argument in more detail, see Michel Ghins, 'Scientific Realism and Invariance', in Enrique Villanueva (ed.), *Rationality in Epistemology*. Atascadero, CA: Ridgeview, 1992, 249–62.

authority of history be greater than that of, say, physics?'[96] The Kuhnian programme thus seems to fall victim to a suppressed self-referential premise concerning the reality of things.

Bruno Latour's arguments for the deconstruction of allegedly 'objective' approaches to nature (such as the idea that nature is transcendent and humanity aims to reflect or interpret its objective reality), also rests on a historical analysis – in this case, a seventeenth-century dispute between Thomas Hobbes and Robert Boyle.[97] Proponents of the 'strong programme' have made this out to be the key scientific debate of the seventeenth century, so that the whiff of social constructivism throughout its course is sufficient to establish the credibility of the constructivist thesis.[98] A postmodern deconstruction of the methods of natural sciences once more rests upon a realist approach to history – although, as Latour's critics have not been slow to point out, an *inaccurate* reading of that history.[99]

A similar issue arises with Michel Foucault, who is best regarded as a philosopher of history, whose explorations of cultural history caused him to become increasingly pessimistic concerning the ability of human language to serve human needs.[100] Language exercises a decisive impact upon human life and thought – yet that language is contoured and structured by relations of power and authority, which calls into question whether it can ever relate to the real world. Now Foucault's conclusions arose from a detailed examination of social history, particularly aspects of the social history of medicine.[101] Yet Foucault's historicizing

---

[96] Paul K. Feyerabend, *Against Method*. 3rd edn. London: Verso, 1993, 271.

[97] Bruno Latour, *We Have Never Been Modern*. Cambridge, MA: Harvard University Press, 1993, 14–21. Latour's analysis rests heavily on the controversial approach to this episode offered by Steven Shapin and Simon Schaffer, *Leviathan and the Air-Pump: Hobbes, Boyle and the Experimental Life*, Princeton, NJ: Princeton University Press, 1985. For a critique of this work, which has become something of an icon of constructivism, see Cassandra L. Pinnick, 'What is Wrong with the Strong Programme's Case Study of the "Hobbes-Boyle Dispute"?', in Noretta Koertge (ed.), *A House Built on Sand: Exposing Postmodernist Myths about Science*. New York: Oxford University Press, 1998, 227–39.

[98] For a correction to this perspective, see Mordechai Feingold, 'When Facts Matter', *Isis* 87 (1996), 131–9.

[99] Margaret C. Jacob, 'Reflections on Bruno Latour's Version of the Seventeenth Century', in Noretta Koertge (ed.), *A House Built on Sand: Exposing Postmodernist Myths about Science*. New York: Oxford University Press, 1998, 240–54.

[100] For a critical cultural appraisal of Foucault's work, see Roger Kimball, *Experiments against Reality: The Fate of Culture in the Postmodern Age*. Chicago: Ivan R. Dee, 2000, 237–57.

[101] See especially Michel Foucault, *Madness and Civilization: A History of Insanity in the Age of Reason*. London: Routledge, 1995; idem, *The Birth of the Clinic: An Archaeology of Medical Perception*. New York: Vintage, 1975; idem, *The History of Sexuality*. New York:

foundation for his radical anti-realistic philosophy is thus paradoxically tied to – indeed, perhaps even dependent upon – the postulate of a real world, which can be investigated historically, and which can be known at least to the extent that the implications of the past real world can be determined for our present real world. The plausibility of the ideas of Kuhn and Foucault thus derive from their being anchored in history, presupposing one form of realism in order to refute another.

Deconstruction is to be viewed as a literary phenomenon, which questions the nature and possibility of discerning or encountering meaning from texts. According to the Yale school of deconstructionist literary critics, exemplified here by J. Hillis Millar, any given text undermines its own claim to possess any determinant meaning; rather, texts are to be seen as open to a potentially infinite number of multiple interpretations.[102] Yet as David Lodge notes, deconstruction seems to have lost its way and its sense of purpose: the reader of the scholarly journals gains the impression that 'deconstruction is played out'.[103] It remains to be seen what will replace it; it is, however, perfectly clear that it offers no secure foundation for any intellectual system. The growth of critical realism in the human sciences is a clear sign that the academy is weary with deconstruction, and longs for an engagement – however stratified and indirect – with something that is *real*.

In the end, the issue of theory change in science is not fatal to scientific realism. In his 1997–8 John Locke Lectures at Oxford University, Lawrence Sklar explored the issues raised by the transience of scientific theories.[104] The problem is partly due to a growing body of experimental data and partly to an increasingly sophisticated conceptual apparatus with which to frame this data.[105]

There have been periods in the history of physics when scientists may very well have believed, and believed with good reason, that they had finally found the stable, true theory of at least a portion of the world. Perhaps the first half of the eighteenth century constitutes such a period,

---

Pantheon, 1978. See further David H. J. Larmour, Paul Allen Miller and Charles Platter, *Rethinking Sexuality: Foucault and Classical Antiquity*. Princeton, NJ: Princeton University Press.

[102] J. Hillis Miller, *The Ethics of Reading: Kant, de Man, Eliot, Trollope, James, and Benjamin*. New York: Columbia University Press, 1987.

[103] David Lodge, 'Through the No Entry Sign: Deconstruction and Architecture', in *The Practice of Writing*. New York: Penguin Putnam, 1996, 260–9.

[104] Lawrence Sklar, *Theory and Truth: Philosophical Critique without Foundational Science*. Oxford: Oxford University Press, 2000, 78–136.

[105] Sklar, *Theory and Truth*, 79.

at least as far as a portion of dynamics is concerned. But after the history of radical expansion, revision and revolution that has constituted theoretical physics over the last centuries, isn't it the case that the only reasonable belief to hold is that our current best theories are ultimately headed for the scrap-heap that has welcomed their predecessors?

In practice, Sklar does not draw this conclusion, and makes some important points about continuity within theory development.[106]

Yet the importance of his point to the project of a scientific theology can hardly be overlooked. Throughout this project, we have stressed that the provisionality of scientific conclusions is to be set alongside the relative stability of working assumptions and methods of the natural sciences. Sklar's analysis demonstrates how important it is not to base an account of a scientific theology upon the allegedly secure *findings* of the natural sciences, but upon *the methods and working assumptions which underlie those sciences* – supremely a belief in the regularity of the natural world, and the ability of the human mind to uncover and represent this regularity in a mathematical manner.

The underdetermination of theory by evidence

An objection often urged against realism by its critics is that the empirical evidence is often not sufficient to identify precisely which of several competing theories is correct. There may, it is argued, be two or more quite distinct metaphysical understandings of reality which have identical or indistinguishable empirical consequences. This being the case, it is not possible to adjudicate between their claims on the basis of the working assumptions and methods of the natural sciences.[107] The doctrine traditionally, yet misleadingly, known as the 'Duhem–Quine thesis' asserts that, if incompatible data and theory are seen to be in conflict, one cannot draw the conclusion that any particular theoretical statement is responsible for this tension, and must therefore be rejected.[108]

> The totality of our so-called knowledge or beliefs, from the most casual matters of geography and history to the profoundest laws of atomic physics . . . is a man-made fabric which impinges on experience only along the edges . . . A conflict with experience at the periphery occasions adjustments in the interior of the field . . . But the total field is so

---

[106] Sklar, *Theory and Truth*, 87–9.
[107] For an extended analysis of this point, see Kukla, *Studies in Scientific Realism*, 58–91.
[108] W. V. O. Quine, *From a Logical Point of View*. Cambridge, MA: Harvard University Press, 1953, 42–3

underdetermined by its boundary conditions, experience, that there is much latitude of choice as to what statements to re-evaluate in the light of any single contrary experience.

Quine's analysis has given rise to what is often referred to as the 'under-determination thesis' – the view, especially associated with sociological approaches to the natural sciences, which holds that there are, in principle, an indefinite number of theories that are capable of fitting observed facts more or less adequately.[109] The choice of theory can thus be explained on the basis of sociological factors, such as interests. According to this view, experimental evidence plays a considerably smaller role in theory generation and confirmation than might be thought. The strongest form of this approach ('maximal under-determination') would take the following form:[110]

> For any theoretical statement S and acceptable theory T essentially containing S, there is an acceptable theory T' with the same testable consequences but which contains, essentially, the negation of S.

The appeal to underdetermination of theory by evidence continues to be widely cited by those wishing to reject a realist approach to the world.

Nevertheless, this objection itself faces formidable difficulties,[111] not least that Pierre Duhem – who arguably can be held to be one of the intellectual sources of the 'underdetermination' thesis – was quite aware of the severe limitations placed upon it. Duhem's point concerned the difficulty confronted when attempting to identify which element in a system of hypotheses was false, and cannot be taken as simply a critique of realism. We may summarize Duhem's thesis as follows.

Let us define a theory, T, which consists of a group of hypotheses, $H_1, H_2, H_3 \ldots H_n$. An example of such a theory might be Newton's theory of optics, or the rival theory proposed by Huygens. Each theory consists of such a group of explicitly stated interrelated hypotheses. It

---

[109] Richard Boyd, 'Realism, Underdetermination, and a Causal Theory of Evidence', *Nous* 7 (1973), 1–12; Larry Laudan and Jarrett Leplin, 'Empirical Equivalence and Under-determination', *Journal of Philosophy* 88 (1991), 449–72; W. Newton-Smith and Steven Lukes, 'The Underdetermination of Theory by Data', *Proceedings of the Aristotelian Society* 52 (1978), 71–91.

[110] Crispin Wright, *Realism, Meaning and Truth*. 2nd edn. Oxford: Blackwell, 1993, 287.

[111] See, for example, Clark Glymour, *Theory and Evidence*. Princeton, NJ: Princeton University Press, 1980; J. D. Greenwood, 'Two Dogmas of Neo-Empiricism: The "Theory-Informity" of Observation and the Duhem–Quine Thesis', *Philosophy of Science* 57 (1990), 553–74.

also consists of a number of auxiliary hypotheses, which are sometimes not formulated explicitly. We might refer to these as $A_1, A_2, A_3 \ldots A_n$. Now consider an observation statement O. What is the impact of this statement on the group of hypotheses? Is it the theory which requires modification? Or merely one of its hypotheses? And if so, which one?

To give a specific historical example: Newton's theory of planetary motion can be thought of as a composition of his three laws of motion and the gravitational principle. Suppose that observation is made which seems inconsistent with this theory – for example, that the observed orbit of the planet Uranus is not consistent with its predicted theoretical values. This therefore calls into question the group of hypotheses consisting of both the explicit hypotheses of the Newtonian theory, H_1, $H_2, H_3 \ldots H_n$ and the auxiliary hypotheses $A_1, A_2, A_3 \ldots A_n$.

But which of these hypotheses is wrong? Is it the entire theory which requires to be abandoned, or is a modification required to only one hypothesis, which allows the theory as a whole to be saved? In this specific case, it was an auxiliary assumption which proved to be incorrect – namely, the assumption that there was no planet beyond Uranus. When a trans-Uranic planet was postulated, the anomalous orbital parameters of Uranus could be explained by the existence of this planet, which exercised a gravitational pull on Uranus. The planet in question (Neptune) was duly discovered independently (but on the basis of the same calculations) by Adams and Leverrier in 1846. No critique of realism is involved or implied; indeed, the discovery of Neptune could be argued to reinforce the credentials of realism at this point. What was initially a hypothesis became an observed reality.[112]

The difficulty therefore resides in the complex relationship of theories to reality, which introduce elements of uncertainty throughout the theoretical matrix. In that theories are never deductively entailed by the data, is not underdetermination to be expected? It has been known since 1603 that pragmatic success can be accounted for by the deductive power of theories which are almost certainly false. This is the essence of Clavius' Paradox, which Rom Harré construes as follows:[113]

> If pragmatic success is understood as the power of a theory to entail those data we take to be observationally or experimentally verified, and not to entail any putative data which experiment or observation shows

---

[112] For a good account of the discovery of Neptune and its background, see Tom Standage, *The Neptune File: Planet Detectives and the Discovery of Worlds Unseen*. London: Allen Lane, 2000.

[113] Harré, *Varieties of Realism*, 53.

to be false, then the paradox demonstrates that this condition is satisfied by infinitely many theories, only one of which is true. One's chance of hitting on that theory if one is restricted to an empiricist attitude to science is nearly nil.

If empirical adequacy is the criterion by which theories are evaluated, then Clavius' paradox forces the conclusion that theories are necessarily underdetermined. The existence of alternative theories empirically equivalent to any given theory can only be guaranteed if the *only* constraint imposed upon the rival theories is that they entail the same data as the original theory. As Harré points out, this overlooks the way in which theories are actually evaluated within the scientific community:[114]

> However, if one looks at the way theories are actually 'determined', without any prior philosophical commitments, theories seem to stand at the intersection of two streams of influence. There is that which stems from experiment and observation, the influence of data. And there is that which has its source in the ontology of theory-families of which the one in question is a member . . . such families are the products of traditions of past scientific and philosophical work. Taking into account all these factors, it is usually the case that the range of alternative theories available to the community as possible explanations of some class of phenomena is very narrow indeed.

For a scientific realist, there is no particular difficulty here. In those situations in which we are confronted with two empirically equivalent yet syntactically inconsistent theories which are equally 'elegant', 'simple' and so forth, there is no compelling reason for choosing between them. The correct epistemic attitude is that of deferring judgement until additional data can be acquired. The 'underdetermination of theory by data' does not in any way compel us to abandon a realist outlook. It does, however, force us to consider why it is that the scientific community has, as a matter of fact, made judgements concerning two theories which appear equally elegant, and are equally able to account for the empirical evidence – as in the case of the general preference for the Copenhagen over the Bohmian interpretation of quantum mechanics.[115] We shall consider this issue in some depth in the third volume of this work, which deals with the genesis, development and reception of theories in science and theology.

---

[114] Harré, *Varieties of Realism*, 75.
[115] See Cushing, *Quantum Mechanics: Historical Contingency and the Copenhagen Hegemony*.

Perhaps the most serious difficulty for the anti-realist is that the underdetermination thesis can be turned against her. If anti-realism is to be 'proved', or the social constructivist or postmodern approach is to be shown to be *the* 'science of science', then a case must be made from the available evidence, including historical case studies. As Cassandra Pinnick and others have pointed out, this inevitably means that such theories are *themselves* underdetermined by the evidence,[116] and hence can never hope to have the explanatory power and appeal which are essential to their gaining acceptance. If the under-determination theory is *itself* underdetermined by evidence, what reasons may be given to prefer this above other accounts of the situation? Underdetermination is thus a two-edged sword. Curiously, social constructivists and anti-realists seem to have assumed that they were immune from its implications. Yet the underdetermination thesis is as vulnerable to the problem of self-referentiality as any other theory. Realism and anti-realism are equally affected by the issue.

Mathematical realism and the mind of God

Mathematics plays a critically important role in both philosophy and theology, even if theologians seem slow to appreciate this. Augustine is one of a relatively small group of theologians who regarded mathematics as having theological significance. While his interest in, for example, the derivation of numbers from the mind is often regarded as a quaint aspect of his 'Pythagoreanism', it is also an important aspect of his understanding of the correlation between the created order and the mind of its creator.[117] Mathematics enables the order within the world to be identified and seen as an aspect of the harmony within the creation, grounded in the being of God.[118]

It is impossible to read Gottlob Frege's *Grundgesetze der Arithmetik* without appreciating that, if Frege is right, mathematics must be seen as a source of indubitable truth – with important and positive impli-cations for foundationalism. Frege may be regarded as setting Descartes' epistemological programme on the new and more secure foundation,

---

[116] George Gale and Cassandra L. Pinnick, 'Stalking Theoretical Physics: An Ethnography Flounders', *Social Studies of Science* 27 (1997), 113–23.

[117] Augustine's thinking here is shaped by the *Introductio Arithmetica* of Nicomachus of Geresa, which he knew in the Latin translation of Apuleius: Aimé de Solignac, 'Doxographies et manuels dans la formation philosophique de Saint Augustin, *Recherches augustiniennes*. vol. 1. Paris: Etudes augustiniennes, 1958, 113–48.

[118] Augustine, *de ordine*, I.ii.4; I.ix.27.

through a radical review of the foundations of mathematics which saw emphasis decisively shift from the *more geometrico* of Descartes and Spinoza to the *more logico* of Frege, Russell and Whitehead. As we noted in an earlier discussion (27–9), the failure of this enterprise has highly significant implications for both theology and philosophy.

Our concern in this chapter, however, has to do with the issue of mathematical realism, which has been seriously neglected by theologians. Frege's foundationalism may well have been discredited by Russell and others; his Platonist approach to mathematical realism, however, remains a powerful stimulus to the philosophy of mathematics. 'Mathematical Platonism' may be defined in terms of the belief that mathematical objects are perfectly real, and exist independently of the human mind. As Frege puts this point:[119]

> [The thought] which we express in the Pythagorean theorem is timelessly true, true independently of whether anyone takes it to be true. It needs no bearer. It is not true for the first time when it is discovered, but is like a planet which, already before anyone has seen it, has been in interaction with other planets.

Platonism thus holds that mathematics is descriptive, rather than prescriptive. The mathematician is an observer, just like an astronomer searching for new planets. Mathematical objects are discovered, not invented, and mathematical theorems aim to describe what has been discovered. Mathematicians such as Kurt Gödel and Roger Penrose have insisted that mathematical truths are discovered in much the same way as explorers discovered new rivers, plants or continents. As G. H. Hardy, who took up the Sadlerian chair of mathematics at Cambridge in 1931, constantly stressed, the language of mathematics and the realities it described were independent of race, politics or creed.[120]

> 317 is a prime, not because we think it is so, or because our minds are shaped in one way rather than another, but *because it is so*, because mathematical reality is built that way.

Or, to use a more recent example, it was demonstrated in 1996 that $(2^{1398269} - 1)$ is a prime number. Yet it would be unreasonable to suggest that this gigantic integer of 420,921 digits was not actually prime until

---

[119] Frege, 'The Thought: A Logical Inquiry'; cited in E. D. Klemke, *Essays on Frege.* Urbana, IL: University of Illinois Press, 1968, 523.

[120] G. H. Hardy, *A Mathematician's Apology.* Cambridge: Cambridge University Press, 1941, 47.

someone came along in 1996 and demonstrated that this was so. This number, it is argued, is prime, irrespective of whether human minds recognized its character as such or not.

Yet perhaps the most remarkable feature of mathematics is its ability to represent the world. Why, many have asked, is it that the external world contains supremely intricate mathematical patterns, as seen in the structure of force field and galaxies? Why is it that this world, which was not constructed by human hands or agency, demonstrates a rich structuring and patterning capable of being represented mathematically, when mathematics is supposedly a free construction of the human mind? Paul Dirac and Sir James Jeans anchored this remarkable ability of mathematics to mirror the world in the mind of a transcendent God. As we saw earlier (vol. 1, 196–218), the Christian doctrine that both the external world and the human observer are the creation of the same God has a highly significant bearing upon what Eugene Wigner famously described as the 'unreasonable effectiveness of mathematics':[121]

> The miracle of the appropriateness of the language of mathematics for the formulation of the laws of physics is a wonderful gift which we neither understand nor deserve.

The ability of mathematics to mirror the structures of the world was called into question through the development of complex numbers during the sixteenth century. Initially seen as a useful working tool, their perceived ontological status underwent a significant development in the closing years of the eighteenth century. The first use of complex numbers to solve quadratic equations by Girolamo Cardano (1501–76) in his *Ars Magna* (1545) caused some concern on account of the puzzling new idea of using the square root of negative numbers to reach these solutions. Numbers such as the square root of minus one were used further by Lodovico Ferrari (1522–65), who regarded them as 'imaginary' yet useful tools. The tradition of referring to these numbers as 'imaginary' continued in the writings of Descartes and Léonard Euler.[122] The reason for this disquiet is not difficult to identify: the ontology seemed highly questionable. Cardano and Ferrari might have developed some useful mathematical tools, but the entities they posited seemed incapable of being regarded as real numbers. How could a negative number conceivably have a square root?

---

[121] Eugene Wigner, 'The Unreasonable Effectiveness of Mathematics', *Communications on Pure and Applied Mathematics* 13 (1960), 1–14; 14.

[122] Morris Kline, *Mathematical Thought from Ancient to Modern Times*. New York: Oxford University Press, 1972, 253–4.

Resistance to treating these complex numbers as 'real' entities developed on two grounds. First, they appeared to bear no relation to the physical world. If mathematics was capable of mirroring the structures of nature, there seemed to be no place – at least, according to Isaac Newton – for these 'imaginary numbers' in the physical description or analysis of the world. Second, they appeared to possess no intra-mathematical application. Both these difficulties were eliminated by the end of the eighteenth century, as physical applications of complex number theory began to emerge, and when J. C. F. Gauss demonstrated the fundamental theorem of algebra in 1799, which made essential reference to complex numbers.[123] The subtle ontological shift involved in moving from speaking of 'imaginary' to 'complex' numbers reflects a growing confidence concerning their ontology. Once these numbers were firmly implicated in the mathematical representation of the world, their ontological status was secured.

A more recent approach concerns us here. In a series of important articles, W. V. O. Quine argued that mathematical entities are indispensable to our best physical theories, and hence that these entities must be regarded as sharing the same ontological status as scientific entities. In his paper 'Success and Limits of Mathematization', Quine argues that the mathematical entities which appear to be implicated in physical theories must be regarded as being as indispensable as the theoretical entities that these posit.[124] It is unreasonable to hold a realist position with reference to the theoretical entities of physical theories, yet to deny this status to the mathematical entities which they pre-suppose. Quine's argument thus takes the following form:

1. The existence of those entities that are indispensable to the best scientific theories should be accepted;
2. Mathematical entities are indispensable to the best such theories;
3. Therefore the existence of mathematical entities is to be accepted.

A related approach is found in the writings of Michael Resnik, who argues for the indispensability of mathematical entities as follows.[125]

[123] Kline, *Mathematical Thought from Ancient to Modern Times*, 594–5; John N. Crossley, *The Introduction of Complex Numbers*. Victoria: Monash University Department of Mathematics, 1978.
[124] W. V. O. Quine, 'Success and Limits of Mathematization', in W. V. O. Quine, *Theories and Things*. Cambridge, MA: Harvard University Press, 1981, 148–55.
[125] Michael Resnik, 'Scientific versus Mathematical Realism: The Indispensability Argument', *Philosophia Mathematica* 3 (1995), 166–74.

The natural sciences, in formally stating their laws and conducting their investigations, assume the truth of mathematics in general, and the existence of mathematical entities in particular. Without these assumptions, a series of important conclusions could not be drawn within the sciences. It therefore follows that we are justified in drawing these scientific conclusions *only* if the mathematics used within the natural sciences is true. Resnik distinguishes his argument from Quine's as follows:

> This argument is similar to [Quine's] confirmational argument except that instead of claiming that the evidence for science (one body of statements) is also evidence for its mathematical components (another body of statements), it claims that the justification for doing science (one act) also justifies our accepting as true such mathematics as science uses (another act).

Resnik thus argues that the *practice* of science demands mathematical assumptions, and avoids some difficulties associated with Quine's confirmational holism.[126]

The history of science is generously populated with cases in which mathematical reasoning surged ahead of scientific experimentation, pointing to entities and relationships which were only confirmed later by experimental observation. We shall consider one in a little detail, on account of its historical and theoretical importance. Paul Dirac's free particle equation resulted from his 1928 attempt to rework Schrödinger's style of quantum mechanics in terms of particle waves, thus allowing it to become consistent with the special theory of relativity. Dirac's equation for an electron in field-free space is given by:

$$(p_0 - \alpha \cdot p - \beta mc)\psi = 0 \qquad 8.1$$

where

$$p_0 = i \; \frac{\hbar}{c} \; \frac{\delta}{\delta t} \qquad 8.2$$

In that the Dirac equation contains operators which require to be presented by 4×4 matrices, the solutions $\{\psi\}$ must be represented by a four-component vector, as follows:

---

[126] For a summary and evaluation of these difficulties, see Mark Colyvan, *The Indispensability of Mathematics*. Oxford: Oxford University Press, 2001, 91–113.

$$\psi = \begin{pmatrix} \psi_1 \\ \psi_2 \\ \psi_3 \\ \psi_4 \end{pmatrix} \qquad 8.3$$

This can be expanded into a set of four coupled differential equations, as follows:

$$(p_0 - mc)\psi_1 - p_z\psi_3 - (p_x - ip_y)\psi_4 = 0 \qquad 8.4$$
$$(p_0 - mc)\psi_2 - p_x + ip_y)\psi_3 + p_z\psi_4 = 0 \qquad 8.5$$
$$-(p_z\psi_1 - (p_x - ip_y)\psi_2 + p_0 + mc)\psi_3 = 0 \qquad 8.6$$
$$-(p_x + ip_y)\psi_1 + p_z\psi_2 + (p_0 + mc)\psi_4 = 0 \qquad 8.7$$

Now the non-relativistic electron wave function has two components, which correspond to the α and β components of the spin angular momentum. The terms which couple with ψ_1 and ψ_2 can be eliminated, since in the non-relativistic limit, p_0 approaches mc. This leaves four eigenvector equations, with approximate values of $m_0 c^2$ for ψ_1 and ψ_2, and $-m_0 c^2$ for ψ_3 and ψ_4.

Now it is clear that ψ_1 and ψ_2 could be interpreted as the α and β components of electron-like solutions. Yet both ψ_1 and ψ_2 are positive, whereas ψ_3 and ψ_4 are identical yet negative. How are these to be interpreted? Dirac's solution was to propose that ψ_1 and ψ_2 are to be interpreted as referring to electrons, whereas ψ_3 and ψ_4 refer to particles which are identical to electrons except that they possess a positive charge. Dirac invented the term 'positron' to refer to this hypothetical entity, which was demanded by the mathematics of his free particle equation. Yet no such entity was experimentally known. The positive electron was a purely theoretical entity, apparently postulated by mathematical analysis, let lacking any observational warrant. Yet three years later, observation confirmed the theory.

A similar principle underlies the insights of James Clerk Maxwell (1831–79), set out in his four equations concerning the behaviour of electric and magnetic fields, and demonstrating their interrelatedness.[127] Maxwell's mathematical demonstration of the interrelatedness of electrical and magnetic fields subsequently led to his realization that light behaved as an electromagnetic wave. For the noted Scottish

---

[127] On the elegance of the mathematics, see Roger Penrose, 'The Role of Aesthetics in Pure and Applied Mathematical Research', *Bulletin of the Institute of Mathematics and Its Applications* 10 (1974), 266–71.

theologian T. F. Torrance, this achievement was of considerable importance, and rested partly on Maxwell's strong Christian belief in God as creator. On 4 November 1979, Torrance preached the sermon at the James Clerk Maxwell memorial service, held at Corsock Parish Church in Kirkcudbrightshire, marking the centenary of Maxwell's death. The sermon offered him the opportunity to set out an expansive reflection on the significance of Maxwell for the development of the natural sciences and theology.

Noting Maxwell's strong Christian faith in the 'divine power and wisdom by which the worlds were created', Torrance pointed out how this led Maxwell to insist that 'nature abhors *partition*, for in nature everything is inwardly connected together', and argued that the specific form of relational thinking which Maxwell developed was grounded in Christian assumptions. For Maxwell, Torrance argues, the Christian doctrine of creation offers a lens through which the rationality and intelligibility of the created order can be understood and pursued further.[128] Maxwell's pursuit of the 'unsearchable riches of creation' was grounded in a 'deep intuitive grasp of God in relation to the world he had created and ceaselessly sustains'. This deep grasp of the contingent rationality of the world as a consequence of its created character gave Maxwell, according to Torrance, his characteristic trust in the ultimate intelligibility of the world, and the ability of the human mind to discern it.

It is clear that there is an ongoing debate within the philosophy of mathematics concerning the existence of mind-independent mathematical entities. Paul Benacerraf has identified a serious difficulty facing such a mathematical realism: if mathematical objects have an existence which is supposedly independent of the human mind, how is the mind able to know them?[129] Yet interestingly, a Christian doctrine of creation is able to offer a response to this specific issue, in much the same way as it can address the difficulty which otherwise arises from the Euthyphro Dilemma (vol. 1, 214–18). However, it is important to note that all philosophies of mathematics suffer from difficulties, and the 'Platonist' approach is no exception, attractive though it may be in other respects.[130]

[128] Thomas F. Torrance, *Transformation and Convergence in the Frame of Knowledge.* Grand Rapids: Eerdmans, 1984, 216–20.

[129] Paul Benacerraf, 'Mathematical Truth', *Journal of Philosophy* 70 (1973), 661–79.

[130] For example, see Michael Jubien, 'Ontology and Mathematical Truth', *Nous* 11 (1977), 135–50; W. W. Tait, 'Truth and Proof: The Platonism of Mathematics', *Synthese* 69 (1986), 341–70; A. Drozdek and T. Keagy, 'A Case for Realism in Mathematics', *The Monist* 77 (1994), 329–44; Mark Balaguer, *Platonism and Anti-Platonism in Mathematics.* New York: Oxford University Press, 1998; Jaap Mansfeld, *Prolegomena Mathematica from Apollonius of Perga to late Neoplatonism.* Leiden: E. J. Brill, 1998.

Retreating from reality: postmodern anti-realism

Realism continues to hold the ascendancy in the natural sciences, and is gaining a growing respect and following in the social sciences through the 'critical realism' of Roy Bhaskar and his circle,[131] to which we shall turn in the following chapter. Anti-realism has been on the retreat throughout the twentieth century. The confident assertions of the positivists have been whittled away to yield a series of increasingly weakened statements. It is difficult to avoid the conclusion that 'the history of anti-realism in the twentieth century exhibits a pattern of progressive attenuation, wherein each version of the doctrine lays claim to strictly less than its predecessor'.[132]

The case for asserting that the natural sciences attempt to respond to reality has thus, in one sense, never been stronger. Despite this, the recently-emerged discipline of 'science studies' has persisted in its view that the natural sciences are to be viewed simply as local social practices, and are devoid of universal significance.[133] The collapse of classical foundationalism is here assumed to entail the collapse of realism. Yet it is clear that this rests upon a series of misunderstandings of the nature of foundationalism (and why it has had to be abandoned) and of realism itself. To reiterate an obvious fact: the natural sciences do *not* rest upon foundationalist assumptions. Quite the reverse: foundationalism attempts to determine in advance what constitutes knowledge, and thus merely inhibits the natural sciences by laying down *a priori* rules for how the sciences ought to operate.

While fully conceding that personal issues, power structures and other social constraints shape the manner in which experiments are undertaken and how theories are assessed and received, I do not see that the view of the natural sciences as local social practices can be maintained without doing serious violence to the integrity of the disciplines, not to mention a certain degree of selectivity concerning the outcome of experimental programmes.

---

[131] Andrew Collier, *Critical Realism: An Introduction to Roy Bhaskar's Philosophy.* London: Verso, 1994. We shall discuss Bhaskar's ideas in detail in chapter 10.

[132] Kukla, *Studies in Scientific Realism,* 151.

[133] See, for example, Joseph Rouse, *Engaging Science: How to Understand its Practices.* Ithaca, NY: Cornell University Press, 1996, which develops an extended argument rejecting both realism and empiricist or constructivist anti-realisms, based upon a minimalist or 'deflationary' conception of truth. I am unpersuaded by this analysis, which seems to me to point towards a Bhaskarian 'critical realism' rather than the solutions that Rouse himself proposes.

In what follows, we shall explore a number of facets of the complex cultural reflections of anti-realism, and attempt to understand why postmodernity has embraced anti-realism as part of its outlook on life.

Working in Plato's pharmacy

The heterogeneity of 'postmodernism' is such that it is actually somewhat pointless to generalize about what constitutes a postmodern attitude to the natural sciences. What is much more interesting, and ultimately intellectually productive, is to explore how anti-realism has become accepted – without any real engagement with the issues – as the working philosophy of postmodernity.

Anti-realism is seen as attractive by certain postmodern writers, not on account of its intellectual *credentials*, but on account of its intellectual *consequences*. It thus serves the agenda of postmodernity well, in that all can be accounted for as a human construction which may immediately be deconstructed by those with the necessary skills to yield a more pleasing intellectual artifice in due course.[134] The natural sciences are thus held to be culturally- or socially-constructed entities, which can be deconstructed to expose and ultimately eliminate the power structures which they embody.[135] This view is expressed rather well in an otherwise rather puzzling and opaque work by sociologist Harvie Ferguson, who suggests that major developments in physics, such as Einstein's theory of relativity, are the direct result of the evolution of 'bourgeois consciousness'. The work takes the form of an elementary introduction to the history of physics overlaid with a bizarre and quite unpersuasive appeal to the near-total explanatory competence of a sociological notion, in turn determined by the Marxist notion of 'commodity relations'.[136]

Modern physics, it seems, has nothing to do with identifying and representing the inner structure of the physical world; it is simply the reflection of deeper sociological forces. Ferguson does not seem to be troubled by this thesis, which he obviously expects to be shared by his (presumably purely sociological) readers. Much the same attitude can

---

[134] See the issues raised by Paul de Man, 'Resistance to Theory', in *The Resistance to Theory*. Minneapolis, MN: University of Minnesota Press, 1986, 3–20.

[135] For an introduction to this theme, see Peter L. Berger and Thomas Luckmann, *The Social Construction of Reality: A Treatise in the Sociology of Knowledge*. Harmondsworth: Penguin, 1971. For a punning riposte, see John R. Searle, *The Construction of Social Reality*. New York: Free Press, 1995.

[136] Harvie Ferguson, *The Science of Pleasure: Cosmos and Psyche in the Bourgeois World View*. London: Routledge, 1990.

be discerned within anti-realist approaches to religion in general, and to Christian theology in particular. Since religion is a social construction, its ideas and rites may be explicated by patterns of power.

Anti-realism is thus seen as opening the door to a welcome pluralism of opinions and world-views. Derrida's proposition that *il n'y a pas de hors-texte* encapsulates the postmodern denial that words may refer to a reality beyond words,[137] which is readily extended to the rejection of the idea that scientific theories or statements refer to anything in the 'real world'. The implications of this are perhaps best studied from his 1971 essay 'La pharmacie de Platon', which rests on a close reading of *Phaedrus*, leading directly to its deconstruction.[138]

'Le pharmacie de Platon' exploits a fundamental ambiguity in the Greek word φάρμαϰον, which can bear the sense of 'drug' (hence, something that heals) and 'poison' (hence, something that kills – as in the hemlock that finally killed Socrates).[139] Derrida's close reading of the *Phaedrus* is allied to this point, in that he intends to demonstrate that there is a close association between writing and φάρμαϰον, in that both are possessed of the 'binary oppositions' that render the engagement with a text so problematic. Even at this early stage in the essay, Derrida is laying the ground for its closing scenes, which invite us to imagine a somewhat flustered Plato scrabbling about in his pharmacy, trying to 'isolate the good from the bad, the true from the false'.[140] Is the substance he possesses the cure for humanity's ills, or a poison which will destroy it? Derrida's point is that we cannot know, so that, in the end, we have to realize that 'nontruth is the truth'.

This is all very well, but it bears no relation to the empirical science that we know as pharmacology, which aims to investigate the molecular basis of how drugs work, so that new drugs may be developed and existing ones adapted for superior or innovative clinical application. Having had occasion to make use of what many regard as the best

[137] Samuel Wheeler, 'Indeterminacy of French Interpretation: Derrida and Davidson', in Ernest LePore (ed.), *Truth and Interpretation: Perspectives on the Philosophy of Donald Davidson*. Oxford: Blackwell, 1986, 477–94.

[138] For an English translation, see Jacques Derrida, *Dissemination*. Chicago: University of Chicago Press, 1981, 63–171. There is a useful study of this work in Andrew J. McKenna, *Violence and Difference: Girard, Derrida and Deconstruction*. Urbana, IL: University of Illinois Press, 1992. I am puzzled by the decision to compare Derrida with Girard, in that the latter does not engage with Derrida to any great extent, and seems to miss that 'Plato's Pharmacy' is basically a criticism of philosophical essentialism. It is certainly true that Derrida explores the idea of a 'scapegoat' (130–4), but this is primarily to demonstrate the indeterminacy of meaning of words.

[139] Derrida, *Disseminations*, 69–71. For the hemlock point, see 126–7.

[140] Derrida, *Disseminations*, 168–9.

account of modern pharmacology, I can report that the work makes no reference whatsoever to Derrida.[141] It does, however, offer an intellectually rigorous account, grounded in extensive empirical investigation, of what is known of the fundamental principles of the action of drugs. Furthermore, it makes the entirely proper point that a drug which can cure in one context can kill in another (usually through overdose). The ambiguity in the Greek term φάρμακον can thus be held to relate to an observed clinical effect, despite Derrida's rather ambitious and puzzling linguistic analysis of the term.

The fact that the anticoagulant properties of warfarin[142] can be used remedially (in dealing with stroke patients) or lethally (as a rat poison) does not for one moment impel anyone to the conclusion that 'nontruth is truth', but demonstrates the importance of understanding how this physiologically active compound works.[143] The same point applies to the pharmacological action of strychnine,[144] a poison in some situations and a palliative in others. Often it is the same physiological action – such as anticoagulance – that preserves health in one context, and destroys it in another. Derrida's musings about the ambivalence of φάρμακον are thus without any real physiological basis.

Roger Kimball identifies the fundamental flaw in Derrida's argument with an elegance I cannot hope to match, when he slyly points out that Derrida's statements on the disconnection of signifier and signified[145]

. . . have the handicap of being continually refuted by experience. When Derrida leaves Plato's pharmacy and goes into a Parisian one, he depends mightily on the fact that there *is* an outside to language, that when he asks for *aspirin* he will not be given *arsenic* instead . . . But of course, if some unscrupulous pharmacist were to substitute arsenic for aspirin, Derrida would learn to reconnect the signifier with the signified right speedily.

Social constructivism: the strong programme

The idea of somehow being 'bound by evidence' is held to be particularly distasteful by some more radical thinkers, who hold that the autonomy of the individual thinker is fatally compromised by the notion of being

---

[141] H. P. Rang, M. M. Dale, J. Ritter and P. Gardner, *Pharmacology*. 4th edn. New York: Churchill Livingstone, 2001.
[142] 3–(α-acetonylbenzyl)–4–hydroxycoumarin.
[143] See the full discussion in Rang, *Pharmacology*, 314–17.
[144] Rang, *Pharmacology*, 324–5.
[145] Kimball, *Experiments against Reality*, 12.

held accountable to an alleged objective reality, or being judged by how faithful an account of its inner workings they offer. Many postmodern writers regard this as an act of crass intellectual servility. Realism demeans, by denying the total creativity and freedom that they regard as the hallmark of academic excellence. Most postmodern thinkers seem to take anti-realism for granted, regarding those who hold realist positions as puzzling hangovers from an earlier and less enlightened era. We construct our own worlds, rather than being obliged to inhabit or inherit those invented by others. The social construction of reality is vastly to be preferred to its empirical investigation.

It will be clear that the phrase 'social construction' here has a much stronger meaning than the sense in which we have used it throughout this volume. The term is used throughout this project to refer to the fact that, when attempting to offer an account of the real world, one is often obliged to use models or constructs as provisional heuristic devices to allow a greater degree of understanding of how a system functions, or how a complex entity is to be mentally pictured. The model or construct is ultimately to be judged in terms of how effectively it accounts for the observational data, and the predictions it allows concerning hitherto unknown or uncorrelated phenomena. In its much stronger sense, however, the term refers to the principle that communities construct ideas and values *to suit their own ends*. These are not understood to be a response to reality, but as a construction which reflects and advances the interests and agendas of a specific social grouping. From a classic Marxist perspective, communities develop ideologies as protective cocoons which shield their ideas and values from erosion precisely because they are *fabricated* from those same ideas and values, and are designed to shield those communities from the truth that would otherwise destroy them.[146] The 'social constructivists' in the natural sciences are thus those who argue that the community of scientists, especially in their practices, demonstrate a propensity to generate ideas which suit their own interests and advance their own agendas.

Yet the implication of social factors in scientific method cannot be ignored, even if it can be overstated to the point of absurdity. We may distinguish between two approaches to the situation:

1. The weak approach, which holds that the development of scientific theories cannot be explained solely with reference to the external world, but must take account of at least some social factors.

---

[146] See the discussion in Berger and Luckmann, *The Social Construction of Reality: A Treatise in the Sociology of Knowledge*.

2. The strong approach, which holds that the nature of the external world plays no role in determining the development of scientific theories.[147]

The weak approach is true in a trivial sense, in that an observer's historical and social location determines her access to the external world. Before the invention of the telescope, it was impossible to see the rings of the planet Saturn, or observe the phases of Venus. And if the socio-economic situation of the observer were such that she could not afford a telescope, these aspects of the external world would remain inaccessible to her, while remaining theoretically observable. It is also true in a more significant manner, in that social factors unquestionably play a part in the reception of scientific theories – a matter to which we shall return in the following volume. For example, Stephen J. Gould suggests that one of the reasons why Darwinism was not well received initially in Victorian England was that Darwin's ideas on sexual selection implied that females were more active in the process of selection than contemporary social mores allowed.[148]

Yet the stronger approach has clear problems, both in terms of its own self-referentiality (how does it account for itself?) and the account it offers of the natural sciences. The suggestion that an attempt to encounter or engage with the external world plays no role in natural scientific methods is patently untrue. Bruno Latour defends this position in his *Science in Action*, a rather uninformed work which intends to set out a series of 'Rules of Method' for the sociologist of science.[149] These take it for granted that nature never exercises a decisive role over how scientific controversies are settled. The real issue is not how the external world shapes theoretical debates, but how *perceptions or representations of the external world* shape such discussions. These human-created perceptions fit neatly into the category of things that sociologists can study.

The importance of this point is brought out in a study by the British sociologist Ted Benton, who argues that sociology has developed a

[147] Peter T. Manicas and Alan Rosenberg, 'Naturalism, Epistemological Individualism and "The Strong Programme" in the Sociology of Knowledge', *Journal for the Theory of Social Behaviour* 15 (1985), 76–101.

[148] Stephen J. Gould, 'The Confusion over Evolution', *New York Review of Books*, 19 November 1992, 47–54.

[149] Bruno Latour, *Science in Action: How to Follow Scientists and Engineers through Society*. Cambridge, MA: Harvard University Press, 1987. For comments and criticism, see Yves Gingras, 'Un air de radicalisme: sur quelques tendance récentes en sociologie de la science et de la technologie', *Actes de la recherches en sciences sociales* 108 (1995), 3–17.

deeply entrenched view of the world which treats 'society' and 'nature' as mutually exclusive categories.[150] This imposition of radically dualist categories upon reality can be argued to be a direct consequence of the neo-Kantian and positivist assumptions which played such a pivotal role in the shaping of modern sociology. It is implicitly assumed within the discipline that the 'human' and 'cultural' take precedence over the 'natural'. As Benton observes:

> Contemporary sociologists mainly work within the broad terms of a conceptual matrix inherited from these founding traditions. This matrix is characterised by a categorial dualism which places 'nature' (and its cognates . . .) on one side of a deep ontological gulf, upon the other side of which are placed 'culture', 'signification', 'meaning', 'society'. The deployment of this dualism is governed by a wide variety of normative and epistemological strategies which privilege the variously defined social, cultural, symbolic domain over the residual 'brute' nature.

This insight allows us to appreciate why sociology maintains an ambivalent attitude towards the natural sciences, at times treating them as something to be mocked and debunked and at others as something to be respected and honoured. The social sciences are marked by a reluctance to talk about 'nature' itself; they prefer to speak of 'discourses about nature', thus placing a human intellectual agency between the sociologist and nature itself. Interestingly, this means that sociologists prefer to speak about or study the natural sciences, rather than nature itself, as this allows them to interpose a 'cultural' or 'social' entity – i.e., the community of natural scientists and its working methods – between themselves and 'nature'. Sociologists are not especially interested in nature, but in the way in which human agencies respond to it.

These considerations combine to yield what Kate Soper has termed a pervasive 'nature-scepticism' within the social sciences, which has contaminated just about every intellectual discipline which interfaces them. Nature is seen as uninteresting and crude; things start to get interesting only when human beings do something with it – whether they just think about it, or do something more transformative with it, such as create works of art (presumably avoiding the severely functional cubic shapes of Corbusier and Gropius), or build cities.[151]

---

[150] Ted Benton, 'Why are Sociologists Naturephobes?', in José López and Garry Potter (eds), *After Postmodernism: An Introduction to Critical Realism.* London: Athlone Press, 2001, 133–45.

[151] Kate Soper, *What is Nature? Culture, Politics and the Non-human.* Oxford: Blackwell, 1995.

There is a valid insight within this criticism of nature, which we have already explored thoroughly in the first volume of this work – namely, that 'nature' is a socially mediated concept, lacking the epistemic independence which is essential if it is to play a foundational or criteriological role in the sciences or theology. Yet there is also a serious shortcoming, which results from the insistence that 'discourse about nature' takes precedence over 'nature' itself, so that it is the manner and mode of the 'discourse about nature' which becomes determinative as to how nature is viewed and represented.

The obvious weakness of this viewpoint is brought out by Paul Gross and Norman Levitt, who offer the following example to counter this idea.[152] Imagine a group of people who are cooped up in a windowless office. A heated discussion breaks out as to whether it is raining or not. This discourse about nature is, of course, likely to be immensely erudite and stimulating, especially if the participants are all sociologists. But how does this discourse about the natural world in any way settle the question of whether it is raining or not? It is only by stepping outside that office and observing whether there are drops of water falling from the sky that we can determine whether it is raining.

A growing number of critics are coming to the conclusion that social constructivism is little more than sociological imperialism, dressed up for the sake of intellectual decency in a rather flimsy philosophical garment. In her careful study of the credentials of the 'strong pro-gramme', Margaret Archer stresses its failure to account for some elementary facts of intellectual life.[153] The insistence upon the social character and social causation of all knowledge means that there is nothing about beliefs themselves that can account for why they are supported or rejected. Furthermore, if all beliefs are relative to their social location, it follows that beliefs held at different times and places are incommensurable, in that they are subject to local idiomatic evaluation rather than being capable of judgement against truth, reason or logic.

In an important critique of the social constructivist account of the natural sciences, Bruno Latour offers a critique of the 'strong pro-gramme' of the sociology of knowledge, as applied to the natural sciences. Latour offers us an important insight which underscores the

---

[152] Paul R. Gross and Norman Levitt, *Higher Superstition: The Academic Left and its Quarrels with Science*. Baltimore, MD: Johns Hopkins University Press, 1998, 58.

[153] Margaret Archer, *Culture and Agency: The Place of Culture in Social Theory*. Cambridge: Cambridge University Press, 1996, 103–42.

importance of the natural sciences as a dialogue partner for theological reflection when he points out that the anti-realist attack on the natural sciences by sociologists merely represents an extension to the natural sciences of procedures already applied to religion and other phenomena that social scientists 'happen to despise'. Having hitherto reserved their constructivist approach to 'soft' targets such as religion, the sociologists now turned it to 'hard' targets, such as the natural sciences. For Latour, this represented a serious misjudgement, in that the obvious failure of the approach in the case of the 'hard' aspects of nature called into question its applicability to the 'soft' parts as well. For Latour, the notion that scientific theories are pure social constructs is as fantastic as it is incredible:[154]

> Society had to produce everything arbitrarily, including the cosmic order, biology, chemistry and the laws of physics. The implausibility of this claim was so blatant for the hard parts of nature that we suddenly realized how implausible it was for the 'soft' ones as well.

Perhaps for this reason, Karl Mannheim famously declared that the natural sciences and mathematics could not be addressed from the perspective of the sociology of knowledge.[155] Although this view reflected a consensus in the immediate post-war era, it was not long before it was challenged by those who argued that science constituted a practice, and was hence open to sociological investigation. The Cambridge crystollographer J. D. Bernal published an important study of the social function of science in 1939, which only received full attention once the war had ended.[156] Despite criticism from Michael Polanyi,[157] Bernal's writings may be argued to have laid the foundation for an increased sociological engagement with the natural sciences, leading to the ultimate conclusion that the natural sciences fell within the scope of

---

[154] Bruno Latour, *We Have Never Been Modern.* Cambridge, MA: Harvard University Press, 1993, 54–5.

[155] Karl Mannheim, *Essays on the Sociology of Knowledge.* London: Routledge & Kegan Paul, 1952. For further discussion, see Gregory Baum, *Truth beyond Relativism: Karl Mannheim's Sociology of Knowledge.* Milwaukee: Marquette University Press, 1977; Brian Longhurst, *Karl Mannheim and the Contemporary Sociology of Knowledge.* Basingstoke: Macmillan, 1989.

[156] J. D. Bernal, *The Social Function of Science.* London: Routledge, 1939. For analysis of this neglected figure, see Günter Kröber, *50 Jahre Bernals 'Die soziale Funktion der Wissenschaft': Programm, Probleme, Perspektiven.* Berlin: Akademie-Verlag, 1990.

[157] Steve Fuller, 'Social Epistemology and the Research Agenda of Science Studies', in Andrew Pickering (ed.), *Science as Practice and Culture.* Chicago: University of Chicago Press, 1992, 390–428.

the 'strong programme' in the sociology of knowledge. David Bloor argued that it was only a 'lack of nerve and will' that stopped sociologists from treating the natural sciences in the same way as religion;[158] indeed, he also insisted that mathematics must be brought within the scope of the 'strong programme'. This must now be seen as a serious misjudgement, in that the overuse of the method calls its general credibility into question. As Latour points out, the overapplication of an already questionable method showed 'how badly constructed were the social theory as well as the epistemology' that accompanied it. While the objects of scientific inquiry – such as religion – are 'much more social, much more fabricated, much more collective, than the "hard" parts of nature', they cannot in any way be regarded as the 'arbitrary receptacles of a full-fledged society'. They are, Latour insists, 'much more real, nonhuman and objective than those shapeless screens on which society needed to be projected'.[159]

Significantly, Latour here writes as one sympathetic to the social constructivist claim. This is evident in his 1988 article on Einstein's theory of relativity, which offers a 'relativistic' reading of Einstein's popular text *Relativity: The Special and General Theory* (1920).[160] Latour's attempt to demonstrate that Einstein's theory of relativity is a social construction has been severely critiqued. John Huth points out how Latour's approach rests on a 'distorted reading' or a 'very sloppy or deliberate misinterpretation' of Einstein's text, and 'a redefinition of terms whose only purpose appears to suit Latour's own ideological needs'.[161] Yet our interest here is not how or whether Latour misrepresents Einstein for constructivist ends; it is to point out that these pertinent criticisms of the constructivist programme come from one of its most significant practitioners.

There can be no doubt that social factors condition, perhaps to an ultimately indeterminate extent, the manner in which reality is represented. The most obvious example of this is the way in which news media, particularly television, seek to portray themselves as offering an 'objective view of the world', while actually offering a socially-

[158] David Bloor, *Knowledge and Social Imagery*. 2nd edn. Chicago: University of Chicago Press, 1991, 4.

[159] Latour, *We Have Never Been Modern*, 55.

[160] Bruno Latour, 'A Relativistic Account of Einstein's Relativity', *Social Studies of Science* 18 (1988), 3–44.

[161] John Huth, 'Latour's Relativity', in Noretta Koertge (ed.), *A House Built on Sand: Exposing Postmodernist Myths about Science*. New York: Oxford University Press, 1998, 181–92; 191.

conditioned angle on matters. Thus a comparative study of news reporting in Italy and the United States indicated that:[162]

> Formal conventions of news reporting often attributed to the technology of television by analysts, or the 'the nature of things' by journalists, in fact stem from features of a country's political culture. All of this work recognizes that news is a form of literature and that one key resource journalists work with is the cultural tradition of storytelling and picture-making and sentence construction they inherit, with a number of vital assumptions about the world built in.

Yet the idea that social factors completely *determine* – as opposed to influence – the perception and representation of reality is faced with serious difficulties, as we shall indicate.

According to the strong social constructivist thesis, reality is actively constructed and reconstructed by individual actors. Sociologists working from within this perspective argue that social phenomena simply do not have an 'objective' existence, but must be interpreted and given meanings by those who encounter them. From this perspective, all knowledge of the world is a human construction rather than a mirror of some independent reality. In that the natural sciences have often portrayed themselves as holding up a mirror by which the natural order may be viewed,[163] it is perhaps little cause for surprise that, from the outset, the movement had a particular animus against the natural sciences. In his major study of the nature of social constructivism, Ian Hacking notes how 'many science-haters and know-nothings latch on to constructionism as vindicating their impotent hostility to the sciences. Constructionism provides a voice for that rage against reason.'[164] Hacking notes how the classic questions of philosophy and the natural sciences are systematically marginalized in the headlong stampede to demonstrate that all is the result of the possession and exercise of power. 'Politics, ideology, and power matter more than metaphysics to most advocates of construction analyses of social and cultural phenomena. Talk of construction tends to undermine the authority of knowledge and categorization.'[165]

---

[162] James Curran and Michael Gurevitch, *Mass Media and Society*. London: Edward Arnold, 2000, 155.

[163] For a critique of this notion in the sciences or philosophy in general, see Richard Rorty, *Philosophy and the Mirror of Nature*. Princeton: Princeton University Press, 1979.

[164] Ian Hacking, *The Social Construction of What?*. Cambridge, MA: Harvard University Press, 1999, 67.

[165] Hacking, *The Social Construction of What?*, 58.

The anti-realism of the social constructivists has been fuelled by what, with the benefit of hindsight, may be seen to have been a careless choice of name for a principle enunciated by Werner Heisenberg – the 'uncertainty principle'. In the hands of social constructivists such as Stanley Aronowitz, this principle becomes an assertion of the epistemological relativism of the natural sciences, a candid admission of the failures of the sciences to grasp the objectivity which they craved and sought to persuade others that they possessed.[166] It need hardly be added that this is not what Heisenberg's principle articulates, nor even what it can reasonably be taken to imply. While some philosophers, such as Michael Dummett and W. V. O. Quine, regard quantum mechanics as warranting a wholesale retreat from realism, others more conversant with the discipline are clear that no such abandonment of realism is required, even by the Copenhagen interpretation.[167]

The Sokal hoax and postmodern interpretations of natural science

The serious misrepresentation of the working methods and assumptions of the natural sciences by social constructivists has been the subject of much comment. In a major analysis of postmodern 'engagements' with the natural sciences, Alan Sokal and Jean Bricmont demonstrate how such postmodern luminaries as Jacques Lacan and Luce Irigaray systematically misrepresent the natural sciences in their attempts to undermine their claims to objectivity.[168] As an example of the pseudo-scientific jibberish produced by Irigaray, we may consider the following:[169]

> If the identity of the human subject is defined in the works of Freud by a *Spaltung*, this is also the word used for nuclear fission. Nietzsche also perceived his ego as an atomic nucleus threatened with explosion. As for Einstein, the main issue he raises, in my mind, is that, given his interest in accelerations without electromagnetic re-equilibrations, he leaves us with only one hope, his God.

Sokal and Bricmont have no difficulty in pointing out the utter confusion and posturing underlying this passage:

---

[166]   See his dense and perplexing work: Stanley Aronowitz, *Science as Power: Discourse and Ideology in Modern Society*. Minneapolis: University of Minnesota Press, 1988.

[167]   See the full analysis of Christopher Norris, *Quantum Theory and the Flight from Realism: Philosophical Responses to Quantum Mechanics*. London: Routledge, 2000.

[168]   Alan Sokal and Jean Bricmont, *Fashionable Nonsense: Postmodern Intellectuals' Abuse of Science*. New York: Picador, 1998.

[169]   Cited and critiqued by Sokal and Bricmont, *Fashionable Nonsense*, 107–8.

Concerning Nietzsche: the atomic nucleus was discovered in 1911, and nuclear fission in 1938; the possibility of a nuclear chain reaction, leading to an explosion, was studied theoretically during the late 1930s and sadly realized experimentally during the 1940s. It is thus highly improbable that Nietzsche (1844–1900) could have perceived his ego 'as an atomic nucleus threatened with explosion' . . . The expression 'accelerations without electromagnetic re-equilibrations' has no meaning in physics; it is entirely Irigaray's invention . . . General relativity bears no relation to nuclear power plants; Irigaray has probably confused it with special relativity.

And so on. The point that Sokal and Bricmont make so powerfully through this documentation in studied ignorance is that postmodern critiques of the natural sciences generally rest upon a stunning lack of knowledge of their methods and theories.

Aware of the absurdities of many postmodern critiques of the sciences, Sokal published a spoof article, mimicking the pretentious and empty phrases of contemporary cultural theorists. The article – portentously entitled 'Transgressing the Boundaries: Toward a Transformative Hermeneutics of Quantum Gravity' – was snapped up by the journal *Social Text*, which was then preparing a special issue to reaffirm the criticisms directed against the natural sciences by an assortment of postmodern thinkers.[170] Sokal's piece seemed an ideal weapon in this battle. Sadly, Sokal revealed the hoax shortly after publication of the May 1996 number of *Social Text*. The hoax has become one of the most celebrated academic pranks of the twentieth century.

Sokal begins his article by establishing his postmodernist credentials for the benefit of his readers. He criticizes natural scientists for continuing to cling to the 'dogma imposed by the long post-Enlightenment hegemony over the Western intellectual outlook'. And what dogma are we talking about there? None other than the notion that there exists an external world, whose properties are independent of human beings, and that human beings can obtain reliable, if imperfect and tentative knowledge of these properties 'by hewing to the "objective" procedures and epistemological strictures prescribed by the (so-called) scientific method'.

Sokal then states – without substantiation – that this 'dogma' has already been thoroughly undermined by the theories of general relativity and quantum mechanics. Physical reality has been shown to be nothing

---

[170] Text reprinted in Sokal and Bricmont, *Fashionable Nonsense*, 212–58.

more than a 'social and linguistic construct'. Even better: once objective values are now realized to be socially-constructed:

> The π of Euclid and the G of Newton, formerly thought to be constant and universal, are now perceived in their ineluctable historicity; and the putative observer becomes fatally de-centred, disconnected from any epistemic link to a space-time point that can no longer be defined by geometry alone.

Recent developments within quantum gravity, he argued, not only affirm postmodern denials of the objectivity of truth, but also mark the beginning of a new kind of physics that would be truly 'liberatory', of genuine service to progressive political causes.

Throughout the article, Sokal mimicked the uncomprehending citation of natural scientists, followed by an overheated and overstated interpretation of its significance for cultural studies. Sokal jumps from correct scientific statements to drawing absurd conclusions concerning their implications, without the benefit of any intermediate reasoning. By doing this, Sokal intended to demonstrate the abuse of natural science by cultural theorists. Thus Niels Bohr's mild observation that in quantum mechanics 'a complete elucidation of one and the same object may require diverse points of view' is immediately interpreted, without any serious argumentation or documentation, to mean the end of the allegedly 'objective' scientific method.

> In such a situation, how can a self-perpetuating secular priesthood of credentialed 'scientists' purport to maintain a monopoly on the production of scientific knowledge? The content and methodology of postmodern science thus provide powerful intellectual support for the progressive political project, understood in its broadest sense: the transgressing of boundaries, the breaking down of barriers, the radical democratization of all aspects of social, economic, political and cultural life.

Sokal concludes by calling for the development of a correspondingly emancipated mathematics which, by setting to one side the restrictions of set theory, would affirm and sustain the progressive and postmodern ambitions of emerging physical science. 'A liberatory science cannot be complete without a profound revision of the canon of mathematics.'

So what is the value of this? Sokal's hoax, after all, did not establish any new facts, or invalidate any existing arguments. In one sense, it was merely a joke which gave those in the know some light relief in the midst of trying to make sense of some of the more turgid forests of postmodern prose. A spoof paper on Einstein's theory of relativity would hardly cause a major re-evaluation of this cornerstone of twentieth-century physics. Sokal's hoax severely undermined credibility in social constructive accounts of the scientific enterprise by raising serious questions as to whether postmodern writers actually understood the scientific notions they brandished about in their discussions, and thence eroded credibility of their judgements concerning them. The public credibility of postmodernism was placed on the line by Sokal's article. The outcome raised serious questions concerning its plausibility. Surely, many asked, there had to be something more sensible. What, they wondered, might replace postmodernity?

After postmodernity – what?

All is not well within postmodern thinking. Anti-realism is in retreat within the social sciences, as the intellectual merits of critical realism gain an increasingly sympathetic hearing. As Garry Potter and José López point out, postmodernity 'was one of, if not *the*, most significant of the intellectual currents which swept the academic world in the last third of the twentieth century'.[171] It has had a major impact on most aspects of western culture during the late twentieth century. Yet its failings and weaknesses have become increasingly apparent, not least because of its failures in relation to the natural sciences. Postmodernism 'seriously bruised the self-confidence to which reason, objectivity and knowledge had become accustomed', extending its criticisms beyond the human to the natural sciences:

> As far as the latter were concerned, postmodernism represented the most radical challenge to its epistemological foundations since the Enlightenment. One could say uncharitably that unfortunately it represented an ultimately intellectually incoherent challenge to those foundations.

The problem, as we have seen, is that the critiques directed by postmodernity against the alleged claims to objectivity of the natural sciences proved embarrassingly self-referential. Most damning of all, postmodernity has signally failed to explain why it is the case that the natural sciences continue to produce useful knowledge. Why do the laws of physics prove resilient to issues of gender, race or social class – to name only the three most obvious factors in a constructivist account?

---

[171] Garry Potter and José López, 'After Postmodernism: The New Millennium', in José López and Garry Potter (eds), *After Postmodernism: An Introduction to Critical Realism*. London: Athlone Press, 2001, 3–16; 4.

And why can these laws be represented by mathematics, when mathematics must also be regarded as a social construction, reflecting the power play of interest groups?

Postmodernity has defeated itself, by deploying weapons that could be used more effectively against it than in its support. As the credibility of postmodern accounts of the natural sciences wanes, an increasingly vigorous critique of its assumptions and methods is gaining momentum.[172] Its failures, inconsistences and special pleadings are falling on increasingly suspicious intellectual terrain, to be picked up and examined with a new critical acumen. The rise of the movement known as 'critical realism' – to which we shall turn in a later chapter – reflects this growing conviction within the social sciences that constructivism has had its day. As Potter and López comment:[173]

> Critical realism puts forward epistemological caution with respect to scientific knowledge, as opposed to a self-defeating relativist scepticism. Science is not pure, and can contain an ideologically distorted element in both explanations and the manner used to arrive at them. There are sociological determinants in the process of knowledge production whether in the social or natural sciences. The production of knowledge itself is a social process and one in which language is deeply embedded. However, knowledge cannot be reduced to its sociological determinants of production.

The interplay of social factors with our perceptions of the real world is complex, both in the natural sciences and in Christian theology, and demands careful attention. Yet the recognition of the role of social factors in the acquisition and representation of knowledge does *not* mean that knowledge is reduced to social determinants.

> We can (and do!) rationally judge between competing theories on the basis of their intrinsic merits as explanations of reality. We do so both scientifically and in everyday life. If we could not, we would not be very frequently successful in our most mundane activities. Science, in one sense at least, is merely a refinement and extension of what we do in the practical functioning of everyday life.

---

[172] See, for example, Calvin O. Schrag, *The Self after Postmodernity*. New Haven, CT: Yale University Press, 1999, which offers a significant critique of deconstructionist and postmodernist views of the self as something ceaselessly changing, and notes in particular the role of religion in defining the 'self'. Schrag's earlier writings include an important affirmation of the notion of rationality in the face of postmodern pluralisms: Calvin O. Schrag, *The Resources of Rationality: A Response to the Postmodern Challenge*. Bloomington, IN: Indiana University Press, 1992.

[173] Potter and López, 'After Postmodernism', 9.

This major paradigm shift within the social sciences opens the way to the recovery of a realist approach to the natural sciences, and supremely to the realism implicit in a scientific theology. We must therefore ask how the critical realist agenda allows the social location of theologizing – and its possible influence on the outcome of that process – to be given its proper place in this process, rather than denied or absolutized. The importance of the role of 'tradition' in this process (chapter 8) is thus affirmed and safeguarded. In the present chapter, we have considered a number of questions focusing on the idea of the scientific project as a response to reality. Yet there is a difficulty implicit within this assertion – a difficulty which demands much further discussion. It has become increasingly common within the natural and social sciences to speak of a *stratified* reality. Why is this so, and what are its implications for a scientific theology? So we turn to consider the notion of 'critical realism', and its consequences for our project.

Chapter 10

Critical Realism: Engaging with a Stratified Reality

The previous chapter set out the case for asserting that there exists a real world, independent of the human mind, which that mind is capable of grasping and representing. The extent to which the knower is involved in that process of grasping and representing has been the matter of debate. It may be helpful to offer a broad-brush depiction of three options, to help locate the issues involved, and the trajectory to be navigated in the present chapter.

1. Naïve realism: Reality impacts directly upon the human mind, without any reflection on the part of the human knower. The resulting knowledge is directly determined by an objective reality within the world.

2. Critical realism: Reality is apprehended by the human mind which attempts to express and accommodate that reality as best it can with the tools at its disposal – such as mathematical formulae or mental models.

3. Postmodern anti-realism: The human mind freely constructs its ideas without any reference to an alleged external world.

In recent years, the term 'critical realism' has come to be used within theological circles to designate a style of realism which is sensitive to the historically situated and personally involved character of theological knowledge, while resolutely declining to let go of the ideals of truth, objectivity and rationality. The essential issue which distinguishes 'naïve realism' from 'critical realism' is often argued to be the latter's recognition of the active involvement of the knower in the process of knowing. The New Testament scholar N. T. Wright offers an excellent account of this general position, which he describes as[1]

> a way of describing the process of 'knowing' that acknowledges the *reality of the thing known, as something other than the knower* (hence 'realism'), while also fully acknowledging that the only access we have to this reality lies along the spiralling path of *appropriate dialogue or conversation between the knower and the thing known* (hence 'critical'). This path leads to critical reflection on the products of our enquiry into 'reality', so that our assertions about 'reality' acknowledge their own provisionality. Knowledge, in other words, although in principle concerning realities independent of the knower, is never itself independent of the knower.

Wright here captures something of the tension that we find in Gadamer's *Truth and Method*. In this work, Gadamer rejects objectifying approaches to attaining knowledge, based upon the natural sciences, and locates 'truth' in the interplay between *interpretandum* and *interpretans*. Truth is not an objective reality in its own right, nor is it the subjective creation of the individual; rather, truth lies in the relationship between text and interpreter. For Gadamer, the fact that 'in the knowing involved . . . the knower's own being is involved' raises fundamental questions concerning the possibility of 'disinterested' or 'objective' knowledge.[2]

Yet perhaps more importantly, we can see in critical realism an attempt to recognize the role of the knower, as set out in William James' celebrated early essay 'Remarks on Spencer's Definition of Mind as Correspondence', which appeared in the *Journal of Speculative Philosophy* in January 1878. Herbert Spencer (1820–1903) is best known for coining the phrase 'the survival of the fittest' to summarize the leading themes of Charles Darwin's theory of natural selection. For James, Spencer's importance lay more in his theory of knowledge,[3] which James regarded as insufficiently attentive to the role of the human agent. James' comments highlight the issues which underlie the critical realist agenda:[4]

---

[1] N. T. Wright, *The New Testament and the People of God*. London: SPCK, 1992, 35.

[2] Hans-Georg Gadamer, *Truth and Method*. London: Sheed & Ward, 1975, 446–7.

[3] For some contemporary assessments, see E. Beckett, 'The Spencerian Philosophy', *Edinburgh Review* 159 (1884), 41–81; A. M. Fairbairn, 'Herbert Spencer's Philosophy and the Philosophy of Religion', *Contemporary Review* 40 (1881), 74–92. These are brought together in the useful collection Michael W. Taylor (ed.), *Herbert Spencer: Contemporary Assessments*. London: Routledge, 1996.

[4] William James, *Essays in Radical Empiricism*. Cambridge, MA: Harvard University Press, 1976, 21.

The knower is an actor, and co-efficient of the truth on the one side, whilst on the other he registers the truth which he helps to create. Mental interests, hypotheses, postulates, so far as they are bases for human action – action which to a great extent transforms the world – help to *make* the truth which they declare.

This insight does not pose a challenge to the notion that there exists a world, independent of the observer. It is to acknowledge that the knower is involved in the process of knowing, and that this involvement must somehow be expressed within a realist perspective on the world. With this point in mind, we may begin to explore the particular style of realism which is regarded as appropriate to a scientific theology.

On exploring realism

Realism remains the most satisfying and resilient account of the outcome of the human engagement with the natural world, despite the rhetoric of scorn directed against it by postmodern thinkers and others. The natural sciences are widely judged to have successfully seen off post-modern criticisms of their fundamental assumptions, helped to no small extent by the disturbing manner in which some French and Belgian postmodern writers have allowed it to be understood that they possess a deep knowledge of this field, while in reality having a painfully superficial acquaintance with the sciences, often limited to its often arcane vocabulary, particularly in the field of quantum mechanics.[5]

Nor has the robustness of realism been limited to the field of the natural sciences. In literature, the confident predictions of the 1960s and 1970s that literary realism would founder have been shown to be premature.[6] Realism – understood as a mimetic representation of experience and the organization of narrative according to a logic of causality and temporal sequence – continues to flourish.[7] It is, however, within the social sciences that some especially interesting developments have taken place, with considerable relevance to any understanding of the nature of religious reality, and its relation to the natural sciences.

In the first volume of this series, we offered a preliminary critique of the form of reductionism found in such works as Willem Drees's

---

[5] See the celebrated exposé of Alan Sokal and Jean Bricmont, *Fashionable Nonsense: Postmodern Intellectuals' Abuse of Science*. New York: Picador, 1998, discussed in the previous chapter.

[6] See the criticisms in Robert E. Scholes, *The Fabulators*. New York: Oxford University Press, 1967.

[7] David Lodge, 'The Novelist Today: Still at the Crossroads?', in *The Practice of Writing*. New York: Penguin Putnam, 1996, 3–19.

Religion, Science and Naturalism (vol. 1, 124–32),[8] and promised a more substantial engagement in the present volume. This engagement takes a form of the exposition and theological application of Roy Bhaskar's 'critical realism', which calls into question the reductionism which lies at the heart of Drees's approach. We shall return to deal with the reductionist rejection of metaphysics in the third volume of this series.[9] We begin by setting the scene for the rise of critical realism in the social sciences.

The new realism in the social sciences

It is clear that there is a new interest in realism within the social sciences. This is evident from John R. Searle's important book *The Construction of Social Reality* (1995). Searle here defends the idea that there exists a real world, consisting of objectivities which can be broadly classified under two categories. First, there are 'brute facts' which exist independently of human thought. For example, Mount Everest has snow and ice at its summit whether I know this or not. This fact is not dependent upon my cognitive activity. Second, there are 'social facts' which, while being objectively true, depend to varying extents upon human intentions, functions and rules. An example of such a fact is 'John Searle is a citizen of the United States of America'. Searle suggests that we should regard such social facts as existing as 'on top of brute physical facts' – in effect, as an overlay.[10] We can see here the beginnings of a stratified approach to reality, which we shall explore in more detail in interaction with Roy Bhaskar.

For Searle, 'social facts' are not inventions, or free constructions of the human mind. They are to be regarded as realities consisting of objective facts. Thus the factual statement 'John Searle is a citizen of the United States of America' rests upon the fact that there is indeed a

---

[8] Willem B. Drees, *Religion, Science and Naturalism*. Cambridge and New York: Cambridge University Press, 1995. Note that Drees and Bhaskar use the term 'naturalism' in quite different senses.

[9] Drees here reflects a widespread consensus within late-twentieth-century liberal Protestant theology that metaphysics is either an impossibility or an irrelevance – see, for example, the superficial dismissal of the notion in Robert H. King, 'The Task of Systematic Theology', in Peter Hodgon and Robert King (eds), *Christian Theology: An Introduction to its Traditions and Tasks*. Philadelphia: Fortress Press, 1982, 1–27, especially 25; or the more considered (but equally critical) assessment in John Macquarrie, *Principles of Christian Theology*. 2nd edn. London: SCM Press, 1977, 15–16.

[10] John R. Searle, *The Construction of Social Reality*. New York: Free Press, 1995, 35. For an introduction to Searle's ideas, see Robert van Gulick and Ernest Lepore, *John Searle and His Critics*. Oxford: Blackwell, 1991.

nation called the United States of America. This is not a 'natural' entity such as a river or mountain, but one depending upon human conventions and laws. Though based upon the 'brute fact' of the landmass of America, the concept of the 'United States of America' represents a political and social overlay on this physical entity.

Searle argues that those who reject realism in favour, for example, of pure social constructivism ultimately depend upon realist assumptions further down the line – for example, by holding that social beings exist, and that they are able to construct entities. Those who argue that things are constructed out of (or in response to) specific contexts are obliged to suppose that these contexts exist in order to explain the process of construction. And so on. Searle's argument, followed through to its logical conclusion, is that alternatives to realism – whether in the natural or social sciences – are ultimately obliged to presuppose the truth of realism in order to carry weight.

Realism, then, is back in fashion. I note this as being of importance; in the end, however, my defence of realism has nothing to do with intellectual fashion, but with the basic conviction that realism offers the best explanation of the successes and strategies of the natural sciences, and that it is clearly presupposed and applied by the classic Christian theological tradition, within which I stand. It has much to offer an orthodox theology, not least through its affirmation that responsible theological statements *about* God can be taken to refer *to* God. This runs counter to those who insist that we must be free to construct our own worlds and representations of the world without being fettered by the oppressive notion of an 'objective reality' which we are somehow obliged to respect in our reflections.

This is not, however, to foreclose the all-important discussion of what *form* of realism is to be adopted in the case of a theological science. 'Realism' designates a family of philosophies, with clear resemblances yet equally obvious divergences. The extent of those divergences is such that Jarrett Leplin once commented that 'realism is a majority position whose advocates are so seriously divided as to appear a minority'.[11] While a scientific theology is unquestionably committed to a realist perspective, it is essential to explore what form of realism is appropriate for its specific concerns and tasks. In the present chapter, we shall expore the 'critical realism' of Roy Bhaskar, which I believe

[11] Jarrett Leplin (ed.), *Scientific Realism*. Berkeley, CA: University of California Press, 1984, 1. See further Rom Harré, *Varieties of Realism: A Rationale for the Natural Sciences*. Oxford: Blackwell, 1986.

has considerable potential in catalysing scientific theological reflection and consolidation.

Critical realism and the autonomy of theology

Yet a difficulty must be considered before proceeding any further. Does not the use of *any* philosophy – whether the critical realism of Roy Bhaskar or the existentialism of Martin Heidegger[12] – run the risk of making theology dependent upon such a philosophy? Is not what is being proposed tantamount to the enslavement of theology to a philosophy – a development that Karl Barth and others so vigorously opposed?

Barth's agenda demands to be taken with the utmost seriousness. His rhetoric of theological freedom refuses to reduce God to one element of a system. In rejecting any and every kind of philosophical foundationalism, Barth subverts the colonization of theology by philosophy or any other discourse. He emphatically rejected the foundationalist claim that philosophy can provide secure universal knowledge. By strenuously insisting on the transcendence and integrity of the divine object of Christian theology, he set out to liberate theology from its bondage to philosophy, bourgeois culture and church tradition.[13] This concern must remain central to a scientific theology. *Yet these concerns may be honoured and accommodated within the ambit of a scientific theology.*

Three points must be made in response to this valid concern, as we prepare to use Roy Bhaskar's critical realism as a means of clarifying how the natural sciences may be deployed as *ancillae theologiae*.

1. As we have stressed, we are not in any way deploying this (or any) philosophy in a *foundational* role. The critical realism we will deploy is not being allowed to act as an *a priori* foundation for theology, determining its base and norms in advance. We have already raised fundamental criticisms of the forms of foundationalism which Barth so feared, and do not propose to deploy any philosophy in such a role.

2. Critical realism will be deployed in an ancillary, not foundational role. The theological modernism Barth opposed can be defined

---

[12] John Macquarrie, *An Existentialist Theology: A Comparison of Heidegger and Bultmann.* London: Collins, 1973.
[13] John Macken, *The Autonomy Theme in the Church Dogmatics of Karl Barth and His Critics.* Cambridge: Cambridge University Press, 1990.

by its fundamental assumption that theologians are obliged to adapt Christianity to the dominant or best available world-view. In contrast, Barth argued that theology should not be in the business of endorsing world-views or any secular theory of existence, still less of depending upon them. This leads me to suggest that, rather than committing itself to any particular world-view, Christian theology should use or appropriate as many world-views and forms of language as are appropriate to explicate the truth of God's Word *without* allowing itself to enter into a relation of dependence upon them.

3. The critical realism we shall be exploring in this section is an *a posteriori* discipline, whose central ideas rest on a sustained engagement with the social and natural structures of the world, rather than a dogmatic *a priori* determination of what those structures should be, and consequently how they should be investigated. Although I would not wish to press this point beyond its limits, it is fair to point out that Bhaskar's critical realism grounds methodology in social or natural ontology in much the same way that Barth grounds theology in the distinctive character and being of the Word of God.

Critical realism and Christian spirituality

A further consideration at this point is the growing importance of the discipline of Christian *spirituality*, which is often held to be distinguished from Christian *theology* on account of its recognition of the transformation of the knower by what is known. The issue is often raised with reference to the writings of Søren Kierkegaard, who argued that to *know* the truth is to be *known by* the truth. 'Truth' is something which affects our inner being, as we become involved in 'an appropriation process of the most passionate inwardness'.[14]

The very idea of a 'disinterested' knowledge of God has been criticized significantly within the classic theological tradition. Calvin may not use the vocabulary of critical realism in his *Institutes*, but most of its leading ideas are unquestionably present. True 'knowledge of God' and 'knowledge of ourselves' may not be had in isolation from one another, in that they interact. By knowing God, the knower is

---

[14] Søren Kierkegaard, *Unscientific Postscript*. London: Oxford University Press, 1941, 169–224. See P. L. Holmer, 'Kierkegaard and Religious Propositions', *Journal of Religion* 35 (1955), 135–46.

transformed.[15] Furthermore, as David F. Wright notes, Calvin is alert
to the importance of the positive role of analogies, metaphors and
models in the mediation of knowledge of God, linking this with his
doctrine of 'accommodation' – itself a response to the doctrine of
creation.[16] Revelation involves accommodated forms of disclosure, rather
than the direct revelation of objective knowledge. The knower is
involved in the process of knowing, in that the relationship of the
accommodated revelation to the objectivities it mirrors requires to be
established in the process of reception and interpretation.

While it is possible to argue that the distinction between 'spirituality'
and 'theology' is artificial, resting on a false construal of theology as an
objective and disinterested academic discipline, there are deeper issues
involved.[17] Thus Edward Farley argues that 'theology' has largely lost
its original meaning as 'sapiential and personal knowledge of divine
self-disclosure' leading to 'wisdom or discerning judgement indispensable for human living'. As classically conceived, theology constitutes
'not just objective science, but a personal knowledge of God and the
things of God'.[18] It will be clear that these concerns are taken up by
Wright's insistence that theological progress takes place 'along the
spiralling path of *appropriate dialogue or conversation between the knower
and the thing known*'. Critical realism might well hold the key to the
reintegration of theology and spirituality.

In what follows, we shall explore some ways of developing this notion
of 'critical realism', before proceeding to a sustained engagement with
and critical appropriation of the insights of Roy Bhaskar.

The variety of critical realisms

The term 'critical realism' has come to designate a variety of positions
within philosophy. The term predominantly refers at the time of

[15] Calvin, *Institutes of the Christian Religion* I.i.i. See further Edward A. Dowey, *The Knowledge of God in Calvin's Theology*. New York: Columbia University Press, 1952; T. H. L. Parker, *Calvin's Doctrine of the Knowledge of God*. Edinburgh: Oliver & Boyd, 1969.

[16] David F. Wright, 'Accommodation and Barbarity in John Calvin's Old Testament Commentaries', in A. Graeme Auld (ed.), *Understanding Poets and Prophets*. Sheffield: JSOT Press, 1993, 413–27.

[17] See the issues noted by Sandra Schneiders, 'Theology and Spirituality: Strangers, Rivals or Partners?', *Horizons* 13 (1986), 253–74; Philip Sheldrake, *Spirituality and Theology: Christian Living and the Doctrine of God*. London: Darton, Longman & Todd, 1998.

[18] Edward Farley, *Theologia: The Fragmentation and Unity of Theological Education*. Philadelphia: Fortress Press, 1983, x; 7. For further discussion of the issues raised by Farley, see Charles M. Wood, *Vision and Discernment: An Orientation in Theological Study*. Atlanta: Scholar's Press, 1985.

publication (2002) to the approach to the natural and social sciences associated with Roy Bhaskar, but which can be seen mirrored in countless other writers who are concerned to affirm the reality of an external world on the one hand, and acknowledge the social location of knowledge of that world on the other. For example, Pierre Bourdieu has stressed that objectivity concerning the natural world – which is to be regarded a real possibility – depends upon identification of the interests, agendas and concerns of the researcher, in order to eliminate unacknowledged biases on her part. An unreflexive investigator who declines to be critical about himself and his own *habitus* will experience difficulty in achieving the objectivity which is otherwise a real possibility.[19]

Despite clear Wittgensteinian 'family resemblances', there are obvious points of divergence between various readings of 'critical realism'. It is perhaps unsurprising that this has caused no small degree of confusion in the discussions of the matter within the literature dealing with the interaction of Christian theology and the natural sciences. In the interests of clarity, it is of no small importance to try to identify the various conceptions of 'critical realism' which are encountered in contemporary writings, and explore their value for the enterprise of a scientific theology. We may begin by offering a brief overview of the senses in which the term was used in the earlier twentieth century.

American critical realism

American critical realism came to prominence during the 1920s and 1930s, and is particularly associated with Arthur Lovejoy (1873–1962) and Roy Wood Sellars (1880–1967). Critical realism was conceived as a co-operative effort to oppose the fundamental ideas of American 'new realism',[20] which was characterized by its commitment to a direct knowledge of physical objects, which avoided the idealism they held to be implicit in alternative accounts of human knowledge. 'New realism' reached its zenith in the years preceding the First World War, and was particularly associated with Ralph Barton Perry (1876–1957). During his long tenure of the chair of philosophy at Harvard, Perry authored a number of important works defending the neutral monism of William James.[21] Despite its initial promise, the movement soon found itself

---

[19] Pierre Bourdieu, *In Other Words: Essays Towards a Reflexive Sociology.* Cambridge: Polity Press, 1990; idem, *Pascalian Meditations.* Cambridge: Polity Press, 2000.

[20] For the manifesto of this movement, see Edwin B. Holt et al., *The New Realism: Cooperative Studies in Philosophy.* New York: Macmillan, 1912.

[21] Most notably, Ralph Barton Perry, *Present Philosophical Tendencies: A Critical survey of Naturalism, Idealism, Pragmatism and Realism.* New York: Longmans Green, 1912.

encountering difficulties, not least in relation to the critical question of how the assertion of identity of the contents of consciousness and its object might be defended. Perry's *General Theory of Value* (1926),[22] which attempted to offer such an account, appeared to late to prevent the decline of the school in the face of a successful assault from the critical realists.

The critical realists opposed the epistemological monism which they deemed characteristic of new realism, and proposed in its place a theory of epistemological dualism, which maintained that content and object were ontologically different, and generally allowed human mental activity to play a greater role than new realism was prepared to concede. Of particular importance is the movement's clear orientation towards the natural sciences, and a principled determination to respond to its apparent explanatory successes. The term 'critical realism' was first coined by Roy Wood Sellars in 1915 to refer to an approach to scientific naturalism that stood in contrast to idealism, pragmatism and realism. These ideas were set out definitively in the 1920 collection *Essays in Critical Realism*, which can be regarded as the manifesto of the movement.[23] Beyond this, the movement achieved little in the way of consensus, and was particularly divided over precisely how one could and should move from content to object without recourse to the idealism they held to be implicit in Lockean theory.[24] Given this lack of consensus on such critical issues, it was inevitable that the movement should lose its coherence. Nevertheless, the movement developed insights of continuing importance. For example, Lovejoy's 1930 analysis of the 'revolt against dualism' led to his formulation of a 'temporalistic realism' which explicitly acknowledged the multilayered structure of the world, and thus entailed a variegated cognitive access to its reality.

This aspect of critical realism is of especial interest to a scientific theology, in that it recognizes the stratification of reality and the epistemological issues which this raises. The recognition of the stratification of reality is an integral aspect of the 'critical realism' of Roy Bhaskar, to which we shall turn presently. However, we must first consider the sense in which this term has come to be used within the science and religion community.

[22] Ralph Barton Perry, *General Theory of Value: Its Meaning and Basic Principles construed in Terms of Interest.* New York: Longmans Green, 1926.
[23] Durant Drake, *Essays in Critical Realism: A Co-operative Study of the Problem of Knowledge.* London: Macmillan, 1920. For an excellent general survey of the movement, see Roderick M. Chisholm, *The Foundations of Knowing.* Minneapolis: University of Minnesota Press, 1982, 109–93.
[24] See, for example, Arthur O. Lovejoy, *The Revolt against Dualism: An Inquiry concerning the Existence of Ideas.* Lasalle, IL: Open Court, 1930.

Critical realism within the science and religion community

The concept of critical realism has found a warm reception within the professional community which focuses on 'science and religion' issues. The key stimulus to this development has been a relatively brief passage in Ian Barbour's seminal work *Issues in Science and Religion* (1966), which with the benefit of hindsight can be seen to have determined the mould of future discussions of this issue. In this work, Barbour devotes a brief section to a discussion of 'the downfall of naïve realism', in which he offers a critical account of those unwise enough to believe that 'scientific theories are *literal descriptions* of nature as it is in itself'.[25] Now nobody likes to be thought of as 'naïve', and what is proposed as an alternative to this has at least a degree of intellectual sophistication which would surely merit the accolade of constituting a 'critical' realism. The distinction between a 'naïve' and 'critical' realism is at times determined more by rhetorical than substantial issues, perhaps creating the impression that this distinction has more to do with the perceived credulity or sophistication of those entertaining these rival theories, rather than their philosophical divergences.

Barbour clarifies his understanding of what is distinctive about a 'critical' realism in a brief yet important discussion of the role of the observer in the natural sciences.[26] A *critical* realism recognizes that the observer modulates the process of observation itself; that the quest for truth modifies the truth that is encountered; that the knower affects what can be known. Barbour holds that whereas older viewpoints believed that there existed an objective world which could be known independently of the observer, the rise of both quantum mechanics and relativity theory have called this into question. What were once 'held to be properties of the world independent of the knower' are now recognized to 'depend on the relationship of the object to the observer'.

This represents an insight which demands careful attention, and which is developed more thoroughly by writers such as Thomas F. Torrance, perhaps the most theologically rigorous exponent of a realist approach to issues in science and theology.[27] The interconnection of

---

[25] Ian G. Barbour, *Issues in Science and Religion*. Englewood Cliffs, NJ: Prentice–Hall, 1966, 284–6.

[26] Barbour, *Issues in Science and Religion*, 285.

[27] See the careful study of P. Mark Achtemeier, 'The Truth of Tradition: Critical Realism in the Thought of Alasdair MacIntyre and T. F. Torrance', *Scottish Journal of Theology* 47 (1994), 355–74; John D. Morrison, 'Heidegger, Correspondence Truth and the Realist Theology of Thomas Forsyth Torrance', *Evangelical Quarterly* 69 (1997), 139–55.

the knower and the known was clearly identified in his Auburn Lectures of 1938–9, and would be developed further at a later stage in his career with reference to the philosophy of Michael Polanyi.[28] This position has also gained increasing support within theological circles in recent decades.

We find such a notion of critical realism picked up and developed in subsequent discussions of the matter from within the science and religion community. Wentzel van Huyssteen offers a thoughtful account of a 'critical-realist perspective' on both the nature and rationality of theological statements, focusing especially on the significance of the category of 'metaphor' as a stimulus to theological conceptualizing.[29] In his useful book *Scientists as Theologians*, John Polkinghorne offers a brief account of the kind of 'critical realism' he finds in his own writings and those of Ian Barbour and Arthur Peacocke. 'It is a *critical* realism that the scientists-theologians defend. No naïve objectivity is involved in either discipline.'[30]

In his 1996 Terry Lectures at Yale University, however, Polkinghorne is much more explicit concerning the essence of a critical realism:[31]

> I believe that the advance of science is not just concerned with our ability to manipulate the physical world, but to gain knowledge of its actual nature. In a word, I am a realist. Of course, such knowledge is to a degree partial and corrigible. Our attainment is verisimilitude, not absolute truth. Our method is the creative interpretation of experience, not rigorous deduction from it. Thus I am a critical realist.

Polkinghorne goes on to set out six distinctive characteristics of the theological critical realism he wishes to commend:[32]

    1. 'Total account' theories of knowledge are to be resisted in favour of 'more piecemeal achievements'. By this, Polkinghorne means that 'we do not need to be right (or agree) about everything in order to be right (or agree) about some things'.

---

[28] Thomas F. Torrance, *Belief in Science and in Christian Life: The Relevance of Michael Polanyi's Thought for Christian Faith and Life.* Edinburgh: Handsel Press, 1980. More generally, see Joseph Kroger, 'Theology and Notions of Reason and Science: A Note on a Point of Comparison in Lonergan and Polanyi', *Journal of Religion* 56 (1976), 157–61.

[29] Wentzel van Huyssteen, *Theology and the Justification of Faith: Constructing Theories in Systematic Theology.* Grand Rapids, MI: Eerdmans, 1989, 125–97.

[30] John Polkinghorne, *Scientists as Theologians: A Comparison of the Writings of Ian Barbour, Arthur Peacocke and John Polkinghorne.* London: SPCK, 1996, 14.

[31] John Polkinghorne, *Belief in God in an Age of Science.* New Haven, CT: Yale University Press, 1998, 104.

[32] Polkinghorne, *Belief in God in an Age of Science*, 105–9.

2. A resistance to attempts to distil the essence of the scientific, usually in order to critique it. Thus the programmes adopted by Bas van Fraassen, Karl Popper or Richard Rorty capture aspects of the scientific programme, yet fail to offer even an adequate, let alone a total, account of its practices.

3. The recognition that 'theory and practice are inexplicably inter-twined in scientific thought', as a result of which scientific facts are to be understood *as having already been interpreted.* 'There is an inescapable self-sustaining circularity in the mutual relationship of theory and experiment.'

4. The recognition that 'there is no universal epistemology, but rather entities are knowable only through ways that conform to their idiosyncratic nature'.

5. Social factors do not determine the character of scientific knowl-edge, although they may accelerate or inhibit its growth – for example, by the perception that certain lines of research are fashionable or of immediate social importance.

6. The doctrine of scientific realism affords the best means of understanding our actual experience of doing science.

Polkinghorne's proposals merit close study, and represent a weighted and thoughtful statement of the possibilities for reclaiming a realist position within theology through a critical dialogue with the natural sciences, particularly physics.

Polkinghorne's thinking on realism is shaped by his experience of the natural sciences as both theory and practice, and takes full account of the critical role of an experimental culture. Elsewhere, however, we find the distinction between various styles of realism being discussed in terms which seem to owe little to the experimental methods and explanatory approaches of the natural science, and seem to constitute a long and wearying footnote to Kant which signally fails to take into account the debate within the philosophical community at large over the merits of the form of critical realism espoused by Roy Bhaskar and his colleagues since the late 1970s. For example, Kees van Kooten Niekerk, writing on what would seem to be the rather significant theme of 'A Critical Realist Perspective on the Dialogue between Theology and Science' in 1998, manages to avoid mention-ing, let alone engaging with, the substantial body of literature resulting from the seminal writings of Roy Bhaskar, to mention only the most significant writer active in this field.[33] To my knowledge, only Janet Martin Soskice has shown any real inclination to engage with Bhaskar's ideas to date, in her insightful defence of realism in relation to the use of 'metaphors' in religious language.[34]

This neglect reinforces the widespread perception that theology has developed an intellectual insularity, in that at least a significant section of the 'science and religion' community has become detached from the debates and resources of the mainline academic community. In his important recent study of 'Theological Critical Realism', Brad Shipway points out the need for serious dialogue between theological critical realists and the remainder of the critical realist community,[35] and notes that the former are 'painfully aware' of their 'quite peripheral position in modern academic dialogue'. This volume is intended to stimulate and encourage this process of discussion by engaging with Bhaskar's critical realism, which seems to offer all the virtues of the themes explored by Barbour and others, while having the considerable advantage of operating within the academic main-stream, rather than what many have regrettably come to view as an unfashionable intellectual backwater.

It is essential to reconnect theological discussion of critical realism with what is happening within the mainline academic community. I therefore propose to turn to the mainline debate over critical realism in philosophy to illuminate the issues encountered in the natural sciences and Christian theology, while honouring the important insights which are to be gained from writers such as Polkinghorne and Torrance. Con-temporary philosophical reflection on critical realism is perfectly capable of embracing all that has been affirmed within the professional community of science and religion writers, while at the same time offering a new stimulus to positive yet critical thinking on the issue, not least through its recognition of the cultural, historical and social factors shaping human perceptions of reality – issues which have yet to be fully addressed within the science and religion community. There is clearly a need for a radical reappraisal of existing approaches and paradigms, which is best achieved by engaging one specific form of

[33] Kees van Kooten Niekerk, 'A Critical Realist Perspective on the Dialogue between Theology and Science', in Niels H. Gregersen and J. Wentzel van Huyssteen (eds), *Rethinking Theology and Science: Six Models for the Current Dialogue.* Grand Rapids, MI: Eerdmans, 1998, 51–86.

[34] Janet Martin Soskice, *Metaphor and Religious Language.* Oxford: Clarendon Press, 1985, 120–3.

[35] Brad Shipley, 'Theological Critical Realism', *Alethia* 3.2 (2000), 29–33.

critical realism which has demonstrable merits for this purpose. As will have become clear from our discussion to date, this is the style of critical realism associated with Roy Bhaskar.

Against reductionism: Roy Bhaskar's critical realism

A new and highly creative phase in the history of critical realism began with the publication of Roy Bhaskar's *A Realist Theory of Science* (1975), and a series of books and articles which followed this over a period of some twenty years.[36] This difficult book is increasingly being recognized as one of the most important philosophical works to have been published in recent years, not least because its method can be extended far beyond the humanities and social sciences, including the natural and applied sciences. Bhaskar's work was hailed as marking a 'Copernican Revolution' in the study of the natural sciences precisely because it transcended an increasingly sterile conflict concerning the achievements of the natural sciences, as well as illuminating the classic conflict between empiricists and rationalists. Bhaskar managed to provide a fresh outlook on these debates largely by attacking the then-dominant positivist conception of science through its flawed understanding of the experimental process. In outlining an alternative, 'transcendental realist' position, Bhaskar allowed critics of positivism to reconceptualize scientific notions such as 'laws', 'tendencies' and 'mechanisms' without abandoning the notion of science itself.

Bhaskar's approach was taken further in 1979 through the publication of *The Possibility of Naturalism*.[37] On the basis of his realist account of science, Bhaskar offered a fresh perspective on the question of whether social and natural objects can be studied in the same 'scientific' manner. Perhaps most significantly, Bhaskar laid a resilient foundation for a definitive critique of the hitherto dominant positivist and hermeneutical approaches to the philosophy of the human sciences, along with the sets of dichotomies with which these had become associated – such as 'society' versus 'the individual', 'facts' versus 'values', 'body' versus 'mind', and 'reasons' versus 'causes'. As Bhaskar made clear in his later

[36] See especially Andrew Collier, *Critical Realism: An Introduction to Roy Bhaskar's Philosophy*. London: Verso, 1994. The most important primary sources are Roy Bhaskar, *A Realist Theory of Science*. 2nd edn. London: Verso, 1997; idem, *Scientific Realism and Human Emancipation*. London: Verso, 1986; idem, *The Possibility of Naturalism: A Philosophical Critique of the Contemporary Human Sciences*. 3rd edn. London/New York: Routledge, 1998.

[37] Roy Bhaskar, *The Possibility of Naturalism: A Philosophical Critique of the Contemporary Human Sciences*. 3rd edn. London/New York: Routledge, 1998.

writings, his understanding of critical realism was eminently open to religious issues. Indeed, in one of his most recent writings, Bhaskar even offers what represents a modest and highly creative argument for the existence of God.[38]

The chief distinguishing feature of Bhaskar's *A Realist Theory of Science* – and arguably also its chief virtue – is his recognition of the importance of the philosophy of sciences, as this has traditionally been conceived, while at the same time taking due account of the social nature of the scientific enterprise. This avoids the weaknesses of a socially abstracted and essentially ahistorical methodology which generally characterizes the classical approaches to the philosophy of science. Bhaskar's close attention to the details of scientific practice, particularly the artificial structuring of the experimental context, avoids the over-statements typical of writers such as Andrew Pickering,[39] while nevertheless giving full weight to the social dimensions of the scientific community – especially the possibility that certain aspects of scientific culture are socially constructed in the laboratory context:[40]

> Constant conjunctions are not in general spontaneously available in nature but rather have to be worked for in the laboratories of science, so that causal laws and the other objects of experimental investigation must, if that activity is to be rendered intelligible, be regarded as ontologically independent of the patterns of events and the activities of human beings alike; and that, conversely, the concepts and descriptions under which we bring them must, if *inter alia* scientific development is to be possible, be seen as part of the irreducibly social process of science. Thus experiences (and the facts they ground) and the constant con-junctions of events that form the empirical grounds for causal laws, are social products. But the objects to which they afford us access, such as causal laws, exist and act quite independently of us.

This complex interplay of the realm of the socially constructed and the ontologically given can be seen in Bhaskar's nuanced affirmation that while the observable facts of the natural sciences are 'real', they are nevertheless 'historically specific social realities'.[41]

Bhaskar explicitly recognizes the importance of ontology in the philosophy of science. Any theory of knowledge, he argues, ultimately

---

[38] Roy Bhaskar, *From East to West: Odyssey of a Soul.* New York: Routledge, 2000, 33–50.
[39] See, for example, Andrew Pickering, *Science as Practice and Culture.* Chicago: University of Chicago Press, 1992.
[40] Roy Bhaskar, *Reclaiming Reality: A Critical Introduction to Contemporary Philosophy.* London: Verso, 1989, 51.
[41] Bhaskar, *Reclaiming Reality,* 61.

presupposes and rests upon an ontological commitment concerning the objects of that knowledge, whether this is explicitly acknowledged or not. The empiricism of the mainstream natural sciences – as opposed to the incautious overstatements of 'empirical' philosophers, such as A. J. Ayer – reflects an implicit ontology of empirical realism. Bhaskar's discontent with an empiricist philosophy of science is particularly evident in his discussion of the relation of scientific observation within the closed context of an experimental context to the more complex open environment outside the laboratory. For Bhaskar, the tensions within existing empiricist philosophies of science were such that the laboratory context could not be adequately correlated with the larger natural world, leading to the absurd conclusion that 'scientists, in their experimental activity, cause and even change the laws of nature'.[42] If the mechanisms which are isolated and identified by experimentation existed only by virtue of the experiment itself, and were not paralleled within the world of nature itself, there would be little point in undertaking experiments in the first place. The process of scientific development can be explained in critical realist terms as the uncovering by experimentation of deeper layers of the causal forces which operate within nature. While these forces exist independently of any scientific investigation of their nature and domains, that scientific investigation itself must be considered to be a historically contingent and socially located process.

For Bhaskar, the experimental successes of the natural sciences could not be explained adequately on the basis of the Humean ontology that was tacitly presupposed by existing philosophies of science. In their place, he posited an understanding of the world as structured, differentiated and changing. The first stage of this programme can be seen in *A Realist Theory of Science*, which argued that the concept of 'being' was an absolutely necessary and irreducible category for any understanding of the natural sciences. Bhaskar re-thematized ontology, arguing for its necessity and irreducibility in any account of the natural sciences. It was in this work that Bhaskar introduced the notion of the 'epistemic fallacy', which reduced issues of ontology to issues of epistemology.[43]

> Empirical realism is underpinned by a metaphysical dogma, which I call the epistemic fallacy, that statements about being can always be transposed into statements about knowledge of being.

[42] Bhaskar, *Reclaiming Reality*, 15–16.
[43] Bhaskar, *A Realist Theory of Science*, 16.

Neither methodology nor epistemology can be allowed to determine matters of ontology. The 'epistemic fallacy' represents a gross confusion of epistemology and ontology, which rests on the false assumption that the structures of the world rest or depend upon human observation. *The world is not limited to what can be observed.* Bhaskar himself develops a critical realist perspective which rests upon the affirmation of an ontology of nature:[44]

> To see science as a social activity, and as structured and discriminating in its thought, constitutes a significant step in our understanding of science. But, I shall argue, without the support of a revised ontology, and in particular a conception of the world as stratified and differentiated too, it is impossible to steer clear of the Scylla of holding the structure dispensable in the long run (back to empiricism) without being pulled into the Charybdis of justifying it exclusively in terms of the fixed or changing needs of the scientific community (a form of neo-Kantian pragmatism exemplified by e.g. Toulmin and Kuhn). In this study I attempt to show how such a revised ontology is in fact presupposed by the social activity of science. The basic principle of realist philosophy of science, viz. that perception gives us access to things and experimental activity access to structures that exist independently of us, is very simple. Yet the full working out of this principle implies a radical account of the nature of causal laws, viz. as expressing tendencies of things, not conjunctions of events. And it implies that a constant conjunction of events is no more a necessary than a sufficient condition for a causal law.

Empiricism, for Bhaskar, purports to offer an account of the natural sciences in terms of experience alone, which fails to offer an adequate distinction between experience, events and mechanisms. Mechanisms must be allowed to exist and operate without manifesting themselves in events, in that their existence cannot be held to be dependent upon their being observed. In the same way, events can occur without this occurrence being observed or experienced. The mechanisms in operation within the natural order are rarely capable of being observed directly, even though those mechanisms exist, and are operative; their existence and nature must be inferred through rigorous critical thought, based on the analysis of the empirical evidence. The observed empirical regularities are not in themselves to be regarded as the primary object of scientific inquiry; this relates more properly to the underlying causal mechanisms which generate the observed regularities.

[44] Bhaskar, *A Realist Theory of Science*, 9.

Whereas many forms of positivism define reality simply in terms of what may be observed, critical realism insists that the world must be regarded as differentiated and stratified, and incapable of being adequately rendered by simple observation. Where Kant's slightly muddled philosophical reflections leave us with a world teeming with mysterious 'things in themselves' about which we can know nothing with any degree of certainty, critical realism affirms that surface appearances are only the experiential, or empirical, aspect of deeper structures and mechanisms which allow the surface appearances to be explained, and about which it is possible to gain knowledge.

There is thus a fundamental ontological distinction to be made between the underlying causal mechanisms of nature and the observable patterns of events within nature, whether these are observed in the natural world itself, or under the somewhat more artificial world of the carefully controlled experiment. The underlying causal mechanisms may be said to be the *intransitive* objects of scientific inquiry, whereas the empirical regularities are the *transitive* products of scientific investigation. The 'epistemic fallacy' leads to the collapse of this fundamental distinction, in effect merging the intransitive and transitive dimensions of scientific investigation.

The attractiveness of Bhaskar's critical realism lies partly in its advantages in dealing with the classic issues of the philosophy of science in the light of the increasing recognition of the socially-conditioned character of scientific practice, and partly in its clear potential as a means of engaging with intellectual disciplines beyond the natural sciences. It is within the social sciences that these ideas have proved especially fruitful. Bhaskar argues that it is possible to offer a 'non-natural but still scientific' account of society without any need to reduce the complexities of social structures to the physical or biological level. 'Society' possesses an ontological status which necessitates a critical realist account of its behaviour, even if analysis must proceed at single levels of explanation, with reference to 'only one relatively autonomous component of the social structure'.[45] Bhaskar's relationship to Marxism is of particular interest at this point.[46] Marxism has long maintained that there exist laws within the social order which can be discovered,

[45] Bhaskar, *Reclaiming Reality*, 87.
[46] For a careful exploration of this issue, see Mats Ekstrom, 'Causal Explanation of Social Action: The Contribution of Max Weber and of Critical Realism to a Generative View of Causal Explanation in Social Science', *Acta Sociologica: Journal of the Scandinavian Sociological Association* 35 (1992), 107–22; Sean Creaven, *Marxism and Realism: A Materialistic Application of Realism in the Social Sciences.* London: Routledge, 2001.

understood and manipulated to the advantage of the ideologically sophisticated observer. In an interesting aside, Bhaskar suggests that Karl Marx was obliged to adopt an unsatisfactory Hegelian dialectical approach to the study of society as his hitherto 'missing methodological fulcrum' because his historical location denied him access to the insights of critical realism.[47]

The development of this new form of critical realism can arguably be anticipated in an important paper published in 1955 by Maurice Mandelbaum.[48] This would not be the only time that Mandelbaum developed ideas that could reasonably be described as 'critically realistic'; a later major study explicitly used the term 'radical critical realism' to refer to an approach which declined to identify the properties of perceived objects with their referents.[49] Developing this point further, Mandelbaum set out his notion of the 'self-excepting fallacy', which argues that most forms of relativism can be shown to depend upon a prior and unacknowledged acceptance of certain objective beliefs.[50] Doubt is thus parasitic upon prior belief. Mandelbaum's ideas were not directly or explicitly developed by Bhaskar; however, as Christopher Lloyd has shown, these ideas are capable of being developed to yield an approach similar, in many respects, to Bhaskar's.[51]

So what are the key features of Bhaskar's approach, and how do they relate to a scientific theology? We shall single out three issues for particular comment. We have already hinted at some of these in this preliminary account of his approach; in what follows, we shall explore them in some detail, laying the ground for their appropriation in a scientific theology.

Realism embraces both natural and social sciences

In our brief exploration of the various types of critical realism, we noted that a central concern was to do justice to the involvement of the knower in the process of knowing, in particular to distance modern philosophy from those approaches to knowledge deriving from the Enlightenment which failed to acknowledge the issue of the subjectivity of knowledge (in the Kierkegaardian sense of that term).

[47] Bhaskar, *The Possibility of Naturalism*, 178.

[48] Maurice Mandelbaum, 'Societal Facts', *British Journal of Sociology* 6 (1955), 305–17.

[49] Maurice Mandelbaum, *Philosophy, Science and Sense-Perception: Historical and Critical Studies*. Baltimore, MD: Johns Hopkins University Press, 1964.

[50] Maurice Mandelbaum, 'The Self-Excepting Fallacy', *Psychologische Beiträge* 6 (1962), 383–6.

[51] Christopher Lloyd, 'Realism and Structuralism in Historical Theory: A Discussion of the Thought of Maurice Mandelbaum', *History and Theory* 28 (1986), 296–325.

Welcome though this development must be, it is not enough to rectify the failings of the Enlightenment world-view, which also failed to take account of the *historical location* of the knower. We have already seen how this has led to a new interest in the notion of tradition-bound rationality, and the development of approaches to knowledge which avoid the aporia of the Enlightenment. Yet it is clear that this only represents the beginning of an engagement with history, and the issue of 'social reality' in general. One of the many merits of Bhaskar's approach is to reintegrate the social and historical within a realist perspective.

Critical realism takes history with the greatest of seriousness. As Peter Manicas points out in an extended discussion of a 'realist social science',[52] the study of history offers the possibility of uncovering the 'social mechanisms' which govern events as diverse as the Great Crash of 1929, the Bolshevik Revolution or the election of an American president. Although some writers have distinguished social science and history, it seems clear that this distinction is ultimately untenable, in that the concept of *time* cannot be eliminated from the social sciences. History thus offers the possibility of engaging with a number of layers of social reality, including ideas, events and dispositions.

From the outset, Bhaskar makes it clear that a central theme of his agenda has been to explore the question of *the extent to which society can be studied in the same way as nature.*[53] In dealing with this critical question, Bhaskar offers definitions of three terms central to his discussion:[54]

> *Naturalism*, which holds that 'there is (or can be) an essential unity of method' between the natural and social sciences;
>
> *Reductionism*, which states that 'there is an actual identity of subject-matter' between the two disciplines;
>
> *Scientism*, which denies that there are 'any significant differences in the methods appropriate to studying social and natural objects,' irrespective of whether these are treated as formally identical or not.

Bhaskar's idiosyncatic use of these terms – particularly 'naturalism' – needs to be noted carefully, as it can give rise to confusion with other styles of 'naturalism'.

---

[52] Peter T. Manicas, *A History and Philosophy of the Social Sciences.* Oxford: Blackwell, 1987, 266–93.

[53] Bhaskar, *The Possibility of Naturalism*, 1.

[54] Bhaskar, *The Possibility of Naturalism*, 2–3.

In view of the proliferation of reductionist approaches to religion in recent years, we may explore how Bhaskar's approach undermines such forms of reductionism. The basic ideas of reductionism are easily stated: every aspect of human thought and behaviour can ultimately be reduced to the laws of physics, and requires no further or additional explanation. Thus Harvard biologist Edward O. Wilson, one of the founders of sociobiology, argues that social behaviour is to be explained by the principles of biology, biology by the principles of chemistry, and chemistry by the principles of physics. Eventually all higher disciplines will be reduced to nothing but the laws of chemistry and physics.[55] Similarly, Nobel Laureate Francis Crick has argued that the goal of the sciences is to reduce all knowledge to the laws of chemistry and physics: 'The ultimate aim of the modern movement in biology is in fact to explain all biology in terms of physics and chemistry.'[56] The human person is to be seen as 'nothing but a pack of neurons' – that is, a collection of neural networks, which once understood, explain all human behaviour.[57]

Bhaskar argues that it does not follow that, because level A is rooted in and emergent from level B, it follows that level A is 'nothing but' level B. Emergent strata possess features that are 'irreducible' – that is, which cannot be conceived solely in terms of lower levels. One cannot 'reduce' biology to chemistry or physics, precisely because the biological stratum possesses characteristics which go beyond those in which it is rooted. If it were possible to explain the origins of biological life in chemical or physical terms, that would not amount to the reduction of biology to either of these disciplines.[58]

> Would biologists lose their object of inquiry? Would living things cease to be real? Our apprehension of them unmasked as an illusion? No, for in as much as living things were capable of acting back on the materials out of which they were formed, biology were not otiose. For a knowledge of biological structures and principles would still be necessary to account

[55] Edward O. Wilson, *Sociobiology: The New Synthesis*. Cambridge, MA: Harvard University Press, 1975. See further Alexander Rosenberg, *Sociobiology and the Preemption of Social Science*. Baltimore, MD: Johns Hopkins University Press, 1980; Peter Koslowski, *Sociobiology and Bioeconomics: The Theory of Evolution in Biological and Economic Theory*. New York: Springer Verlag, 1999.

[56] Francis Crick, *Of Molecules and Men*. Seattle, WA: University of Washington Press, 1966, 10.

[57] Francis Crick, *The Astonishing Hypothesis: The Scientific Search for the Soul*. New York: Charles Scribner's Sons, 1994, 3.

[58] Roy Bhaskar, *A Realist Theory of Science*, 113.

for any determinate state of the physical world. Whatever is capable of producing a physical effect is real and a proper object of scientific study.

Bhaskar insists that each stratum – whether physical, biological or cultural – is to be seen as 'real', and capable of investigation using means appropriate to its distinctive identity.

On Bhaskar's specific reading, 'naturalism' offers an account of the relation of the natural and social sciences which affirms their methodological commonalities, while respecting their distinctions, particularly when these arise on account of their objects of investigation.[59]

> Naturalism holds that it is possible to give an account of science under which the proper and more or less specific methods of both the natural and social sciences can fall. But it does not deny that there are significant differences in these methods, grounded in real differences in their subject-matters and in the relationships in which these sciences stand to them. . . . It is the nature of the object that determines the form of its possible science.

We see here a clear recognition of each science being determined by the nature of its object, and being obligated to respond to it κατὰ φυσίν, in a manner which is appropriate to its distinctive nature.

To illustrate this point, we may turn to a recent analysis of British politics since the Second World War, focusing particularly on the politics and economics of the Thatcher era. While the book is of considerable interest for its judgements – for example, on the root causes of British decline in the post-war years – it is also notable for methodological reasons, in that it challenges positivist and relativist perspectives on these issues, insisting that British society must be seen as an independently existing reality with deep structures and causal relations which are open to a critical realist analysis.[60]

Bhaskar's approach forbids the sociological imperialism which insists upon the reduction of everything to social categories. It demands that methodology be specifically linked to ontology – that is, to an identification of the distinctive nature of the reality under investigation, and the formulation of an appropriate methodology which is respective of and responsive to the nature of that reality. The natural and social sciences are obligated to use different approaches, precisely because 'natural reality' and 'social reality' are different. 'Natural' and 'social'

---

59 Bhaskar, *The Possibility of Naturalism*, 3.
60 David Marsh, *Post-War British Politics in Perspective*. Cambridge: Polity Press, 1999, 1–14.

structures must be distinguished in three specific manners. Social structures:[61]

1. Do not exist independently of the activities which they govern;

2. Do not exist independently of the agents' conceptions of what they are doing in their activity;

3. May be transient, in that the tendencies they ground may not be universal in terms of space-time invariance.

These considerations necessitate that the social and natural sciences be accorded the right to exercise different methodologies, in accord with their differing subject matters. The recognition of the stratification of reality legitimates a diversity of methodologies, precisely because methodology is determined by ontology.

Epistemology is to be distinguished from ontology

Existence is not dependent on observation, or being observable. Bhaskar insists that generative mechanisms may exist yet not be observed or observable, so that their powers may exist unexercised or be exercised without being realized – that is, that there may exist variable outcomes which cannot be the subject of experimental closure, due to the variety of intervening contingencies affecting them.

Bhaskar defines the epistemic fallacy as the view 'that statements about being can be reduced to or analysed in terms of statements about knowledge'.[62] This runs counter to the verificationist theory of meaning, such as that espoused so vigorously – if ultimately inconsistently – by A. J. Ayer. For Ayer, the question of the existence or non-existence of God is to be reduced to the more modest question of what may be known and not known. Strictly speaking, Ayer's views lead to neither theism nor atheism, but simply to the insistence that both positions are defined in terms of a meaningless word.

It will be clear that this has important theological consequences. The epistemic fallacy regards statements about being as equivalent to statements about knowledge. Bhaskar relates this to the *ontic* fallacy, which holds that knowledge is to be analysed as a direct, unmediated relation between a subject and being. The ontic fallacy ignores the cognitive and social mechanisms by which knowledge is produced from antecedent knowledge, leaving an ontology of empirical knowledge

---

[61] Bhaskar, *The Possibility of Naturalism*, 38.
[62] Bhaskar, *A Realist Theory of Science*, 36.

events (raw perceptions) and a de-socialized epistemology. Bhaskar argues that the epistemic fallacy results in the projection of the external world onto a subjective phenomenal map, whereupon the ontic fallacy projects the phenomenal entities of that subjective map back out on the world as objective sense data, of which we are held to have direct perceptual knowledge. On this account, a reality independent of thought is first *subjectified*, prior to these subjectified elements being *objectified* to explain and justify our knowledge.[63]

Reality is stratified

The idea that reality is multi-layered can be found in a number of theological and philosophical writings of the twentieth century. We have already noted how this notion can be found in the 'American critical realism' of the early twentieth century, especially in the writings of Arthur Lovejoy. In his important work *The Tacit Dimension* (1966), Michael Polanyi developed the idea of a 'hierarchical universe', composed of many levels. The world is 'stratified,' and is to be thought of as a 'universe of levels', each of which operates under the 'marginal control' of the level immediately above it.[64] Bhaskar does not engage with Polanyi in any detail, and I would judge it unwise to posit any relational dependence on Bhaskar's part here.

Bhaskar's own account of the stratification of reality represents one of his most distinctive contributions to the development of critical realism. The image of a 'stratum' suggests a difference in depth, allowing a causal explanatory link to be posited between different strata. The image allows an immediate distinction to be drawn between surface phenomena and what may initially be argued – and subsequently perceived – to lie beneath that surface. The impetus to go deeper – to identify causal mechanisms which lie beneath the surface of what we observe or experience – is fundamental to any natural science.[65]

> One has in science a three-phase schema of development in which, in a continuing dialectic, science identifies a phenomenon (or range of phenomena), constructs explanations for it and empirically tests its explanations, leading to the identification of the generative mechanism at work, which now becomes the phenomenon to be explained, and so on. In this continuing process, as deeper levels or strata of reality are successfully unfolded, science must construct and test its explanations

---

[63] Bhaskar, *Scientific Realism and Human Emancipation*, 253.
[64] Michael Polanyi, *The Tacit Dimension*. Garden City, NY: Doubleday, 1966, 29–32; 37.
[65] Bhaskar, *The Possibility of Naturalism*, 12.

with the cognitive resources and physical tools at its disposal, which in this process are themselves progressively transformed, modifed and refined.

Rival metaphors lack this ability to deal with the engagement with increasing depths of reality. The metaphor of 'perspectives' suggests the image of walking around a mountain, or a great medieval cathedral, identifying the different façades and viewpoints which are possible through this process of perambulation. Yet the perspectives all express the same *level of engagement.*

A similar difficulty arises from Althusser's metaphor of the 'continents', in which he likens areas of human knowledge to continents which are opened up to human exploration. For Althusser, Thales opened up the first 'continent' of mathematics; Galileo opened up the 'continent' of physics; and finally, Marx opened up the 'continent' of history.[66] Pushing the metaphor a little further, Althusser divides these continents into 'regions'. Chemistry and biology thus sit alongside each other in the 'continent' of physics. Yet, as Andrew Collier points out, this completely fails to account for the fact that there is a stratified relationship between these scientific disciplines. Chemistry, physics and biology are here grouped together, *on the same level* and in contiguous regions, whereas most natural scientists would argue that the relationship is best stated in terms of biology depending upon chemical laws, which in turn depend upon physical laws.[67]

The notion of strata picks up some themes found in Marxist theory. Although Marx himself appears to have adopted a simple 'base-superstructure' framework, which held that ideas were ultimately determined by their socio-economic substructure, these ideas were developed more fully by his later followers. Georgii Plekhanov argued for a five-level model of a modern society, as follows:[68]

1. The state of the productive forces;

2. The economic relations that these forces engender;

---

[66] Louis Althusser, *Lenin and Philosophy, And Other Essays.* London: New Left Books, 1971, 42. On Althusser, see further Margaret A. Majumdar, *Althusser and the end of Leninism?* London: Pluto, 1995.

[67] For comments, see Andrew Collier, *Scientific Realism and Socialist Thought.* Hemel Hempstead: Harvester Wheatsheaf, 1988, 43–5. For additional comments on such approaches, see Arthur Peacocke, *Creation and the World of Science.* Oxford: Oxford University Press, 1979, 112–19.

[68] G. V. Plekhanov, *Fundamental Problems of Marxism.* New York: International Publishers, 1969, 80. On this writer, see Samuel H. Baron, *Plekhanov: The Father of Russian Marxism.* Stanford, CA: Stanford University Press, 1963.

3. The socio-political system that develops on this economic base;

4. The mentality of people living within this system, reflecting both its economic conditions and its socio-political system;

5. The ideologies that arise among these people, embodying that mentality.

Plekhanov thus argues that everything ultimately depends upon economics, but distinguishes a series of levels at which the fundamental economic forces operate. The link between 'productive forces' and 'ideologies' is not quite as straightforward as Marx suggests, and involves the identification and analysis of the interaction of the various strata.

Bhaskar argues that a similar pattern of stratification can be discerned within the natural sciences. He offers the following example by way of illustration.[69] Consider the observable reaction of sodium metal coming into contact with hydrochloric acid, yielding the evolution of hydrogen and the production of sodium chloride. This reaction can be represented and explained at four different levels, as follows:

Stratum I $2Na + 2HCl = 2NaCl + H_2$
            which is explained by
Stratum II theory of atomic number and valency   Mechanism 1
            which is explained by
Stratum III theory of electrons and atomic structure   Mechanism 2
            which is explained by
Stratum IV (competing theories of subatomic structure) (Mechanism 3)

The observation of the behaviour of sodium metal in hydrochloric acid can thus be explained at a series of levels. This does not mean that this epistemological stratification is grounded in contingent aspects of human cognitive capacities, in that the real grounds of this lies in the real ontological stratification of the object of the sciences. For Bhaskar, the plurality of sciences is the inevitable and proper outcome of of the irreducibly stratified character of the structure of the real world, and the mechanisms at work within it. A unity of methodology presupposes a simple philosophical ontology, which is inattentive to the structuring of reality.

Bhaskar thus draws a distinction between 'experience', 'events' and 'mechanisms', and represents their relationship in tabular form:[70]

---

[69] Bhaskar, *A Realist Theory of Science*, 169.
[70] Bhaskar, *A Realist Theory of Science*, 13.

	Domain of Real	Domain of Actual	Domain of Empirical
Mechanism	√		
Events	√	√	
Experiences	√	√	√

The domain of the 'empirical' embraces what can be experienced. Yet Bhaskar makes it absolutely clear that not all events may be experienced; it is not necessary for us to observe something for it to be real. Similarly, mechanisms cannot be observed, but are nonetheless real. Bhaskar vigorously contests any suggestion that reality is contingent upon observation, and posits his three domains in an effort to break free from the straitjacket of positivism. Bhaskar opposes any attempt to collapse the domains of the real, the actual and the empirical into one, arguing that a failure to recognize the ontological depth of reality inevitably leads to superficial engagements with society and the world.

So how do these strata relate to each other? In his analysis of Bhaskar's philosophy, Andrew Collier identifies some relations that may exist between strata, of which we note two.[71]

1. Ontological presupposition. Here, one stratum ontologically pre-supposes another, in that the former could not exist without the other. Biological strata thus ontologically presuppose physical strata, and social strata presuppose biological strata.

2. Vertical explanation. Here, mechanisms operating at one stratum explain those operating at another. The explained stratum clearly ontologically presupposes that which explains. Nevertheless, this is not a transitive relation: chemistry may explain biology, and biology sociology – yet this does not mean that chemistry explains sociology.

The potential of Bhaskar's approach has been examined with particular reference to the social sciences by a number of writers. William Outhwaite has pointed out how the 'stratification of reality into the domains of the real, the actual and the empirical' presupposes an ontology; nevertheless, the specific nature of this ontology cannot be determined in advance, but must be established for each individual science.[72]

---

[71] Collier, *Critical Realism*, 131–2.
[72] William Outhwaite, *New Philosophies of Social Science: Realism, Hermeneutics and Critical Theory*. New York: St Martin's Press, 1987, 44–60.

The problems and possibilities opened up by Bhaskar's approach can be seen in his attempt to apply them to the study of society. In dealing with this question, Bhaskar draws a careful distinction between the ontological question (what properties do societies possess?) and the epistemological question (how do these properties make them possible objects of knowledge for us?).[73] The positivist insistence upon 'unity of methodology' is rejected in that *methodology is determined by ontology*. The importance of this distinction, and the order in which the questions are posed, is made clear by Bhaskar as follows:[74]

> This is not an arbitrary order of development. It reflects the condition that, for transcendental realism, it is the nature of objects that determines their cognitive possibilities for us; that in nature it is humanity that is contingent and knowledge, so to speak, accidental.

This point may be illustrated by that fact that a stone may be picked up and thrown *because* it is solid; it is not solid because it can be picked up and thrown. While Bhaskar concedes that the fact that stones may be handled in this way 'may be a contingently necessary condition for our *knowledge* of their solidity', his basic point is that the ontology of the object determines how we know and use it.

Having established this general principle, Bhaskar moves on to explore how the appropriate method and object of social thought is to be established. Arguing that concepts of *method* are determined by *ontology*, and that concepts of *object* are determined by an *epistemology*, Bhaskar differentiates four influential models of social thought according to their approaches to both categories:[75]

School of Social Theory	Method	Object
Utilitarianism	Empiricist	Individualist
Weber	Neo-Kantian	Individualist
Durkheim	Empiricist	Collectivist
Marx	Realist	Relational

---

[73] Bhaskar, *The Possibility of Naturalism*, 25–71.
[74] Bhaskar, *The Possibility of Naturalism*, 25.
[75] Bhaskar, *The Possibility of Naturalism*, 31.

Certain schools of sociology argued that 'natural reality' and 'social reality' could be collapsed into the latter, so that human knowledge can be fundamentally reduced to social theory. In marked contrast, Bhaskar insists upon an ontological difference between them, and thus breaks with the sociological school of thought which held that social reality ultimately embraced everything, which could and should be investigated by fundamentally empirical methods.

Bhaskar's social ontology is determined by his 'transformational model of social activity', which casts important light on the critical distinction between nature and society.[76] Bhaskar seems to identify at least four strata as follows:[77]

Psychological sciences
Social sciences
Biological sciences
Molecular sciences.

So how do the methods appropiate to the lower strata relate to the upper strata? Given Bhaskar's critical insight that a proper methodology is determined by the ontology of what is to be investigated, methods that might be appropriate for biology might not be for the social sciences. The essential point is that each stratum must be investigated by a methodology which is determined *a posteriori* by its ontology. This is an important bulwark against reductionism.

Against reductionism in theology – or anything else
It will be obvious that Bhaskar's critical realism offers a scientific theology resources to:

- *consolidate* its position as a distinctive and legitimate intellectual discipline;
- *develop* its own understanding of its sources and methods; and
- *clarify* its relationship to other disciplines in the natural and social sciences.

In appropriating Bhaskar's approach in this way, I have not made a scientific theology dependent upon an understanding of the nature of reality which has been imported from outside the Christian tradition,

---

[76] Collier, *Critical Realism*, 141–51.
[77] Collier, *Scientific Realism and Socialist Thought*, 45.

still less committed the culpable error of linking theology to a secular philosophy. Rather, I am using the framework developed by Bhaskar as a means of exploring and appreciating the insights of a scientific theology, which exist and apply independently of Bhaskar's analysis.

The main consequences of Bhaskar's analysis is to confirm the intellectual viability of the leading themes of a scientific theology, especially the following:

1. A scientific theology may legitimately be regarded as a response to an existing reality, whose existence is independent of the actuality or possibility of human observation.

2. Each intellectual discipline must adopt a methodology which is appropriate to, and determined by, the ontology of its specific object. Its methodology is thus determined *a posteriori* rather than *a priori*.

It is particularly important to note how 'critical realism' undermines the plausibilty of any form of reductionism. As the main points have already been made in this chapter, this concluding section will merely reiterate the points made elsewhere. One of the most important aspects of Bhaskar's approach is that it demands that the different levels of reality be fully acknowledged. It is impossible to reduce reality to one ontological level, or to insist that what is 'real' is determined by whether it can be 'known' – often by the improper use of only one methodology, corresponding to the one level of reality that such a reductionism recognizes. Theology and the natural sciences recognize a plurality of levels of reality, and refuse to reduce everything to one level.

This calls into question the agenda of the strong social constructivists, who insist that everything is to be reduced to issues of power, vested interests and authority. Perhaps more importantly, it challenges those who insist that reality is to be defined as 'what can be known through the natural sciences' – an approach which is intrinsically anti-religious and anti-metaphysical in its outlook. A number of points may be made against this reductionism.

1. It is historically conditioned, in that 'what is known through the natural sciences' changes with improvements in observational techniques and technological advances. This leads to the unacceptable idea that the nature of reality changes in accordance with our ability to know it.

2. It falls victim to the fallacy, so heavily criticized by Bhaskar, that ontology is determined by epistemology – that is to say, that the reality of something is determined by whether we can observe it. This is fraught with difficulties, as the present and previous chapter indicate.

Bhaskar's analysis also allows us to construct a framework by which we may identify and explore the various strata of the Christian faith, and reflect on their importance for a scientific theology. To gain something of an appreciation of the potential of this technique, we may consider how Karl Barth and T. F. Torrance make use of the notion of stratification. As we shall see, both understand the notion to refer primarily to ideational stratification in response to theological reality. We shall develop this approach in a somewhat different way, in that we shall set out how a scientific theology responds to a stratified reality.

The recognition of the stratification of reality allows critical realism to make a distinction between *vertical* explanation and *horizontal* explanation.[78] The former refers to a relationship between different strata of reality – for example, where a physical law affects the behaviour of a biological entity. Bhaskar speaks of the higher level mechanism as being 'rooted in' or 'emergent from' a lower level. Bhaskar's approach at this point allows him to challenge both reductionist approaches which collapse reality into a single observable stratum, and pluralist theories which affirm the existence of different strata, but decline to see them as dependent upon each other.[79]

The stratification of theological reality: some preliminary comments

The present and previous chapters have made the case for a critical realism in the natural and social sciences, noting the increasing attenuation of anti-realist positions throughout the twentieth century. Yet one point remains to be established. Why does the demonstration that some form of realism is the preferred philosophy of the natural sciences have any bearing on theology whatsoever? It is fatally easy to make the simplistic assumption that there exists a direct mapping from the natural

---

[78] Collier, *Critical Realism*, 107–15.
[79] For the argument, see Bhaskar, *The Possibility of Naturalism*, 97–107.

sciences to Christian theology, so that what holds for the former automatically applies to the latter as well. In what follows, we shall map out the converging lines of thought which establish the legitimacy of this connection.

It must be recalled that we have argued for the tradition-mediated rationality of the Christian faith including a series of assumptions concerning the nature of the world as creation, and the distinctively Christian understanding of the role of Christ as the agent of creation, linked with the doctrine of creation *ex nihilo*. As we stressed earlier (vol. 1, 59–60) at least one of these assumption would be totally rejected by most Jewish and Islamic writers, who might otherwise share many common theistic assumptions with their Christian colleagues. My concern is not to defend Christianity at this point, but rather to respect its integrity and the inner logic of its interconnected assumptions.

There is a correspondence between the reality of the created world and the reality of its creator. From a Christian standpoint, the existence (*existentia*) of the creation is dependent upon the prior existence (*essentia*) of God. As reality is stratified, the remaining issue is to determine what mode of inquiry is appropriate to each level. The Christian revelation holds that God's revelation is to be located in nature, in history, in personal experience, in the life of the church, and especially in Scripture. As we shall see, each of these can be regarded as a 'level of reality' open to investigation.

Within the Christian tradition, there is a *created correpondence* between creation and creator – that is to say, that the reality of God is rendered in the created order, including humanity as its apex. In that the reality of the created order is affirmed by scientific realism, it follows that reflection on this reality offers insights into the nature of God. Notice how this insight is arrived at on the basis of the parameters of the Christian tradition; it is not an autonomous or self-evident truth, but something whose truth depends upon the prior truth of a Christian doctrine of creation.

The stratified understanding of reality affirmed by critical realism thus allows us to argue that the natural sciences investigate the stratified structures of contingent existence *at every level open to human inquiry*, while a theological science addresses itself to God their creator *who is revealed through them*. The doctrine of the incarnation – the affirmation that the God who created space, time and history entered into this created zone in the person of Jesus Christ – affirms both historical and theological realities.

Creation exists because God exists; the reality of creation both mirrors and models the reality of God. Natural sciences address the creation; a scientific theology addresses the creator, who is known through the creation. Though these terse statements demand amplification and qualification, they identify the fundamental isomorphism of the scientific and theological enterprises, provided that *nature* is seen from a specifically Christian perspective as *creation*. The reality of God and the derived and contingent reality of the creation can thus be seen as distinct, yet clearly related, strata of reality, whose ontology determines the methodology to be used in their investigation. Critical realism is therefore as appropriate to the study of the reality of the creator as it is to the ensuing created reality of the natural order.

So where is theology to be located in a stratification of reality? Most theologians to have explored this question place theology at the pinnacle of a hierarchy of disciplines,[80] perhaps as an unconscious repristination of the scholastic vision of theology as the 'queen of the sciences'. This is certainly an interesting insight – though not one that might be expected to be shared outside the Christian community of discourse. I do not, however, believe that it is correct.

The proper role of theology is to posit that *the creative and redemptive being of God is the most fundamental of all strata of reality*. A Christian vision of the entire panoply of creation depends upon seeing that vista through the informing and interpretative lens of a web of doctrinal insights, especially the doctrine of creation. The manner in which each stratum of reality is viewed will reflect the informing world-view brought to bear upon it. A fundamental distinction must be made between the nature of God as the one who causes contingent reality to emerge, and the existence of the created order itself – a distinction classically expressed in terms of the dialectic between *essentia* and *existentia*.[81] God is not simply one who exists; God is one who causes all else to exist.

Once this point is established, the rest falls into place. It is not the position of *theology* within the stratification of reality which is of critical

[80] See, for example, George F. Ellis and Nancey C. Murphy, *On the Moral Nature of the Universe: Theology, Cosmology, and Ethics.* Minneapolis, MN: Fortress Press, 1996, 65; 204; Peacocke, *Creation and the World of Science*, 367–71.

[81] Alexander Altmann, *Essence and Existence in Maimonides.* Manchester: Manchester University Press, 1953; Francis A. Cunningham, *Essence and Existence in Thomism.* Lanham, MD: University Press of America, 1988; Amélie-Marie Goichon, *La distinction de l'essence et de l'existence d'après Ibn Sina (Avicenne).* Paris: Desclée de Brouwer, 1937.

importance, but the position of *God*. If ontology is to determine methodology, it therefore follows that theology is to be regarded as lying at the base, not the apex, of the sciences. Nevertheless, the blunt assertion that 'theology is the science of God' fails to take cognizance of the manner in which Christian theology understands God to be revealed and encountered – for example, in nature, history and personal experience, to say nothing of the engagement with Scripture which is so central a task of the Christian tradition.

An analogy from the world of medicine may help make the difficult point under discussion clearer. The failure of a single-level approach to the concerns of the natural sciences is best demonstrated by considering what is meant by the notion of 'illness'. Models of illness are of critical importance in the analysis and understanding of clinical cases, and the determination of what form of rehabilitation is necessary following any given illness.[82] Yet 'illness' is a highly complex notion, including both pathological elements (such as damage to the liver, or the presence of a tumour) and socially constructed elements (such as radical changes in the individual's social role consequent to this).

Recognizing both the complexity of the situation and the importance of identifying the various levels of the notion of 'illness' for the construction of health services and the design of research, the World Health Organization set out an 'International Classification of Impairments, Disabilities and Handicaps' (ICIDH) in 1980.[83] This model originally treated illness in terms of impairments, disabilities and handicaps; this has now been revised (ICIDH–2) in terms of the more socially acceptable notions of 'activity' and 'participation'.[84] As Wade sets out the model, four 'levels of illness' may be discerned, as tabulated overleaf:[85]

---

[82] Derick T. Wade, 'Recent Advances in Rehabilitation', *British Medical Journal* 320 (2000), 1385–8.

[83] *International Classification of Impairments, Disabilities and Handicaps: A Manual of Classification Relating to the Consequences of Disease*. Geneva: World Health Organization, 1980. For comment and analysis, see E. M. Bradley, 'An Introduction to the Concepts and Classifications of the International Classification of Impairments, Disabilities and Handicaps', *Disability and Rehabilitation* 15 (1993), 161–78.

[84] *ICIDH–2: International Classification of Functioning and Disability*. Geneva: World Health Organization, 1997.

[85] Wade, 'Recent Advances in Rehabilitation', 1386.

Level of Illness	Alternative Terms	Comments
Pathology	Disease; diagnosis	Abnormalities in the structure or function of an organ or organ system
Impairment	Symptoms; signs	Abnormalities or changes in the structure or function of the the whole body
Activity	Function; observed behaviour	Abnormalities, changes or restrictions in the interaction between a person and his or her environment or physical context
Participation	Social positions and roles	Changes, limitations or abnormalities in the position of the person in their social context

Exploring this in a little more detail will help explain the basic point at issue. At the *pathological* level, someone might develop a brain tumour. This leads to *impairment* in the form of certain observable changes in the functioning of the human body, including potential memory loss or other loss of cognitive functions. At the level of *activities*, this leads to the individual experiencing difficulties with certain – but not all – routine tasks, which have implications for her lifestyle. At the level of *participation*, this could lead to loss of social role and unemployment if the person's job required good memory and cognitive skills.

Illness can therefore be studied and addressed at several different levels. It would be absurd to suggest that one level is 'real', and the others not. Unemployment may be argued to be a social construction; it is, nevertheless, decidedly real for those unfortunate enough to experience it. Each of the levels demands a different mode of investigation, and in turn a different manner of remediation. The model illustrates neatly how an essentially pathological factor leads to increasingly socially constructed issues. The nature and specific interaction of these levels will depend upon the pathology, the nature of the individual affected, and the social position which she occupies. Only when all these are taken into account can the illness be said to have been fully understood and addressed.

The ICIDH–2 model makes it clear that each level of illness demands a different methodology, in accordance with its distinctive nature. The method used at present to investigate whether an individual has a brain tumour (such as magnetic resonance imaging) is quite distinct from those techniques used to determine loss of memory (such as the WISC battery of tests), which in turn differs radically from those which monitor changes in the social role of individuals. A stratified reality thus leads to a plurality of methods of investigation. *Each stratum demands its own methodology.* A reductionist approach which demands that everything is stated and investigated only in terms of the most basic stratum cannot hope to do justice to the real life situations which critical realism aims to explore and illuminate. The same point is true of religions, such as Christianity, which embody ideational, social, historical and experiential domains, each demanding to be investigated on its own terms, and refusing to be sidelined in the interests of a reductionist agenda.

The ICIDH–2 'model of illness' neatly illustrates the need to identify the various aspects of a complex entity, and ensure that each is fully considered. The individual levels each demand to be studied using their own distinctive methodologies, leading to the conclusion that a complex system – such as illness – be recognized to consist of a plurality of levels, and hence demand a pluriformity of methodologies, both in investigation and remediation.

It is clear that the task facing theology can be stratified in a similar way. The ICIDH–2 model of illness posits that, while one may speak of the 'root cause' of illness as being pathological – that is, resulting from an abnormality in a human organ or its functioning – it is impossible to limit the definition of illness, its empirical investigation or its remediation to this basic level. In a similar way, we can offer a stratified account of theological reality, which identifies the complexity of the reality which theology aims to represent and portray. To illustrate this, we shall consider how theological explanation is stratified both horizontally and vertically, and offer some preliminary reflections on the importance of this observation.

The horizontal stratification of theological explanation

Christian reflection on the different 'levels' of theological analysis to date has generally tended to take the form of 'horizontal' explanation – that is to say, it has focused on clarifying the relation between various theological entities within a single stratum. This is an important discussion, and is to be honoured. However, it needs to be extended to allow discussion of the role of the various strata of reality for the theological agenda. In what follows, we shall consider how Karl Barth and T. F. Torrance offer such horizontal accounts of the theological task.

Karl Barth on the threefold form of the Word of God

A central feature of Barth's theology is his concept of the 'Word of God'. Barth's fundamental contention is that theology is essentially the obedient orientation of the theologian towards the being and act of God in Jesus Christ, which constitutes the perspective from which all of theology may and must be surveyed. To think theologically is thus essentially to take seriously the fact that the being of God is prior to the enterprise of human theological speculation and questioning. Reacting against approaches to Christology such as that represented by A. E. Biedermann, Barth explicitly rejects any deductive Christology based upon a 'Christ-principle' in favour of one based upon 'Jesus Christ himself as witnessed to in Holy Scripture'.[86]

Every theological proposition in the *Church Dogmatics* thus has its point of departure in Jesus Christ. It is this feature of Barth's later thought which has led to it being described as 'Christological concentration' or 'Christomonism'.[87] Barth is not actually suggesting that the doctrine of either the person or work of Christ (or both, if they are deemed inseparable) should stand at the centre of a Christian dogmatics, nor that a Christological idea or principle should constitute the systematic speculative midpoint of a deductive system. Rather, Barth is arguing that the act of God which is Jesus Christ underlies theology in its totality. A 'Church Dogmatics' must be 'Christologically determined' in that the very possibility and reality of theology are determined in the first place by the actuality of the act of divine revelation, by the speaking of the Word of God, by the event of Jesus Christ.

The central concept which guides Barth's reflections at this point is the 'Word of God'.[88] The concept comes to play a critical role in the

---

[86] For a general introduction, see S. W. Sykes, 'Barth on the Centre of Theology', in S. W. Sykes (ed.), *Karl Barth – Studies of His Theological Methods*. Oxford: Oxford University Press, 1979, 17–54.

[87] Jacques de Senarclens, 'La concentration christologique', in *Antwort: Karl Barth zum siebzigsten Geburtstag*. Zurich: Zollikon, 1956, 190–207.

[88] For this concept in Barth's mature thought, see Barth, *Church Dogmatics* I/1, 125–98.

Göttingen Dogmatics (1924–5), in which Barth begins to tease out the elements of God's self-disclosure as revelation, Scripture and preaching. The Word of God is[89]

> one in three, and three in one: revelation, scripture, and preaching – the Word of God as revelation, the Word of God as scripture, the Word of God as preaching, neither to be confused nor separated. One Word of God, one authority, one power, and yet not one but three addresses. Three addresses of God in revelation, scripture and preaching, yet not three Words of God, three authorities, truths or powers. Scripture is not revelation, but from revelation. Preaching is not revelation or scripture, but from both. But the Word of God is scripture no less than it is revelation, and it is preaching no less than it is scripture.

It is important to note how Barth's threefold conception of the Word of God is ecclesiologically orientated. The process of theological authentication thus does not concern individuals in isolation or abstraction from the church, for the Word discloses itself through the church's canonical Scripture and in its proclamation. Barth's doctrine of the threefold Word implies simultaneously the indissoluble unity of the Word with the texts, tradition and present life of the church, along with the necessity of always distinguishing between the Word and the text, the text and the community.

Barth's concept of the threefold nature of the Word of God thus involves the linking of a divine event (revelation), a historically-mediated text (Scripture), and a social activity (preaching). At first sight, this represents an excellent example of the stratification of theological reality, involving a recogition of the different levels of social and cultural embeddedness of revelation. On closer examination, however, Barth appears to treat these notions as essentially ideational – that is to say, as representing networks of ideas which, though clearly interconnected through their mutual grounding in and witness to the fundamental reality *Deus dixit!*, are not differentiated in terms of the cultural or historical strata in which they are embedded. Dogmatics is a critical measuring of the church's speech about God against God's own word of self-communication.

A similar issue arises in relation to T. F. Torrance's approach to theological reflection, as we shall indicate below.

---

[89] Karl Barth, *The Göttingen Dogmatics: Instruction in the Christian Religion.* Grand Rapids, MI: Eerdmans, 1991, 14–15.

T. F. Torrance on multi-levelled theological reflection and the Trinity

Torrance is one of the most important interpreters of Barth, and it is therefore to be anticipated that Torrance's theology represents a sustained engagement with the category of revelation. In addition to echoing Barth's concerns, Torrance shows an awareness of the need to explore the different levels of theological articulation. Torrance – who here reflects some themes found in Polanyi's *Tacit Dimension*[90] – argues that human knowledge is multi-levelled and corresponds with the multi-levelled system of observable reality. According to Torrance, modern science has distilled this hierarchy of truths to three basic levels:[91]

> As Einstein, Polanyi, and others have shown us, the stratified structure of scientific knowledge usually comprises three levels of thought co-ordinated with one another: the primary or basic level, which is the level of our ordinary day-to-day experience and the loosely organised natural cognitions it involves; the secondary level of scientific theory with its search for a rigorous logical unity of empirical and conceptual factors; and the tertiary level where we develop a more refined and higher logical unity with a minimum of refined concepts and relations.

This three-tiered structure of knowledge within science can be applied in the same way to theology, leading to Torrance's conception of levels of theological reflection. For Torrance, the primary object of theological reflection is Jesus Christ. We shall presently explore (297–314) how there appears to be a genuine connection between a scientific and a Christocentric or incarnational conception of the Christian faith. The process of theological reflection is necessarily multi-levelled, in that the reality which is to be analysed is stratified. Torrance discerns three levels of reflection, as follows.

The first level (which could be defined as 'incipient theology') is the evangelical and doxological level.[92] This could be thought of as the basic level of Christian experience and living; 'the level of our day-to-day worship and meeting with God in response to the proclamation of the Gospel'. Torrance here cites approvingly the dictum of Hugh Ross

---

[90] For an assessment of the impact of Polanyi's ideas on T. F. Torrance's concept of 'levels', see Colin Weightman, *Theology in a Polanyian Universe: The Theology of Thomas F. Torrance*. New York/Berne: Peter Lang, 1994. But see the corrections to his interpretation at Alister E. McGrath, *Thomas F. Torrance: An Intellectual Biography*. Edinburgh: T&T Clark, 1999, 229–32.

[91] Thomas F. Torrance, *The Christian Doctrine of God: One Being, Three Persons*. Edinburgh: T&T Clark, 1996, 84.

[92] Torrance, *The Christian Doctrine of God*, 88–90.

Mackintosh, to the effect that the inner life of God 'is apprehended by us for the sake of its redemptive expression, not for the internal analysis of its content'.[93] At this level, the Christian believer has an experience of the reality of God as a 'basic undefined cognition which informally shapes our faith'. The Christian experience of worship, reading of Scripture, and an intuitive awareness of the reality of God constitutes the point of departure for further theological reflection.[94]

> Our minds become inwardly and intuitively adapted to know the living God. We become spiritually and intellectually implicated in patterns of divine order that are beyond our powers fully to articulate in explicit terms, but we are aware of being apprehended by divine Truth as it is in Jesus which steadily presses for increasing realization in our under-standing, articulation and confession of faith.

Through participation in the worship of the Christian community and engaging with the Scriptures (Torrance occasionally speaks of 'in-dwelling' Scripture, thereby stressing the personal engagement he envisages), the 'trinitarian pattern of God's self-revelation implicit in them becomes stamped in our minds'.

Torrance thus argues that the second stage in this process of engage-ment is the theological level. This secondary level of engagement involves moving on from the primary level of 'experiential apprehension' of God, and discerning the structures which lie within it.[95]

> By forming appropriate intellectual instruments with which to lay bare the underlying epistemological patterns of thought, and by tracing the claims of connection throughout the coherent body of theological truths, [theologians] feel their way forward to a deeper and more precise knowledge of what God has revealed of himself, even to the extent of reaching a reverent and humble insight into the inner personal relations of his Being. Our concern at this secondary level, however, while distinctly theological, is not primarily with the organic body of theological knowledge, but with penetrating through it to apprehend more fully the economic and ontological and trinitarian structure of God's revealing and saving acts in Jesus Christ as they are presented to us in the Gospel.

The theologian thus progresses from the Christian *experience* of God to grasp at least something of the *general theological structures* which underlie this experience. It will be clear that this can be understood to apply to a series of Christian doctrines; in the specific case of the Trinity,

---

[93] Torrance, *The Christian Doctrine of God*, 91.
[94] Torrance, *The Christian Doctrine of God*, 89.
[95] Torrance, *The Christian Doctrine of God*, 91.

Torrance argues that the transition in question is from 'the intuitive incipient form of an understanding of the Trinity' to 'the economic Trinity'.[96]

The third level (the 'higher theological level) involves 'moving from a level of economic trinitarian relations' to 'what [God] is ontically in himself'.[97] While the notion of the 'economic Trinity' may be said to belong to the second level of discourse, that of the 'essential Trinity' belongs to the third.

> In advancing from the second to the third epistemological level, we move from an ordered account of the economic activity of God toward us as Father, Son and Holy Spirit, to an ultimate set of fundamental concepts and relations whereby we seek to formulate in forms of thought and speech the hypostatic, homoousial and perichoretic relations in the eternal dynamic Communion.

In the course of this third and final phase, some significant developments in theological vocabulary take place, with implications which need to be noted.

1. New words require to be invented, in order to give expression to the new insights resulting from such theological speculation.

2. Words already in usage develop new associations, or have existing associations refined or redefined within the controlling paradigm of trinitarian thought. For example, the terms 'spirit' and 'being' underwent a radical shift in meaning away from a hitherto impersonal association towards 'an intensely personal meaning'.[98]

3. The acknowledged fragility of theological terms must not be taken to mean that they are inappropriate in this respect, nor as implying that their referent shares their ambiguity. 'All true theological concepts and statements invariably fall short of the God to whom they refer so that . . . their fragility and inadequacy as concepts and as human statements about God must be regarded as part of the correctness and truthfulness of their reference to God.'[99]

4. Despite the fragility of human language as a means to refer to God, there is no need to use purely negative modes of discourse when speaking of or thinking about God. The nature of God is such that 'committed rational worship and praise through godly

---

[96] Torrance, *The Christian Doctrine of God*, 91–8.
[97] Torrance, *The Christian Doctrine of God*, 93; 98–107.
[98] Torrance, *The Christian Doctrine of God*, 103.
[99] Torrance, *The Christian Doctrine of God*, 110–11.

ways of thought and speech that are *worthy* of God' is an essential element of a responsible Christian theology.[100]

Torrance regards this terminological evolution as an essential aspect of this theological engagement, and warns against the danger of using such *redefined* terms in their original pre-Christian senses. A further concern which Torrance notes in relation to this third level of theologizing is that it runs the risk of becoming detached from its moorings in God's self-revelation in history, and become little more than speculation and possible invention.[101]

> We must keep a constant check on these refined theological concepts and relations to make sure that they are in definite touch with the ground level of God's actual self-revelation to us and our evangelical experience of his saving activity in history, and that they remain empirically correlated with the saving truths and events of the Gospel, otherwise they tend to pass over into mythological projections of our own rationalizations into Deity.

The pattern of trinitarian theological reflection and formulation set out by Torrance can be represented as follows:

Experience of God $\Rightarrow$ Economic Trinity $\Rightarrow$ Essential Trinity

These three levels are mutually correlated; while, for example, the ontological Trinity is revealed in Christian experience, that experience is ultimately grounded in the ontological Trinity. The ontological Trinity in turn cannot be regarded as independent of either the economic Trinity, or of Christian trinitarian experience. Nor is Torrance for one moment suggesting that lower levels within the stratification of truth are to be regarded as false or redundant; they are all to be regarded as interconnected responses to their object. A failure to recognize the mutual interconnectedness of these levels of discourse can lead to theological reflection becoming divorced from Christian experience on the one hand, or from its proper ontological foundations on the other.

As we noted above, Torrance's approach in his *The Christian Doctrine of God* is primarily an account of the stratification of theological explanations. That is to say, Torrance has rightly demonstrated how an engagement with reality leads to a stratification of theological responses. While Torrance's engagement with Christian experience of God indicates a willingness to address issues of ontological depth, the emphasis is still primarily upon the horizontal aspects of explanation. In contrast, Bhaskar's approach focuses primarily on *the stratification of the reality which generates theories,* rather than *stratification within the resulting theories.* This therefore raises the question of how Christian theology relates to the various strata to which it responds. In what follows, we shall set out a provisional agenda which allows the importance and potential fruitfulness of such a stratified approach to theology to be developed.

The vertical stratification of theological explanation

Reality is read, interpreted and approached and encountered on the basis of a provisional understanding of what is being approached and encountered – an understanding which will be modified and developed in the light of successive iterations of this encounter. How this encounter with reality is related to the genesis, development and reception of theory is a matter of considerable interest in its own right, and will be the subject of the third and final volume in this project.

For our purposes here, we need to note the implications for such an iterative encounter with reality of the failure of the Enlightenment project – more specifically, that our 'readings' of reality are constituted and shaped, not simply by the reality that we believe that we are encountering, but by the tradition-mediated and tradition-constituted rational framework that we bring to bear upon it (see 64–97). Thus we *see* nature *as* creation, in that the Christian tradition authorizes and conditions us to do so. Yet in another sense, we recognize the need to concede and explore rival readings of nature, and aim to allow our reflections on nature to impact upon our theology. This point would be conceded by most, whether operating from within a Thomist tradition of natural theology, or a more generally Reformed perspective, informed by the dialectic between general and special revelation.[102]

The issue is that of the hermeneutical circle, a familiar problem in theology and literary theory – for example, in the manner in which the eighteenth-century Venetian playwright Carlo Goldoni understood the interplay of 'theatre' and 'world'.[103] The 'circle' arises through a text (or metaphorical textual equivalent, such as the 'book of nature') being located within a particular literature or language. As a result, the text is

[100] Torrance, *The Christian Doctrine of God,* 111.
[101] Torrance, *The Christian Doctrine of God,* 109.
[102] See G. C. Berkouwer, *General Revelation.* Grand Rapids, MI: Eerdmans, 1955; Bernard Ramm, *Special revelation and the Word of God.* Grand Rapids, MI: Eerdmans, 1961.
[103] Jackson I. Cope, 'The Spiral Return: From Stylistics to Theatre in Goldoni', *Eighteenth-Century Studies* 22 (1988), 70–7.

used to redefine the character of that literature (or language), while the refined language then permits a deeper engagement with the text in question. In Goldoni's case, *teatro* is based upon *mondo*, yet then offers a new way in which *mondo* is seen, and hence leads to a new way of representing and engaging it in *teatro*.[104] Theatre thus provides (at least, for Goldoni) a lens by which the world can be viewed, understood and changed.

Interpretans and *interpretandum* are thus related, not as linear cause and effect, but as points on a hermeneutical circle. An enhanced understanding thus arises through an iterative procedure, in which *interpretans* and *interpretandum* are constantly correlated to each other.[105] There is thus a 'hermeneutical spiral' arising from the interplay of the interpreter and the text (or textual equivalent), leading to both an enhancement of the interpretative framework being deployed and the quality of the insights being developed.[106] The issue is thus that of identifying the strata of reality which need to be involved in this process of creative interplay, and ensuring that these are connected to the theological task. Theology does not just address history, nor does it just address nature – it addresses *and is addressed* by these and other strata of reality, and has the responsibility of coordinating these different levels of being, and showing how they are coherent with its overall vision of reality.

In the final volume of this series, we shall address the question of how theology shapes its theories; our concern at this point is with the manner in which these theories shape our interaction with reality. This concluding section thus undertakes the task of exploring how the stratification of reality can be handled within the context of a scientific theology. Roy Bhaskar's critical realism both enables and encourages theology to engage with different levels of the world. Two points need to be highlighted:

1. Critical realism denies that reality may be reduced to any specific level of reality – such as religious experience, culture or the social

---

[104] See the fine study '"Teatro" e "mondo" nella poetica del Goldoni', in Mario Baratto, *Tre studi sul teatro: Ruzante, Aretino, Goldoni.* Venice: Pozza, 1964.

[105] This theme is explored in the difficult study of Ray L. Hart, *Unfinished Man and the Imagination: Toward an Ontology and a Rhetoric of Revelation.* New York: Herder & Herder, 1968.

[106] Anthony C. Thiselton, *The Two Horizons: New Testament Hermeneutics and Philosophical Description.* Grand Rapids, MI: Eerdmans, 1980, 104. For a useful study of this image, see Grant Osborne, *The Hermeneutical Spiral: A Comprehensive Introduction to Biblical Interpretation.* Downers Grove, IL: InterVarsity Press, 1991, 6.

concept of religion – thus challenging reductionist approaches to theology in particular, and Christianity in general.

2. Critical realism encourages a connectivist approach to theology, by insisting that its correlation with the various strata of reality be explored, both as a means of intellectual enrichment and as a matter of intellectual responsibility. Thus to explore the relationship between theology and one such stratum – let us say, 'experience' – does not preclude recognizing the importance of other such relationships, involving other strata such as 'history'.

In the remainder of this chapter we shall briefly note some aspects of the stratified reality to which Christian theology must relate, before moving on to deal with the issue of a theological response to reality in general.

Nature

We have already seen how the natural order plays an important role in a scientific theology. From the perspective of a scientific theology, *nature is seen as creation* (vol. 1, 135–240). Christian theology thus addresses a publicly accessible reality, which requires to be interpreted in certain ways. Thus Michael E. Soulé identifies nine 'distinct cognitive formations' of nature in western culture, including:[107]

- Nature as a mindless force, causing inhumanity inconvenience to humanity, and demanding to be tamed;

- Nature as an open-air gymnasium, offering leisure and sports facilities to affluent individuals who want to demonstrate their sporting prowess;

- Nature as a wild kingdom, encouraging scuba-diving, hiking and hunting;

- Nature as a supply depot – an 'ageing and reluctant provider' which produces (although with increasing difficulty) minerals, water, food and other services for humanity.

As we have seen (72–97), Christian theology offers a tradition-mediated reading of the 'book of nature' as God's creation which offers considerable potential as a means of explaining meta-traditional beliefs.

---

[107] Michael E. Soulé, 'The Social Siege of Nature', in Michael E. Soulé and Gary Lease (eds), *Reinventing Nature: Responses to Postmodern Deconstruction*. Washington, DC: Island Press, 1995, 137–70.

History

The philosophy which arguably is best grounded in history and thence offers an interpretation of that same history is Marxism.[108] The classic summary of Marx's views is to be found in the 'Preface' to Marx's *A Contribution to the Critique of Political Economy*, which sets out his vision of history as the locus of the 'conflict between the social forces of production and the relations of production'.[109] Marx's view that history was going somewhere, and that committed socialists could accelerate that process through appropriate action, gave Marxism an intellectual and political appeal which few could hope to match, particularly in the socially-alienated West Germany of the 1960s. It certainly interested me, and I have always valued the sense of intellectual rigour and commitment which my Marxist mentors encouraged.

The importance of addressing history was recognized by Augustine, not least on account of the problems raised by the 'imperial theology' of Eusebius of Caesarea, which saw the Roman empire as the climax of God's redemptive purposes. With the conversion of the Roman emperor Constantine in the fourth century, a new era in Christian history had dawned. Some Christian writers, most notably Eusebius, portrayed Constantine as an instrument chosen by God for the conversion of the empire.[110] Eusebius' 'Rome-theology' appears to have had a deep impact upon Christian thinking in this crucial period, not least in rendering Rome virtually immune from reflective criticism on the part of Christian writers. Indeed, so intimate was the connection which came to be presupposed between empire and gospel that the sack of Rome (410) endangered the future of western Christianity. The fall of Rome raised a series of potentially difficult questions for the imperial theology. Why had Rome been sacked?

Augustine addresses such questions in *The City of God*, partly to discredit a 'theology of history' which had become influential in Christian circles, and to liberate Christianity from this straitjacket which had been imposed upon it.[111] *The City of God* topples Rome from its position in Eusebius' theology of history. No longer is Rome portrayed

---

[108] Heinrich Popitz, *Der entfremdete Mensch: Zeitkritik und Geschichtsphilosophie des jungen Marx*. Frankfurt am Main: Europaische Verlagsanstalt, 1967.

[109] Karl Marx, *A Contribution to the Critique of Political Economy*. Chicago: Charles H. Kerr & Company, 1904, 11–12.

[110] Glenn F. Chesnut, *The First Christian Histories: Eusebius, Socrates, Sozomen, Theodoret and Evagrius*. Macon, GA: Mercer University Press, 1986.

[111] For the issues, see R. A. Markus, *Saeculum: History and Society in the Theology of St Augustine*. Cambridge: Cambridge University Press, 1970.

as God's chosen instrument for the salvation of the world, and the preservation of the gospel. The restrictive (and highly distorting) controlling influence of an imperial ideology upon the Christian exposition of Scripture was thus removed. As a result, the fall of Rome did not entail the fall of the gospel itself. By enslaving itself to a prevailing ideology, the dominant form of Christian thought had ensured its survival – indeed, its ascendancy – in the short term. But when that ideology collapsed, it brought its allies down with it. At least a substantial section of Christian theology had come to depend upon this ideology. Augustine's great contribution was to allow it to rediscover its true legitimation and foundation in Scripture, as read and received within the church.

While Augustine saw it as essential to offer a Christian theology of history, others were less persuaded. The *philosophes* of the Enlightenment had little time for history, regarding it as epistemically incapable of conveying knowledge. G. E. Lessing's famous assertion that 'accidental truths of history can never become the proof of necessary truths of reason' reflects the view of his generation, not simply his personal views.[112]

A somewhat overdue theological 'return to history' was signalled with the publication of the collection of essays, edited by Wolfhart Pannenberg, entitled *Revelation as History*. Fundamental to Pannenberg's argument is the idea that God's self-revelation is indirect, rather than direct; and that this indirect revelation takes place within the publicly accessible flux of history.[113] One of the most distinctive features of Pannenberg's early theology is the seriousness of his engagement, not simply with history, but with the *philosophy* of history – something which had hitherto been neglected by theologians, but taken with the utmost seriousness by Marxist theoreticians.

Christian theology is thus based upon, and offers an interpretation of, an analysis of universal and publicly accessible history. For Pannenberg, revelation is essentially a public and universal historical event which is seen as an 'act of God'. This seemed to reduce faith to an understanding of history, and deny any role to the Holy Spirit in

---

[112] G. E. Lessing, 'On the Proof of the Spirit and Power', in H. Chadwick (ed.), *Lessing's Theological Writings*. Stanford: Stanford University Press, 1956, 53–5.

[113] Wolfhart Pannenberg, 'Redemptive Event and History', in *Basic Questions in Theology*, London: SCM Press, 1970, vol. 1, 15–80. For the original pubication, see Wolfhart Pannenberg (ed.), *Revelation as History*. London: Macmillan, 1968.

the event of revelation.[114] Yet it is possible to argue that Pannenberg's essential insight is this: *history is to be seen as an arena of divine revelation*. Once more, we see the pattern of seeing a publicly accessible resource in a way consonant with the rationality of the Christian tradition.

Experience

Following the Enlightenment critique of Christian theology on the basis of its rationality – which was held to be particularist, rather than universal – Schleiermacher made an appeal to the religious experience of the individual and the Christian community as a potential means of grounding theology. Once more, a general resource – in this case, of course, a subjective entity – is being seen in a certain way. The general human consciousness of 'being dependent' is, according to Schleiermacher, recognized and interpreted within the context of the Christian faith as a sense of being dependent *upon God*. This 'feeling of absolute dependence (*das Gefühl schlechthinniger Abhängigkeit*)' thus constitutes the starting point for Christian theology.

Some seem to believe that a theology may be grounded in experience simply as a means of progressing beyond experience, and reaching out to new and more relevant intellectual pastures. Yet the key to engagement with any aspect of reality is not to leave it behind, abandoning it in favour of some more attractive goal. Rather, it is to be incorporated into the vision of reality that theology offers; it is to be transfigured, not discarded. This applies as much to experience as to history or nature. Having *seen* nature *as* creation, the theologian does not abandon interest in nature, but is able to see it in a new and heightened manner, in which it is appreciated and respected more fully. The same is true of experience.

The importance of this point can be see in a sadly neglected monograph on the origins and development of the New England theology published in the 1930s by Joseph Haroutinian. In his careful study of the theology of Jonathan Edwards, Haroutinian stressed how Edwards constructed 'the theology of Calvinism upon the basis of an empirical piety', while defending its doctrines both theologically and philosophically.[115] The strongly experiential aspects of Edwards' piety were

---

[114] For the hostile initial reaction to this notion of revelation, see Paul Althaus, 'Offenbarung als Geschichte und Glaube', *Theologische Literaturzeitung* 87 (1962), 321–30; Lothar Steiger, 'Offenbarungsgeschichte und theologische Vernunft', *Zeitschrift für Theologie und Kirche* 59 (1962), 88–113. For Pannenberg's response to Althaus, see Wolfhart Pannenberg, 'Einsicht und Glaube: Antwort an Paul Althaus', *Theologische Literaturzeitung* 88 (1963), 81–92.

[115] Joseph Haroutunian, *Piety versus Moralism: The Passing of the New England Theology*. New York: H. Holt & Co., 1932, xxi.

integrated within his overall vision of the Christian faith, and given a new sense of theological significance through his doctrine of creation. Edwards' experience – or 'sensation' – of the beauty of God was thus an integral aspect of his theological system. Yet Edwards' successors broke the link between theology and piety, reverting to 'governmental and legalistic conceptions of Calvinism'.[116] His experience-based piety was sidelined, in favour of a morality without any experiential or aesthetic dimension.

The trajectory of this subversion of Edwards' theological vision led relentlessly from experience to moralism. Edwards' successors – such as William Hart, Joseph Bellamy and Samuel Hopkins – tended to regard his interest in aesthetic religious experience as a dispensable starting point, which might be set to one side when the greater issues of morality had been secured. What Edwards regarded as the source of religion was thus displaced by one of its derivatives.

Yet there is no need for this development. Experience remains an important aspect of the Christian life, which is placed on a new foundation through the interposition of a theological framework. Theology allows experience to be experienced as something, and thus offers a new perspective on an existing phenomenon. As T. S. Eliot put it in 'The Dry Salvages':

> We had the experience but missed the meaning,
> And approach to the meaning restores the experience.

The present chapter has shown how the basic insights of scientific realism may be consolidated through Roy Bhaskar's 'critical realism', which allows theological engagement with the various levels of reality, and raises fundamental objections to reductionist approaches to theology which insist that only one stratum of reality should be addressed. It is clear that the exploration of the theological potential of Bhaskar's approach merits much closer and deeper examination, and it is hoped that this preliminary encounter will encourage others to undertake this more thorough engagement.

Having explored aspects of the realist agenda in some detail, it is now appropriate to set out the basic characteristics of a scientific theology as an engagement with reality.

---

[116] Haroutunian, *Piety versus Moralism*, xxii.

Chapter 11

The Encounter with Reality:
The Contours of a
Scientific Theology

W
e are now in a position to explore the contours of a scientific theology, conceived as an encounter with reality. Previous chapters have laid the groundwork for this final chapter in the present volume, particularly through exploring how the Christian tradition embodies a tradition-mediated rationality which regards nature as God's creation, and history as the sphere of divine revelation. We have placed particular emphasis on the role of natural theology as a meta-traditional device (72–97), which confirms the explanatory fecundity of the Christian tradition while simultaneously allowing it to connect up with the agendas and insights of other traditions.

A fundamental assumption of a scientific theology is that, since the ontology of the natural world is determined by and reflects its status as God's creation, the working methods and assumptions of those natural sciences which engage most directly with that natural world are of direct relevance to the working methods and assumptions of a responsible Christian theology. The basic theme of 'encountering reality' runs throughout both these natural sciences and a scientific theology, and is rooted in the Christian doctrine of creation. This is not to say that the natural sciences and Christian theology are identical, either in substance or method; the notion of an 'engagement with reality' contains within itself the related notion of engaging with each stratum of that reality *according to its distinct nature.*

The present chapter sets out four major characteristics of a scientific theology. It is argued that a scientific theology:

1. takes the form of a coherent response to an existing reality;
2. is an _a posteriori_ discipline;
3. takes account of the unique character of its object;
4. offers an explanation of reality.

In the remainder of this chapter, we shall explore these fundamental characteristics of a scientific theology in more detail.

The four points made above are, in my view, relatively uncontroversial. Once the central theme is accepted, the remaining aspects fall into place with relative ease. My research in this field has, however, led me to an additional conclusion, which I believe to be correct, yet am aware is potentially controversial. I have therefore decided to include this fifth element as a _postulate_ – a hypothesis which I believe to be warranted from within the standpoint of the Christian tradition, and which coheres with the remaining four fundamental characteristics of a scientific theology. The fifth postulate is that a scientific theology is, by virtue of the inner logic of the Christian faith, _Christocentric_. This has considerable implications for reflection on the nature and purpose of theory in Christian theology, as we shall see in the final volume of this series.

It may be objected at this point that such a conclusion represents a hindrance to the dialogue between the sciences and religion in general. I see no merit in this point. If this dialogue is to proceed without due attentiveness and consideration for the very different beliefs of the various religions, it is unlikely to be of any great significance. In making this observation concerning the distinctive nature of Christianity, I am merely respecting the integrity of the Christian faith, and making the entirely reasonable point that true dialogue depends upon a willingness to acknowledge such distinctives, rather than suppress or ignore them in the interest of some hidden agenda. If my analysis of the inner logic of the Christian faith is incorrect, I will gladly respond accordingly. There is, however, no case to be made for failing to identify and honour that inner logic, particularly by those whose view of things is determined by the mantra 'all religions say the same thing, really'. They do not, unless they are _made_ to do so by those who prefer to construct reality rather than investigate it respectfully and faithfully, as it actually is.

Scientific theology as a response to reality

We have already considered the strength of the case for some form of realism, based on an analysis of the theory and practice of the 'hard sciences', and noted that most anti-realist writers tend to limit themselves to criticisms of realism rather than offering sustained accounts of a viable anti-realist position. As we noted earlier, the theme of 'responding coherently to reality' brings together the idea that any science worthy of the name is under an obligation to ground itself in an engagement with the real world, and to offer a coherent account of what it encounters (123–35).

The theological affirmation of reality

If there does indeed exist a reality independent of the human recognition of this situation, is not theology also obligated to respond to that reality, and give an account of what it finds? Is there not the most fundamental of congruities between theological and natural sciences at this critical point?

One objection to such an approach must be noted immediately. Is this not a deplorable example of a methodologically confused discipline seeking to hitch itself to the methods of another, widely agreed to be immensely successful? Theology is hardly the subject of admiration and envy throughout the academic community on account of its ontological and epistemological triumphs. Why not rely on someone else's – preferably one that has a long history of success? Is not the whole idea of a 'scientific theology' little more than a disingenuous attempt to conceal the manifest intellectual failures of theology?

Now perhaps that represents a slight overstatement of the issue. Yet caricatures *work* precisely because there is a recognizable resemblance to their objects of criticism. The history of theology since about 1750 has often seemed, at least to its more critical observers, to represent a panic-stricken scramble to find a *fundamentum inconcussum* for reliable knowledge of God and the world[1] – or at least something that everyone else wouldn't laugh at. Some of the more puzzling experiments in theology over this period represent rather desperate attempts to hitch theological wagons to philosophical horses that would not drop dead from exhaustion round the next corner.

Yet one of the most important themes of a scientific theology is its vision of the unity of reality. Reality is to be apprehended in various ways and at different levels, with various disciplines offering themselves as the more appropriately qualified to explore certain aspects of that

---

[1] Although, to be fair, the same issue troubled most philosophers at some point or other. See the discussion with particular reference to Husserl in Bruno Paradis, 'Schémas du temps et philosophie transcendantale', *Philosophie* 12 (1995), 10–27.

reality than others. The Christian doctrine of creation insists that the dual affirmation of the created status of the natural order and of the human mind leads to the recognition that there is an ontological imperative for the epistemological enterprise – that is, that the nature of reality is such that the question of how it is to be known is imposed upon us. The Christian vision of reality is such that knowledge of creator and creation, redeemer and redeemed, are interlocked. Perhaps different methods of investigation are appropriate for different purposes; yet the fundamental Christian vision is that of a creator, redeemer and creation which are all possessed of the same intrinsic rationality through the act of creation itself.

Against the agenda of a radical idealism – as it is encountered, for example, in the writings of Descartes – a scientific theology affirms the reality of a world outside and apart from human perception of that world, and the obligation to give an account of that world on the basis of how that world is experienced and encountered. Ernest Gellner sets out the point at issue with particular clarity when he points to the radical idealist project as proposing and resting upon 'the transfer of ultimate legitimacy inwards to man, to human cognitive powers'. Knowledge is thus not controlled or determined, either in theory or practice, by an objective ordering within the world; rather, it is 'constructed by our cognition and its principles'.[2]

A scientific theology is not a free creation of the human mind, an expression of unrestrained creativity and innovation, an affirmation of the inward authority of the Cartesian *cogito*. It is a response to reality, a deliberate and principled attempt to give a faithful and adequate account of the way things are, subject to the limits placed upon human knowledge on account of our status as sinful creatures, and our location in history. In short, it is *responsible*, in two senses of that term:

1. It represents a *response to reality*, rather than a creation of that reality. A scientific theology is a theology which accepts the existence of a creator and creation, even when humanity fails to recognize either. We do not bring such concepts into existence through our mental activity, but recognize and respond to a situation which already exists, independent of and prior to our reflections. There is an all-important question here, which will require further consideration – namely, whether such a moment of recognition is to be viewed as a genuinely human insight, a

[2] Ernest Gellner, *Legitimation of Belief.* Cambridge: Cambridge University Press, 1975, 28–9.

disclosure resulting from an accumulation of insight; or whether the disclosure is to be seen as an *unveiling*, a revelation.

2. It is *accountable* for its insights and themes. That is to say, there are criteria against which it may be judged; there is a community who may judge how faithful that theology is as a positive yet critical affirmation of its insights and beliefs; and ultimately, in the Christian way of viewing things, a God who will hold the theologian accountable for the manner in which this specific God's character and nature are rendered.

The notion of theology as a scientific discipline which gives an account of its apprehension of reality is thoroughly traditional. In more recent times, the theme of such a theology has been stressed within the important theological tradition which takes its bearings from the substantial theological project of Karl Barth. For Barth, theology is an exercise in *Nachdenken*, a following through of the objectivity of reality.[3] Such an objectivity exists prior to any operation of the human mind; such an operation discloses and illuminates the structures of this reality. In part, Barth's emphasis on theology as *Nachdenken* can be seen as a response to those who insisted upon determining the possibility of revelation in advance of its taking place, by laying down *a priori* the conditions under which revelation might occur, and the form it must take. Yet Barth also had a fundamental concern to maintain a form of theological realism, over and against the Feuerbachian theological anti-realism which was such a significant force within German-language theology of his day.

To appreciate the importance of Barth's agenda, we may turn to consider some forms of theological anti-realism, before offering responses to them.

Theological anti-realism: Don Cupitt

Theological anti-realism can be traced back to Ludwig Feuerbach (1804–71),[4] whose reading of Hegel's account of concept formation led him to postulate that religious notions were essentially the improper

---

[3] We find a similar theme in Eberhard Jüngel's massive exploration of the doctrine of God, in which the question of how God is to be conceived (*Denkbarkeit Gottes*) assumes a pivotal role: Eberhard Jüngel, *Gott als Geheimnis der Welt: Zur Begründung der Theologie des Gekreuzigten im Streit zwischen Theismus und Atheismus*. 4th edn. Tübingen: J. C. B. Mohr, 1982, 224–5.

[4] For what follows, see Heinz Fastenrath, *Ein Abriss atheistischer Grundpositionen: Feuerbach, Marx, Nietzsche, Sartre*. Stuttgart: Klett, 1993; Max Wartofsky, *Feuerbach*. Cambridge: Cambridge University Press, 1982.

objectification of human feelings or longings. We have already considered how Feuerbach's critique of theism may be met through an appeal to a Christian doctrine of creation (vol. 1, 204–9). It is also important to note that the significance of Feuerbach's anti-realism derives largely from the context in which it is set – namely, the pivotal role assigned to feeling (*das Gefühl*) in Schleiermacher's theological system. Feuerbach's argument decouples *das Gefühl* from any transcendent realm, at both the epistemological and ontological levels. Far from providing a connection with the transcendent, *das Gefühl* is merely a manifestation of the depths of the human heart.

Feuerbach represents a modern theological anti-realism, heavily conditioned by the assumptions of the Enlightenment. With the fragmentation and decline of this movement, theological anti-realism has increasingly come to be associated with postmodernity. The British philosopher of religion Don Cupitt represents a particularly fascinating instance of a postmodern theological anti-realist, whose ideas may profitably be explored at this point. Cupitt is also of interest on account of his tendency to mirror the trends of dominant western cultural ideologies.[5] Since the publication of his *Taking Leave of God* (1981), Cupitt has generally embraced a tag-along theology, which takes its cues and derives its intellectual legitimation from whatever happened to be interesting or fashionable at the time he was writing.[6] The anti-realist trend of his thought led him to abandon any belief in an 'objective' God at a relatively early stage. However, this anti-realism came to be articulated increasingly in terms of deconstruction, with a growing interest in the ideas of certain leading French postmodern writers. Thus from about 1985, we find Rolandes Barthes, Jacques Derrida and Michel Foucault playing an increasingly significant role in his thinking, leading him to abandon any reference to God even as an internal symbol of faith.[7]

[5] For the best assessments of Cupitt's development and significance, see Anthony C. Thiselton, *Interpreting God and the Postmodern Self: On Meaning, Manipulation and Power.* Edinburgh: T&T Clark, 1995, 81–117. See further Scott Cowdell, *Atheist Priest? Don Cupitt and Christianity.* London: SCM Press, 1988; Stephen Ross White, *Don Cupitt and the Future of Christian Doctrine.* London: SCM Press, 1994.

[6] Don Cupitt, *Taking Leave of God.* London: SCM Press, 1981. For a critique of this work, see Keith Ward, *Holding Fast to God: A Reply to Don Cupitt.* London: SPCK, 1982.

[7] Don Cupitt, *The Long-legged Fly: A Theology of Language and Desire.* London: SCM Press, 1987. The use of Lacan is interesting, not least because the internal difficulties raised by Lacan's position seem to be overlooked. See Don Cupitt, *The Time Being.* London: SCM Press, 1992. As Thiselton comments, this seems to represent a 'rather hurried reading' of Lacan. For the problems with Lacan's flawed critique of realism, see François Roustang, *The Lacanian Delusion.* New York: Oxford University Press, 1990, 59–102.

My decision to use Cupitt to illustrate some issues arising from post-modern anti-realism is open to severe and justifiable criticism. Let me mention several potential grounds of complaint before proceeding further. Cupitt is in the habit of stating, rather than arguing, his position, causing intense frustration to those who are trying to work out what the intellectual merits of his position might be. Furthermore, he tends to avoid the systematic engagement with either a major thinker or position, tending instead to generalize or offer highly rhetorical and simplistic accounts of writers such as Immanuel Kant, Blaise Pascal, D. F. Strauss and Ludwig Wittgenstein, and evade difficulties that his position encounters.[8] Cupitt's tag-along theology seems to be regarded as so intellectually derivative and ephemeral that it has not been taken with great seriousness even by academic theologians, let alone the academy in general.

While fully conceding the force of these objections, I believe that it is appropriate to consider Cupitt as a representative of theological anti-realism precisely because such anti-realism can be seen to take its cues from an increasingly beleagured postmodernism, whose credibility is now seriously in doubt. The cumulative force of internal contradictions and external failures is such that a Kuhnian paradigm shift cannot be far away. Cupitt tends to equate 'simplistic' and 'realist' approaches to the Christian faith, apparently unaware of the varieties of realism, and the vulnerability of the specific anti-realist approaches he favours.

Cupitt's appropriation of postmodern agenda has been subjected to rigorous scrutiny by Anthony Thiselton.[9] Setting to one side the question of whether Cupitt has actually understood the writers on whom he draws, Thiselton laments the way in which Cupitt regularly commends 'authoritative rhetoric' in place of 'exploratory argument', substituting 'aggressively propandist stances' for the cool rational discourse which the situation so evidently demands.

> 'Recent literary theory has shown that absolute integrity . . . is a myth.' Quite apart from lumping together the theories of Derrida, Lacan and others as 'recent literary theory in general', Cupitt openly utilizes this principle for a double purpose. He uses it on the one had to advise radicals that 'deception', 'evasion' and other such manipulative strategies may enable them to disguise their stance as 'playing the game' in the eyes of

[8] See, for example, White, *Don Cupitt and the Future of Doctrine*, 122–3. See also the points made by Brian Hebblethwaite, *The Ocean of Truth: A Defence of Objective Theism.* Cambridge: Cambridge University Press, 1988, 43–52, in response to Don Cupitt, *The Sea of Faith.* London: BBC Publications, 1985.

[9] Thiselton, *Interpreting God and the Postmodern Self,* 105–17.

the orthodox. On the other side he universalizes the recommendation that the 'religious teacher *must* [his italics] use language manipulatively, rhetorically and deceitfully'.

Thiselton is especially critical of Cupitt's refusal to respond to criticisms of his positions on the basis of the ephemerality of those views: by the time the critics have submitted their judgements, Cupitt has moved on. Presumably Cupitt believes that he remains permanently ahead of the opposition, and is thus invulnerable to criticism. In *The Time Being* (1992), Cupitt insists that the 'world of signs' is endlessly transient, making it impossible to reach firm and permanent conclusions. All is shifting; nothing endures. Yet this virtue rapidly becomes a weakness, in that Cupitt's views are seen to be transient, rather than of permanent value.[10]

The general tone of Cupitt's anti-realism can be seen from the following statements, taken from *The Sea of Faith*:[11]

> Does this amount to saying that God is simply a humanly constructed ideal, such that when there are human beings no longer there will be God no longer? The question is improper, because it is framed from the obsolete realist point of view. The suggestion that the idea of God is man-made would only seem startling if we could point by contrast to something that has not been made by men. But since our thought shapes all its objects, we cannot. In an innocuous sense, all our normative ideas have been posited by ourselves, including the truths of logic and mathematics as well as all our ideals and values. How else could be have acquired them? Thus God is man-made only in the sense that everything is.

In later writings, Cupitt goes on to develop these ideas more radically, arguing that the world has been completely cut adrift from the moorings of realism. Instead of responding to reality, we create whatever we choose to regard as real. Reality is something which we construct, not something to which we respond. 'We constructed all the world-views, we made all the theories . . . They depend on us, not we on them.'[12] Over the years, Cupitt has gradually shifted from a form of critical realism (which recognizes that what we say about God never fully represents the reality of God) to an anti-realism (which insists that there is no objective reality 'out there': all our language about 'reality' – including God – is really about ourselves.

---

[10] Thiselton, *Interpreting God and the Postmodern Self*, 113–14.
[11] Cupitt, *Sea of Faith*, 270–1.
[12] Don Cupitt, *Only Human*. London: SCM Press, 1985, 9.

Yet this position is untenable. It embodies the worst excesses and misunderstandings of the 'linguistic turn' in philosophy, which refuses to acknowledge that language is in any way shaped or determined by the external world.[13] We are trapped within a linguistic matrix, over which we have no control. Language itself is the sole shaper of the world. The mind plays no 'constructive' role in shaping our 'experience'. Yet there is ample empirical evidence that language shifts and develops in order to accommodate an enhanced grasp of the natural world. One of the reasons for the general abandonment of analytical philosophy is its manifest failings when confronted with the acheivements of the natural sciences, and their ability to transcend the limitations of language through an enhanced grasp of the external world.

Cupitt assumes – for he most certainly has not demonstrated – that realism is 'obsolete', and hence draws the premature conclusion that all our thoughts about the world must be the arbitrary products of the human mind. If there is no external restraint upon our thought – for example, conforming to reality, or agreeing with Cupitt because his arguments are so compelling – then we are free to think and act as we choose, creating the intellectual and moral world which we inhabit. Where previously the nature of God had dictated what could and could not be said about God, now the nature of language dictates what can and cannot meaningfully be said of anything – God included.[14] Yet Cupitt seems to confuse epistemology and ontology in some of these assertions, and seems to eliminate any meaningful ground for someone to actually agree with him. We are presented with what appears to be a playful Foucaultian rhetorical montage which seeks to persuade without providing any context of justification, and – in a classic example of the fallacy of self-referentiality – assumes it is immune to criticism.

Throughout his later writings, we find a studied reluctance to engage with the natural sciences, despite Cupitt's earlier interests in this field.[15] His anti-realist rhetoric never quite seems to manage to engage with the critical questions thrown up by the explanatory and predictive successes of the natural sciences, or the growing discontent with anti-realist philosophies. Instead, we find a studied evasion of such questions, buttressed by a manipulative rhetoric which describes realism as 'simplistic' and 'outmoded'. Yet Cupitt does not justify this. He seems to assume that, since prestigious writers like Wittgenstein

[13] For his radical approach to this question, see Don Cupitt, *The Last Philosophy*. London: SCM Press, 1995; idem, *Solar Ethics*. London: SCM Press, 1995.
[14] White, *Don Cupitt and the Future of Doctrine*, 63.
[15] See Don Cupitt, *The Worlds of Science and Religion*. London: Sheldon Press, 1976.

are anti-realists, everyone else ought to follow suit.[16] But Wittgenstein is not quite as straightforward as Cupitt makes out; furthermore, Wittgenstein's views can hardly be allowed to determine the outcome of this debate, as if he represents the final word in the realism debate. Roy Bhaskar's critical realism seems to many to deal perfectly well with the Wittgensteinian agenda.[17]

The failure of Cupitt's approach is best seen in the sections of *The Sea of Faith* in which he surveys the radical changes that have come about in our understanding of the world as the result of Newtonian mechanics and Darwin's theory of evolution. These new insights have transformed the religious situation, making it impossible to go back to earlier ways of conceiving and practising the Christian faith. Yet Cupitt assumes that these scientific insights are *valid* – that Darwin's theory of evolution is (at least approximately) true, and that it offers a reliable account of the real world which forces Christianity to rethink its ideas and methods. The fact is that a form of scientific realism has been smuggled in; indeed, without it, Cupitt would have to speak merely of arbitrary shifts in intellectual fashion, rather than permanent changes in our understanding of the world. To discredit theological realism, Cupitt is obliged to assume its historical or scientific counterparts. So it seems that all of our ideas are not free creations of the autonomous human mind: at least some are the response to what we might call 'facts'.

Cupitt's puzzling account of our intellectual situation appears to presume that events outside the human mind have no capacity to shape or reshape our language or thoughts. This baffling idea makes it impossible to explain how our ideas of the world develop in response to scientific progress. As Frederick Will pointed out, the world does have any ability to shape our language and thoughts, and we must ensure this is reflected in our thinking about our language, as well as the world it attempts to represent.[18]

> The world, of which we are a part, and various of its features, states or objects continue to have the capacity to affect our language and conceptual systems. Things – to speak thus loosely and collectively – can guide us in our epistemic endeavors, if we have the good fortune and wit

---

[16] See the puzzlingly simplistic account of Wittgenstein in *The Sea of Faith*, 213–25. For comments, see Thiselton, *Interpreting God and the Postmodern Self*, 108–9.

[17] Nick Hostettler, 'How Wittgenstein got Bhaskar Wrong', *Alethia* 3.1 (2000), 22–8. For the contrary view, see Nigel Pleasants, *Wittgenstein and the Idea of a Critical Social Theory: A Critique of Giddens, Habermas and Bhaskar*. London: Routledge, 1999.

[18] Frederick L. Will, *Pragmatism and Realism*. Lanham, MD: Rowman & Littlefield, 1997, 37.

to discern their guiding signs. They can nudge us, frustrate us and so prompt us to bring our conceptual and linguistic procedures into conformity with aspects of the world which we at the time may only dimly recognize. They can signal us through the retrograde motion of Jupiter that revisions are needed in our astronomy and our conception of the relations of earth, sun and moon. They can prompt us by means of the peculiar properties of newly isolated deuterium that alteration is due in the way we think of a physical element.

I can only assume that Cupitt and I live in different worlds, and will leave the reader to determine which is more 'real'. The world in which I live is one in which human ways of thinking demonstrably have been, and continue to be, changed by events and changing understandings of the way the world actually is. The Lisbon earthquake of All Saints' Day, 1755, which destroyed thirty thousand persons in six minutes and was followed by a ten metre tidal wave which flooded most of the city, raised the most serious of questions concerning Alexander Pope's naïve optimism, as expressed in his famous dictum from *An Essay on Man:* 'What is, is right.' Voltaire's *Candide* and his *Poem on the Disaster of Lisbon* represent a reaction against this optimism, occasioned to no small degree by this natural disaster.[19] An event in nature – which was certainly real enough for the thirty thousand persons who died – thus had a highly significant impact on the ways of thinking of the Enlightenment. Far from being bound to a pre-existing static world of language, the writers of the Enlightenment proved perfectly capable of responding to this stimulus to their thinking.[20]

The world in which I live and work as both natural scientist and theologian has been shaped through a tightening grip on the nature of the external world, which forced abandonment of the medieval view that the earth stood at the centre of the solar system (see the works of Copernicus, Kepler and Galileo), and raised questions about the nature of the world and our place within it (see Darwin's *The Origin of Species* and subsequently *The Ascent of Man*). I assume that Cupitt knows about this world, as he often refers to it in his writings, arguing that these changes have forced us to abandon traditional religious beliefs. This rather hasty and premature conclusion nevertheless rests on the premise

---

[19] Giovanni Gullace, *Il Candide nel pensiero di Voltaire.* Napoli: Societa editrice napoletana, 1985.
[20] For the literature, see Judite Nozes, *The Lisbon Earthquake of 1755: Some British Eye-Witness Accounts.* Lisbon: British Historical Society of Portugal, 1987; T. D. Kendrick, *The Lisbon Earthquake.* London: Methuen, 1956. For specifically religious reflections, see John Wesley, *Serious thoughts occasioned by the earthquake at Lisbon.* London: n.p., 1756.

that an improved human understanding of the real world demands that we change our ways of thinking about some of its aspects.

In his haste to rubbish traditional religious beliefs as being 'out-moded', Cupitt seems to overlook the awkward fact that what he believes to *render* them outmoded originates from outside the human mind, and gains its credibility and intellectual force precisely because it is clearly part of the 'way the world is' (Voltaire) rather than the way we choose to view the world. For Voltaire, the way that Pope chose to view the world was rendered obselete by the Lisbon earthquake. Yet Cupitt's world-view appears impervious to such awkward intrusions. This allows him the liberty to think and believe what he likes. Yet it must be asked, in all seriousness, whether such intellectual liberty has any correlation whatsoever with the reliability of the judgements that he thus reaches.

Perhaps the best indicator of the implications of Cupitt's anti-realist conception of religion is found in a 1991 essay 'After Liberalism'.[21] Religion is here portrayed as a purely human creation, which is open to endless re-creation without limits, whether imposed from within or without.

> Post-modern religion is religion that fully accepts that it is just human, being made of human signs, and which after having gone through the fires of nihilism knows that it must now continually remake itself as art.

Old-fashioned liberal Christianity thus cannot be taken seriously any more. In its place, we must affirm the fundamental insight of the human construction of all ideas and values:

> The main theme is very simple: it is the realization that our knowledge systems, our beliefs, our myths, our meanings, even our values, are as human and local and transient as we are. *That* is the thought that freezes the blood. The older liberalism could not bear it, and turned away. But the post-liberal sort of theology I have been trying to describe will be nihilistic. It will head determinedly into the darkness.

This is rhetoric masquerading as argument. Let us look at a belief, and see whether it is quite as 'local and transient' as Cupitt suggests – namely, the insight that underlies Newton's mechanics, which Cupitt rightly believes to have been of fundamental importance in shaping the modern

---

[21] Don Cupitt, 'After Liberalism', in D. W. Hardy and P. H. Sedgwick (eds), *The Weight of Glory: A Vision and Practice for Christian Faith*. Edinburgh: T&T Clark, 1991, 251–6.

world. According to Newton, the gravitational attraction F_{grav} between two bodies of masses m_1 and m_2, separated by a given distance d is given by the equation:

$$F_{grav} = \frac{G\, m_1\, m_2}{d^2}$$

where G is the universal gravitational constant. So what does Cupitt want us to believe? That G is a *local* gravitational constant, which varies from one location and era to another – the suggestion that Alain Sokal made in his glorious spoof paper, celebrating the fashionable nonsense of postmodern science? In the end, the plausibility of Cupitt's anti-realism rests on the rhetoric he deploys in commending it, and on his readers avoiding thinking too much about the implications and presuppositions of his assertions.

So what kind of response is made to such suggestions by theologians committed to realism? In what follows, we shall consider the realist theological programmes of Karl Barth and T. F. Torrance, and consider how they meet some of the issues we have just been considering.

Theological realism: Karl Barth and T. F. Torrance

It is difficult to conceive of two more diametrically opposed positions on the issue of theological realism than those of Ludwig Feuerbach (1804–72) and Karl Barth (1886–1968). For Feuerbach, the concept of God was the product of the human imagination, which objectified human emotions and faculties. 'Knowledge of God' is nothing more and nothing less than human self-knowledge. For Barth, God exists over and above human knowledge of God, and is only to be known authentically through the divine self-revelation. Barth here took up an exposed position running counter to the norms of the prevailing culture,[22] even if it accorded well with the norms of mainstream Christianity. Given the importance of the issue of theological realism in its own right, and the continued scholarly interest in the precise manner in which Feuerbach is implicated in the complex trajectory of

---

[22] Barth seems to have had little idea that the natural sciences might have provided an important ally in his work. I assume that this can be put down to his concern to avoid any hint of a philosophically-determined theology, perhaps coupled with a lack of knowledge of the nature sciences. For detailed discussion, see Harold P. Nebelsick, 'Karl Barth's Understanding of Science', in John Thompson (ed.), *Theology beyond Christendom: Essays on the Centenary of the Birth of Karl Barth*. Allison Park, PA: Pickwick Publications, 1986, 165–214.

Barth's theological development, it seemed appropriate to develop the issues of theological realism by allowing the Barth–Feuerbach debate to act as a catalyst for reflection on the issue.

In recent years, the existing scholarly consensus over Barth's theological development – which can broadly be thought of as an early dialectical phase, giving way to a 'theology of the Word' in the aftermath of his 1931 engagement with Anselm of Canterbury in *Fides quarens intellectum* – has been challenged, perhaps most significantly by Bruce L. McCormack.[23] The older view of Barth's development rested in part on Barth's own musings on his theological development. However, a more subtle and complex factor which shaped this was the perception that the early dialectical and polemical Barth can be sharply distinguished from the mature Barth. This distinction between an early 'dialectical' and a more mature 'analogical' phase rests partly on a seminal 1951 work of Hans Urs von Balthasar.[24] However, it needs to be noted that von Balthasar did not have access to the all-important lecture notes from Barth's Göttingen period, which point to an emergent theological programme which does not readily fit the 'dialectical-analogical' scheme.[25]

John Webster notes that the older consensus founded on von Balthasar's work is increasingly being recognized as being based on a selective approach to Barth's writings, in which a few of Barth's occasional writings (such as those gathered together in *The Word of God and the Word of Man* and *Theology and Church*) are given priority, and the all-important lecture cycles of the 1920s are marginalized. A careful study of these lecture notes suggests that, from the moment he began his teaching career, Barth was a serious constructive thinker, rather than the iconoclast that the 'dialectical' model demands.[26] These lecture notes point to the major themes of the *Church Dogmatics* already being in place by the 1920s, especially some of the issues relating to prolegomena, such as the doctrine of the Trinity and revelation. This, can be seen in his 1925 lecture on Hermann:[27]

---

[23] Bruce L. McCormack, *Karl Barth's Critically Realistic Dialectical Theology: Its Genesis and Development 1909–1936*. Oxford: Clarendon Press, 1995.

[24] Hans Urs von Balthasar, *Karl Barth: Darstellung und Deutung seiner Theologie*. Cologne: Hegner, 1951. For variations on this, see T. F. Torrance, *Karl Barth, Biblical and Evangelical Theologian*. Edinburgh: T&T Clark, 1990, 27–82. This 'developmental' reading of Barth represents a shift away from Torrance's earlier work *Karl Barth: An Introduction to His Early Theology 1910–1931*. London: SCM Press, 1961, 48–104.

[25] McCormack, *Karl Barth's Critically Realistic Dialectical Theology*, 327–74.

[26] John Webster, *Barth*. London: Continuum, 2000, 23.

[27] Karl Barth, *Theology and Church: Shorter Writings, 1920–1928*. London: SCM Press, 1963, 256.

> But the fact remains that if one has once had the idea that at the beginning
> and end of the pageant, where we theologians are amusing ourselves
> with such things, there stands the majesty of the Triune God, the Father
> whom none sees except in the Son who is One with him and through
> the Spirit who again is one with him, if one has once thought that God
> is eternally Subject and never object, that he determines himself and is
> knowable exclusively through himself in 'pure act' (*actus purissimus*) of
> his Triune personality – then one has thought it and must continue to
> think it. The thought cannot afterwards be put into brackets as just a
> 'reflection of faith'.

Webster argues that the later phases of Barth's work involve not so
much a decisive turn away from what came earlier but the giving of a
greater profile to and a massive amplification of the affirmations which
'Barth's earlier rhetoric sometimes obscures from less careful readers'.[28]
The development of Barth's theology cannot be schematized simply as
polemical rhetorical de-construction without positive affirmations on
the one hand, or as reaction against philosophy in general (or perhaps
certain styles of philosophy in particular). Both these readings of Barth's
development tend to present the early Barth – as opposed to the mature
Barth – as allowing no relationship between the transcendent God of
revelation and the contingent material world. They stress the negative
aspects of the dialectic between God and humanity, rather than the
positive affirmation of God's covenant towards humanity. It could,
however, be reasonably argued that Barth was first and foremost a
theologian grappling with the presentation of the biblical God revealed
in Jesus Christ, and that this principle can be discerned as underlying
the development of his theology. Given such serious debates over the
general trajectory of Barth's theological trajectory, it is inevitable that
the more specific question of Barth's relation to Feuerbach should
require a fresh analysis.

Two main positions can be discerned within the secondary literature
dealing with Barth's relationship to Feuerbach, with significant differences in terms of both the importance which Barth attached to
Feuerbach, and the specific issues to be addressed. One school of
thought holds that Barth's knowledge of and interest in Feuerbach is
both substantial and formative to his theological development. Joseph
Weber, a prominent representative of this position, sees Barth's *Church
Dogmatics* as a sustained critique of Feuerbach's anthropologically
focused anti-theology, in effect representing a *Nein!* directed against

---

[28] Webster, *Barth*, 23.

Feuerbach.[29] More recently, W. Waite Willis has developed a similar theme arguing that the doctrines of the Trinity found in Barth, and subsequently in Moltmann, are best to be viewed as a defence against 'protest atheism'.[30] Willis sees the essence of this movement as lying in its 'protest against God grounded in the misery of the concrete human situation'. The ultimate grounds for rejection of God here do not lie in any alleged intellectual incoherence of theism, but in the perception that 'the divine is responsible for and does nothing to transform the human condition'.[31] Willis argues that the its epistemological roots of 'protest atheism' must be seen to lie in Feuerbach's rejection of God on the grounds that 'the divine is constituted only at the expense of the human'.[32] Willis argues that the general thrust of this anti-theological polemic lies behind Barth's positive theological formulations.[33]

> In forming his theology Barth is constantly aware of Feuerbach's critique. Demonstrating this awareness is the doctrine of the Trinity which as developed by Barth serves an apologetic function in that it incorporates Feuerbach's major epistemological position. . . . This Trinitarian appropriation of Feuerbach's epistemology enables Barth to use the doctrine of the Trinity as the basis for argumentation against other theological systems.

Both Weber and Willis regard Feuerbach's atheology as playing a substantive role in the emergence and formulation of Barth's theological programme. Barth's entire theological project is to be viewed as a systematic rejection and critique of an anthropological approach to theology. While Barth may well fulminate against Schleiermacher, his real enemy is to be seen as Feuerbach, whose concept of the 'humanization of God' determines the inherent anthropology of all statements concerning God.

A second line of argument within the literature sees Barth's specific reaction against Feuerbach as embodying a more broadly-based critique of an entire modern experientially-based theological tradition, whose origins are ultimately to be traced back to Martin

---

[29] Joseph C. Weber, 'Feuerbach, Barth and Theological Methodology', *Journal of Religion* 46 (1966), 24–36; 29.

[30] W. Waite Willis, *Theism, Atheism and the Doctrine of the Trinity: The Trinitarian theologies of Karl Barth and Jürgen Moltmann in Response to Protest Atheism.* Atlanta, GA: Scholars Press, 1987.

[31] Willis, *Theism, Atheism and the Doctrine of the Trinity*, 3.

[32] Willis, *Theism, Atheism and the Doctrine of the Trinity*, 4.

[33] Willis, *Theism, Atheism and the Doctrine of the Trinity*, 27.

Luther, which Feuerbach pressed to its logical conclusions. This approach is represented by Manfred Vogel, who argues that Feuerbach's theology is to be seen as 'the necessary outcome of the theological orientation of the modern era'. In critiquing Feuerbach, Barth is thus indirectly criticizing the entire theological project of modernity.[34] According to this perspective, Feuerbach is viewed as a representative, or perhaps a central legitimating resource for a theological programme to which Barth took particular exception, raising the possibility that Barth may have projected or retrojected issues associated with modernity in general onto Feuerbach in particular.

This possibility is explored by John Glasse, who argues that Barth's attitude to Feuerbach underwent a significant development around the time of the Anselm book, and is linked with a growing awareness of the Christological aspects of revelation. In his early phase, Barth concentrated on a polemic against anthropologically grounded conceptions of religion through his insistence that God is *totaliter aliter*. Whatever Feuerbach and his colleagues may choose to call the outcome of any human objectification or projection of feelings, it cannot be equated with God. While never offering a response to Feuerbach's critique of religion, Barth nevertheless formalizes a Christologically focused conception of revelation which he regards as undercutting any anthropological critique of revelation as objectified human self-consciousness.[35]

If this were the case, Barth could be argued to treat Feuerbach simply as a convenient representative of a methodology he wished to confute, rather than dealing with his philosophy of religion in any detail. Given Barth's misgivings over paying undue attention to issues of philosophy, this would result in Feuerbach being less than fairly treated, especially in relation to his central thesis concerning the genesis of the concept of 'God' through the objectification of human feelings. Rather than address this central issue, Barth in effect conducts an internal reorientation of the debate, shifting the grounds of contention from the content to the actuality of revelation. The idea of the divine self-interpretation of revelation, implicit in Barth's notion of *Offenbarkeit*, is treated as in itself offering an adequate response to the Feuerbachian agenda.

This has not satisfied Barth's critics, who not unreasonably point to the intrinsic circularity of Barth's arguments at this point. As Weber

---

[34] Manfred H. Vogel, 'The Barth–Feuerbach Confrontation', *Harvard Theological Review* 59 (1966), 27–52.

[35] John Glasse, 'Barth on Feuerbach', *Harvard Theological Review* 57 (1964), 69–96.

argues, Barth could be argued to do little more than assert that his concept of revelation lies beyond Feuerbach's critique:[36]

> Barthian theology may regard itself to be more secure from the attacks of Feuerbach because it in no way tries to establish the validity of talking about revelation in some human possibility. But when Barth shows that faith is not open to normal means of verification, this could mean that it is in no way verifiable, it would then be meaningless to try to understand revelation as Barth does. When we look closer at Barth's theology we see that ultimate verification of revelation seems to be in the faith of the believer who confesses that this faith is not his own possibility. Rather, it is grounded in God's revelation in Jesus Christ. But can one then not respond by pointing out that in fact the actuality of revelation is just the actuality of the subjective faith of the believer? . . . Feuerbach has spoken a word in our modern culture that cannot be ultimately refuted by rational argumentation.

The real difficulty is that Barth does not seem to regard Feuerbach's agenda as worthy of detailed criticism. His theological priorities seem to lie in the positive articulation of his own position, and differentiating this from the rival position of Schleiermacher, which he clearly regards as inadequate and vulnerable to the charge of anthropocentrism. Barth asserts that divine revelation lies beyond Feuerbach's critique, and in his 'strident theological rhetoric of the real'.[37]

Three points can be made in Barth's defence. First, if we take a purely coherentist view of human knowledge, Barth's demonstration of the internal consistency of his view must be given considerably more weight than his critics allow. If there is no external 'reality' of God, then the reliability of a theological system cannot be judged by the alleged extent to which it is grounded in or mirrors this reality. Those siding with Feuerbach thus have a distinct disadvantage, in that they have no alternative foundation on which to base a rival system. Theological anti-realists, like their philosophical cousins, tend to find themselves in the position of critiquing realists, rather than offering viable alternatives. To reiterate the issue: if there is *no* foundation for human knowledge of God, other than what we ourselves construct – whether individually or collectively – then the

---

[36] Weber, 'Feuerbach, Barth and Theological Methodology', 32. For similar criticisms, see Wolfhart Pannenberg, *Anthropology in Theological Perspective*. Edinburgh: T&T Clark, 1985, 15; Dorothee Sölle, *Political Theology*. Philadelphia: Fortress Press, 1974, 11–39, 94–5.

[37] I borrow this phrase from Richard H. Roberts, *A Theology On Its Way? Essays on Karl Barth*. Edinburgh: T&T Clark, 1991, 196.

coherence of the resulting ideas is one of the few criteria by which their merits may be judged.

Yet more importantly, in the second place Barth is able to point to the person of Jesus Christ, as set within the biblical matrix, as the *fundamentum* of Christian theology. Barth's theological realism is firmly anchored Christologically. God *is*;[38] God's revelation does not need to be demonstrated, but its character and consequences require to be unfolded. 'In the doctrine of God we have to learn what we are saying when we say "God". In the doctrine of God we have to learn to say "God" in the correct sense.'[39] And for Barth, that revelation of God is inextricably linked with Christ and Scripture:[40]

> When Holy Scripture speaks of God, it does not permit us to let our attention or thoughts wander at random . . . When Holy Scripture speaks of God, it concentrates our attention and thoughts upon one single point and what is to be known at that point . . . If we ask further concerning the one point upon which, according to Scripture, our attention and thoughts should and must be concentrated, then from first to last the Bible directs us to the name of Jesus Christ.

The strongly incarnational – dare we even say 'sacramental'? – character of Barth's concept of revelation is everywhere apparent. We know God as God is revealed in Christ, or we do not know God at all:[41]

> God gives himself to be known – and this is the limitation that we have to bring out in the idea of impartation – in an objectivity different from his own, in a creaturely objectivity. He unveils himself as the One he is by veiling himself in a form which he himself is not . . . The basic reality and substance of the creatureliness which he has commissioned and empowered to speak of him, the basic reality and substance of the sacramental reality of his revelation, is the existence of the human nature of Jesus Christ . . . Because the eternal Word himself became flesh, because the revelation of God took place once and for all in Jesus Christ, we know the same revelation of God wherever it is attested in expectation and recollection.

This 'Christological concentration' involves the assertion of actuality over possibility – that is to say, reflecting and 'after-thinking' on who God is and what God has actually done, rather than speculating on how it might be possible for God to exist or act. Barth's theological realism may therefore be said to be grounded in Christ.

---

[38] Barth, *Church Dogmatics* II/1, 257.
[39] Barth, *Church Dogmatics* II/1, 3.
[40] Barth, *Church Dogmatics* II/2, 52–3.
[41] Barth, *Church Dogmatics* II/1, 52–4.

Thirdly, it must be stated that it is indeed an essential part of Barth's programme to counter the philosophical and theological trends of modernity. This means that Feuerbach and a range of other writers are dealt with, perhaps not necessarily in depth or individually, but as a *collective* witness to the autonomous human attempt to determine the conditions under which revelation may occur, and the content which it should take.[42] This cannot be taken to mean that Barth is a 'postmodern' thinker *tout simple*; the issues are rather more complex than this designation allows.[43] The essential point is that Barth registers, in the name of theological integrity, a fundamental challenge to the styles of theology which were initiated and derived their legitimization from the Enlightenment project. The specificities of Barth's reaction against the Enlightenment are such that he cannot conceivably be bracketed together with Derrida or Levinas, except in the most general of terms.

Nevertheless, despite the points which may be made in Barth's defence, the critical reader will feel a sense of slight unease. Barth's famous reluctance to engage in philosophical debate inevitably means that he can only counter philosophical criticism with theological assertion. Granted that Barth's theological critique of the Enlightenment was visionary, and must be acknowledged as such, might not there be a case for engaging in a dialogue, however critical, with the natural sciences, when seen in an ancillary role? Barth's ferocious critique of natural theology, coupled with his general disinterest in the natural sciences, suggests that Barth himself would not see such an undertaking as particularly useful or appropriate. Yet one of his most significant interpreters thought otherwise. We may therefore turn to the writings of the noted Scottish theologian T. F. Torrance for further reflections on our theme.

T. F. Torrance can be seen as an inspirational figure for the project of a 'scientific theology', and it is thus unsurprising that he should play

---

[42] John Macken, *The Autonomy Theme in the Church Dogmatics of Karl Barth and His Critics*. Cambridge: Cambridge University Press, 1990; Thies Gundlach, *Selbstbegrenzung Gottes und die Autonomie des Menschen: Karl Barths Kirchliche Dogmatik als Modernisierungschrift evangelischer Theologie*. Frankfurt/Bern: Peter Lang, 1992.

[43] See some interesting, yet rather speculative, lines of thought in William Stacy Johnson, *The Mystery of God: Karl Barth and the Postmodern Foundations of Theology*. Louisville, KY: Westminster/John Knox Press, 1997. For specific comparisons of Barth and postmodern writers, see Isolde Andrews, *Deconstructing Barth: A Study of the Complementary Methods in Karl Barth and Jacques Derrida*. Frankfurt am Main: Peter Lang, 1996; Johannes F. Goud, *Levinas en Barth: een godsdienstwijsgerige en ethische vergelijking*. Amsterdam: Rodopi, 1984; Graham Ward, *Barth, Derrida and the Language of Theology*. Cambridge: Cambridge University Press, 1995.

a prominent role in any discussion of theological realism.[44] While firmly maintaining Barth's stance on the reality of God prior to and independent of any human recognition of this fact, Torrance is much more aware of (and sensitive to) potential dialogue partners for a scientific theology in its quest for the affirmation of theological reality. The following points are of particular importance:

1. Torrance adopts a more positive attitude to natural theology, rehabilitating it by insisting upon its proper role and context within a systematic theology (see vol. 1, 279–86). By doing so, he opens the way to a critical apropriation of insights from other intellectual disciplines which adopt realist perspectives on nature or life.

2. From his earliest phase, Torrance has been aware of the theological significance of the theological interaction with the natural sciences. During his studies at New College, Edinburgh (1934–7), Torrance had come to appreciate the insights of one of his mentors, Daniel Lamont, on this matter,[45] and had sought to express these in his 1938–9 lectures at Auburn Theological Seminary, in the state of New York.[46]

3. At a later stage in his career, Torrance began to develop a particular interest in the form of theological realism associated with Alexandrian writers, such as Athanasius, which he found especially expressed in the doctrine of the *homoousion*. Torrance's theological realism thus reflects, in part, Barth's 'Christological concentration', but moves beyond this through his emphasis upon the physical nature of the incarnation, and its consequences for the centrality of an incarnational Christology *as God's word and act* for a scientific theology.

4. Torrance establishes a rigorous theological connection between the incarnation and creation, allowing cross-connections to be posited between the sciences which recognize Christ as their proper object, and those which address the creation itself as their object.

In what follows, we shall explore the third of these points, which is of particular interest to our project, before moving on to the fourth.

---

[44] For the best account to date of this aspect of Torrance's thought, see John Douglas Morrison, *Knowledge of the Self-Revealing God in the Thought of Thomas Forsyth Torrance.* New York: Peter Lang, 1997.

[45] The key writing here is Daniel Lamont, *Christ and the World of Thought.* Edinburgh: T&T Clark, 1934.

[46] Alister E. McGrath, *Thomas F. Torrance: An Intellectual Biography.* Edinburgh: T&T Clark, 1999, 199–205.

The significance of the incarnation for a realist approach to theology is set out in some detail in the Richards Lectures, which Torrance delivered at the University of Virginia at Charlottesville during 1978.[47] Torrance remarked that the substance of these lectures could best be expressed in the somewhat cumbersome but nonetheless illuminating phrase 'the ground and grammar of a realist theology in the perspective of a unitary understanding of the creation'. This immediately helps us distinguish Torrance's approach to Christian theology from Lindbeck's coherentist approach, which allows that theology has its *grammar* but not an ultimate *ground* with reference to which it may be justified and corrected.

Torrance points to the need for Christian theology to return to its traditional understanding of its ground and grammar, in the light of the questions and issues thrown up by the scientific revolution. Such a return to 'the foundations of knowledge carried through by classical Christian theology on the ground of the revealed inherence of Word and Act in the Being of God' demands an engagement with the classical doctrine of the incarnation. We must 'allow objective being to reveal itself to us' out of 'its own inner *logos* or intelligibility'.[48] An approach to theology which recognizes the incarnation as its 'ground and grammar' is thus essentially realist in its orientation. Adopting Athanasius as his dialogue partner, Torrance argues that theology takes its proper form 'in movements of thought in which we seek to know God strictly in accordance with his nature, and in terms of his own internal relations as they become disclosed to us through the incarnation'.[49] The orthodox doctrine of the incarnation enables us to affirm that, since 'God's *Logos* inheres in his own being eternally, and that *Logos* has become incarnate in Jesus Christ, then it is in and through Christ that we have cognitive access into the being of God, into his inner divine intelligibility or *Logos*'. Torrance places particular importance on the *homoousion* for a scientific theology, in that the doctrine that Christ is *homoousios* with God negates any notion that Christ is 'a mere symbol, some representation of God detached from God', and instead affirms that:[50]

> In our relations with Jesus Christ, we have to do directly with the ultimate reality of God. As the epitomized expression of that fact, the *homoousion*

[47] Published as Thomas F. Torrance, *The Ground and Grammar of Theology*. Charlottesville, VA: University of Virginia Press, 1980.

[48] Torrance, *The Ground and Grammar of Theology*, 95–7.

[49] Torrance, *The Ground and Grammar of Theology*, 151.

[50] Torrance, *The Ground and Grammar of Theology*, 160–1.

is the ontological and epistemological linchpin of Christian theology. . . . What God is to us in his saving economic activity in space and time through Christ and in the Holy Spirit, he is antecedently and eternally in himself.

It is instructive to note how both Barth and Torrance ground their realist theologies in Christology, holding that Christ reveals and embodies who and what God actually is.[51]

Torrance thus argues that theology is under an obligation to respond to the way things actually are, making use of the correlation between human modes of thought and the inner structure of reality itself which is expressed and affirmed in the Christian doctrines of creation and redemption through Christ. It is from the doctrine of creation that we learn that the order we discern within it is *contingent*, the result of the creative ordering of a God who was free to impose divine patterning and ordering on the creation without any external restructions or compulsion.[52] 'In creating the universe out of nothing, God has conferred on it a created or contingent rationality of its own.'[53] Yet the Christian doctrine of creation cannot be separated from the *homoousion* on account of the credal insistence that creation took place *through Christ*. There is a connection, an interrelationship, between creation and the incarnation. 'In the last analysis, the birth of the creation hinges upon the *homoousion*, that is, upon whether it was through Jesus Christ who is of one substance with the Father that "all things were made", as the Nicene creed laid down.'[54]

With this insistence upon the correlation of creation and incarnation, Torrance is able to make the connection that establishes the foundation of a realist theology. The order that the natural sciences identify within creation is not of their own invention, nor the product of an order-loving human mind, but is intrinsic to the created order by virtue of its divine creation. The divine ordering and rationality, which is *embedded* in nature is also *embodied* in Christ as God incarnate. The *logos* that can be discerned, however weakly, within nature is disclosed fully in Christ. The realism that is mandated by the natural sciences is thus

[51] See further Thomas F. Torrance, *Space, Time and Incarnation*. London: Oxford University Press, 1969, 75–8.

[52] For comment, see Colin E. Gunton, *The Triune Creator: A Historical and Systematic Study*. Edinburgh: Edinburgh University Press, 1998, 112–13.

[53] Thomas F. Torrance, *Divine and Contingent Order*. Oxford: Oxford University Press, 1981, 3. This entire work should be consulted for the explication of the relation of this 'created' rationality to the 'divine rationality' itself.

[54] Thomas F. Torrance, *The Trinitarian Faith: The Evangelical Theology of the Ancient Catholic Church*. Edinburgh: T&T Clark, 1988, 109.

correspondingly mandated for a scientific theology, in that both seek
to uncover a *ratio* or *logos* which is peculiar to their object, and which
exists prior to and independent of their investigations. Torrance is thus
able to argue that a realist approach to theology both remains faithful
to the classical Christian tradition, while accounting for the explanatory
and predictive successes of the natural sciences. The key assumptions
and working methods that the empirical sciences bring to the study of
nature, seen as creation, are to be brought by a scientific theology to
the study of Jesus Christ, seen as God incarnate.

The use of the critical phrase 'seen as' deserves comment. As we noted
in considering the notion of tradition-constituted and -mediated
rationality (64–72), the Christian tradition offers a lens by which nature
is viewed as creation, and Christ as God incarnate, through whom the
world was created. As Torrance constantly stresses, this is a fundamental
credal insight of the Christian churches, not some idiosyncratic formulation of potentially unrepresentative theologians.[55] The Christian
tradition has been shaped by this incarnational insight, which affects the
manner in which both nature and Jesus Christ are perceived and comprehended. As the history of western thought makes abundantly clear, both
nature and Jesus Christ have been the subject of an astonishing variety
of interpretations and ideational constructions down the centuries.[56] The
Christian tradition identifies specifically Christian readings of both,
which demarcates them from their non-Christian interpretations. Given
the failure of the Enlightenment project to establish and impose a
universal rationality, the Christian tradition's rendering of nature and
Christ must be regarded as offering a rationality – that is, a discernment
of an underlying *ratio* or *logos* – which is entirely appropriate to the
distinctive nature of the Christian revelation. Viewed from within the
Christian tradition, nature and Christ are construed in certain specific
manners which lead to precisely the conclusions which Torrance draws.

Scientific theology as an *a posteriori* discipline

If there exists a reality independent of us – so that its existence is prior
to our recognition or acceptance of that reality – then we are obligated

---

[55] See the extended discussions found throughout Thomas F. Torrance, *The Christian
Doctrine of God: One Being, Three Persons*. Edinburgh: T&T Clark, 1996; idem, *The
Trinitarian Faith*.
[56] On nature, see the analysis in vol. 1, 81–133. On Jesus Christ, see such works as Jaroslav
Pelikan, *Jesus through the Centuries: His Place in the History of Culture*. New Haven, CT:
Yale University Press, 1985.

to respond to that reality, offering as best an account of it as we can. While fully conceding that theological formulations are incapable of capturing the fullness of the divine realities, such an approach to theology will insist that there *are* such divine realities, and that a scientific theology represents a principled attempt to describe and comprehend them under the limiting conditions that are imposed upon humanity by virtue of our created character and fallen nature.

A scientific theology takes the view that theological reflection paradoxically *begins* with an actual knowledge of God, and in the light of this, proceeds to inquire as to how this knowledge might be possible. It inverts the order which many would regard as natural – 'natural' here, of course, meaning 'conforming to a set of assumptions inherited from the Enlightenment' – which would regard the question of how God may be known to be chronologically and logically prior to the question of what can be known of God. Any theory which lays down in advance how, or to what extent, God can be known predetermines that knowledge through a set of *a priori* assumptions which have been allowed to exercise a critical and controlling function in theological reflection. How God can be known constitutes a question which may only be answered in the light of the way in which God is known through revelation.

This runs counter to a highly influential approach to theology, which reached its zenith during the Enlightenment. This approach lays down certain beliefs as axiomatic, and proceeds to deduce a series of theological propositions from these axioms. In a 'revolutionary moment in Western philosophy',[57] Descartes defined God as *entis summe perfecti*, and proceeded to make certain deductions from this that would shape the future direction of philosophical theology.[58] Descartes held that it was possible to deduce the critical ideas of existence and veracity from this definition of God. If God is defined as a perfect being, the existence of God must be taken as implied within this definition.

As Michael Buckley points out, 'in the demonstration *a priori*, the deduction of the existence of God mirrors the deduction of mathematics: the notion or nature of the existence of the supremely perfect entails proportionately its own necessary existence'.[59] But is the approach viable? The awkward question of the link between Descartes' approach

[57] Michael J. Buckley, *At the Origins of Modern Atheism*. New Haven, CT: Yale University Press, 1987, 92.
[58] René Descartes, *Mediationes de Prima Philosophia*. Paris: Librarie Philosophique J. Vrin, 1944, 65–6.
[59] Buckley, *At the Origins of Modern Atheism*, 94.

and the development of modern atheism aside, is there not a vulnerability here? Does not the idea of an incontestable *a priori* rest upon the *contested* notion of a universal rationality?

A theological science follows the natural science in insisting that such *a priori* approaches are ultimately incoherent. Most *a priori* approaches to theology and philosophy covertly rest upon *a posteriori* assumptions.[60] Kant's philosophical reflections were partly shaped by the ideas of Euclidian geometry and Newtonian mechanics.[61] Kant regarded Euclidian geometrical axioms as *a priori* ideas which had the status of universal and necessary truths. In the same way, the axioms of Euclidian geometry were held to give rise to a set of necessarily true beliefs, which were not subject to the contingency of statements derived from experience. Furthermore, Kant accepts Newton's problematic notion of 'absolute space' without any critical engagement, and assumes that this must be regarded as 'pure *a priori* experience'.[62]

The categories that Kant believed to be *a priori* truths – and thus universal and necessary – are in reality those of Euclidian geometry and Newtonian mechanics, which simply do not have the universal character that Kant clearly believed them to have. As Kant's appropriation of Newtonian mechanics makes clear, it has proved remarkably easy to assume that generally accepted *a posteriori* ideas are actually *a priori* in character, thus converting historically contingent and epistemologically provisional ideas into the 'necessary truths of reason'.

A priori approaches to theology hold that any attempt to develop a scientific theology must begin by laying down ontological and epistemological axioms, and then proceeding to derive insights on their basis. As has often been pointed out, the experimental methodology of the natural sciences precedes reflection on what ontology and epistemology might be appropriate in their light. The critical successes of the natural sciences can be argued to rest upon their principled refusal to make *a priori* prejudgements concerning what may be known, and the manner by which that knowledge is established. By thus refusing to be limited by the presuppositions of critical forms of inquiry, the natural

---

[60] On *a posteriori* elements in Descartes, see Buckley, *At the Origins of Modern Atheism*, 92–4.

[61] Michael Friedman, *Kant and the Exact Sciences*. Cambridge, MA: Harvard University Press, 1992, xi–xii.

[62] Immanuel Kant, *Kritik der reinen Vernunft*. Frankfurt am Main: Suhrkamp Verlag, 1968, 73. 'Also ist die ursprüngliche Vorstellung vom Raume Anschauung a priori, und nicht Begriff.' Note that Newton states this principle in the form of a corollary, not an axiom.

sciences have been able to respond to the implications of a growing body of experimental and observational knowledge without the incumbrance of preconceived theories of knowledge or being.

A posteriori *analysis in the natural sciences*

Within the natural sciences, understandings of reality arise primarily in an *a posteriori* manner, in that they are chronologically and logically to be regarded as consequent to the empirical evidence upon which the natural sciences are grounded. This point is made repeatedly by Edmund Husserl (1859–1938). Husserl defines phenomenology as 'the general doctrine of essences', stressing that it is a 'presuppositionless descriptive science' which investigates consciousness after having systematically eliminated any prior assumptions about the relationship of consciousness to anything in the world. Husserl distinguishes between 'science of the natural sort' and 'science of the philosophic sort' (phenomenology). The former is grounded in what Husserl terms the 'natural attitude', which regards the mind as a natural thing in the objective world. 'Science of the natural sort' takes cognition for granted, regarding it as an *actuality*, whereas 'science of the philosophic sort' explores the question of the *possibility* of cognition. Phenomenology can therefore be regarded as a method for uncovering the preconditions of cognition, on the assumption that cognition has already taken place.[63] Husserl states this point as follows:[64]

> The right attitude to take in the pre-philosophical and, in a good sense, dogmatic sphere of inquiry, to which all the empirical sciences (but not these alone) belong is, in full consciousness, to discard all scepticism together with all 'natural philosophy' and 'theory of knowledge', and find the data of knowledge where they actually face you, whatever difficulties epistemological reflection may subsequently raise concerning the possibility of such data being there.

Husserl adopted a similar tone in his 'Inaugural Lecture' at Freiburg im Breisgau (1917), noting that 'phenomenology claims to be the science of pure phenomena' – that is, primarily the 'sphere of those sensuously given realities (*der sinnendinglichen Gegebenheiten*) through which Nature is evinced in perceiving'.

---

[63] John J. Drummond, *Husserlian Intentionality and Non-Foundational Realism: Noema and Object*. Dordrecht: Kluwer Academic Publishers, 1990; Friederike Kuster, *Wege der Verantwortung: Husserls Phänomenologie als Gang durch die Faktizität*. Dordrecht: Kluwer Academic, 1996.

[64] Edmund Husserl, *Ideas: General Introduction to Pure Phenomenology*. New York: Macmillan, 1931, 95–6.

The fundamental point to be made here is that the natural sciences have not allowed themselves to be inhibited by a preconceived epistemology, which lays down what can and what cannot be known in advance of an engagement with the natural world. The history of science repeatedly demonstrates that such *a priori* posturing does little beyond temporarily restraining advances in scientific understanding, and generally causing natural scientists to take a less than positive view of the place and propriety of philosophy in their scientific enterprises. The way in which a rigid Aristotelianism inhibited advance in the fields of mechanics and astronomy in the late sixteenth and early seventeenth century represents a classic instance of this difficulty.

The incarnation and a priori *notions of God*

The same general issue is encountered throughout the history of theology. *A priori* philosophical notions are repeatedly alleged to constitute barriers or difficulties for central Christian affirmations. Perhaps the most illuminating theological episode in this respect is the recurrent philosophical objection to the idea of the incarnation – namely, that it is illogical or inconceivable that God should become incarnate in Christ. The development of the Christian understanding of Christ in the Greek-speaking world of the first four centuries is a particularly illuminating instance of how preconceived ideas of God came into collision with rather different ideas, deriving from an experience of God.[65]

The dangers of depending upon, or accidentally incorporating, any *a priori* ideas into Christological reflection is set out clearly by Charles Gore, both in his 1891 Bampton Lectures at Oxford University,[66] and in a volume published some years later, following through some of the leading ideas developed in that work.[67] Gore contrasts two approaches to Christology which he believes to be *a priori* and unhistorical: the *dogmatic* insistence that Christ's human mind was such that it was impossible for him to 'grow in knowledge', and the *humanitarian* position that Christ was sinful. Both of these, Gore argues, rest on preconceived ideas about true divinity and humanity which find themselves in conflict with the historical materials provided in 'the evangelical

---

[65] Wolfhart Pannenberg, 'The Appropriation of the Philosophical Concept of God as a Dogmatic Problem of Early Christian Theology', in *Basic Questions in Theology II*. London: SCM Press, 1971, 119–83.

[66] Charles Gore, *The Incarnation of the Son of God*. London: John Murray, 1922.

[67] Charles Gore, *Dissertations on Subjects Connected with the Incarnation*. London: John Murray, 1895.

narrative'.[68] It is the task of Christian theology to ground itself upon that narrative, responding to what it discerns within its witness to the identity of Christ, rather than determining its views on God and humanity in advance of any such engagement.[69] As Gore stresses, the true nature of both humanity and divinity require to be revealed to us – and the locus of both aspects of that revelation is Christ.[70] It is through *a posteriori* reflection on the biblical witness to Christ that we come to know what is truly meant by 'God' and by 'humanity'.

A related concern can be found in the writings of Karl Barth. Barth's strident views on the impropriety of constructing a philosophical or anthropological foundation for theology ultimately rested upon his belief that such a procedure entailed determining the conditions under which divine revelation could take place, rather than responding to a revelation that had already taken place. Barth's anxiety was that *a priori* philosophical assumptions would 'police' the possibility of revelation. A theological science – not, incidentally, a phrase with which Barth feels entirely comfortable – thus takes the form of *a posteriori* reflection on a revelation that has already taken place. As Barth states this point in his 1924–5 Göttingen lectures:[71]

> The problem of the possibility of revelation can only be seriously raised and treated where its *reality* is known. The possibility of revelation can, as a matter of principle, only be comprehended *a posteriori*. All reflection on how God *can* reveal himself is really only a thinking-after of the fact that God *has* revealed himself.

This same principle can be seen in operation in Barth's reflections on the significance of Jesus Christ, where we again find Barth taking a strong line on the *a posteriori* character of theological reflection on the identity of Christ. Such reflection is a 'thinking after', a *Nachdenken*, consequent to the actuality of revelation, rather than a piece of metaphysical speculation based on *a priori* notions. Barth is clear that the 'empty space where the great truth of the incarnation belongs' is none other than 'the concept of revelation':[72]

> What I have constructed, namely, the empty space that denotes the problem before which we stand, was obviously a construction *a posteriori*. How could I have attained to the idea of incarnation, that unheard-of

[68] Gore, *Dissertations on Subjects Connected with the Incarnation*, 95–7.
[69] Gore, *The Incarnation of the Son of God*, 80–112.
[70] Gore, *The Incarnation of the Son of God*, 142.
[71] Karl Barth, *The Göttingen Dogmatics: Instruction in the Christian Religion.* Grand Rapids, MI: Eerdmans, 1991, 151.
[72] Barth, *Göttingen Dogmatics*, 141.

idea, except by abstraction from a fact that is even more unheard-of? I have not been talking hypothetically about a hypothetical entity, but about the actually existent possibility of revelation, about Jesus Christ, about the way that God comes to us as it is known and confessed in the Christian church. I could not speak specifically about the condition without finally, as you have noted, adopting the terms of the Chalcedonian Definition, in which the church gave classical formulation, not to a deduction of Christ *a priori*, but to an account of the actual reality of Christ.

It is extremely important to grasp the point of Barth's critique of metaphysics at this point. Barth objects vigorously to any account of God's revelation which rests upon or presupposes certain metaphysical foundations; he is perfectly prepared, however, to allow certain metaphysical consequences to flow from human reflection on the actuality and content of that divine revelation. It is quite understandable that some scholars should have referred to Barth as 'anti-metaphysical', thereby intending to convey his outright rejection of any metaphysical *foundation* to divine revelation. It is beyond dispute that Barth holds that God does not require the assistance of philosophers or anthropologists in order to speak.

Yet the question of how the content of that divine revelation is to be articulated remains open. Barth's discussion of the doctrines of the Trinity and the 'two natures' of Christ suggest that he has no fundamental difficulty with the metaphysical elaboration of the implications or content of the threefold form of the Word of God, and is thus not strictly 'anti-metaphysical' at this point. Barth's critique of any *a priori* role for metaphysics in theology does not preclude the inclusion of metaphysical notions *a posteriori*, provided that these can be shown to be legitimated by revelation itself.

For Barth, the notion of revelation attempts to articulate and give substance to the pervasive Christian sense of the divine initiative which precedes, enables and demands a human response. Before we speak, we are conscious of being addressed or called. At the soteriological level, this sense of the initiative lying with God is expressed in Augustine's concept of prevenient grace; at the epistemological level, it finds its expression in the notion of revelation. The history of Jesus of Nazareth represents an initiative which is not ours; indeed, it can be argued to take the initiative away from us, inviting us to enter into a conceptual world which we ourselves did not fashion. Taking the notion of revelation seriously thus legitimates, even demands, an *a posteriori* approach to theology.

We shall give thought to what this complex and nuanced notion of 'revelation' might mean in due course. In the twentieth century, the notion has often been articulated specifically as the notion of divine self-revelation, particularly within the Barthian tradition. However, it is important to note that this is not the only model available. At the purely historical level, it may be argued to represent a departure from an older Protestant tradition;[73] at a more theological level, it risks reducing the concept of revelation to a single-layered reality, overlooking the multiple levels at which it impacts. Nevertheless, however revelation is to be understood, it denotes some generative event which triggers off a cascade of ideas and reinterpretations – the process of *Nachdenken*. Revelation is thus inextricably bound up with the memory of the generative event which precipitates a 'hermeneutical spiral'.[74] If one was to take the view that, for the sake or argument, the generative event and primary *explicandum* of Christian theology is Jesus of Nazareth, it follows that we are invited to reshape our mental horizons and reconsider any prior understandings of God and human nature in the light of the story of Jesus of Nazareth. The history of Jesus of Nazareth once forced, and still forces, the redrawing of conceptual boundaries and mental horizons, demanding that we rethink and refashion our understanding of such matters as God, and human nature and destiny.

A feisty defence of an *a posteriori* approach to theology can be found throughout the substantial theological programme of Thomas F. Torrance. Although indebted to Barth at many points, Torrance can be seen (particularly in his later writings) as appropriating Barth against the backdrop of the ontological realism of the Greek patristic tradition, especially Athanasius. In his landmark work *Theological Science* (1969), Torrance sets out this approach as follows:[75]

A genuine theology is distrustful of all speculative thinking or of all *a priori* thought. Theological thinking is essentially positive, thinking that keeps its feet on the ground of actuality; *a posteriori*, thinking that follows and is obedient to the given and communicated Word and Act of God as the material for its reflection; and *empirical*, thinking out of real experience of God determined by God. It is because it is through

[73] Wolfhart Pannenberg, *Revelation as History*. New York: Macmillan, 1968, 4, where this development is put down to the influence of German idealism.

[74] Ray L. Hart, *Unfinished Man and the Imagination: Toward an Ontology and a Rhetoric of Revelation*. New York: Herder & Herder, 1968, 83–105.

[75] Thomas F. Torrance, *Theological Science*. London: Oxford University Press, 1969, 33–4.

this given fact that theological knowledge has reality, and on its basis alone that it can be established as knowledge.

Torrance makes it clear that the epistemological centre and focus of responsible Christian theology is, in his view, Jesus Christ. To engage with Christ is to concede that he is possessed of an intrinsic rationality which the human mind can uncover through obedient reflection on what is given to us in the actuality of that divine self-revelation.[76]

> We direct our minds to the self-giving of God in Jesus Christ and allow our minds to fall under the power of the divine rationality that becomes revealed in him. It is a rationality inherent in the reality of the incarnate Word before it takes shape in our apprehension of it (*a posteriori*), but as we allow it to become disclosed to us under our questions and find that it is opened out before us in an objective depth that far transcends what we can specify of it in our formulations (disclosure models).

This approach does not command universal assent in modern theology. Many would still argue that *a priori* ideas have a central role to play in theology, and that they should be accorded normative status as standing outside the contingencies of history and culture. *A priori* ideas are thus seen by at least some as possessing a privileged status, denied to any idea of revelation or *Nachdenken* within the historical process itself. This is to bring ready-made ideas of God (whatever their intellectual pedigrees) to the person of Jesus, and attempt to accommodate him to them.

The demand that Christ be interpreted on the basis of *a priori* ideas is often linked with an explicit rejection of the idea of incarnation as a 'philosophical impossibility'. This view is stated by Karl Jaspers with a confidence which is perhaps inversely related to his grounds for doing so.[77] This strident affirmation is best regarded as an assertion that the doctrine of the incarnation, and the view of God which it reflects or embodies, is to be deemed to be inconsistent with a certain rather different preconceived idea of the nature of God. It is an unacknowledged assertion, not merely of a conflict of concepts of divinity – a conflict which requires resolution by inquiry concerning the intellectual pedigrees, frameworks of rationality and empirical justification of the conceptualities implicated – but of the need to clarify the manner in which frameworks of rationality are generated and transmitted.

Jaspers is unlikely to be satisfied with this deconstruction of his *a priori* convictions, not least because he seems so sure of them. However,

---

[76] Thomas F. Torrance, *God and Rationality*. London: Oxford University Press, 1971, 45.
[77] Karl Jaspers, *Philosophical Faith and Revelation*. New York: Harper & Row, 1967, 145.

it is essential to appreciate that Jaspers has not shown that the incarnation is 'wrong' – simply that it is inconsistent with a particular *a priori* notion of God. One way of responding to this observation would indeed be to suggest that the doctrine of the incarnation is 'wrong', and ought therefore to be abandoned. Yet there is another response, perhaps offering rather more intriguing possibilities – namely, that this preconceived idea of God is to be called into question, allowing the rather different God who is made known *a posteriori* through revelation to be discovered and encountered.

Yet the history of twentieth-century theology makes it clear that there is an important question which remains to be addressed. Given that a scientific theology adopts an *a posteriori* approach, can it be anything other than *critical*? Our brief flirtation above with the approach of Karl Jaspers might be instructive here. An *a posteriori* approach to the incarnation undermines Jaspers' conception of God, in effect arguing – in the nicest possible way, of course – that this may well be Jaspers' personal view of things, but wouldn't it be nice to listen to God instead? If there is indeed a God, and that God chooses to self-disclose, then surely that disclosure will have somewhat greater weight than Jaspers' personal ideas on the matter?

On this view, a scientific theology interposes a check on unrestrained human speculation by demanding that this be anchored in the realities of the world. It insists that philosophical and theological reflections are earthed. It constitutes a rock against which some rather ambitious theological vessels founder. It seeks to apply to theology the same general approach found in the natural sciences – namely, that theories and hypothesis must be constantly checked out against what they purport to represent or describe. Our discussion of the *a posteriori* character of a scientific theology has once more highlighted the importance of Christology to a scientific theology. The familiar argument that the incarnation is *a priori* impossible is a telling indication of the continuing influence of preconceived ideas of the nature and character of God upon Christian theology. A scientific theology offers the opportunity to challenge such ideas, raising the question of whether the *a priori* is simply a social construction, or is so radically historically located that it is devoid of universal significance.

Luther's theology of the cross as a critique of a priori notions of God

One of the most significant theological developments of the Reformation was the formulation of Martin Luther's *theologia crucis* over the period 1515–19.[78] This has proved remarkably fertile, with a number of twentieth-century theologians adopting it as a point of departure for their own theological reflections.[79] Yet it must be appreciated that Luther's *theologia crucis* is more than an attempt to correlate theology and experience, especially the experience of suffering;[80] it represents a calculated and systematic attack on the role of *a priori* notions of God in any Christian theology. Luther does not have any particular difficulties with the role of metaphysics in theology; his concern is to ensure that preconceived metaphysical ideas are allowed no role as a foundation or criterion of authentically Christian theology.

Luther's radical theology of the cross represents a systematic critique of any approach to theology which permits human preconceptions of the locus, nature and possibility of divine revelation to determine those issues in advance. Luther argues, perhaps at times more passionately than rigorously, that the assertion that God is revealed through the shame, weakness and foolishness of the cross represents a divine decision to overturn human preconceptions of the divine nature. By forcing humanity to admit that, as a matter of fact, divine revelation has occurred at a place and in a manner which subverts rational judgements on what is appropriate for such a revelation, Luther interprets God as obliging that puzzled humanity to admit the incompetence of its slender theological resources. We are unable to determine in advance what God is like; *we need to be told.*

Luther develops a revelational counterpart to a doctrine of grace. Just as Luther insists that humanity lacks the soteriological resources to justify itself, and is forced to rely on the grace of God for salvation, so humanity lacks the epistemic resources to discover and grasp God unaided. Whether in matters of salvation or revelation, humanity needs to be helped to a full knowledge of God. And, just as fallen and sinful needs divine grace to know God, so that same grace is required to know *about* God. For Luther, the first step to encountering the grace of God is to abandon any pretensions that one possesses any righteousness whatsoever; in the same way, the essential prerequisite for a true knowledge of God is the abandonment of any preconceived

[78] Alister E. McGrath, *Luther's Theology of the Cross: Martin Luther's Theological Breakthrough.* Oxford: Blackwell, 1985.

[79] Obvious examples here include Jürgen Moltmann, *The Crucified God: The Cross of Christ as the Foundation and Criticism of Christian Theology.* London: SCM Press, 1974; Eberhard Jüngel, *God as the Mystery of the World.* Edinburgh: T&T Clark, 1983.

[80] See Pierre Böhler, *Kreuz und Eschatologie: Eine Auseinandersetzung mit der politischen Theologie, im Anschluss an Luthers Theologia Crucis.* Tübingen: J. C. B. Mohr, 1981.

ideas concerning God's nature, or the manner and place of God's revelation.[81]

Luther thus rejects any *a priori* metaphysical speculation in theology, insisting that an authentically Christian theology takes the form of *a posteriori* reflection on a revelation which has already taken place. That is to say, theology is concerned with the unfolding of the actuality of revelation, not speculation concerning its possibility. Interestingly, Luther links both the actuality and the substance of revelation with the person of Jesus Christ, continuing the pattern of the convergence of realism with Christocentrism which we noted with both Torrance and Barth:[82]

> God does not want to be known except through Christ; nor can he be known in any other way. Christ is the offspring promised to Abraham; on him God has grounded all his promises. Therefore Christ alone is the means, the life, and the mirror through which we see God and know his will. Through Christ God declares his favour and mercy to us. In Christ we see that God is not an angry master and judge but a gracious and kind father, who blesses us, that is, who delivers us from the law, sin, death, and every evil, and gives us righteousness and eternal life through Christ. This is a certain and true knowledge of God and divine persuasion, which does not fail, but depicts (*depingit*) God himself in a specific form, apart from which there is no God.

It is thus the task of Christian theology to respond to this 'specific form' taken by God in this self-revelation, rather than relying on native human instinct for guidance at this point.[83]

Scientific theology as a response to its distinctive object

Thus far, we have argued that a scientific theology represents an *a posteriori* response to an existing reality, which it attempts to describe, represent and communicate. Yet there is a further issue which arises from this theme of an engagement with an existing reality – namely, the extent to which the distinctiveness of the object of a science must be reflected in the methodology of that science. The Enlightenment

---

[81] Enrico de Negri, *Offenbarung und Dialektik: Luthers Realtheologie*. Darmstadt: Wissenschaftliche Buchgesellschaft, 1973.

[82] *D. M. Martin Luthers Werke: Kritische Gesamtausgabe*, Weimar: Böhlau, 1911, vol. 40, 602–3.

[83] For a fuller treatment of some of these issues, see Ernst Wolf, 'Die Rechtfertigungslehre als Mitte und Grenze reformatorischer Theologie', *Evangelische Theologie* 9 (1949), 298–308.

tended to assume that all sciences were committed to using the same working methods and assumptions; a scientific theology insists that the distinctive identity of the object of a science is reflected in its response to that object.

To suggest that theology is a distinct discipline with its own integrity might at first sight appear to call into question any unitary conception of knowledge, or any conception of 'the real', as opposed to an aggregate of discrete realities. This is an issue of considerable importance; indeed, it could be argued that any attempt to construct a unitary conception of reality or of human knowledge must be able to offer a satisfactory response to this concern. We may therefore open our discussion of this point by considering its grounding and application in the natural sciences.

Objects, levels and language in the natural sciences

The force of the problem is greatly alleviated through a phenomenological survey of the natural sciences, which indicates that a wide variety of methodologies are deployed across the spectrum of these disciplines. Physics, evolutionary biology and psychology each have their own vocabularies, methods and procedures, and engage with nature at their own distinctive levels. This point has long been understood, and is not controversial. For example, consider Robert Oppenheimer's comments:[84]

> Every science has its own language . . . Everything the chemist observes and describes can be talked about in terms of atomic mechanics, and most of it at least can be understood. Yet no one suggests that, in dealing with the complex chemical forms which are of biological interest, the language of atomic physics would be helpful. Rather it would tend to obscure the great regularities of biochemistry, as the dynamic description of gas would obscure its thermodynamic behaviour.

The merits of the point that Oppenheimer wishes to make would be recognized by any working scientist. Each science develops a vocabulary and a working method which is appropriated or adapted to its object. The more complex that object, the more levels of explanation are required. A classic example is the human body, which can be investigated at a series of levels – anatomical, physiological and psychological – each of which illuminates one aspect of the greater whole, but none of which is adequate by itself to give a full account.

---

[84] J. Robert Oppenheimer, *Science and the Common Understanding*. London: Oxford University Press, 1954, 87.

The issue of levels of explanation or multilayered description is well established in the natural sciences. To illustrate this point, we may consider the case of physics, widely regarded as 'the ideal of scientific knowledge'.[85] Over the years, physics has found it necessary and appropriate to recognize the different manners in which it has had to engage with the systems of the natural world. It has developed 'explanations of different levels of reality', such as hydrodynamics for the explanation of the behaviour of macroscopic liquids, and quantum mechanics to account for events at the submicroscopic end of the spectrum.[86]

In his careful study of the epistemological aspects of theoretical physics, Abner Shimony notes that 'one of the remarkable features of the physical world is the existence in many situations of several well-defined levels of description for the same physical system'.[87] Shimony sets these out as follows:

1. Relativistic field theory. Shimony regards this as the deepest level of description, widely used by condensed-matter physicists.

2. Non-relativistic quantum-mechanical many-body treatment of interacting electrons and nuclei.

3. Macroscopic description, which is the coarsest level of description. Here, fundamental variables can be defined by averages over large regions.

We live, move and have our being in one world; yet this world is possessed of many levels or layers, and requires investigation, explanation and representation at every level – a point which we considered in greater depth earlier (209–30). While the world may indeed be capable of being reduced to the level of atoms, molecules and forces which can be discussed by the natural sciences, it would be premature and simplistic to suggest that such a reductionist engagement with the many levels of the world is intellectually adequate. This point is stressed by John Searle in his important essay *The Construction of Social Reality.* Conceding that the 'fundamental features of that world are as described by physics, chemistry and the other natural sciences', Searle notes the

---

[85] John Ziman, *Reliable Knowledge: An Exploration of the Grounds for Belief in Science.* Cambridge: Cambridge University Press, 1978, 28.

[86] Brian Goodwin, *How the Leopard Changed Its Spots.* London: Weidenfeld & Nicolson, 1994, x.

[87] Abner Shimony, *Search for a Naturalistic World View.* 2 vols. Cambridge: Cambridge University Press, 1993, vol. 2, 212.

existence of phenomena within that world which are *not* physical or chemical.[88]

> How can there be an objective world of money, property, marriage, governments, elections, football matches, cocktail parties and law-courts in a world that consists entirely of physical particles in fields of force, and in which some of these particles are organized into systems that are conscious biological beasts, such as ourselves?

Searle's point is that physics concerns itself with one particular stratum of the real world; it does not – indeed, it cannot – exclude there being other levels which demand different approaches and levels of explanation. As John Ziman points out, 'there is nothing wrong with physics as such, but it is an inappropiate model for all consensible and potentially consensual knowledge'.[89]

A similar issue can be identified in the development of psychological models of humanity in the early part of the twentieth century. A number of schools of thought emerged, offering divergent understandings of human nature. In part, this reflects the fact that each developed theories and methods which were appropriate to the level of human behaviour it wished to investigate.[90] Four schools may be noted in making this point:

1. *Behaviourism* had its origins in a desire to understand the simplest aspects of human behaviour, such as the reflex and conditioned reflex.

2. *Gestalt theory* arose from the investigation of human perception and cognition.

3. *Psychoanalysis* attempted to explore the issue of human personality as a whole, initially through focusing on neurotic conflict.

4. *Factor analysis* dealt with human intellect and character.

These disciplines arose in a somewhat fragmentary manner, and can be argued to have left later generations with the task of attempting an integration of their insights and approaches.

We may illustrate this point further by considering Daniel Dennett's cognitive theory of consciousness. In his *Content and Consciousness*,

---

[88] John R. Searle, *The Construction of Social Reality*. London: Allen Lane, 1995, 1. See further his earlier work, John Searle, *The Rediscovery of the Mind*. Cambridge: MIT Press, 1992.

[89] Ziman, *Reliable Knowledge*, 28.

[90] R. B. Joynson, 'Models of Man: 1879–1979', in Anthony J. Chapman and Dylan M. Jones (eds), *Models of Man*. Leicester: British Psychological Society, 1980, 1–12.

Dennett introduced an important distinction between personal and sub-personal levels of explanation.[91] At the sub-personal level, explanation is understood in primarily mechanistic and physiological terms, formulated in terms of brain events and neural networks and concerned with the question of how sensory input is transformed into behavioural output. At the personal level, however, mental phenomena and purposive actions are explained through categories properly descriptive of the activities of persons, rather than the activities of systems within the brain. This dual approach seems to avoid some of the difficulties involved in radical reductionist approaches to theories of consciousness. The fact that two different 'levels of explanation' are proposed is not considered problematic, and is maintained in Dennett's later works.[92]

It will be clear from the analysis thus far that there is then no generalized scientific methodology which can be applied without variance and uncritically to all sciences. While certain general principles may be argued to lie behind the specific approaches found in any given natural science, the point is that the nature of the field to be investigated shapes the approach to be adopted. In that each science deals with a different object, it is under an obligation to respond to that object according to its distinctive nature. The methods which are appropriate to the study of one object cannot be abstracted and applied uncritically and universally. Each science develops procedures which it deems or discovers to be appropriate to the nature of its own particular object in which it 'has solved its own inductive problem of how to arrive at a general conclusion from a limited set of particular observations'.[93] In what follows, we shall explore this with reference to an important issue in quantum mechanics.

Quantum phenomena: the Heisenberg uncertainty principle

The case of quantum phenomena illustrates the particular limitations which they place upon scientific disciplines which seek to study them. Heisenberg's 'uncertainty principle' has been the subject of interest by fashionable French intellectuals, who have altered a fundamental postulate concerning the limitations placed upon our knowledge of the quantum world to a global statement of relativism in all matters of

---

[91] Daniel C. Dennett, *Content and Consciousness*. London: Routledge, 1993.
[92] Daniel C. Dennett, *Kinds of Minds: Towards an Understanding of Consciousness*. London: Weidenfeld & Nicolson, 1996.
[93] A. D. Ritchie, *Studies in the History and Methods of the Sciences*. Edinburgh: Edinburgh University Press, 1963, 7.

truth, objectivity and judgement. Brian Appleyard cites the principle as evidence that science has abandoned the quest for objective knowledge.[94] Stanley Aronowitz cites the principle as not merely legitimating, but *demanding*, relativism in matters of knowledge.[95] As Paul Gross and Normann Levitt note, by the time Aronowitz has finished messing around with this idea – which he clearly does not understand – it becomes a relativist manifesto, referring to[96]

> a kind of epistemological and spiritual malaise, plaguing the minds and souls of contemporary physicists. The argument, roughly but accurately paraphrased (and all too familiar from New Age tracts, among other things) is that since physics has discovered the uncertainty principle, it can no longer provide reliable information about the physical world, has lost its claim to objectivity, and is now embedded in the unstable hermeneutics of subject-object relations.

The reality of the situation is much more interesting. It has little to do with relativism, and everything to do with identifying and respecting the limits placed upon scientific knowledge by the nature of what is to be known. Far from saying that 'all is uncertain', Heisenberg's article specified precisely the limits of uncertainty involved in making measurements of sub-atomic events. The Heisenberg uncertainty principle specifies that the product of the uncertainties in the position (Δq) and momentum (Δp) of the electron can never be smaller than Planck's quantum of effect. A similar relationship exists between uncertainties in energy and time. As the principle was finally stated:

$$\Delta q . \Delta p \geq h / 2\pi$$

where h is Planck's constant. It thus follows that the principle has virtually no relevance to the macroscopic world with which we are familiar. Consider an object weighing one kilogram, whose speed can be determined with an error of one millimetre per second. Applying Heisenberg's uncertainty principle, it follows that there will be a maximum error in determining its position of roughly 10^{-29} millimetres – which is completely insignificant. But if the scenario is shifted from the macroscopic to the quantum world, such errors become highly significant.

---

[94] Bryan Appleyard, *Understanding the Present: Science and the Soul of Modern Man*. New York: Doubleday, 1994, 157–9.

[95] Stanley Aronowitz, *Science as Power: Discourse and Ideology in Modern Society*. Minneapolis: University of Minnesota Press, 1988.

[96] Paul R. Gross and Norman Levitt, *Higher Superstition: The Academic Left and its Quarrels with Science*. Baltimore, MD: Johns Hopkins University Press, 1998, 51.

The origins of the uncertainty principle go back to a 27-page paper by Werner Heisenberg, dealing with the 'perceptual content of quantum theoretical kinematics and mechanics'.[97] The paper set out clearly the following fundamental principle: if the position of an electron is determined by irradiation with high energy gamma rays, the electron undergoes a change in its momentum as a consequence of this process of irradiation. As a result, an uncertainty exists concerning both its position and momentum. 'The more precisely the position is determined, the less precisely the momentum is known in this instant, and vice versa.' Heisenberg insisted that it was meaningless to speak of the position of an electron without being able to specify how that position was to be determined. 'If one wants to be clear about what is meant by the "position of an object", for example of an electron . . . then one has to specify definite experiments by which the "position of an electron" can be measured; otherwise this term has no meaning at all.'

The issue concerns the limitations placed upon observation, and hence upon knowledge, by the entities it is proposed to observe. Heisenberg's uncertainty principle represents the theoretical outcome of the application of the principle that we must encounter reality on its own terms, and accept the limitations which this entails. Electrons, Heisenberg insists, are not *anschaulich*, in that they cannot be 'perceived'. The question of how this affected the manner in which they were studied now became a matter of critical importance, in that the procedures of measurement and observation – which were virtually unproblematic in classical physics – encountered fundamental difficulties in relation to quantum phenomena. If these phenomena are to be investigated, the fundamental limitations imposed upon the processes of observation and measurement by the nature of the quantum entities must be respected. Entities are known only in ways that correspond to their idiosyncratic identities, which must be acknowledged and respected.

The Barth–Scholz debate over theological science

This insight allows us to revisit one of the more interesting theological debates of the twentieth century – the controversy between Karl Barth and Heinrich Scholz over whether Christian theology is *wissenschaftlich*. In 1931, Heinrich Scholz published an article dealing with the question of whether Protestant theology could possibly be a science

---

[97] Werner Heisenberg, 'Über den anschaulichen Inhalt der quantentheoretischen Kinematik und Mechanik', *Zeitschrift für Phyisk* 43 (1927), 172–98.

(*Wissenschaft*). The article was prompted by Karl Barth's insistence that Christian theology was *wissenschaftlich* in that it responded to its object in an appropriate manner. It was not appropriate, he insisted, to develop a universal method, capable of being applied across disciplines; rather, it was necessary to identify the object of Christian theology, and respond in a manner which was consonant with its distinctive characteristics. Although the rudiments of this idea can be seen in earlier writings, the idea is set forth with particular clarity in the 1927 *Christliche Dogmatik.*

In this important work, Barth launched an attack on the views of Hans Heinrich Wendt, who had argued that *wissenschaftlich* knowledge did not depend upon its subject matter. A more or less identical method was appropriate to all intellectual disciplines.[98] Wendt here follows the general neo-Kantian consensus of the period, and did not see himself as making particularly controversial or outrageous statements. It was not a universal viewpoint, and was opposed by Martin Kähler among others who held that the object of a discipline must determine its methods.[99] Nevertheless, his views prompted Barth to launch a sustained attack on the notion of a universal *wissenschaftlich* method, using Wendt as a foil. For Barth, it was essential to respect the unique subject matter of Christian theology, and respond accordingly.[100]

> The choice of the means of establishment of the objective truth, the type of epistemic connection, the critical norm, and possibility of proof in any discipline (*Gebiet*) must be determined by the distinctiveness of the relevant object (*Eigenart des betreffenden Gegenstandes*) – not the inverse, in which the object is forced to conform to predetermined concepts of method and science (*Wissenschaftlichkeit*).

In his 1931 article, Scholz contested Barth's approach.[101] Scholz approached the question from the standpoint of a philosopher of religion who was not entirely hostile to Barth's theological position, yet had serious misgivings concerning Barth's hostility to engagement between theology and other disciplines, including philosophy.[102] He

---

[98] Hans Heinrich Wendt, *System der christlichen Lehre*. Göttingen: Vandenhoeck & Ruprecht, 1907, 2–3.

[99] See Martin Kähler, *Die Wissenschaft der christlichen Lehre*. Leipzig: Deichert, 1893, 5.

[100] Karl Barth, *Die christliche Theologie im Entwurf*. Munich: Kaiser Verlag, 1927, 115.

[101] Heinrich Scholz, 'Wie ist eine evangelische Theologie als Wissenschaft möglich?', *Zwischen den Zeiten* 9 (1931), 8–51.

[102] See Heinrich Scholz, *Religionsphilosophie*. Berlin: Reuther & Reichard, 1921, 130–1, for an interesting criticism of Feuerbach. For a specific critique of the 'scientific' nature of Schleiermacher's theology, see Heinrich Scholz, *Christentum und Wissenschaft in Schleiermachers Glaubenslehre: Ein Beitrag zum Verständnis der Schleiermacherschen Theologie*. Berlin: A. Glaue, 1909.

set out three 'minimum conditions' for any theology to possess 'scientific' status:

1. That any scientific discipline must be capable of stating its beliefs as propositions whose truth is asserted.
2. That all such propositions must be related to a single aspect of reality.
3. That the truth claims made by theological statements should be capable of being tested and confirmed against the critical principles used in their formulation.

To this, Scholz then adds the most important condition of all – the requirement that a science (*Wissenschaft*) must be able to state its propositions as axioms (or fundamental propostions) and as theorems which are deduced from these axioms. In 1932, Barth rejected these criteria, although without casting all that much light on why he was so vigorously opposed to them.[103]

On the basis of our earlier analysis of tradition-mediated rationalities, and anticipating our discussion of the multilayered natural of the natural scientific project, it is possible to see that there are nuggets of truth in each thinker's approach. Scholz, for example, is surely right to insist that the principles which lead to theological statements being formulated require investigation and should be open to testing.[104] Theological statements do not appear magically from nowhere; their historical origins (rather de-emphasized by Scholz, by the way) and intellectual coherence must be open to critical examination.[105]

Yet there is a major problem. Underlying Scholz's works appears to be a foundationalist view of knowledge, with priority being given to deduction from fundamental propositions. While the demise of foundationalism does not require us to reject the idea of a foundation for Christian theology, it frees us from any obligation to insist that theology mimics other disciplines, such as analytical philosophy. Scholz's supreme demand – that theology should be able to formulate axioms, apparently by analogy with mathematics and logic – rests upon an understanding of method which seems firmly anchored in the Enlightenment. While

---

[103] Barth, *Church Dogmatics*, I/1, 8–9. For an analysis of the controversy, see Arie L. Molendijk, 'Ein heidnische Wissenschaftsbegriff: Der Streit zwischen Heinrich Scholz und Karl Barth um die Wissenschaftlichkeit der Theologie', *Evangelische Theologie* 52 (1992), 527–45.

[104] Scholz, 'Wie ist eine evangelische Theologie als Wissenschaft möglich?', 21.

[105] Scholz, 'Wie ist eine evangelische Theologie als Wissenschaft möglich?', 45–8.

Scholz is no uncritical rationalist, the tapestry of his article is shot through with the assumption that at least some degree of universality of method is possible.

Barth is right to challenge this. It is impossible to lay down *a priori* what conditions must apply to theology as the science (*Wissenschaft*) of God, or to assume that norms and working assumptions drawn from other disciplines can be transposed to theology without doing violence to its integrity. The point at issue is made well by T. F. Torrance, who can be seen as developing Barth's notion of 'theological science' in a positive yet critical manner:[106]

> Scientific procedure will not allow us to go beyond the boundary set by the object, for that would presume that by the inherent powers of our own 'autonomous reason' we can gain mastery over it. We have to act within the limits imposed by the nature of the object, and avoid self-willed and undisciplined speculative thinking. It would be uncontrolled and unscientific procedure to run ahead of the object and prescribe just how it shall or can be known before we actually know it, or to withdraw ourselves from actual knowing and then in detachment from the object lay down the conditions upon which valid knowledge is possible.

Torrance's point is that the natural sciences make it clear that we cannot settle questions of scientific knowledge *a priori*, must instead recognize that such knowledge is *a posteriori*, and conditioned by the specific nature of the scientific discipline and its object. Torrance's concern here is reinforced through the recognition – explored in depth in chapter 7 – that there is no 'universal rationality', no universal method or foundations, which allow us to lay down in advance what form a discipline should take, still less to apply the methods and foundations of another intellectual tradition to Christian theology.

Torrance develops this point further in an important study of the theological method of Athanasius, to which we may now turn. Torrance's studies of the scientific method of the school of Alexandria persuaded him that the Greek fathers were perfectly aware of the general principle that knowledge depended upon the inherent structure or nature of the realities under investigation. A science can only investigate an object in accordance with its distinct nature (κατὰ φύσιν). Torrance discerns this principle in operation in both the scientific and more formally theological writings of John Philoponus of Alexandria. Torrance argued that the theological and scientific thinking

---

[106] Torrance, *Theological Science*, 26.

of Philoponus took shape within the scientific tradition of Alexandria, where considerable attention had been given, not least by Clement of Alexandria, to the inner connection between faith and scientific knowledge, and the appropriate method of inquiry. According to Clement, we must seek to know and understand something strictly in accordance with what it actually is – that is, κατὰ φυσίν in accordance with its distinctive nature as it becomes disclosed in the course of inquiry, and thus in accordance with what it really is.

Torrance argues that this 'kataphysical' approach to theology is evident in the writings of Athanasius, who insisted that Christian theology should learn to ask questions and develop a vocabulary in response to the realities it engaged with.[107]

> So far as scientific theology is concerned, this means that we are forced to adapt our common language to the nature and reality of God who is disclosed to us in Jesus Christ, and even where necessary to coin new terms, to express what we thus apprehend. Hence Athanasius insisted that when our ordinary terms are applied to God, they must be *stretched* beyond their natural sense and reference, and must be employed in such a way that they indicate more than the actual terms can naturally specify.

Whether theology coins its own vocabulary, or borrows terms from other contexts, it is essential to ensure that they are used and understood as they relate to the object of the Christian faith, rather that recapitulating the presuppositions of their original context.

The history of theology offers many illuminating episodes which illustrate the importance of this point. An excellent example is provided by the development of the notion of 'the righteousness of God' (*iustitia Dei*) in the western theological tradition.[108] In attempting to clarify what biblical writers meant when speaking of God's 'righteousness' or 'justice', many western writers found it natural to assume that there was a correspondence between the senses of the term as applied to God and to humans. Writers such as Julian of Eclanum argued that the Ciceronian notion of justice as 'rendering people their due entitlement' (*reddens unicuique quod suum est*) applied to God as well as to humanity, and thus developed an understanding of the process of salvation which entailed the divine reward of humanity as a consequence of, and in recognitition of, moral excellence.

---

[107] Thomas F. Torrance, 'Athanasius: A Study in the Foundations of Classical Theology', in *Theology in Reconciliation*. London: Geoffrey Chapman, 1975, 215–66; 241.

[108] For documentation of what follows, see Alister E. McGrath, *Iustitia Dei: A History of the Christian Doctrine of Justification*. 2nd edn. Cambridge: Cambridge University Press, 1998, 51–70.

This trend was consolidated during the Middle Ages, and reached its theological zenith in the *via moderna* of the fourteenth and fifteenth centuries. Martin Luther's 'theology of the cross' is to be seen both as a critique of the doctrine of analogy which led to the belief that divine and human justice could be regarded as analogous in this context, and to the recovery of a more authentically biblical notion of *iustitia Dei*.[109] The basic point which this case study illustrates is the need to ensure that there is an appropriate match between theological vocabulary and the object it purports to represent. Part of the task of a scientific theology is to critique the vocabulary of faith and correct misunderstandings which could lead to the loss of the integrity of faith.

The nature of the knowledge of God

A scientific theology is concerned with the knowledge of God. Yet we have seen how the nature of the object to be known has a decisive influence upon the nature of that knowledge. The philosophers of the Enlightenment were not entirely enthusiastic over speaking about God, and tended to leave this to pietist pastors. Where the question of the knowledge of God was discussed, the model proposed was generally that of discovering an object. An active human being, through the exercise of the critical faculty of reason, was capable of finding God within the universe, in much the same way as the German archaeologist Heinrich Schliemann discovered the lost city of Troy in 1870, or the astronomer J. E. Bode discovered the first asteroid in 1801. Knowledge of God is thus assumed to be informational in character, and to arise from the activity of the human agent as discoverer.

This way of thinking about God is profoundly unsuited to traditional Christian reflection on God. While the Christian tradition holds that some knowledge of God may arise through nature, it is emphatic that full and authentic knowledge of God arises through divine self-disclosure – that is, through divine revelation rather than human investigation.[110] Furthermore, the Christian tradition held that this 'knowledge of God' did not take the form solely of information about God, but was also

---

[109] Alister E. McGrath, *Luther's Theology of the Cross: Martin Luther's Theological Breakthrough.* Oxford: Blackwell, 1985.

[110] For an overview of the issues and some useful case studies, see Avery Dulles, *Models of Revelation.* Dublin: Gill & Macmillan, 1983; Colin E. Gunton, *A Brief Theology of Revelation.* Edinburgh: T&T Clark, 1995; Walter Kickel, *Vernunft und Offenbarung bei Theodor Beza: Zum Problem der Verhältnisses von Theologie, Philosophie und Staat.* Neukirchen-Vluyn: Neukirchener Verlag, 1967; J. A. Veitch, 'Revelation and Religion in the Thought of Karl Barth', *Scottish Journal of Theology* 24 (1971), 1–22; Wolfgang Wieland, *Offenbarung bei Augustinus.* Mainz: Matthias–Grünewald–Verlag, 1978.

possessed of a capacity to actualize a relationship with God. In other words, true knowledge of God is a fundamentally relational and transformative notion,[111] incapable of being fully expressed in categories more appropriate to knowing about everyday life in ancient Troy, or knowing the orbital characteristics of asteroids such as Ceres.

The full realization of the importance of this point in western theology dates from the aftermath of the First World War, and is particularly associated with the rise of dialogical personalism in the early 1920s.[112] The basic features of this philosophy were laid out in two major works of this period: Ferdinand Ebner's *Das Wort und die geistigen Realitäten* ('The Word and Spiritual Realities', 1921), and Martin Buber's *Ich und Du* ('I and Thou', 1923). Both works developed a powerful critique of contemporary idealism, and particularly of the concept of the isolation of the self and the notion of a generic *wissenschaftliche Philosophie* applicable across the entire frame of human knowledge.[113] Instead, it is suggested that all human existential life should be analysed in *dialogical* terms. Buber analyses human experience as follows:[114]

> The world is twofold for humanity according to our twofold attitude.
>
> The attitude of humanity is twofold according to the two basic words we can utter.
>
> The basic words are not single words, but pairs of words.
>
> One basic word is the word pair I–Thou (*Ich–Du*).
>
> The other basic word is the word pair I–It (*Ich–Es*).

For Buber, the I–It relationship defines the world of experience (*Erfahrung*), which may be regarded as the interaction of a subject and object. The I–Thou relationship, however, establishes the world of encounter (*Begegnung*), which must be regarded as the mutual inter- action of two subjects. The fundamental difference between 'I–It' and 'I–Thou' attitudes lies with how the knowing agent interprets the other.

---

[111] For the use of the term 'mystical' to refer to this knowledge, as in the writings of Thomas Merton, see Raymond Bailey, *Thomas Merton on Mysticism.* Garden City, NY: Doubleday, 1975; John A. T. Vazhakoottathil, *Thomas Merton's Mystical Quest for the Union with God.* St Ottilien: EOS Verlag, 1993. For a more evangelical approach, see J. I. Packer, *Knowing God.* London: Hodder & Stoughton, 1973.

[112] Bernhard Langemeyer, *Der dialogische Personalismus in der evangelischen und katholischen Theologie der Gegenwart.* Paderborn: Verlag Bonifacius–Druckerei, 1963.

[113] Hermann Oberparleiter, *Martin Buber und die Philosophie: Die Auseinandersetzung Martin Bubers mit der wissenschaftlichen Philosophie.* Frankfurt am Main: Peter Lang, 1983.

[114] Martin Buber, *I and Thou.* Edinburgh: T&T Clark, 1970, 53. For an excellent study, see Steven T. Katz, 'Dialogue and Revelation in the Thought of Martin Buber', *Religious Studies* 14 (1978), 57–68.

In an 'I–It' experience, the knower does not interpret the other as having any possibilities beyond those which the self has determined for it. In other words, the knowing agent is to be understood as constructing an image of the other in which it imposes possibilities on the other and does not recognize it as having any other possibilities of its own. The knower thus relates to its image of the other instead of the other as it actually is. On the other hand, in the 'I–Thou' encounter the knower recognizes that the other has possibilities of its own beyond those which the self expects or imposes.

Whereas in the world of experience the subject is active and the object passive, the world of encounter opens up the possibility of both activity and passivity on the part of the subject as the subject engages in a dynamic relationship with another subject. It is this concept of the mutual interaction of two subjects which Buber attempts to encapsulate in the untranslatable formula *Ich-wirkend-Du und Du-wirkend-Ich*, which, despite its verbal clumsiness, conveys effectively the idea of the involvement of the knower in the process of knowing.

Buber thus emphasizes the importance of the relationship between the 'I' and the 'Thou', which prevents the improper reification or hypostasization of either. As Buber stresses, 'actuality' (*Wirklichkeit*) cannot be objectified. While Buber locates the world of encounter primarily in human relationships, he is clearly aware of its potential application to the relationship between God and humanity, and it is not surprising that several major theologians sought to apply its insights as a means of reappropriating more authentically Christian ideas of 'knowing God' than those permitted by the Enlightenment.

The development of Buber's dialogical critique of the subject–object dichotomy was a major theme of the theology of the second quarter of the twentieth century, and its most significant Christological application may be found in Brunner's 1938 *Truth as Encounter*, which had its origins as a series of lectures to theological students in Sweden.[115] In this work, Brunner argues that faith is primarily a personal encounter with the God who meets us personally in Jesus Christ. For Brunner, 'truth' is itself a personal concept, and the subject–object dichotomy a destructive element within Christian theology. The biblical revelation lies 'beyond objectivism and subjectivism', in that revelation is understood to be an event in history. This should not be interpreted to

---

[115] Emil Brunner, *Truth as Encounter*. 2nd edn. London: SCM Press, 1964, 18–30. See further Roman Roessler, *Person und Glaube: Der Personalismus der Gottesbeziehung bei Emil Brunner*. Munich: Kaiser Verlag, 1965, 19–20; Stephan Scheld, *Die Christologie Emil Brunners*. Wiesbaden: Franz Steinbeck, 1981, 48–92.

mean that history reveals God, but that God reveals himself within the historical process, and supremely in the work and person of Jesus Christ. Brunner uses the phrase 'personal correspondence' to convey the fact that revelation cannot be conceived propositionally or intellectually, but must be understood as an act of God, and supremely the act of Jesus Christ.

God reveals himself personally and historically, by communicating himself in Jesus Christ. The concept of 'truth as encounter' thus conveys the two elements of a correct understanding of revelation: it is in the first place *historical* and in the second place *personal.* By the former, Brunner wishes us to understand that truth is not something permanent within the eternal world of ideas which is disclosed or communicated to us but something which *happens* in space and time. Truth comes into being as the act of God in time and space. By the latter, Brunner intends to emphasize that the content of this act of God is none other than God himself, rather than a complex of ideas or doctrines concerning God.

Brunner's conception of knowing God as 'Thou' rather than as 'It' allows him to reaffirm two themes which he believes to be central to the authentic Christian understanding of 'knowing God', which arise directly from the specific nature and character of God.

1. Truth comes to us; it is not in us. In other words, we need to be told what God is like in and through divine self-revelation.

2. Truth *about God* takes the form of encounter *with God,* which includes both informational and personal elements.

It can be seen immediately how Brunner's approach reaffirms the involvement of the knower in the process of knowing, and marks a necessary and appropriate break with the Enlightenment conception of 'knowing ideas about God' – a notion which, in fairness, it probably inherited from Lutheran Orthodoxy. The criticism of Orthodoxy on this point by Pietist writers often stressed the 'personal involvement' of the believer with God, and is thus a criticism as much of later Orthodoxy's views of what knowledge of God represented as how it was to be obtained.[116] Brunner's appropriation of Buber is one strategy

---

[116] For the general themes, see Martin Greschat, *Orthodoxie und Pietismus.* Stuttgart: Kohlhammer, 1982; for specific case studies, see Hans Martin Rotermund, *Orthodoxie und Pietismus: Valentin Ernst Löschers 'Timotheus Verinus' in der Auseinandersetzung mit der Schule August Herman Franckes.* Berlin: Evangeslische Verlagsanstalt, 1959; Stefan Luft, *Leben und Schreiben für den Pietismus: Der Kampf des pietistischen Ehepaares Johanna Eleonora und Johann Wilhelm Petersen gegen die lutherische Orthodoxie.* Herzberg: Bautz, 1994.

among others for reclaiming what T. F. Torrance regarded as the most fundamental insight of Kierkegaard:[117]

> When the question of truth is raised in an objective manner, the knower is related directly to the truth as to an object to which he is related, but attention is not focused on the relationship. When the question is raised subjectively the knower is directed subjectively to the truth, and then the attention is focused on the nature of his relationship to the truth.

Brunner's dialogical personalism represents only one possibility for formulating the distinctive Christian understanding of the knowledge of God, and it is not my intention to defend or criticize it. The point I have tried to make in exploring the Buber–Brunner strategy is that it is *accommodated* to the specific nature of God, rather than representing a generic universal theology of knowledge which is regarded as being as applicable to God as it is to asteroids or lost cities. Precisely because it is so generic, a *wissenschaftliche Philosophie* (and a *wissenschaftliche Theologie*) is prone to neglect, if not to evade, the issues of both the distinctive character of the object of knowledge and the involvement of the knower in the process of knowing. Both are integral to a *naturwissenschaftliche Theologie*.

Scientific theology offers an explanation of reality

The notion of explanation plays an important role in Christian theology. 'Why?' is an important and legitimate question, the force of which cannot be ignored. Why are things the way they are? Themes such as the following play no small role in the biblical tradition, particularly in relation to the meaning of events.

> When your children ask you in time to come, 'What is the meaning of the decrees and the statutes and the ordinances that the Lord our God has commanded you?' then you shall say to your children, 'We were Pharaoh's slaves in Egypt, but the Lord brought us out of Egypt with a mighty hand. The Lord displayed before our eyes great and awesome signs and wonders against Egypt, against Pharaoh and all his household.' (Deuteronomy 6:20–2)

Here the various cultic institutions of Israel are being explained to future generations as memorials of foundational events in the history of Israel,

---

[117] Torrance, *Theological Science*, 5. Torrance's appreciation of this point is partly due to James Brown's Croall Lectures given in the University of Edinburgh in 1953: see James Brown, *Subject and Object in Modern Theology*. London: SCM Press, 1955.

and especially as affirmations of the saving work of God in history.[118] In much the same way, the Christian eucharist is explained by New Testament writers as a memorial of the death of Christ (1 Corinthians 11:23–6), and the suffering of Christians as a process of 'disciplining' which demonstrates that they are truly children of God (Hebrews 12:6).

The history of the Christian tradition offers us countless examples of theology being conceived as – among other things – an explanatory framework which enables believers to make sense of the world in which they live. Seen at a purely functional level, theology aims to establish a link between the beliefs and derived practices of the Christian community and the contemporary experience of Christians. This trend can, as we have noted, be seen in both Old and New Testaments, and is an important feature of the Christian theological tradition subsequently. The doctrine of creation can be seen as offering an explanation for the regularities observed within the natural order, just as the doctrine of the 'two natures' aims to explain the significance of Jesus Christ.

It is beyond dispute that Christian theology has seen itself as having an explanatory role, and that it continues to do so. But should it? Some have argued that the notion of 'explanation' is not an integral aspect of religious identity. To put it crudely: religion is not primarily about explaining things. This view has been defended by a number of writers, perhaps most significantly the philosopher of religion D. Z. Phillips.[119] The approach adopted by Phillips is derived from the writings of Wittgenstein, especially his caustic remarks on Sir James Frazer's *Golden Bough*. This view has, however, been subjected to serious criticism in a number of recent works specifically engaging with the relationship of Christianity and the natural sciences.

In his careful study *Explanation from Physics to Theology* (1989), Philip Clayton brings out the significance of 'the meaning dimension' in religion.[120] A number of different levels of explanation may be discerned; nevertheless, a phenomenological approach to the question definitely discloses an explanatory imperative within the religious traditions:[121]

[118] See also Exodus 13:14–15; Joshua 4:6–7. For the points at issue, see H. J. Kraus, 'Gilgal: Ein Betrag zur Kulturgeschichte Israels', *Vetus Testamentum* 1 (1951), 181–99.

[119] D. Z. Phillips, *Religion without Explanation*. Oxford: Blackwell, 1976. For an exploration of this theme in the writings of Wittgenstein, see his *Wittgenstein and Religion*. London: Macmillan, 1993.

[120] Philip Clayton, *Explanation from Physics to Theology: An Essay in Rationality and Religion*. New Haven, CT: Yale University Press, 1989, 131–45.

[121] Clayton, *Explanation from Physics to Theology*, 118.

> An important task is posed by the need to view one's life as meaningful, and religious explanations are in the first place (but not solely) responses to this task . . . Religious beliefs are grounded at the outset in their ability to make the experience of an individual or group meaningful. The believer understands the world in a certain way; that is to say, he perceives a significance in certain (or all) objects or situations that others do not.

Similarly, Michael Banner offers a related approach in his *Justification of Science and the Rationality of Religious Belief* (1990). Banner argues that the objections against explanation advanced by Phillips can be countered and refuted, both on account of internal difficulties within his approach, and the need for a more nuanced account of the nature of faith than that which he offers.[122]

The considerations set out by writers such as Banner and Clayton are widely regarded as at least neutralizing the objections to a 'religion as explanation' model. It is not my intention to argue that Christian theology is primarily about offering explanations of the way things are. My concern is simply to note that one of the uses to which theology is put is to offer at least some explanation of the nature of things, irrespective of the degree of comprehensiveness of that explanation or the emphasis which would be placed upon 'explanation' alongside other aspects of Christian life and thought, such as 'salvation'. Thus Richard Swinburne's carefully argued defence of the existence of God makes a judicious appeal to the explanatory power of theism in relation to such matters as the existence and ordering of the universe.[123] The world displays phenomena which 'cry out for explanation'; part of the coherence of Christian theism is its (alleged) ability to offer an explanation for what is observed.

We shall return to this issue in much greater detail in the final volume of this trilogy, which will consider the question of how competing explanations are to be evaluated. Our concern at this stage is simply to register that there is an explanatory dimension to a scientific theology.

We now turn to the fifth postulate concerning a scientific theology. As I have already made clear, I believe that this postulate is warranted, yet that its plausibility rests entirely on the inner logic of the Christian faith.

---

[122] Michael C. Banner, *The Justification of Science and the Rationality of Religious Belief.* Oxford and New York: Oxford University Press, 1990, 67–118.

[123] Richard Swinburne, *The Existence of God.* Oxford: Clarendon Press, 1979, 277–90.

Why a scientific theology is Christocentric

The theological approach which has dominated the significant 'science and religion' constituency to date has focused on the doctrine of creation.[124] The reasons for this are not difficult to discern, and may be summarized as follows:

1. The notion of the world being 'created' is common to most of the world's religions. To use the generalized language of creation is therefore to avoid any embarrassing and potentially awkward claims for Christian distinctiveness, which might hinder the generic 'science and religion' dialogue by pointing up the differences between, for example, Christian and Jewish concepts of creation.

2. An emphasis on creation allows an immediate appeal to a very generalized concept of divinity, capable of being reconciled with the Platonic tradition on the one hand, other monotheistic faiths, and especially the insights of the philosophy of religion.

At first sight, the vision of a scientific theology set out in these volumes endorses this trend, in that a Christian doctrine of creation can be seen to be of fundamental importance to the credibility and intellectual viability of a scientific theology (vol. 1, 241–305). Yet it also raises a question concerning it, in that a Christian doctrine of creation which is prepared to affirm its distinctiveness as a *Christian* statement includes an explicit reference to Christ. My concern throughout this project has been to insist upon respecting the integrity of the Christian tradition – a procedure which in no way interferes with the process of dialogue with other traditions, unless it is held that such dialogue may only be undertaken by suppressing or overlooking each religion's distinctive features.

Christ and the distinctive nature of the Christian faith

'Christianity is radical monotheism.' That, at any rate, was the judgement of H. Richard Niebuhr in a series of lectures delivered in 1957 at the University of Nebraska as the 'Montgomery Lectures on

Contemporary Civilization.'[125] Niebuhr's agenda here is dictated by his desire to distinguish three categories of faiths. In addition to his category of 'radical monotheism', Niebuhr recognizes polytheism and henotheism, and sets out to explore their interrelationship. It should be noted that Niebuhr does not limit his analysis to what traditionally might be designated as 'religions', but includes such phenomena as communism, fascism, racism and nationalism which he declares to be 'polytheism and henotheism in their modern, nonmythological guise'. Niebuhr's designation of Christianity as 'radical monotheism' is thus determined by the set of categories he chose as a means of distinguishing various cultural systems he wished to analyse. This is a pity, as Niebuhr's designation has proved influential in shaping popular conceptions of Christianity.[126] In reality, it is profoundly misleading to refer to Christianity in this way, for the simple reason that it fails to take account of the centrality of Christ to the Christian tradition.

The idea that Jesus Christ should have any real impact on Christianity was strongly resisted by Enlightenment writers, whose commitment to the notion of a universal rationality and set of moral values led them to deny that Christ could have any constitutive role in shaping Christian thought. He might be permitted to illustrate or embody already existing moral values or religious ideas; he could not, however, be allowed to determine them.[127] That privilege was to be accorded to the universalities of human reason alone. The idea that Christianity possessed distinctive ideas that were true was dismissed as a self-contradictory statement. Christianity might echo or reflect the rational faith of the Enlightenment. But if it was *distinctive*, it was for that reason *wrong*. The demise of the Enlightenment has led to a rediscovery of the critical foundational role of Christ in Christian theology, ethics and spirituality, and a reappropriation of the themes of the 'great tradition' of Christian reflection prior to the Enlightenment.

The foundational role of Christ to Christian life and thought can be summarized under four general headings, as follows.

1. JESUS CHRIST IS THE HISTORICAL POINT OF DEPARTURE FOR CHRISTIANITY

It is a simple matter of historical fact that the coming of Jesus Christ brought the Christian community into being. Thus Albrecht Benjamin

---

[125] H. Richard Niebuhr, *Radical Monotheism and Western Culture*. New York: Harper, 1960.

[126] See, for example, the way in which this category is used rather uncritically in James W. Fowler, *Stages of Faith*. San Francisco: Harper, 1981, 22–3.

[127] Alister E. McGrath, *The Genesis of Doctrine: A Study in the Foundations of Doctrinal Criticism*. Oxford: Blackwell, 1990, 132–45.

Ritschl argued that Jesus of Nazareth brought something new to the human situation, something which reason had hitherto neglected. Jesus was conscious of a *new and hitherto unknown relation to God.* Where the Enlightenment believed in a universal rational religion, of which individual world religions were at best shadows, Ritschl argued that this was little more than a dream of reason, an abstraction without any historical embodiment. Christianity possesses certain definite theological and cultural characteristics as a historical religion, partly due to Jesus of Nazareth. The coming of Jesus thus marks both the historical point of departure and the subsequent moral shaping of the Christian church.[128]

2. JESUS CHRIST REVEALS GOD

Christian theology affirms that Jesus Christ makes God known in a particular and specific manner, distinctive to Christianity. This is expressed in the New Testament at various levels, including through reference to Christ as the 'image of the invisible God' (Colossians 1:15). This conviction has been central to mainstream Christianity down the ages.[129] Thus the writer of the second Letter of Clement, probably to be dated from the middle of the second century, opens his letter with the affirmation that 'we must think of Jesus Christ as of God'.

3. JESUS CHRIST IS THE BEARER OF SALVATION

A central theme of mainstream Christian thought is that salvation, in the Christian sense of the term, is manifested in and through, and constituted on the basis of, the life, death, and resurrection of Jesus Christ. The historical development of 'theories of the atonement' is perhaps best seen as an attempt to formalize or correlate the various ways in which the New Testament articulates the idea that, in some way, the death and resurrection of Jesus Christ open up a new relationship to God, and hence a new way of life.[130]

---

[128] For the issues this raises, see Hans-Georg Link, *Geschichte Jesu und Bild Christi: die Entwicklung der Christologie Martin Kählers in Auseinandersetzung mit der Leben-Jesu-Theologie und der Ritschl-Schule.* Neukirchen-Vluyn: Neukirchener Verlag, 1975; Clive Marsh, *Albrecht Ritschl and the Problem of the Historical Jesus.* San Francisco: Edwin Mellen Press, 1992.

[129] See, for example, Pierre Claverie, *Le livre de la foi: révélation et parôle de Dieu dans la tradition chrétienne.* Paris: Cerf, 1996; William L. Portier, *Tradition and Incarnation: Foundations of Christian Theology.* New York: Paulist Press, 1994.

[130] See F. W. Dillistone, *The Christian Understanding of Atonement.* London: Nisbet, 1984; Colin E. Gunton, *The Actuality of Atonement: A Study of Metaphor, Rationality and the Christian Tradition.* Edinburgh: T&T Clark, 1988; Martin Hengel, *The Atonement: A Study of the Origins of the Doctrine in the New Testament.* London: SCM Press, 1981.

4. JESUS CHRIST DEFINES THE SHAPE OF THE REDEEMED LIFE

Christian spirituality and ethics affirm that the shape of Christian existence, in relation to both its spiritual and its ethical dimensions, is shaped by Jesus Christ. The New Testament itself is strongly *Christomorphic* in its view of the redeemed life – that is to say, it affirms that Jesus Christ not only makes that life possible; he also determines its shape. The New Testament imagery of 'being conformed to Christ' expresses this notion well. The rise of narrative theology has given especial importance to this point, through the recognition that the narrative of Jesus Christ which exercises controlling influence over the Christian community. Christian belief, and especially Christian ethics, are shaped by the narrative of Jesus Christ. This gives flesh and substance to otherwise abstract ideas of values and virtues.[131]

This analysis could be extended at some length, demonstrating the manner in which the distinctive nature of the Christian faith is inextricably linked with its principled determination faithfully to render Christ in its confessional statements. It is of no small importance to note that the aspects of the Christian faith which are found particularly objectionable by revisionists wishing to promote the simplistic agenda that 'all religions say the same thing' are the divinity of Christ, the doctrine of the incarnation, the resurrection of Christ, and the doctrine of the Trinity – all of which are clearly grounded in the unique person of Christ.

Christ as the foundation of faith

Earlier, we noted the importance of communities and traditions for the mediation of rationalities and values. As classically conceived, the Christian tradition regards Christ as embodying the wisdom of God, and as the foundation and criterion of other Christian doctrines. Perhaps the most obvious such case is the doctrine of the Trinity, widely regarded as representing the distinctively Christian vision of God. Yet the formalization of that doctrine was the result of a prior engagement with the identity of Jesus Christ, culminating in the definitive Chalcedonian statement declaring that Jesus Christ was 'consubstantial' with God. This represented more than an affirmation concerning Christ; it necessitated a clarification of the Christian concept of God, especially in the face of its rivals within the Greek philosophical

---

[131] The work of Stanley Hauerwas is of particular importance here. See Emmanuel Katongole, *Beyond Universal Reason: The Relation between Religion and Ethics in the Work of Stanley Hauerwas.* Notre Dame, IN: University of Notre Dame Press, 2000.

tradition.[132] At both the historical and theological levels, the doctrine of the Trinity articulates the identity and character of the God who is made known and made available through Christ. The Trinity may therefore be regarded as a doctrine about Christ, as much as a doctrine about God.[133]

To engage with, or operate faithfully within, the Christian tradition thus demands a recognition of the central role of Christ in Christian life, thought and devotion. It may be attractive to treat Christianity simply as a variant of theism; this, however fails to do justice to its trinitarian morphology, which in turn represents its incarnational foundations. A scientific theology, by seeking to do justice to Christianity *as it actually is* – rather than some reconstructed variant – will thus have to take the centrality of Christ with the uttermost seriousness.

If the classic Christian tradition – as represented from Irenaeus to Athanasius – is given full weight, the distinctive Christian understandings of God, creation, the grounds and nature of salvation, human nature and destiny are all understood to be disclosed and grounded Christologically. It is not merely that salvation is grounded in Christ; the *shape* of that salvation is determined Christologically. Thus the theme of 'union with Christ' plays a central role in both the anthropology and soteriology of writers as diverse as Luther, Calvin and Bernard of Clairvaux.[134] It can therefore be argued that the central themes of the Christian faith are grounded in *a posteriori* reflection on the biblical witness to Christ, not derived from *a priori* ideas about God or humanity.

If the centrality of Christ to the grounding of Christian theology is conceded, it follows that the coherence of any resulting theology will be determined by the adequacy of its representation of Christ within that system. Earlier, we stressed the importance of the theme of 'responding coherently to reality', pointing out how both the foundation

[132] R. P. C. Hanson, *The Search for the Christian Doctrine of God: The Arian Controversy 318–381.* Edinburgh: T&T Clark, 1988; Edmund J. Fortman, *The Triune God: A Historical Study of the Doctrine of the Trinity.* Philadelphia: Westminster, 1972. In more recent times, the doctrine has served to distinguish the Christian conception of God from the apathetic deity so severely criticized by 'protest atheists': W. Waite Willis, *Theism, Atheism and the Doctrine of the Trinity: The Trinitarian Theologies of Karl Barth and Jürgen Moltmann in Response to Protest Atheism.* Atlanta, GA: Scholars Press, 1987.

[133] Basil Studer, *Trinity and Incarnation: The Faith of the Early Church.* Collegeville, MN: Liturgical Press, 1993.

[134] Carl E. Braaten and Robert W. Jenson, *Union with Christ: The New Finnish Interpretation of Luther.* Grand Rapids, MI: Eerdmans, 1998; E. Tamburello Dennis, *Union with Christ : John Calvin and the Mysticism of St Bernard.* Louisville, KY: Westminster/John Knox Press, 1994, 23–40.

and inner coherence of a theological or scientific system were of critical importance. If a scientific theology is indeed grounded in Christ, directly or indirectly, then the question of the foundation of that theology must force us to move on to address the question of the inner coherence of the resulting system.

It is therefore important to note that the great heresies of the Christian tradition, in both east and west, are inextricably linked with the question of the internal coherence of the accounts they offer of the significance of Christ. The most compelling study of this remains that of F. D. E. Schleiermacher, and we shall consider his reflections in what follows.

Christ and the coherence of faith: Schleiermacher on the four natural heresies of Christianity

In his *The Christian Faith* (1834), F. D. E. Schleiermacher offers one of the most important analyses of the place of Christ in the Christian theological tradition.[135] One of the central insights that Schleiermacher develops is that a Christian dogmatics must attribute to Jesus the 'dignity' which his 'activity' demands. That is to say, the Christain understanding of the person of Jesus (which Schleiermacher expresses in terms of his *dignity*), must be commensurate with and grounded in his work (or *activity*), and vice versa.[136]

> They must be most intimately related and mutually determined. So that it is vain to attribute to the Redeemer a higher dignity than the activity at the same time ascribed to him demands, since nothing is explained by this surplus of dignity. It is equally vain to attribute to him a greater activity than follows naturally from the dignity which one is ready to allow him . . . Therefore every doctrine of Christ is inconsistent, in which this equality (of dignity and activity) is not essential, whether it seeks to disguise the detraction from the dignity by praising him in great but really alien activities, or, conversely, seeks to compensate for the lesser influence which it allows him by highly exalting him, yet in a fashion which leads to no result.

The doctrines of the person and work of Christ are thus so intimately connected that it is impossible to isolate them; a statement about the identity or dignity of Jesus is simultaneously a statement about his function or activity. As a result, there is an implicit affirmation of the

[135] Maureen Junker, *Das Urbild des Gottesbewüsstseins: Zur Entwicklung der Religionstheorie und Christologie Schleiermachers von der ersten zur zweiten Auflage der Glaubenslehre.* Berlin: Walter de Gruyter, 1990.

[136] F. D. E. Schleiermacher, *The Christian Faith.* Edinburgh: T&T Clark, 1928, 375.

coherence of Christ's person and work, which must be reflected in theological reflection.

Schleiermacher argues that a sharp distinction must be drawn between 'heresy' and 'unbelief'. Unbelief, according to Schleiermacher, consists in the rejection or denial of the principle that God has redeemed us through Jesus Christ. To deny that God has redeemed us through Jesus Christ is to deny the most fundamental truth claim which the Christian faith dares to make. The distinction between what is Christian and what is not lies in whether this principle is accepted: the distinction between what is *orthodox* and what is *heretical*, however, lies in how this principle, once conceded and accepted, is understood. In other words, heresy is not a form of unbelief; it is something that arises within the context of faith itself.

Heresy is to be thought of *as an ultimately incoherent form of Christian belief*, which preserves the appearance of Christianity, yet implicitly contradicts its essence through rendering it internally inconsistent:[137]

> If the distinctive essence of Christianity consists in the fact that in it all religious emotions are related to the redemption wrought by Jesus Christ, there will be two ways in which heresy can arise. That is to say: this fundamental formula will be retained in general . . . but *either* human nature will be so defined that a redemption in the strict case cannot be accomplished, *or* the Redeemer will be defined in such a way that he cannot accomplish redemption.

If the distinctive essence of Christianity consists in the fact that God has redeemed us through Jesus Christ (that is, through no one else and in no other way), it must follow that the Christian understanding of God, Jesus Christ and human nature should be coherent with this understanding of redemption. Thus:

1. The Christian understanding of God must be such that God can effect the redemption of humanity through Christ;
2. The Christian understanding of Christ must be such that God may effect our redemption through him;
3. The Christian understanding of humanity must be such that redemption is both possible and genuine.

The Christian understanding of God, Christ, and humanity must therefore cohere with the principle of redemption through Christ alone.

---

[137] Schleiermacher, *The Christian Faith*, 98. For further discussion, see Klaus M. Beckmann, *Der Begriff der Häresie bei Schleiermacher*. Munich: Kaiser Verlag, 1959, 36–62.

Inconsistency within the system at this point leads to incoherence and instability.

According to Schleiermacher heresy arises through accepting the foundational Christological principle of the Christian faith, but interpreting it in such a way that incoherence results. The principle that 'all religious emotions are related to the redemption wrought by Jesus Christ' may be accepted, and yet be interpreted in such a way that either:

1. Christ cannot effect the redemption of humanity; or
2. Humanity – the object of redemption – cannot be redeemed, in the proper sense of the term.

On the basis of this analysis, Schleiermacher proceeds to argue that what he terms the four 'natural heresies in Christianity' – Docetism and Ebionitism; Manicheanism and Pelagianism – result from incoherent accounts of the identity and significance of Jesus Christ.

Schleiermacher first turns to consider the question of the identity of 'the Redeemer' (his characteristic way of referring to Christ in this context). According to Schleiermacher, the answer given to this critical question must be capable of accounting for the uniqueness of his office and for his ability to mediate between God and humanity. This, he argues, presupposes an essential similarity between Christ and humanity. If the Redeemer is to mediate between humanity and God, there must be some similarity between Christ and humanity which makes this contact possible – and yet at the same time there must be something fundamentally *different* about Christ, which distances him from the human need for redemption. No human being is a redeemer, whereas all require to be redeemed.

Mediation demands similarity and dissimilarity. If the superiority of Jesus Christ over humanity is emphasized *without* maintaining his essential similarity to them, his ability to reconcile humanity to God is lost, in that he no longer has a point of contact with those whom he is supposed to redeem. On the other hand, if his similarity to humanity is emphasized *without* acknowledging that in at least one respect he is fundamentally different, then the Redeemer himself requires redemption. If the Redeemer is treated as being similar in every respect to humanity, he must be acknowledged to share the human need for redemption. Therefore *either* every human being must be thought of as a potential or actual redeemer, to a greater or lesser extent, *or else* the Redeemer cannot himself redeem.

Schleiermacher concludes that the doctrine of redemption through Christ requires that he should share the basics of the common human condition, except its need for redemption. According to Schleiermacher, orthodox Christianity has upheld this crucial insight by insisting that Jesus Christ is at one and the same time both God and human. It would be much simpler to suggest that Jesus was just God, or just human; but to uphold the possibility and actuality of our redemption, it is necessary to insist that they are both true.

Two heresies may arise through upholding the principle of redemption through Christ, but interpreting the person of Christ in such a way that this redemption becomes incoherent. On the one hand, Jesus Christ loses his point of contact with those he is meant to redeem, thus giving rise to *Docetism*. On the other, he loses his essential dissimilarity from those whom he came to redeem, and comes to be treated simply as a particularly enlightened human being, thus giving rise to the heresy which Schleiermacher styles *Ebionitism*.[138]

In a similar manner, Schleiermacher explores the identity of the redeemed. The answer to this question must be capable of explaining why redemption is necessary from outside humanity itself – in other words, why we cannot redeem ourselves. The object of redemption must both require redemption in the first place, and be capable of accepting that redemption when it is offered. These two aspects of the question must be maintained at one and the same time, just like the humanity and divinity of Christ. Schleiermacher argues that Manicheanism and Pelagianism arise through an incoherent account of the identity of the redeemed.

The four heresies described above, according to Schleiermacher, are to be understood to arise through an incoherent interpretation of the person and work of Christ. For Schleiermacher, it is no accident that these were by far the most important heresies to be debated in the early church. Christological considerations are thus shown to lie at the heart of the Christian faith. A defective Christology thus turns out to be tantamount to a deficient and inadequate conception of Christianity itself. Within the context of Schleiermacher's conception of theology, Christology can thus be seen to be of central and defining importance both to the Christian faith and to its resulting theology.

It must be made clear that Schleiermacher's account of heresy is deficient precisely because it is purely ideational, and makes no reference

---

[138] Schleiermacher stresses that his systematic account of these heresies does not correspond precisely to the specific historical forms of the heresies.

to cultural or social factors, including the issue of ecclesiastical power, which Walter Bauer (controversially) discerned as being of critical importance in this matter.[139] As accounts of the development of heretical movements in the early church make clear, the situation is far more complex than Schleiermacher allows.[140] Donatism, for example, can be interpreted as a cultural movement, asserting the rights of the indigenous Berber peoples of North Africa over and against the Roman colonists in the region. Similarly, many of the 'heresies' of the Middle Ages represented nationalist challenges to the political authority of the papacy at a time when this was seen as increasingly important to the coherence of Christendom.[141] There is no doubt that some heresies are grounded in specific religious ideas – perhaps most significantly, the dualist notion that the cosmos and humanity are in constant conflict through opposing forces of good and evil.[142] Yet even these are often modulated by social factors, so that an intellectual core acquires a significant overlay of cultural notions and values. This failure to recognize the social and cultural embeddedness of heresy is one of the weaknesses of any purely ideational approach to theology, and can be remedied by the adoption of a 'critical realism', such as that which we explored in an earlier chapter.

That, however, is another story. Our concern here is to note how Schleiermacher's analysis demonstrates that both the foundation and coherence of Christian theology can be said to be determined Christologically. In other words, within a classic conception of the Christian faith, Christ functions as both the *foundation* and *criterion* of an authentically Christian theology. This point has been made by many writers, some of whom would distance themselves from Schleiermacher in other respects. For example, Jürgen Moltmann's celebrated study *The Crucified God* argues that it is the cross of Christ – rather than some indeterminate aspect of Christ's person and work – which functions in this dual role.[143] Similarly, the Anglican scholar and

[139] Walter Bauer, *Orthodoxy and Heresy in Earliest Christianity*. London: SCM Press, 1972. See further A. Robinson Thomas, *The Bauer Thesis Examined: The Geography of Heresy in the Early Christian Church*. Lewiston, NY: Edwin Mellen Press, 1988.

[140] Everett Ferguson, *Orthodoxy, Heresy and Schism in Early Christianity*. New York: Garland, 1993.

[141] W. H. C. Frend, *Heresy and Schism as Social and National Movements*. Cambridge: Cambridge University Press, 1972; Gordon Leff, *Heresy in the Later Middle Ages: The Relation of Orthodoxy to Dissent, c.1250 – c.1450*. Manchester: Manchester University Press, 1967.

[142] P. F. M. Fontaine, *The Light and the Dark: A Cultural History of Dualism*. Amsterdam: J. C. Gieben, 1998; Yuri Stoyanov, *The Other God: Dualist Religions from Antiquity to the Cathar Heresy*. New Haven, CT: Yale University Press, 2000.

[143] Jürgen Moltmann, *The Crucified God: The Cross of Christ as the Foundation and Criticism of Christian Theology*. London: SCM Press, 1974.

theologian Charles Gore argued that deficiencies in Christology result in a wider incoherence within the Christian faith.[144]

The eastern tradition: scientific theology and Christology

It is fatally easy for a theologian who is steeped primarily in the rich intellectual and spiritual pastures of the western theological tradition to underplay the heritage of the eastern church. In turning to deal with the question of whether a scientific theology is necessarily – or merely appropriately – a Christocentric theology, I shall turn to explore one of the most serious and systematic theological engagements of the Christian tradition, focusing on Athanasius and the Cappadocian fathers.[145] Writing against a complex and variegated Hellenistic cultural and intellectual background, these writers sought to maintain faithfulness to the Christian tradition on the one hand, with a fruitful engagement with its intellectual environment on the other.[146]

In his double treatise *contra Gentes – de incarnatione Verbi* – which are probably best seen as two parts of a single work, the first a work of apologetics, and the second a work of systematic theology[147] – Athanasius sets out to demonstrate the rationality of the Christian faith – including its central tenet of the incarnation of the Word – in the face of the criticisms and apparent misunderstandings of the notion prevalent within late classical pagan culture. Athanasius offers a coherent view of the world, which links together the creation of the world by God, the creation of humanity by God, and the incarnation of the same Word of God after whose likeness the world and humanity was fashioned.[148]

[144] See Charles Gore, 'Our Lord's Human Example', *Church Quarterly Review* 16 (1883), 282–313. The most striking example of this is Gore's critique of the 'New Theology' of R. J. Campbell, which he judged to be flawed Christologically – and hence incoherent throughout, not least in regard to its doctrine of God: Charles Gore, *The New Theology and the Old Religion*. London: John Murray, 1907.

[145] For general introductions, see Khaled Anatolios, *Athanasius: The Coherence of His Thought*. New York: Routledge, 1998; Anthony Meredith, *The Cappadocians*. Crestwood, NY: St Vladimir's Seminary Press 1996; Philip Rousseau, *Basil of Caesarea*. Berkeley, CA: University of California Press, 1994.

[146] On this background, see Henry Chadwick, *Early Christian Thought and the Classical Tradition*. Oxford: Clarendon, 1966; Arnaldo Momigliano, *Il conflitto tra paganesimo e cristianesimo nel secolo IV*. Torino: Einaudi, 1975; Ramsay MacMullen, *Christianity and Paganism in the Fourth to Eighth Centuries*. New Haven, CT: Yale University Press, 1997, 103–49.

[147] Johannes Quasten, *Patrology*. 4 vols. Westminster, MD: Newman Press, 1952–86, vol. 3, 24–6.

[148] For the close connection between his anthropology and his Christology, see Johannes Roldanus, *Le Christ et l'homme dans la théologie d'Athanase d'Alexandrie: étude de la conjonction de sa conception de l'homme avec sa christologie*. Leiden: E. J. Brill, 1977.

Athanasius' starting point is his doctrine of creation, which locates a fundamental consonance or resonance between human rationality and its creator, thus laying the foundations of both a natural theology and a soteriology.[149]

> [God] has created humanity according to his own image through his own Word, our Saviour Jesus Christ, so that humanity is perceptive and knowledgeable of reality on account of its likeness to him, also giving it a conception and knowledge of its own eternity.

The fact that humanity has been created according to the 'image of God' is then supplemented with the doctrine that creation has been structured in accordance with the λόγος, so that the same humanity who has been created according to the divine image might discern God's work within that creation. 'God ordered creation through his own Word in such a way that, while he is invisible by nature, he might nevertheless be known to humanity through his works.'[150]

This leads to what, for Athanasius, is a critical step – namely, the assertion that the divine λόγος which was responsible for the ordering of creation became incarnate, assuming human nature within the flux of human history. Athanasius explores the soteriological and epistemological implications of this event. God became human in order that humans might become God.[151] Since only God can save, the agent of salvation – Jesus Christ – must be recognized as divine, distinct from the remainder of God's creation. Yet our concern in this section is primarily with the epistemological aspects of the incarnation. As Athanasius points out in *contra Gentes*, the Word of God is the basis of the ordering and stability of the universe; that same Word became incarnate in Christ.[152]

> I am here speaking of the very Word itself (λόγος), which is the living and acting God, the Word of the good God of the universe, who is to be distinguished from the things that are made, and all of the creation. He is the proper and the only (ἴδιος δὲ καὶ μόνος) Word of the good Father, who has ordered all the universe.

In that Christ is the Word incarnate, humanity has direct access to the nature of the Father and to the ordering of the universe through him. Christ is the perfect image and issue (καρπός) of the Father, and thus

[149] Athanasius, *contra Gentes*, 2.
[150] Athanasius, *contra Gentes*, 35.
[151] Athanasius, *de incarnatione Verbi*, 54.
[152] Athanasius, *contra Gentes*, 40.

intentionally and substantially – not accidentally – discloses and embodies the patterning and structuring of the created order.[153]

There is thus a resonance – but most emphatically not an identity – between natural theology and the incarnation. Athanasius holds that, by virtue of its creation, the soul is 'naturally' (κατὰ φυσίν) orientated towards God, and that a turning away from God is thus to be regarded as 'contrary to nature' (παρὰ φυσίν) – an idea which finds support from many other writers of this period.[154] The concept of God's pre-existent word (λόγος ἄσαρκος) functions as the basis of a natural theology which allows humanity at least some idea of the existence and character of God – ideas which were 'fleshed out' through the coming of the Word incarnate. It must, of course, be noted that Athanasius qualifies any suggestion that humanity can come to a full knowledge of God through nature by stressing that humanity, as we now know it, is sinful. While God has indeed endowed the creation with the possibility of disclosing knowledge of the divine nature, human sin obscures that knowledge. For Athanasius, this is a fundamental motivation for the incarnation. God was not prepared to abandon humanity, but chose to enter into the creation, thus making possible true knowledge of God and human transformation through divinization.[155]

The correlation of the theological roles of the pre-existent and incarnate Word – λόγος ἄσαρκος and λόγος ἔνσαρκος – establishes a fundamental link between apologetics and dogmatics, between a natural and a systematic theology – and most importantly of all, for our purposes, between the study of *nature* and the study of *Christ*. The rational ordering of creation is directly correlated with the incarnation. Within a Christian perspective, to study creation is to study the same λόγος that was incarnated in Christ, and which has also shaped the contours of human rationality. Human reason, creation and Christ are thus interlinked and interlocked through their relationship with the divine λόγος.

The view that Christology is central to Christian theology, both in terms of its method and substance, is found in T. F. Torrance's *Theological Science*. This work affirms the centrality of the 'logic of

---

[153] Athanasius, *contra Gentes*, 46.

[154] See, for example, Irenaeus, *adversus haereses* V.i.1; Gregory of Nazianzen, *Oratio Theologica* 2. For an excellent account of the role of natural theology at this time, see Jaroslav Pelikan, *Christianity and Classical Culture: The Metamorphosis of Natural Theology in the Christian Encounter with Hellenism*. New Haven, CT: Yale University Press, 1993.

[155] Athanasius, *de incarnatione Verbi*, 6. See further Roldanus, *Le Christ et l'homme dans la théologie d'Athanase d'Alexandrie*.

Christ' – note the implicit reference to the coherence of faith – in the theological enterprise:[156]

> We do not seek to impose a pattern upon theological knowledge, but rather to discern the pattern inhering in its material content, or to let reveal itself to us as we direct our questions toward it to find out its central frame of reference. When we do that we are directed to Jesus Christ, to the Incarnation, to the hypostatic union, the unique together-ness of God and man in Christ which is normative for every other relationship between man and God. . . . It is from that centre that we take our bearings as we consider the doctrine of the Trinity, of the Father and of the Holy Spirit as well as of the Son, and therefore of creation as well as of redemption.

There are clear parallels here with the eastern Christian tradition, and it is therefore perhaps not surprising that Athanasius' *contra Gentes* and *de incarnatione Verbi* play an important role within Torrance's scientific theology, as can be seen from his *Ground and Grammar of Theology*.[157] Torrance argues that Athanasius' approach does not involve any attempt to 'find a way of reaching God by rational argument'; rather, he insists, the intention is to 'point out a way of communing with the regulative and providential activity of God in the rational order of the universe'. The order which pervades the universe does not derive from some autonomous rational principle, but from the creative activity of the λόγος of God:[158]

> We may [thus] find a way into the central unity or order of things, that is then allowed to throw light upon the whole manifold of connections with which we are concerned in the knowledge of God in his interaction with the creation – and not least the distinctive kind of intelligible relation appropriate to its actual subject matter.

Creation, Christology, eschatology and the observability of God

Throughout the long debate on realism, the question of whether an entity is *observable* plays a central role. While it would be simplistic to equate 'the real' with 'the observable', there is no doubt that there is considerable truth in that simplification. So may God be observed?

---

[156] Torrance, *Theological Science*, 216. See also Torrance, *The Christian Doctrine of God*, 1, where the incarnation is held to prescribe both the 'proper matter and form' of an authentic Christian theology.

[157] Torrance, *The Ground and Grammar of Theology*, 76–8. For criticism of Torrance at this point, see Richard A. Muller, 'The Barth Legacy: New Athanasius or Origen Redivivus? A Response to T. F. Torrance', *The Thomist* 54 (1990), 673–704, especially 687–8.

[158] Torrance, *The Ground and Grammar of Theology*, 77.

In beginning to answer this question, we must draw together three related elements of classic Christian theology, noting how they are correlated in the work of creation and redemption.

1. God may be observed *indirectly* in the world, through the lens of a natural theology. Once the world is 'seen as' God's creation, the wisdom and character of God may be discerned indirectly through the natural order. In that there is a direct link between the doctrine of creation and Christology, Christ may be argued to be indirectly implicated in this indirect vision of God.

2. In that Jesus Christ is God incarnate, God may be said to be 'observed' in the person of Jesus Christ. 'No one has ever seen God' (John 1:18). Yet in that Christ is the 'image of the invisible God (Colossians 1:15), the New Testament is able to affirm that anyone who has seen Christ has seen God (John 14:1–9; see also 1 John 1:1–4).

3. At the eschatological consummation, God will be 'observed' through the beatific vision.

The first point has already been dealt with at some length, and need not be discussed further (vol. 1, 193–240). The second and third points require some extended discussion. The New Testament uses the language of 'observation' when it insists that God may be seen in Christ. This theme has been of immense importance throughout the Christian tradition, but has held an especially significant place in the theology and spirituality of Byzantine theology. During the eighth century, John of Damascus made the critical point that the incarnation of God in Christ allows the hitherto invisible God to be seen in and through a visible medium.[159]

> [Prior to the incarnation] there was absolutely no way in which God, who has neither a body nor a face, could be represented by any image. But now that he has made himself visible in the flesh and has lived with people, I can make an image of what I have seen of God . . . and contemplate the glory of the Lord, his face having been unveiled.

The theology of the incarnation immediately establishes a link between Christ and the 'beholding' of God.[160] Christ renders God visible as an anticipation of the final disclosure of God at the end of history.

---

[159] John of Damascus, *contra imaginum calumniatores* I, 16.
[160] For an exploration of the issues, see Aidan Nichols, *The Art of God Incarnate: Theology and Image in Christian Tradition.* London: Darton, Longman & Todd, 1980.

The eschatological dimension of the question is traditionally explored through the theme of 'the beatific vision'. On account of the transformation of human nature through the resurrection, believers are able to directly behold God. As Benedict XII defined this doctrine in 1336:[161]

> We declare that the souls of all the saints in heaven have seen and do see the divine essence by direct intuition and face to face (*visione intuitiva et etiam faciali*), in such a way that nothing created intervenes as an object of vision, but the divine essence presents itself to their immediate gaze, unveiled, clearly and openly; moreover, that in this vision they enjoy the divine essence, and that, in virtue of this vision and this enjoyment, they are truly blessed and possess eternal life and eternal rest.

This doctrine perhaps receives its most familiar and greatest exposition in Dante's *Divine Comedy*, in which the great cycle of poems ends with the poet finally beholding[162]

the love that moves the sun and the other stars.

Yet the essential point to be made here is that the God who is known directly through intuition eschatologically is the same God who was made known in history *Christologically*.

Our concern here is primarily with the question of under what circumstances God can be said to be 'visualizable' or 'observable'. As will be clear from even this brief analysis, the classic Christian theological tradition insists that God is *disclosed* and *embodied* in Christ – again, pointing to the key role of Christology in a scientific theology.

This is the conclusion reached by T. F. Torrance in his analysis of the relationship of the scientific and theological enterprises.[163] Torrance's argument at this point begins with the recognition that God 'has endowed his creation with a rationality and beauty of its own in created correspondence to his transcendent rationality and beauty'.[164] That is to say, there is a correspondence – not identity – between the rationality and beauty of the world and those qualities as they are found and

---

[161] Benedict XII, 'Benedictus Deus,' in H. Denzinger (ed.), *Enchiridion Symbolorum*. 24–5 edn. Barcelona: Herder, 1948, 230.

[162] *Paradiso* XXXIII.145. For further comment, see Paul Priest, 'Allegory and Reality in the *Commedia*', *Dante Studies* 96 (1978), 127–44.

[163] C. Baxter Kruger, 'The Doctrine of the Knowledge of God in the Theology of Thomas F. Torrance', *Scottish Journal of Theology* 43 (1990), 366–89; Kang Phee Seng, 'The Epistemological Significance of Homoousion in the Theology of Thomas F. Torrance', *Scottish Journal of Theology* 45 (1992), 341–66.

[164] Thomas F. Torrance, *Reality and Evangelical Theology*. 2nd edn. Downers Grove, IL: InterVarsity Press, 1999, 10–11.

grounded in God, revealed in Scripture and embodied in Christ. The theologian's 'evangelical commitment to Jesus Christ "through whom and for whom the whole universe has been created"' offers a framework by which the true wisdom and wonder of the created order may be appreciated to the full, in that[165]

> it compels us to give the empirical reality of the created order its full and proper place in theological interpretation of divine revelation, especially in its incarnate form and reality in Jesus Christ. That is the inescapable *realism* of evangelical theology.

It therefore seems that, if the correlation between the creator God, the creation, human nature (and above all, human rationality) and the doctrine of the incarnation are anything like what classic Christian theology has held to be the case, there is a strong case for arguing that a scientific theology is grounded and governed, founded and guided, by the logic of the incarnate Word. *A scientific theology is thus a Christocentric theology.* The λόγος through whom creation received its distinctive form is the same λόγος who became incarnate in Christ. The ordering and rationality embedded in nature, and capable of being discerned by the human mind as created *in imagine Dei*, is embodied in Christ. With this insight, the intimate links between creation and Christ on the one hand, and between creation, redemption and consummation on the other, become luminously transparent. The coherence of Christian theology is such that these are interlocked in a web of beliefs, which embrace all aspects of the intellectual and spiritual tasks.

Let the last word in this discussion go to a nineteenth-century Anglican writer, who has been sorely neglected since his death. In his 1871 Hulsean Lectures at Cambridge University, F. J. A. Hort (1828–92) declared that 'it is not too much to say that the Gospel itself can never be fully known till nature as well as man is fully known; and that the manifestation of nature as well as man in Christ is part of his manifestation of God'.[166] Given the inner logic of the Christian tradition, true knowledge of both ourselves and of nature as God's creation can only be had to the full when seen in Christ. A scientific theology which is truly a *Christian* theology can be so only when it focuses on Christ, as it is in Christ that the fulness of the God who is known partially through the created order is to be encountered (Colossians 2:9).

---

[165] Torrance, *Reality and Evangelical Theology*, 11.

[166] F. J. A. Hort, *The Way, The Truth, The Life: The Hulsean Lectures for 1871*. Cambridge: Cambridge University Press, 1893, 83. See further E. G. Rupp, *Hort and the Cambridge Tradition: An Inaugural Lecture*. London: Cambridge University Press, 1970.

Moving On: Anticipating the Development of Theory

The present volume has explored the issue of realism in science and theology, and mapped out a critical realist approach which I regard as being both intellectually habitable and theologically responsible. However, the emphasis placed upon the interaction of knower and known within critical realism leads to a corresponding emphasis being required on the manner in which reality is portrayed and represented. We must therefore move on, and consider how scientific theories and Christian doctrines are developed in response to reality, including the difficult questions of the role of metaphysics in theory development and the place of social constructs in theology and the natural sciences.

The issue of the genesis, reception and development of doctrine is one of the most important issues in Christian theology, and has considerable importance in ecumenical discussion between Catholic, Protestant, Orthodox and evangelical theologians. A scientific theology proposes a direct convergence between the way in which the scientific and theological communities develop, formulate and confirm their theories as to how reality is to be grasped and represented. Both the natural sciences and theology propose that development in theory is governed by attentiveness to reality, so that it is the same ultimate reality that is expressed and conceived in different ways at different times. The third and final volume in this project thus moves on to engage with the issue of theory in the natural sciences and Christian theology.

Bibliography

ACHTEMEIER, P. MARK, 'The Truth of Tradition: Critical Realism in the Thought of Alasdair MacIntyre and T. F. Torrance', *Scottish Journal of Theology* 47 (1994), 355–74.

ACKERMANN, ROBERT, 'Experiment as the Motor of Scientific Progress', *Social Epistemology* 2 (1988), 327–35.

——, 'The New Experimentalism', *British Journal for the Philosophy of Science* 40 (1989), 185–90.

AESCHLIMAN, MICHAEL D., *The Restitution of Man: C. S. Lewis and the Case against Scientism*. Grand Rapids, MI: Eerdmans, 1998.

ALSTON, WILLIAM P., 'What's Wrong with Immediate Knowledge?', *Synthese* 55 (1983), 73–96.

ALTMANN, ALEXANDER, *Essence and Existence in Maimonides*. Manchester: Manchester University Press, 1953.

ARBIB, MICHAEL A., and MARRY B. HESSE, *The Construction of Reality*. Cambridge: Cambridge University Press, 1986.

ARCHER, MARGARET, *Culture and Agency: The Place of Culture in Social Theory*. Cambridge: Cambridge University Press, 1996.

ARKES, HADLEY, 'That "Nature Herself Has Placed in Our Ears a Power of Judging": Some Reflections on the "Naturalism" of Cicero', in Robert P. George (ed.), *Natural Law Theory: Contemporary Essays*. Oxford: Clarendon Press, 1992, 245–77.

ARONOWITZ, STANLEY, *Science as Power: Discourse and Ideology in Modern Society*, Minneapolis: University of Minnesota Press, 1988.

AYER, A. J., *Language, Truth and Logic*. London: Victor Gollancz, 1946.

——, 'What is a Law of Nature?', in A. J. Ayer (ed.), *The Concept of a Person*. London: Macmillan, 1956, 209–34.

BAIGRIE, BRIAN S., 'The Justification of Kepler's Ellipse', *Studies in History and Philosophy of Science* 21 (1991), 633–64.

BALAGUER, MARK, *Platonism and Anti-Platonism in Mathematics*. New York: Oxford University Press, 1998.

BALDWIN, THOMAS, 'The Identity Theory of Truth', *Mind* 100 (2001), 35–52.

BANNER, MICHAEL C., *The Justification of Science and the Rationality of Religious Belief*. Oxford and New York: Oxford University Press, 1990.

BARBOUR, IAN G., *Issues in Science and Religion*. Englewood Cliffs, NJ: Prentice–Hall, 1966.

BARRETT, LEE C., 'Theology as Grammar: Regulative Principles or Paradigms and Practices', *Modern Theology* 4 (1988), 155–72.

BARTH, KARL, *Church Dogmatics*. 14 vols, Edinburgh: T&T Clark, 1957–75.

BAUM, GREGORY, *Truth beyond Relativism: Karl Mannheim's Sociology of Knowledge*. Milwaukee: Marquette University Press, 1977.

BEGBIE, JEREMY S., *Voicing Creation's Praise: Towards a Theology of the Arts*. Edinburgh: T&T Clark, 1991.

BEISER, FREDERICK C., *The Sovereignty of Reason: The Defense of Rationality in the Early English Enlightenment*. Princeton, NJ: Princeton University Press, 1996.

BENACERRAF, PAUL, 'Mathematical Truth', *Journal of Philosophy* 70 (1973), 661–79.

BENTON, TED, 'Why are Sociologists Naturephobes?', in José López and Garry Potter (eds), *After Postmodernism: An Introduction to Critical Realism*. London: Athlone Press, 2001, 133–45.

BERGER, PETER L., and THOMAS LUCKMANN, *The Social Construction of Reality: A Treatise in the Sociology of Knowledge*. Harmondsworth: Penguin, 1971.

BERNAL, J. D., *The Social Function of Science*. London: Routledge, 1939.

BERNSTEIN, RICHARD J., *Beyond Objectivism and Relativism: Science, Hermeneutics and Praxis*. Philadelphia: University of Pennsylvania Press, 1991.

BERNSTEIN, RICHARD J., *Philosophical Profiles: Essays in a Pragmatic Mode.* Philadelphia: University of Pennsylvania Press, 1986.

BHASKAR, ROY, *From East to West: Odyssey of a Soul.* New York: Routledge, 2000.

——, *The Possibility of Naturalism: A Philosophical Critique of the Contemporary Human Sciences.* 3rd edn. London: Routledge, 1998.

——, *A Realist Theory of Science.* 2nd edn. London: Verso, 1997.

——, *Reclaiming Reality: A Critical Introduction to Contemporary Philosophy.* London: Verso, 1989.

——, *Scientific Realism and Human Emancipation.* London: Verso, 1986.

BIGELOW, JOHN C., and ROBERT J. PARGETTER, *Science and Necessity.* Cambridge: Cambridge University Press, 1990.

——, BRIAN ELLIS and CAROLINE LIERSE, 'The World as One of a Kind: Natural Necessity and Laws of Nature', *British Journal for Philosophy of Science* 43 (1992), 371–88.

BLOOR, DAVID, *Knowledge and Social Imagery.* 2nd edn. Chicago: University of Chicago Press, 1991.

BONJOUR, LAURENCE, 'Externalist Theories of Justification', *Midwest Studies in Philosophy* 5 (1980), 53–73.

——, *The Structure of Empirical Knowledge.* Cambridge, MA: Harvard University Press, 1985.

BOURDIEU, PIERRE, *In Other Words: Essays Towards a Reflexive Sociology.* Cambridge: Polity Press, 1990.

——, *Pascalian Meditations.* Cambridge: Polity Press, 2000.

BOYD, RICHARD, 'The Current Status of Scientific Realism', in Jarrett Leplin (ed.), *Scientific Realism.* Berkeley: University of California Press, 1984, 41–82.

——, 'Scientific Realism and Naturalistic Epistemology', in Peter D. Asquith and Ronald N. Giere (eds), *Proceedings of the Philosophy of Science Association.* vol. 2. East Lansing, MI: Philosophy of Science Association, 1980, 613–62.

BOYLE, JOSEPH, 'Natural Law and the Ethics of Traditions', in Robert P. George (ed.), *Natural Law Theory: Contemporary Essays.* Oxford: Clarendon Press, 1992, 3–30.

BROWN, JAMES ROBERT, *Philosophy of Mathematics: An Introduction to the World of Proofs and Pictures.* London: Routledge, 1999.

BUCKLEY, JAMES J., 'Doctrine in the Diaspora', *The Thomist* 49 (1985), 443–59.

BURKE, J. G., *Promoting Experimental Learning: Experiment and the Royal Society 1660–1727*. Cambridge: Cambridge University Press, 1991.

BURRELL, DAVID B., 'An Introduction to *Theology and Social Theory*', *Modern Theology* 8 (1992), 319–30.

CAMPBELL, JOHN ANGUS, 'The Polemical Mr Darwin', *Quarterly Journal of Speech* 61 (1975), 375–90.

CARNAP, RUDOLF, *Der logische Aufbau der Welt*. Hamburg: Felix Meiner Verlag, 1998.

——, *Logical Aspects of Probability*. Chicago: University of Chicago Press, 1950.

CECCARELLI, LEAH, *Shaping Science with Rhetoric: The Cases of Dobzhansky, Schrödinger and Wilson*. Chicago: University of Chicago Press, 2001.

CHISHOLM, RODERICK M., *The Foundations of Knowing*. Minneapolis: University of Minnesota Press, 1982.

——, *Theory of Knowledge*. 3rd edn. Englewood Cliffs, NJ: Prentice-Hall International, 1989.

CHRISTIAN, WILLIAM A., *Doctrines of Religious Communities: A Philosophical Study*. New Haven, CT: Yale University Press, 1987.

CLAYTON, JOHN P., *The Concept of Correlation: Paul Tillich and the Possibility of a Mediating Theology*. Berlin: De Gruyter, 1980.

COLLIER, ANDREW, *Critical Realism: An Introduction to Roy Bhaskar's Philosophy*. London: Verso, 1994.

COLYVAN, MARK, *The Indispensability of Mathematics*. Oxford: Oxford University Press, 2001.

COOKE, VINCENT M., 'Moral Obligation and Metaphysics', *Thought* 66 (1991), 65–74.

COUVALIS, GEORGE, *Feyerabend's Critique of Foundationalism*. Aldershot: Avebury, 1989.

CREATH, RICHARD, 'Taking Theories Seriously', *Synthese* 62 (1985), 317–45.

CUNNINGHAM, FRANCIS A., *Essence and Existence in Thomism*. Lanham, MD: University Press of America, 1988.

CUSHING, JAMES T., *Quantum Mechanics: Historical Contingency and the Copenhagen Hegemony*. Chicago: University of Chicago Press, 1994.

DANKER, FREDERICK W., 'Graeco-Roman Cultural Accommodation in the Christology of Luke–Acts', in K. H. Richards (ed.), *Society of Biblical Literature 1983 Seminar Papers*. Chico, CA: Scholars Press, 1983, 391–414.

DENNEHY, RAYMOND, 'The Ontological Basis of Human Rights', *The Thomist* 42 (1978), 434–63.

DEVITT, MICHAEL, 'Aberrations of the Realism Debate', *Philosophical Studies* 61 (1991), 43–63.

——, *Realism and Truth*. Oxford: Blackwell, 1984.

DOUVEN, IGOR AND JAAP VAN BRAKEL, 'Is Scientific Realism an Empirical Hypothesis?', *Dialectica* 49 (1995), 3–14.

DRAKE, DURANT, *Essays in Critical Realism: A Co-operative Study of the Problem of Knowledge*. London: Macmillan, 1920.

DREES, WILLEM B., *Religion, Science and Naturalism*. Cambridge: Cambridge University Press, 1995.

DROZDEK, A., and T. KEAGY, 'A Case for Realism in Mathematics', *The Monist* 77 (1994), 329–44.

DU BOIS-REYMOND, EMIL HEINRICH, *Über die Grenzen des Natur-erkennens: Die sieben Welträtsel – Zwei Vortrage*. Leipzig: Veit, 1907.

EVANS, GILLIAN R., *Alan of Lille: The Frontiers of Theology in the Later Twelfth Century*. Cambridge: Cambridge University Press, 1983.

FALES, EVAN, 'Plantinga's Case against Naturalistic Epistemology', *Philosophy of Science* 63 (1996), 432–51.

FARRER, AUSTIN, *A Rebirth of Images: The Making of St John's Apocalypse*. London: Dacre Press, 1949.

FEINGOLD, MORDECHAI, 'When Facts Matter', *Isis* 87 (1996), 131–9.

FEYERABEND, PAUL K., *Against Method*. 3rd edn. London: Verso, 1993.

——, *Farewell to Reason*. London: Verso, 1987.

——, *Science in a Free Society*. London: Verso, 1983.

FINE, ARTHUR, *The Shaky Game: Einstein, Realism and the Quantum Theory*. Chicago: University of Chicago Press, 1986.

FINNIS, JOHN, *Natural Law and Natural Rights*. Oxford: Clarendon Press, 1980.

FÖLSING, ALBRECHT, *Albert Einstein: A Biography*. New York: Viking, 1997.

FORBES, CHRISTOPHER, 'Comparison, Self-Praise and Irony: Paul's Boasting and the Conventions of Hellenistic Rhetoric', *New Testament Studies* 32 (1986), 1–30.

FOWLER, D. H., *The Mathematics of Plato's Academy: A New Reconstruction.* New York: Oxford University Press, 1999.

FRAASSEN, BAS VAN, 'Empiricism in the Philosophy of Science', in P. Churchland and C. Hooker (eds), *Images of Science: Essays on Realism and Empiricism.* Chicago: University of Chicago Press, 1985, 245–308.

——, *Laws and Symmetry.* Oxford: Clarendon Press, 1989.

——, 'The Pragmatics of Explanation', *American Philosophical Quarterly* 14 (1977), 143–50.

——, *The Scientific Image.* Oxford: Oxford University Press, 1980.

FRANKLIN, ALLEN, *The Neglect of Experiment.* Cambridge: Cambridge University Press, 1986.

GADAMER, HANS-GEORG, *Truth and Method.* London: Sheed & Ward, 1975.

GALE, GEORGE, and CASSANDRA L. PINNICK, 'Stalking Theoretical Physics: An Ethnography Flounders', *Social Studies of Science* 27 (1997), 113–23.

GARDNER, MICHAEL R., 'Realism and Instrumentalism in Nineteenth Century Physics', *Philosophy of Science* 46 (1979), 1–34.

——, 'Realism and Instrumentalism in Pre-Newtonian Astronomy', *Minnesota Studies in the Philosophy of Science* 10 (1983), 201–65.

GERRISH, BRIAN A., 'The Nature of Doctrine', *Journal of Religion* 68 (1988), 87–92.

GIERE, RONALD N., 'The Skeptical Perspective: Science without the Laws of Nature', in Freidel Weinert (ed.), *Laws of Nature: Essays on the Philosophical, Scientific and Historical Dimensions.* New York: de Gruyter, 1995, 120–38.

GILBERT, G. NIGEL, and MICHAEL MULKAY, 'Warranting Scientific Belief', *Social Studies of Science* 12 (1982), 383–408.

GLICK, THOMAS F., *The Comparative Reception of Darwinism.* Austin: University of Texas Press, 1972.

GOICHON, AMÉLIE-MARIE, *La distinction de l'essence et de l'existence d'après Ibn Sina (Avicenne).* Paris: Desclée de Brouwer, 1937.

GOODING, DAVID, TREVOR PINCH, and SIMON SCHAFFER, *The Uses of Experiment: Studies in the Natural Sciences.* Cambridge. Cambridge University Press, 1989.

GORE, CHARLES, *The Incarnation of the Son of God.* London: John Murray, 1922.

GREENWOOD, J. D., 'Two Dogmas of Neo-Empiricism: The "Theory-Informity" of Observation and the Duhem–Quine Thesis', *Philosophy of Science* 57 (1990), 553–74.

GRIFFIN, DAVID RAY, 'A Richer or Poorer Naturalism? A Critique of Willem Drees's *Religion, Science and Naturalism*', *Zygon* 32 (1997), 595–616.

GROSS, ALAN G., *The Rhetoric of Science.* Cambridge, MA: Harvard University Press, 1996.

GROSS, PAUL R., and NORMAN LEVITT, *Higher Superstition: The Academic Left and its Quarrels with Science.* Baltimore, MD: Johns Hopkins University Press, 1998.

——, NORMAN LEVITT, and MARTIN W. LEWIS (eds), *The Flight from Science and Reason.* New York: New York Academy of Sciences, 1996.

GROSSMANN, REINHARDT, 'Russell's Paradox and Complex Properties', *Nous* 6 (1972), 153–64.

GRUBE, DIRK-MARTIN, 'Religious Experience after the Demise of Foundationalism', *Religious Studies* 31 (1995), 37–52.

GRÜNBAUM, ADOLF, 'Is Falsifiability theTouchstone of Scientific Rationality? Karl Popper versus Inductivism', in R. S. Cohen, P. K. Feyerabend and M. W. Wartofsky (eds), *Essays in Memory of Imre Lakatos.* Dordrecht: Reidel, 1976, 213–52.

HACKING, IAN, *The Social Construction of What?* Cambridge, MA: Harvard University Press, 1999.

HAECKEL, ERNST, *Die Welträtzel: Gemeinverstandliche Studien über monistische Philosophie.* Bonn: Emil Strauss, 1899.

HALL, A. RUPERT, *The Scientific Revolution, 1500–1800: The Formation of the Modern Scientific Attitude.* London: Longmans, Green & Co., 1954.

HANSEN, VAGN LUNDSGAARD, *Geometry in Nature.* Wellesley, MA: A. K. Peters, 1993.

HARDY, G. H., *A Mathematician's Apology.* Cambridge: Cambridge University Press, 1941.

HARRÉ, ROM, *Varieties of Realism: A Rationale for the Natural Sciences.* Oxford: Blackwell, 1986.

HARRISON, CAROL, *Beauty and Revelation in the Thought of Saint Augustine.* Oxford: Oxford University Press, 1992.

HEMPEL, CARL G., *Aspects of Scientific Explanation.* New York: Free Press, 1965.

HENSLEY, JEFFREY, 'Are Postliberals Necessarily Antirealists?: Re-examining the Metaphysics of Lindbeck's Postliberal Theology', in T. R. Philips and D. L. Okholm (eds), *The Nature of Confession: Evangelicals and Postliberals in Conversation.* Downers Grove, IL: InterVarsity Press, 1996, 69–80.

HERSH, REUBEN, 'Some Proposals for Reviving the Philosophy of Mathematics', *Advances in Mathematics* 31 (1979), 31–50.

HIEBERT, ERWIN, 'The Genesis of Mach's Early Views on Atomism', in R. Cohen and R. Seeger (eds), *Ernst Mach: Physicist and Philosopher.* Dordrecht: D. Reidel, 1970, 79–106.

HITTINGER, RUSSELL, 'Natural Law and Virtue: Theories at Cross Purposes', in Robert P. George (ed.), *Natural Law Theory: Contemporary Essays.* Oxford: Clarendon Press, 1992, 42–70.

HOFSTADTER, RICHARD, *Social Darwinism in American Thought.* Boston: Beacon, 1955.

HOITENGA, DEWEY J., *Faith and Reason from Plato to Plantinga: An Introduction to Reformed Epistemology.* Albany, NY: State University of New York Press, 1991.

HOLLAND, J., et al., *Induction: Process of Inference, Learning and Discovery.* Cambridge, MA: MIT Press, 1986.

HOLMER, PAUL, 'Wittgenstein and Theology', in D. M. High (ed.), *New Essays on Religious Language.* New York: Oxford University Press, 1969, 25–35.

HOLT, EDWIN B., et al., *The New Realism: Cooperative Studies in Philosophy.* New York: Macmillan, 1912.

HON, GIORA, 'Is the Identification of Experimental Error contextually dependent? The Case of Kaufmann's Experiment and its Varied Reception', in Jed Z. Buchwald (ed.), *Scientific Practice: Theories and Stories of Doing Physics.* Chicago: University of Chicago Press, 1995, 170–223.

HORT, F. J. A., *The Way, The Truth, The Life: The Hulsean Lectures for 1871.* Cambridge: Cambridge University Press, 1893.

HOSTETTLER, NICK, 'How Wittgenstein got Bhaskar Wrong', *Alethia* 3.1 (2000), 22–8.

HOYNINGEN-HUENE, PAUL, 'Kuhn's Conception of Incommensurability', *Studies in History and Philosophy of Science* 21 (1980), 481–92.

——, *Reconstructing Scientific Revolutions: Thomas S. Kuhn's Philosophy of Science*. Chicago: University of Chicago Press, 1993.

HUTH, JOHN, 'Latour's Relativity', in Noretta Koertge (ed.), *A House Built on Sand: Exposing Postmodernist Myths about Science*. New York: Oxford University Press, 1998, 181–92.

HUYSSTEEN, J. WENTZEL VAN, *Essays in Postfoundationalist Theology*. Grand Rapids, MI: Eerdmans, 1997.

——, 'Experience and Explanation: The Justification of Cognitive Claims in Theology', *Zygon* 23 (1988), 247–61.

——, *The Shaping of Rationality: Toward Interdisciplinarity in Theology and Science*. Grand Rapids, MI: Eerdmans, 1999.

——, *Theology and the Justification of Faith: Constructing Theories in Systematic Theology*. Grand Rapids, MI: Eerdmans, 1989.

IRZIK, GÜROL, and TEO GRÜNBERG, 'Carnap and Kuhn: Arch Enemies or Close Allies?', *British Journal for the Philosophy of Science* 46 (1995), 285–307.

JACKSON, TIMOTHY, 'The Theory and Practice of Discomfort: Richard Rorty and Pragmatism', *The Thomist* 51 (1987), 270–98.

JACOB, MARGARET C., 'Reflections on Bruno Latour's Version of the Seventeenth Century', in Noretta Koertge (ed.), *A House Built on Sand: Exposing Postmodernist Myths about Science*. New York: Oxford University Press, 1998, 240–54.

JONES, L. GREGORY, 'Alasdair MacIntyre on Narrative, Community and the Moral Life', *Modern Theology* 4 (1987), 53–69.

JUBIEN, MICHAEL, 'Ontology and Mathematical Truth', *Nous* 11 (1977), 135–50.

JÜNGEL, EBERHARD, *Gott als Geheimnis der Welt: Zur Begründung der Theologie des Gekreuzigten im Streit zwischen Theismus und Atheismus*. 4th edn. Tübingen: J. C. B. Mohr, 1982.

KANTOROVITCH, AHARON and YUVAL NE'EMAN, 'Serendipity as a Source of Evolutionary Progress in Science', *Studies in History and Philosophy of Science* 20 (1989), 505–30.

KELLENBERG, BRAD J., 'Unstuck from Yale: Theological Method after Lindbeck', *Scottish Journal of Theology* 50 (1997), 191–218.

KERR, FERGUS, *Immortal Longings: Versions of Transcending Humanity.* London: SPCK, 1997.

KIMBALL, ROGER, *Experiments against Reality: The Fate of Culture in the Postmodern Age.* Chicago: Ivan R. Dee, 2000.

KITCHER, PHILIP, *Abusing Science: The Case against Creationism.* Cambridge: MIT Press, 1982.

——, 'The Naturalists Return', *Philosophical Review* 101 (1992), 53–114.

——, *The Nature of Mathematical Knowledge.* New York: Oxford University Press, 1983.

KLEINER, SCOTT A., 'A New Look at Kepler and Abductive Argument', *Studies in History and Philosophy of Science* 14 (1983), 279–313.

KLINE, MORRIS, *Mathematical Thought from Ancient to Modern Times.* New York: Oxford University Press, 1972.

KORNBLITH, HILARY, 'Justified Belief and Epistemically Responsible Action', *Philosophical Review* 92 (1983), 33–48.

KRÖBER, GÜNTER, *50 Jahre Bernals 'Die soziale Funktion der Wissenschaft': Programm, Probleme, Perspektiven.* Berlin: Akademie–Verlag, 1990.

KRUGER, C. BAXTER, 'The Doctrine of the Knowledge of God in the Theology of Thomas F. Torrance', *Scottish Journal of Theology* 43 (1990), 366–89.

KUHN, THOMAS S., *Black-Body Radiation and the Quantum Discontinuity.* Oxford: Clarendon Press, 1978.

——, *The Copernican Revolution.* New York: Random House, 1959.

——, *The Structure of Scientific Revolutions.* Chicago: University of Chicago Press, 1962.

KUIPERS, THEO A. F., *From Instrumentalism to Constructive Realism: On Some Relations between Confirmation, Empirical Progress and Truth Approximation.* Dordrecht: Kluwer Academic, 2000.

KUKLA, ANDRÉ, 'Scientific Realism, Scientific Practice and the Natural Ontological Attitude', *British Journal for the Philosophy of Science* 45 (1994), 955–75.

——, *Studies in Scientific Realism.* Oxford: Oxford University Press, 1998.

KURZ, WILLIAM S., 'Hellenistic Rhetoric in the Christological Proof of Luke–Acts', *Catholic Biblical Quarterly* 42 (1980), 171–95.

LACHNER, RAIMUND, *Zwischen Rationalismus und Traditionalismus: Offenbarung und Vernunft bei Jakob Frohschammer*. Münster: Lit, 1995.

LAUDAN, LARRY, 'Realism without the Real', *Philosophy of Science* 51 (1984), 156–62.

——, 'Explaining the Success of Science: Beyond Epistemic Realism and Relativism', in James T. Cushing, C. F. Delaney and Gary M. Gutting (eds), *Science and Reality*. Notre Dame: University of Notre Dame Press, 1984, 83–105.

——, *Progress and its Problems: Towards a Theory of Scientific Growth*. Berkeley: University of California Press, 1977.

—— and JARRETT LEPLIN, 'Empirical Equivalence and Underdetermination', *Journal of Philosophy* 88, (1991) 449–72.

LAUDISA, FREDERICO, 'Einstein, Bell and Nonseparable Realism', *British Journal for the Philosophy of Science* 46 (1995), 309–29.

LEPLIN, JARRETT, 'Methodological Realism and Scientific Rationality', *Philosophy of Science* 53 (1986), 31–51.

——, (ed.) *Scientific Realism*. Berkeley, CA: University of California Press, 1984.

LIDDON, H. P., *The Divinity of our Lord and Saviour Jesus Christ*. London: Longmans, Green & Co., 1903.

LINDBECK, GEORGE, *The Nature of Doctrine*. Philadelphia: Westminster, 1984.

LINDSTROM, PER, 'Quasi-realism in mathematics', *The Monist* 83 (2000), 122–49.

LISSKA, ANTHONY J., *Aquinas's Theory of Natural Law: An Analytic Reconstruction*. Oxford: Clarendon Press, 1996.

LONGAIR, M. S., and ROGER PENROSE, *The Large, The Small, and The Human Mind*. Cambridge: Cambridge University Press, 1999.

LONGHURST, BRIAN, *Karl Mannheim and the Contemporary Sociology of Knowledge*. Basingstoke: Macmillan, 1989.

LOUGHLIN, GERARD, 'Christianity at the End of the Story or the Return of the Master-Narrative', *Modern Theology* 8 (1992), 365–84.

LOUTH, ANDREW, *Discerning the Mystery: An Essay on the Nature of Theology*. Oxford: Clarendon Press, 1983.

MACH, ERNST, *Contributions to the Analysis of the Sensations.* Chicago: Open Court, 1897.

——, *History and Root of the Principle of the Conservation of Energy.* Chicago: Open Court Publishing Co., 1911.

MACINTYRE, ALASDAIR, *After Virtue,* 2nd edn. Notre Dame, IN: University of Notre Dame Press, 1984.

——, *Whose Justice? Which Rationality?,* London: Duckworth, 1988.

MACKEN, JOHN, *The Autonomy Theme in the Church Dogmatics of Karl Barth and His Critics.* Cambridge: Cambridge University Press, 1990.

MACKINTOSH, H. R., *The Doctrine of the Person of Jesus Christ.* Edinburgh: T&T Clark, 1913.

MACQUARRIE, JOHN, *An Existentialist Theology: A Comparison of Heidegger and Bultmann.* London: Collins, 1973.

MAKIN, GIDEON, *The Metaphysics of Meaning: Russell and Frege on Sense and Denotation.* London: Routledge, 2000.

MANDELBAUM, MAURICE, *Philosophy, Science and Sense-Perception: Historical and Critical Studies.* Baltimore, MD: Johns Hopkins University Press, 1964.

MANDELBROT, BENOIT B., *The Fractal Geometry of Nature.* New York: W. H. Freeman, 1982.

MANICAS, PETER T., and ALAN ROSENBERG, 'Naturalism, Epistemological Individualism and "The Strong Programme" in the Sociology of Knowledge', *Journal for the Theory of Social Behaviour* 15 (1985), 76–101.

MANNHEIM, KARL, *Essays on the Sociology of Knowledge.* London: Routledge & Kegan Paul, 1952.

MANSFELD, JAAP, *Prolegomena Mathematica from Apollonius of Perga to late Neoplatonism.* Leiden: E. J. Brill, 1998.

MARITAIN, JACQUES, *The Rights of Man and the Natural Law.* San Francisco: Ignatius Press, 1986.

MASCALL, ERIC L., *Existence and Analogy.* London: Darton, Longman & Todd, 1966.

MAXWELL, GROVER, 'The Ontological Status of Theoretical Entities', in Herbert Feigl and Grover Maxwell (eds), *Minnesota Studies in the Philosophy of Science.* vol. 3. Minneapolis: University of Minnesota Press, 1962, 3–15.

MCGRATH, ALISTER E., *The Genesis of Doctrine: A Study in the Foundations of Doctrinal Criticism.* Oxford: Blackwell, 1990.

McKelvey, Charles, *Beyond Ethnocentrism: A Reconstruction of Marx's Concept of Science*. New York: Greenwood Press, 1991.

McKenna, Andrew J., *Violence and Difference: Girard, Derrida and Deconstruction*. Urbana, IL: University of Illinois Press, 1992.

McMullin, Ernan, 'A Case for Scientific Realism', in Jared Leplin (ed.), *Scientific Realism*. Berkeley, CA: University of California Press, 1984, 8–40.

Meijering, E. J., *Die Hellenisierung des Christentums im Urteil Adolf von Harnack*. Amsterdam: Kampen, 1985.

Michaelson, Gordon E., 'The Response to Lindbeck', *Modern Theology* 4 (1988), 107–20.

Midgley, Mary, *Science and Poetry*. London: Routledge, 2001.

Milbank, John, 'Knowledge: The Theological Critique of Philosophy in Hamann and Jacobi', in John Milbank, Catherine Pickstock and Graham Ward (eds), *Radical Orthodoxy*. London: Routledge, 1999, 21–37.

——, '"Postmodern Critical Augustinianism": A Short *Summa* in Forty Two Responses to Unasked Questions', *Modern Theology* 7 (1991), 225–37.

——, *Theology and Social Theory: Beyond Secular Reason*. Oxford: Blackwell, 1993.

Millikan, R. A., 'Quantenbeziehungen beim photoelektrischen Effekt', *Physikalische Zeitschrift* 17 (1916), 217–21.

Millikan, Ruth G., *Language, Thought and other Biological Catagories: New Foundations for Realism*. Cambridge, MA: MIT Press, 1984.

Moore, James R., *The Post-Darwinian Controversies: A Study of the Protestant Struggle to come to terms with Darwin in Great Britain and America, 1870–1900*. Cambridge: Cambridge University Press, 1979.

Moser, Paul K., *Knowledge and Evidence*. Cambridge: Cambridge University Press, 1989.

Murphy, Nancey C., 'From Critical Realism to a Methodological Approach: Response to Robbins, van Huyssteen and Hefner', *Zygon* 23 (1988), 287–90.

Musgrave, Alan, 'Constructive Empiricism Versus Scientific Realism', *Philosophical Quarterly* 32 (1982), 262–71.

Nagel, Ernest, *The Structure of Science: Problems in the Logic of Scientific Explanation*. London: Routledge & Kegan Paul, 1979.

NORRIS, CHRISTOPHER, *Against Relativism: Philosophy of Science, Deconstruction and Critical Theory*. Oxford: Blackwell, 1997.

——, *Quantum Theory and the Flight from Realism: Philosophical Responses to Quantum Mechanics*. London: Routledge, 2000.

O'NEILL, COLMAN, 'The Rule Theory of Doctrine and Propositional Truth', *The Thomist* 49 (1985), 417–42.

PANNENBERG, WOLFHART, 'The Appropriation of the Philosophical Concept of God as a Dogmatic Problem of Early Christian Theology', in *Basic Questions in Theology II*. London: SCM Press, 1971, 119–83.

PENROSE, ROGER, *The Emperor's New Mind: Concerning Computers, Minds and the Laws of Physics*. London: Vintage, 1990.

——, 'The Role of Aesthetics in Pure and Applied Mathematical Research', *Bulletin of the Institute of Mathematics and Its Applications* 10 (1974), 266–71.

——, *Shadows of the Mind: A Search for the Missing Science of Consciousness*. London: Vintage, 1995.

PERRY, RALPH BARTON, *Present Philosophical Tendencies: A Critical survey of Naturalism, Idealism, Pragmatism and Realism*. New York: Longmans, Green, 1912.

PHILLIPS, D. Z., 'Lindbeck's Audience', *Modern Theology* 4 (1988), 133–54.

PINNICK, CASSANDRA L., 'What is Wrong with the Strong Programme's Case Study of the "Hobbes-Boyle Dispute"?', in Noretta Koertge (ed.), *A House Built on Sand: Exposing Postmodernist Myths about Science*. New York: Oxford University Press, 1998, 227–39.

PLACHER, WILLIAM C., 'Revisionist and Postliberal Theologies and the Public Character of Theology', *The Thomist* 49 (1985), 392–416.

——, *Unapologetic Theology: A Christian Voice in a Pluralistic Conversation*. Louisville, KY: Westminster/John Knox Press, 1989.

PLANTINGA, ALVIN, 'Is Belief in God Properly Basic?', *Nous* 15 (1981), 41–52.

——, 'Reason and Belief in God', in Alvin Plantinga and Nicholas Wolterstorff (eds), *Faith and Philosophy: Reason and Belief in God*. Notre Dame: University of Notre Dame, 1983, 16–93.

——, *Warrant and Proper Function*. New York: Oxford University Press, 1993.

PLANTINGA, ALVIN, *Warrant: The Current Debate.* Oxford: Oxford University Press, 1993.

POLKINGHORNE, JOHN, *Belief in God in an Age of Science.* New Haven, CT: Yale University Press, 1998.

———, *One World: The Interaction of Science and Theology.* Princeton: Princeton University Press, 1986.

———, *Scientists as Theologians: A Comparison of the Writings of Ian Barbour, Arthur Peacocke and John Polkinghorne.* London: SPCK, 1996.

POTTER, GARRY, and JOSÉ LÓPEZ, 'After Postmodernism: The New Millennium', in José López and Garry Potter (eds), *After Postmodernism: An Introduction to Critical Realism.* London: Athlone Press, 2001, 3–16.

PRELLI, LAWRENCE J., *A Rhetoric of Science: Inventing Scientific Discourse.* Columbia, SC: University of South Carolina Press, 1989.

PSILLOS, STATHIS, *Scientific Realism: How Science Tracks Truth.* London: Routledge, 1999.

PUTNAM, HILARY, 'Mathematics without Foundations', *Journal of Philosophy* 64 (1967), 5–22.

———, *Representation and Reality.* Cambridge, MA: MIT Press, 1991.

———, 'Three Kinds of Scientific Realism', *The Philosophical Quarterly* 32 (1982), 195–200.

QUINE, W. V. O., 'Five Milestones of Empiricism', in W. V. O. Quine (ed.), *Theories and Things.* Cambridge, MA: Harvard University Press, 1981, 67–72.

———, *From a Logical Point of View.* Cambridge, MA: Harvard University Press, 1953.

———, 'Success and Limits of Mathematization', in W. V. O. Quine (ed.), *Theories and Things.* Cambridge, MA: Harvard University Press, 1981, 148–55.

RATNER, JOSEPH, 'The Correspondence Theory of Truth', *Journal of Philosophy* 32 (1935), 141–52.

REDHEAD, MICHAEL, *From Physics to Metaphysics.* Cambridge: Cambridge University Press, 1995.

———, 'The Nature of Reality', *British Journal for the Philosophy of Science* 40 (1989), 429–41.

REISCH, GEORGE A., 'Did Kuhn kill Logical Empiricism?', *Philosophy of Science* 58 (1991), 264–77.

RESCHER, NICHOLAS, *The Coherence Theory of Truth*. Washington, DC: University Press of America, 1982.

——, 'Conceptual Idealism Revisited', *Review of Metaphysics* 44 (1991), 495–523.

——, *Scientific Realism: A Critical Appraisal*. Dordrecht: D. Reidel, 1987.

——, 'Some Issues regarding the Completeness of Science and the Limits of Scientific Knowledge', in G. Radnitzky and G. Andersson (eds), *The Structure and Development of Science*. Dordrecht: D. Reidel, 1979, 19–40.

——, *A System of Pragmatic Idealism*. Princeton, NJ: Princeton University Press, 1992.

RESNIK, MICHAEL, 'Scientific versus Mathematical Realism: The Indispensability Argument', *Philosophia Mathematica* 3 (1995), 166–74.

ROBBINS, J. WESLEY, 'Is Belief in God properly basic?', *International Journal of Philosophy of Religion* 14 (1985), 241–8.

ROBERTS, JON H., *Darwinism and the Divine in America*. Madison: University of Wisconsin Press, 1988.

ROGERS, ARTHUR KENYON, *What is Truth? An Essay in the Theory of Knowledge*. New Haven, CT: Yale University Press, 1923.

ROLDANUS, JOHANNES, *Le Christ et l'homme dans la théologie d'Athanase d'Alexandrie: étude de la conjonction de sa conception de l'homme avec sa christologie*. Leiden: E. J. Brill, 1977.

RORTY, RICHARD, *Consequences of Pragmatism*. Minneapolis, MN: University of Minneapolis Press, 1982.

——, *The Linguistic Turn: Essays in Philosophical Method*. Chicago: University of Chicago Press, 1992.

——, *Philosophy and the Mirror of Nature*. Princeton: Princeton University Press, 1979.

ROSENFIELD, L., 'The Epistemological Conflict between Einstein and Bohr', *Zeitschrift für Physik* 171 (1963), 242–5.

——, 'Niels Bohr's Contribution to Epistemology', *Physics Today* 16 (1963), 47–54.

ROTH, P. A., and R. B. BARRETT, 'Deconstructing Quarks: Rethinking Sociological Constructions of Science', *Social Studies of Science* 20 (1990), 579–632.

RUDWICK, MARTIN J. S., *The Great Devonian Controversy: The Shaping of Scientific Knowledge among Gentlemanly Specialists.* Chicago: University of Chicago Press, 1985.

RUSE, MICHAEL, *Taking Darwin Seriously: A Naturalistic Approach to Philosophy.* New York: Prometheus Books, 1998.

SALMON, WESLEY, 'Epistemology of Natural Science', in Jonathan Dancy and Ernest Sosa (eds), *A Companion to Epistemology.* Oxford: Blackwell, 1992, 280–99.

SATTERTHWAITE, PHILIP E., 'Acts against the Background of Classical Rhetoric,' in Bruce W. Winter and Andrew D. Clark (eds), *The Book of Acts in its First Century Setting 1: Ancient Literary Setting.* Grand Rapids, MI: Eerdmans, 1993, 337–80.

SAUER-THOMPSON, GARY, and JOSEPH WAYNE SMITH, *The Unreasonable Silence of the World: Universal Reason and the Wreck of the Enlightenment Project.* Aldershot: Ashgate, 1997.

SCHEFFLER, ISRAEL, *Science and Subjectivity.* Indianapolis: Bobbs Merrill, 1967.

SCHRAG, CALVIN O., *The Resources of Rationality: A Response to the Postmodern Challenge.* Bloomington, IN: Indiana University Press, 1992.

SEARLE, JOHN R., *The Construction of Social Reality.* New York: Free Press, 1995.

SENG, KANG PHEE, 'The Epistemological Significance of Homoousion in the Theology of Thomas F. Torrance', *Scottish Journal of Theology* 45 (1992), 341–66.

SHIPLEY, BRAD, 'Theological Critical Realism', *Alethia* 3.2 (2000), 29–33.

SIMON, YVES, *The Tradition of Natural Law.* New York: Fordham University Press, 1965.

SKLAR, LAWRENCE, *Theory and Truth: Philosophical Critique without Foundational Science.* Oxford: Oxford University Press, 2000.

SMART, J. J. C., *Philosophy and Scientific Realism.* London: Routledge & Kegan Paul, 1963.

SOKAL, ALAN, and JEAN BRICMONT, *Fashionable Nonsense: Postmodern Intellectuals' Abuse of Science.* New York: Picador, 1998.

SOPER, KATE, *What is Nature? Culture, Politics and the Non-human.* Oxford: Blackwell, 1995.

SOSKICE, JANET MARTIN, *Metaphor and Religious Language*. Oxford: Clarendon Press, 1985.

——, 'Theological Realism', in W. J. Abraham and S. Holtzer (eds), *The Rationality of Religious Belief.* Oxford and New York: Clarendon Press, 1987, 105–19.

STEINER, MARK, 'The Application of Mathematics to Natural Science', *Journal of Philosophy* 86 (1989), 449–80.

STELL, STEPHEN L., 'Hermeneutics in Theology and the Theology of Hermeneutics: Beyond Lindbeck and Tracy', *Journal of the American Academy of Religion* 61 (1993), 679–703.

STEWART, IAN, *Nature's Numbers: Discovering Order and Pattern in the Universe*. London: Weidenfeld & Nicolson, 1995.

STOUT, JEFFREY, *The Flight from Authority: Religion, Morality and the Quest for Autonomy*. Notre Dame, IN: University of Notre Dame Press, 1981.

STOVE, DAVID, *Scientific Irrationalism: Origins of a Postmodern Cult*. New Brunswick, NJ: Transaction Publishers, 2001.

TAIT, W. W., 'Truth and Proof: The Platonism of Mathematics', *Synthese* 69 (1986), 341–70.

TAN, LEI, *The Mandelbrot Set: Theme and Variations*. Cambridge: Cambridge University Press, 2000.

THAGARD, PAUL R., 'The Best Explanation: Criteria for Theory Choice', *Journal of Philosophy* 75 (1976), 76–92.

——, *Conceptual Revolutions*. Princeton, NJ: Princeton University Press, 1993.

THIELICKE, HELMUT, *Offenbarung, Vernunft und Existenz: Studien zur Religionsphilosophie Lessings*. Gütersloh: Gerd Mohn, 1959.

THIEMANN, RONALD E., *Revelation and Theology: The Gospel as Narrated Promise*. Notre Dame, IN: University of Notre Dame Press, 1985.

TORRANCE, THOMAS F., *The Ground and Grammar of Theology*. Charlottesville, VA: University of Virginia Press, 1980.

——, *The Christian Doctrine of God: One Being, Three Persons*. Edinburgh: T&T Clark, 1996.

——, *Reality and Evangelical Theology: The Realism of Christian Revelation*. 2nd edn. Downers Grove, IL: InterVarsity Press, 1999.

TORRANCE, THOMAS F., 'The Transcendental Role of Wisdom in Science', in Evandro Agazzi (ed.), *Science et sagesse: Entretiens de l'Académie Internationale de Philosophie des Sciences, 1990.* Fribourg: Universitätsverlag Freiburg Schweiz, 1991, 63–80.

——, *The Trinitarian Faith: The Evangelical Theology of the Ancient Catholic Church.* Edinburgh: T&T Clark, 1988.

——, *Theological Science.* London: Oxford University Press, 1969.

TOULMIN, STEPHEN, *The Uses of Argument.* Cambridge: Cambridge University Press, 1958.

TRACY, DAVID, 'Lindbeck's New Program for Theology: A Reflection', *The Thomist* 49 (1985), 460–72.

TRIGG, ROGER, *Rationality and Science: Can Science Explain Everything?.* Oxford: Blackwell, 1993.

——, *Reality at Risk: A Defence of Realism in Philosophy and the Sciences.* 2nd edn. London: Harvester Press, 1989.

VAN KOOTEN NIEKERK, KEES, 'A Critical Realist Perspective on the Dialogue between Theology and Science', in Niels H. Gregersen and J. Wentzel van Huyssteen (eds), *Rethinking Theology and Science: Six Models for the Current Dialogue.* Grand Rapids, MI: Eerdmans, 1998, 51–86.

VATTIMO, GIANNI, *The End of Modernity: Nihilism and Hermeneutics in Post-modern Culture.* Cambridge: Polity Press, 1991.

VEATCH, HENRY, *For an Ontology of Morals: A Critique of Contemporary Ethical Theory.* Evanston, IL: Northwestern University Press, 1973.

WAGNER, STEVEN J., 'Why Realism Can't Be Naturalized', in Steven J. Wagner and Richard Warner (eds), *Naturalism: A Critical Appraisal.* Notre Dame, IN: University of Notre Dame Press, 1993, 211–53.

WAINWRIGHT, GEOFFREY, 'Ecumenical Dimensions of George Lindbeck's "Nature of Doctrine"', *Modern Theology* 4 (1988), 121–32.

WALKER, RALPH C. S., *The Coherence Theory of Truth: Realism, Anti-Realism, Idealism.* London: Routledge, 1989.

WEDBERG, ANDERS, *Plato's Philosophy of Mathematics.* Westport, CT: Greenwood Press, 1977.

WESTMAN, ROBERT S., 'Proof, Poetics and Patronage: Copernicus' Preface to *De Revolutionibus*', in David C. Lindberg and Robert S. Westman (eds), *Reappraisals of the Scientific Revolution*. Cambridge: Cambridge University Press, 1990, 167–205.

WEYER-MENKHOFF, STEPHAN, *Aufklärung und Offenbarung: zur Systematik der Theologie Albrecht Ritschls*. Göttingen: Vandenhoeck & Ruprecht, 1988.

WHEELER, SAMUEL, 'Indeterminacy of French Interpretation: Derrida and Davidson', in Ernest LePore (ed.), *Truth and Interpretation: Perspectives on the Philosophy of Donald Davidson*. Oxford: Blackwell, 1986, 477–94.

WIGNER, EUGENE, 'The Unreasonable Effectiveness of Mathematics', *Communications on Pure and Applied Mathematics* 13 (1960), 1–14.

WILL, FREDERICK L., *Induction and Justification: An Investigation of Cartesian Procedure in the Philosophy of Knowledge*. Ithaca, NY: Cornell University Press, 1974.

——, *Pragmatism and Realism*. Lanham, MD: Rowman & Littlefield, 1997.

WILLIAMS, ROWAN, 'Does it make sense to speak of pre-Nicene orthodoxy?', in Rowan Williams (ed.), *The Making of Orthodoxy*. Cambridge: Cambridge University Press, 1989, 1–23.

WILSON, EDWARD O., *Sociobiology: The New Synthesis*. Cambridge MA: Harvard University Press, 1975.

WITTGENSTEIN, LUDWIG, *Philosophical Investigations*. 3rd edn. Oxford: Blackwell, 1968.

——, *Tractatus Logico-Philosophicus*. London: Routledge & Kegan Paul, 1992.

WOLF, MIROSLAV, 'Theology, Meaning and Power: A Conversation with George Lindbeck on Theology and the Nature of Christian Difference', in T. R. Philips and D. L. Okholm (eds), *The Nature of Confession: Evangelicals and Postliberals in Conversation*. Downers Grove, IL: InterVarsity Press, 1996, 45–66.

WOLTERSTORFF, NICHOLAS, 'Can Belief in God Be Rational if it has no Foundations?', in Alvin Plantinga and Nicholas Wolterstorff (eds), *Faith and Rationality*. Notre Dame, IN: University of Notre Dame Press, 1983, 135–86.

WORRALL, JOHN, 'Fresnel, Poisson and the White Spot: The Role of Successful Predictions in the Acceptance of Scientific Theories', in David Gooding, Trevor Pinch and Simon Schaffre (eds), *The Uses of Experiment: Studies in the Natural Sciences.* Cambridge: Cambridge University Press, 1989, 135–57.

WRIGHT, CRISPIN, *Realism, Meaning and Truth.* 2nd edn. Oxford: Blackwell, 1993.

WRIGHT, N. T., *The New Testament and the People of God.* Minneapolis, MN: Fortress Press, 1992.

YEO, RICHARD R., 'William Whewell's Philosophy of Knowledge and its Reception', in Menachem Fisch and Simon Schaffer (eds), *William Whewell: A Composite Portrait.* Oxford: Clarendon Press, 1991, 175–99.

Index